NEXTGEN MARXISM

T0281806

NEXTGEN MARXISM
WHAT IT IS AND HOW TO COMBAT IT

MIKE GONZALEZ
KATHARINE CORNELL GORKA

Encounter
BOOKS

NEW YORK & LONDON

First American hardcover edition published in 2024 by Encounter Books,
an activity of Encounter for Culture and Education, Inc.,
a nonprofit, tax-exempt corporation.
Encounter Books website address: www.encounterbooks.com

Manufactured in the United States and printed on acid-free paper.
The paper used in this publication meets the minimum requirements of
ANSI/NISO Z39.48-1992 (R 2009) (*Permanence of Paper*).

LIBRARY OF CONGRESS CATALOGING-IN-PUBLICATION DATA IS AVAILABLE
Information for this title can be found
at the Library of Congress website under the following
ISBN 978-1-64177-353-9 and LCCN 2024001390.

FIRST AMERICAN EDITION
Printed in the United States of America

CONTENTS

	Introduction	7
1.	Background of the Present Crisis	25
2.	The Cultural Awakening	53
3.	The (Old) New Left	89
4.	The Metamorphosis	113
5.	The Takeover	141
6.	Organizing for Revolution	165
7.	Sexualizing Children and the Attack on the Family	189
8.	"In the Belly of the Beast"	205
9.	What to Do	235
	Acknowledgments	277
	Endnotes	279

DEDICATION

*To my husband, Sebastian, whose loving heart and unrelenting quest
to tell the truth inspire me to be courageous every day*

KATHARINE GORKA

To the loving memory of my parents, Miguel Angel and Graziella

MIKE GONZALEZ

INTRODUCTION

IN EARLY SUMMER 2020, protests erupted in more than two thousand cities and towns across the United States in response to the killing of George Floyd by Minneapolis police officer Derek Chauvin. All told, between fifteen million to twenty-six million people participated in the demonstrations and more than six hundred riots. Black Lives Matter (BLM) signs went up in neighborhoods and store windows across the country. Whole streets were emblazoned with the words "Black Lives Matter." Statues of historical American figures were torn down. Schools and streets were renamed. History was rewritten. Diversity, equity, and inclusion became the national creed. In the short four years since those protests, America has become nearly unrecognizable. Teachers are instructing children that they may have been born in the wrong body; school librarians and school boards are defending the right to have books containing lurid sex scenes in school libraries; college campuses have become centers of aggressive intolerance and purveyors of speech codes; once again in America, your race counts for more than your achievements when it comes to hiring and promotion; colleges ritualistically make "indigenous land acknowledgement" statements; and the lie that America is "systemically racist" has become a belief that must be taken on faith. Indeed, in 2023, Americans were again shocked to see students rally on campuses across the country, but especially on the supposedly elite ones, in defense of Hamas's killing spree in Israel in October (a massacre that included gang rapes). What has happened to America? Were the George Floyd protests and riots simply a spontaneous response to the unjust death of one man, or was something more at work? Is the United States functioning as its Founders intended, or have insidious forces tipped the balance? Are Americans sovereign over their own lives, or are they being subjugated by forces they did not choose and over which they have little control?

This book makes the case that the social upheaval we are experiencing in the United States today is the result of a zero-sum view of the world, a world of irreconcilable antagonisms, one in which the open exchange of ideas is replaced by a rigid orthodoxy, in which there is no room for dissent, in which people are reduced to their skin color or sexual orientation. It is a worldview that sees the United States as fundamentally flawed and for which the sole antidote is its destruction and rebuilding. The BLM leaders who shared this view well before they founded BLM made use of Floyd's tragedy to try to deliver a knockout blow against the US constitutional order in 2020 and were able to convince the managers and leaders of all our top institutions to buy in to the idea that the United States is systemically racist and oppressive, and thus in need of total transformation. It is this phenomenon that accounts for what has happened to American society. Now, this worldview has numerous antecedents, but its most important and enduring is the German radical Karl Marx. Some may argue that what we are seeing today is not Marxism, because central to Marxism is the idea that man is a purely economic being. But Marxism has gone through an iterative process, as this book explains, and the primacy of "material relations" in Marx no longer holds. The conflict we are experiencing today is rooted in ideas put forth by Karl Marx and then refined and adapted over the years. Some may argue, equally, that the woke element of society—the shock troops of the new Marxism—represent a minority of society. We agree with that, but we also agree with the political thinkers Gaetano Mosca and Vilfredo Pareto that a determined elite can turn society upside down. The Bolsheviks were a tiny minority in Russia in 1917.

One of the great ironies of this new version of Marxism, what we call Next-Gen Marxism, is that it began its current ascendancy in the years when most of us thought communism was breathing its last. In 1989, as the world feted the collapse of Soviet communism and the victory of free people in Eastern Europe, the specter of Marxism was finding other vicinities to haunt. It came in different garb—no longer was communism clothed in the smocks and aprons of the proletariat but in the tweeds and khakis of the college professor or in the informal chic of the community organizer. It was also less hung up on "material forces"; instead, it had learned that culture and racial forces were what inspired men. Lastly, the ghost of communism was no longer a violent spirit, seeking to spill the blood of the bourgeoisie; rather, it believed in grabbing power by re-educating the children of the bourgeoisie in colleges and universities, sending the adults to reeducation camp in the form of "antiracism" training, and liquidating their cultural habitat. The factory floor gave way to the faculty lounge and the community-organizing workshop as loci of resistance, as American academia led other cultural institutions in adopting the new Marxism. Race, sex, gender, climate change, and sundry other causes substituted for class consciousness as cudgels of transformation.

In the essentials, however, Marxism remained unchanged. It was still animated by the same "revolutionary mentality" that the conservative Brazilian thinker Olavo de Carvalho once described as "the state of spirit in which an individual or a group believes himself capable of remodeling the whole of society—if not human nature in general—through political action."¹ The destruction of the ruling order still needed to be global. God, the family, the nation, and private property remained the enemy, as they had been when communism was first codified in 1848 by Karl Marx. Reality is conceptual and thus mutable (nonexistent). Human nature, to the NextGen Marxists, is malleable, "the ensemble of human relations," as Marx wrote in 1845.² NextGen Marxists, whether practitioners of the radical theories of race, sex, or climate, agree with Marx's cultural explainer Antonio Gramsci that man "changes continuously with the changing of social relations."³ Most importantly, NextGen Marxists completely sign on to Marx's view in the *Manifesto* that "the history of all hitherto existing society is the history of class struggle"⁴—except that, to them, class is not economic but rooted in the immutable characteristics of race, sex, and so on.

This change of tactics, while retaining Marxism's eternal strategy and goals, has proved to be much more durable and effective than Stalin, the State Department spy Alger Hiss, or the ham-fisted Gus Hall, the longtime leader of the Communist Party USA, ever hoped to be. In the third decade of the present century, because of a sustained destabilization campaign organized by Marxists in the United States and abroad and masquerading as a movement for "social justice," this new formula has made inroads into all of our institutions.

It's not just universities and K–12 schools that today feel the impact of Next-Gen Marxists but also workplaces, military barracks, museums, sports leagues and other forms of entertainment, and even houses of worship. Few elementary school teachers, human-resources employees, or museum curators would call themselves Marxists (though a surprisingly high number of college professors do⁵), but far too many of them have been instructed in the ideas of Marx and such followers as Antonio Gramsci, Paolo Freire, and Kimberlé Crenshaw.

That means that, whether they know it or not, every time they promote the view that society is broken up between oppressors and their oppressed, or that Americans need to overhaul their conceptual framework, or that capitalism is killing the planet, they are spreading a new version of Marxism. These ideas have gathered force since the 1980s and are now on steroids. Reeling from the shock of the 2020 riots, the gatekeepers of our key cultural institutions have adopted the narrative of BLM's revolutionary network that America is oppressive and systemically racist and thus that the entire system itself needs a complete overhaul.

The revolutionary overhaul of the conceptual apparatus, or of the entire system (a Greek-origin word that means an organized set of doctrines, ideas, or principles used to explain the whole), can be seen at work especially in settings that instruct us about who we are. The promotion by the Smithsonian's "Latino Exhibit," a precursor to the new National Museum of the American Latino, of the idea that Hispanics are victims in America serves to curate grievances.[6] The disfigurement of the presidential homes at Monticello and Montpellier tarnishes not just the legacies of Thomas Jefferson and James Madison but all of American history. As Brenda Hafera puts it, "when those traditions, our heritage of republican principles, are sufficiently and irredeemably stained, the American regime will be ready for its transformation. Undermining the Founding generation is part of that revolutionary project."[7] The suddenly cascading emergence of new sexual frontiers, from Lia Thomas to drag queen story hour and the Genderbread Person, sow doubt about what was once an unshakable conviction: the sex to which one belonged. Sex Ed for Social Change (SIECUS)—an organization so powerful that it writes guidelines on comprehensive sex education for the Centers for Disease Control[8]—tells us in its very name that what it seeks is societal transformation. "Sex education has the power to spark large-scale social change," SIECUS emphasizes on its website.[9]

In other words, Nikita Khrushchev's boast that he would demolish the West turned out to be empty, but NextGen Marxists have done a good job of pulling out the threads of the Western cultural fabric, to the point perhaps of dissolving it. There may not be pictures of Marx, Friedrich Engels, or Vladimir Lenin hanging in neon-lit government offices, but Marxism has triumphed beyond what we were led to expect when history allegedly ended in 1989.

The Year 1989

THE YEAR 1989 was pivotal in this transformation, so much so that both the evolution and the relocation of communism were recorded by the newspaper that still regarded itself as the "paper of record." An eagle-eyed reporter at *The New York Times* penned in late 1989 an article noting that Marxist professors were taking over American academia at precisely the same time that millions who had lived under its brutal consequences were finally throwing off their yoke. "As Karl Marx's ideological heirs in Communist nations struggle to transform his political legacy, his intellectual heirs on American campuses have virtually completed their own transformation from brash, beleaguered outsiders to assimilated academic insiders. It could be considered a success story for the students of class struggle, who were once regarded as subversives,"[10] began the article, which ran under the headline "Education; the Mainstreaming of Marxism in US Colleges."

The article was written by a journalist trained in understanding communists, the paper's 1985–88 Moscow bureau chief, Felicity Barringer. Her piece highlighted an important turning point in the history of modern Marxism, shining a spotlight on emerging trends and evolutions that, a generation later, have now blossomed into full flower in the third decade of the twenty-first century.

The year the Berlin Wall came down was a turning point in other ways. It was also the year when legal scholars who were black, Asian, and, in at least one case, Mexican American officially founded, and named, the discipline of critical race theory (CRT). A mishmash of ideas at first contained within the law schools, CRT was to give ideological ballast to changes that would come decades later. CRT was self-consciously a revolutionary strategy—seen and discussed as such by its founders. "As I see it, Critical Race Theory recognizes that revolutionizing a culture begins with the radical assessment of it," CRT's intellectual godfather Derrick Bell wrote in 1995.[11] CRT marked a step forward both for the idea that the revolution would be waged on the basis of race, sex, the environment, and so on and also for the push to completely revamp society's conceptual framework.

And 1989 was also the year when a former member of the domestic terror group the Weather Underground, who had earlier spent time in prison for assault and battery, opened a center in Los Angeles to instruct the revolution's new foot soldiers in community organizing and in Marxism–Leninism. Eric Mann named his new creation the Labor Community Strategy Center, and though it was little heralded at the time, it was to prove deeply consequential. A few years after opening its doors, the center recruited a seventeen-year-old who would go on to ignite a movement that, more than any other before it, would shake the US way of life to its foundation: Patrisse Cullors, the cofounder of BLM.

Mann did not mince words about what he intended to do with young minds like Cullors'. He wrote in the *Boston Review*, "The Labor/Community Strategy Center is a leftist initiative, which was launched in 1989, around the time of the fall of the Berlin Wall, to figure out what revolutionary organizing in the age of reaction would look like. Our work focuses on training a new generation of black and Latino activists in the traditions of black revolutionary, Third World, and communist organizing."[12]

What Mann, CRT, and Barringer's academics had in common was a focus on instructing future generations into Marxist ways of thinking. Marxists, now fully liberated from Moscow's shackles, were implementing a blueprint for revolution through the culture. Today's strategy is thus being carried out by cultural Marxists—that is, revolutionaries who agree with Gramsci that, at least in the West, revolution can come only after years of cultural indoctrination, dismantling society's existing cultural narrative and instilling a new one, rather than relying on economic or social fissures to spark revolt.

Cultural Marxists liberate themselves even from Marx, or at least from some of his tactics, while retaining his original strategic goals of destroying "everything that exists,"[13] replacing capitalism with central planning and removing the checks and balances of representative democracy. Thus cultural Marxists improve on Marx's belief that changes in "the material forces of production" dictate the timing of revolution. Cultural beliefs are also material forces, as Gramsci put it. The worker takes a back seat. Where the leftist of yore spoke of saving the working class or the proletariat, the twenty-first-century leftist speaks of the "marginalized" or the "members of underserved communities." This is bureaucratic speak for non-whites, which becomes useful when government tries to conceal race-conscious policies. Or they simply speak of "people of color" when they don't have to conceal anything.

Today's cultural Marxists use race, sex, climate, or any number of other social issues to instill in the young a sense of grievance against the existing system and thus stoke an urge to reject tradition and opt for radical change. To achieve this deprogramming and reprogramming, the Marxists would have to infiltrate and then capture the institutions that constitute the commanding heights of the culture. The year the Wall fell, 1989, this takeover had finally advanced to such a degree that it was recorded by the paper of record.

Barringer was particularly keen-eyed in her assessment of these and other crucial trends that distinguished the new Marxism from orthodox Marxism.

She noted that as a result of the change in focus from economic to social grievances, communism's defeat in the Soviet Union and its captive nations behind the Iron Curtain seemed not to faze the Marxist academics she quoted. Indeed, they were celebratory. "I'm very happy with what's happening in these countries. I think it's going to save socialism, rather than kill it," said John Roemer, professor of economics at the University of California, Davis.

Another tendency was a recognition of the fact that capitalism was clearly superior in its ability to satisfy man's needs and wants, one of communism's greatest failures. Jonathan M. Wiener, professor of history at the University of California, Irvine, said that "Marxism needs to account for the continuing vitality of capitalism as capitalism embraces more and more of the world." To be sure, the professors relegated capitalism's victory to this one advantage, and they did not extol the freedom that went with capitalism. They never contrasted the free market's ability to liberate the creative spirit and allow individuals to pursue human flourishing with Marxism's inevitable despotism (something that Karl Marx himself had warned would be necessary).[14] Capitalism's economic advantage was moreover described as an illusory benefit: prosperity came at the expense of having to conform to the drab dictates of the marketplace and therefore forced people to live lives of quiet desperation. Capitalism's superior ability to provide goods and services was cast by new Marxists as the harbinger of ugly consumerism.

Still, the recognition that communism just couldn't compete with capitalism economically was important. Again, this is something that had begun in the 1960s. Max Horkheimer, the third and most important director of the Frankfurt School and the founder of critical theory, told an interviewer in 1969, right before his death, that Marx had been wrong in believing

> capitalist society would necessarily be overcome by the solidarity of the workers due to their increasing impoverishment. This idea is false. The society in which we live doesn't impoverish workers but helps them toward a better life. And moreover, Marx didn't see at all that freedom and justice are dialectical concepts: The more freedom, the less justice, and the more justice, the less freedom.[15]

BUT BY the late 1980s, this was no longer just an old man raving about philosophy—this was borne out by incontrovertible evidence. Capitalism was better at supplying men's needs, and therefore the worker would never revolt. Wiener advanced as a solution that "we need to look more at how the ideology of consumerism has overpowered class consciousness."[16] But that was not how communism would save itself. There were other ways.

A Communist Division of Labor

A KEY insight of Barringer's article was that it sketched out the way Marxism was reckoning with the failure of class consciousness to inspire revolution. She noted that inside the academy, Marxism was growing, especially in those disciplines that delved into cultural interpretation:

> *Where Marxism is thriving, these scholars say, is less in social science courses, where there is a possibility of practical application than in the abstract world of literary criticism. It is also in this field that new radicals—from feminists who say class analysis leaves women out, to deconstructionists who say historical truth does not exist—have posed the sharpest challenge to those who back Marx's theories of class struggle.*[17]

AS PROFESSOR Wiener himself explained, "Marxism and feminism, Marxism and deconstruction, Marxism and race—this is where the exciting debates are." Eric Mann calls this "a little division of labor" that communists create as they carry out their goal of overthrowing the United States. In an interview with Venezuela's teleSUR station, Mann recalled that he once had asked a gay rights leader, "'How did you come up with the idea of the Gay Liberation Fund?' He says, 'Why do you think we called it that? Because we believed in the National Liberation Fund of Vietnam. We weren't just wanting gay marriage, we wanted to overthrow the government as part of being queer.'" Mann added, "I come out of the tradition where wherever you started, we're all trying to make the same revolution. We had maybe a little division of labor."[18]

Mann is hardly alone. In fact, communists and their socialist brethren tell us again and again that they indiscriminately use race, sex, climate, or other issues to advance revolutionary goals. The recanted Marxist David Horowitz is fond of quoting a member of Students for a Democratic Society, the radical 1960s group, who said, "The issue is never the issue. The issue is always the revolution." As Horowitz explained, "in other words the cause—whether inner city blacks or women—is never the real cause, but only an occasion to advance the real cause which is the accumulation of power to make the revolution."[19] This is an important point to understand. Go to any gathering where Marxists strategize, any online platform that promotes such planning, and you will find the espousal of causes that outwardly range from race, sex, gender, sexual orientation, and transgenderism to indigenism, environmentalism, animalism, or ableism. Behind it all, the accretion of raw power is the goal. This power is to be used for civilizational transformation. They are all "trying to make the same revolution," to use Mann's words.

Cornel West, the Harvard professor who wrote the foreword for the main text of CRT in 1995, also picked up in a 1991 article for *The New York Times* on how the progressive movement would operate on several fronts. West called it "the inchoate, scattered yet gathering progressive movement that is emerging across the American landscape. This gathering now lacks both the vital moral vocabulary and the focused leadership that can constitute and sustain it. Yet it will be rooted ultimately in current activities by people of color, by labor and ecological groups, by women, by homosexuals."[20]

The Marxists' little division of labor is employed to its fullest extent by the networks that have spawned to spread NextGen Marxism in the world and inside the United States. The US Social Forum (USSF), the Left Forum, LeftRoots, and many others bring together environmentalists, feminists, racial warriors, and transgender-rights activists to make sure they all work together under a big anticapitalist Red Tent.

At the 2015 conference of Left Forum, a premier gathering of global Marxists, there was, for example, a panel on "Climate Justice and Energy Democracy," another on "The Climate Mobilization: A Route to Reclaiming Democracy and Preventing Ecological Collapse," and yet one more on "The Climate Crisis Is a Democracy Crisis: Why We Need a Democratic Revolution in the US and Beyond," to name but three of several devoted to environmentalism. The short film *Climate Justice: The US Left and the Problem of the State* was screened. There was a panel titled "'The Transgender Tipping Point Is Crushing Us': Trans Politics in the Era of Visibility." Yet one more panel was an all-you-can-eat buffet: "Restorative Justice for All? Race, Class, Gender, Disability, and Animal Liberation."[21] Race was, of course, one of the main topics of the conference. But the emphasis on climate should hardly surprise. As we will see in chapter 9, the man who founded Greenpeace, Patrick Moore, said he walked away from environmentalism in the late 1980s because the same process that Barringer recorded as happening in academia was being duplicated in environmentalism—all the pro-Soviet people started to move to climate work when they saw the Iron Curtain collapsing.

The USSF is probably the most important "network of networks" and is covered extensively in chapter 7. It started out in Atlanta in 2007 as an offshoot of the global World Social Forum, which was founded in Porto Alegre, Brazil, in 2001. In Atlanta, panels were organized around all the different fronts of the revolution. There was, for example, a workshop on "The Sky as a Common Resource: Fighting Global Warming by Asserting Equal Rights to Our Atmosphere";[22] the Women's Working Group of the USSF, in coordination with SisterSong, "organized over 70 gender-specific workshops and events";[23] and yet another group held a panel on "Beyond Reform or Revolution: Economic Transformation in the US"[24] and another on "Race, Gender, Nationality: A Fight for the Right to the City."[25]

But this is just tactics. The connecting tissue is Marxism, as we can see from the 2007 Atlanta workshop titled "The Red Tent; the Court of Women; Feminism Race and Class."[26] These conferences are about how to harness power to destroy capitalism and change everything. One of the largest workshops in Atlanta, which lasted four hours, dealt with "revolutionary strategy and organization" and was organized by Freedom Road Socialist Organization, the League of Revolutionaries for a New America, Eric Mann's Labor Community Strategy Center, Bring the Ruckus, and Marxist study groups from the Bay Area and New York City.[27]

The 2015 Left Forum gathering, which was held in New York, came after BLM was already formed, came in fact some six months after the explosive riots that followed the police shooting of Michael Brown in Ferguson, Missouri, a months-long destabilization campaign that BLM used to organize and strategize with other far-left groups. The Left Forum conference was a continuation of that mission and was in fact titled "No Justice, No Peace," one of the main slogans that was in evidence in Ferguson. And one of the main events of the conference was a speech by the BLM cofounder Alicia Garza, in which she went straight to the point. "It's not possible for a world to emerge where black lives matter if it's under capitalism, and it's not possible to abolish capitalism without a struggle against national oppression and gender oppression," Garza said to huge applause. "Black Lives Matter is much more than a hashtag. In fact, Black Lives Matter is an organized network, in twenty-six cities, globally."

Garza added that "our task is to build the Left" but warned that the Marxists gathered around her would not get "actual political power, actual economic power, social power, with slogans and newsletters." What was needed to defeat capitalism was "an organized, consolidated, multi-issue, multitendency Left."[28]

This Book

IF YOU have ever gotten the sneaky suspicion that all the ways the Left uses to transform society and (it hopes) human nature may be linked, this book is here to tell you that you're right and to help you connect the dots. It will tell you that, no, you are not crazy, nor a conspiracy theorist. The use of race, sex, sexual orientation, climate, social justice, gender, and animal rights; the denigration of beauty and the sublime; the consequent elevation of ugliness, chaos, and disorder; the decimation of the family and the abandonment of God—these and many other diverse struggles are fronts in a larger war. As Germán Parodi of Disabled in Action in Pennsylvania put it to Venezuela's teleSUR media network, the reason he helped organize the USSF in Philadelphia in 2015 was that "we all are being oppressed and we know that, but that leaves many of us fighting for scraps. We are very fractioned and we are working on different issues but the Social Forum brings us all together."[29] NextGen Marxists who know what they are doing organize people under all these disparate causes, all sharing the ultimate goal of seeking to dismantle capitalism and the political order. The organizations devoted to furthering the separate causes retain distinct sets of experts and activists, but they are united in their shared aim of reordering society.

NextGen Marxism is, therefore, the new frontier in a 170-year-old war that has wreaked havoc in all corners of the world. It is the cultural Marxism of Gramsci—the idea that to obtain civilizational transformation, you must first undermine the existing culture; the manipulation of a raft of causes to ignite grievances; the use of grassroots organizing to create foot soldiers for focused campaigns, demonstrations, or even riots; and, crucially, the creation of revolutionary networks to strategize and coordinate. Gramsci was of course building on Lenin's organizational structure, but it was Gramsci's goal and strategy for transforming an entire culture that built a bridge from Lenin's successful revolution in backward Russia to what we are seeing today in the United States and other industrialized societies: the speech codes, cancel culture, and elevation of victimhood to a national cult. These are the products of NextGen Marxism, and one of the central purposes of this book is to help Americans clearly understand that the phenomena around them have a Red Tent.

To see this clearly is not to be a conspiracy theorist, and it is the opposite of "hysteria." Hysteria is what the Left has whipped the country into for years now, by constantly claiming, for example, as Garza did at the Left Forum in New York, that there is now "a plan to subvert, to oppress, and in some cases, in many cases especially now, to extinguish black lives, to get rid of us."[30] Hysteria is telling people that the world is going to end because of climate change unless we reverse centuries of progress, starting right now. And hysteria is insisting that "language does not merely represent violence, but enacts its own type of violence."[31]

When we were fighting Soviet Marxism and its fellow travelers here in America, the Left pretended, too, that anti-communists were spreading, or had fallen for, a conspiracy theory. In *The Right: The Hundred-Year War for American Conservatism*, Matthew Continetti credited Hannah Arendt's 1951 book *The Origins of Totalitarianism* for demonstrating that "anticommunism was not some right-wing fantasy or a 'reflexive,' 'knee-jerk' 'hysteria' but a considered position among intellectuals across the spectrum."[32]

With this book, we strive to explain that liberals who want to improve society, but not redo it, have as much an interest in fighting NextGen Marxism as do conservatives whose interest is to conserve tradition. Americans today are confronted with a NextGen Marxism that is "multitendency" to accumulate power. The NextGen Marxists carrying out these strategies have gotten very far already. This book explains in detail what can be done to reverse their gains. We connect the dots as a means to alert the reader that we need to have a consequential battle of ideas, as well as a practical plan of action, or we will certainly lose the country.

At the same time, we must not lose sight that NextGen Marxists are Americans with constitutional rights. We must expose what they are doing with evidence, explain the reasoning behind our conclusions, and fight their ideas with better ideas. We must also do so without falling into the mistakes that Joe McCarthy and the John Birch Society made while fighting communist infiltration in the 1950s. The Birchers' frothy conspiracy theories were unsubstantiated, and the group was rightly drummed out of polite society by Barry Goldwater, Bill Buckley's *National Review*, and others with impeccable anti-communist bona fides who did not want their cause sullied. McCarthy was often on the

NEXTGEN MARXISM | 19

mark, but by making wild accusations, he, too, eventually lost the support of the American public. Thus a quick perusal of our notes will reveal that we mostly quote NextGen Marxists themselves on what they say they want to do, and their reason for doing it, unlike members of the media, who ignore what NextGen Marxists say and pretend what is happening is all part of a struggle for social justice, racial equity, and market-friendly climate programs.

The reasons to battle NextGen Marxism are compelling, and they are the same as for combating the old Soviet Marxism. Marxism is legalized robbery; it is exploitive and manipulative. Its superimposed collectivism robs the individual of agency, leaving him an empty shell. The revolutionary mindset inevitably leads to tyranny because it lacks a limiting principle or an inherent mechanism that clicks in and checks its appetite for change and power. As Carvalho reminds us, the revolutionary mindset is "totalitarian and genocidal in itself, independently from its ideological content in different circumstances and occasions. By refusing himself to be accountable to anything except a hypothetical future of its own invention, and firmly disposed to destroy by cunning or by force every obstacle to the remodeling of the world to his own image and likeness, the revolutionary is the worst enemy of the human species."[33] Or as George Will puts it, "wokeness, which lacks limiting principles, limits opposition to itself."[34]

We see many examples of this, but an easy one to comprehend is to be found in the change in sexual mores. In a short twenty-five years, we have cascaded from the Defense of Marriage Act (which prohibited same-sex marriage) getting eighty-four votes in the Senate in 1996, including Senator Joe Biden's; to the US Supreme Court declaring same-sex marriage constitutional in *Obergefell v. Hodges* in 2015; to President Biden appointing two high-profile transvestites to his administration in 2021;[35] to the proliferation of Americans identifying as LGBT, evidenced by a rise to 21 percent among those born between 1997 and 2003 in 2021, or double what it had been just four years earlier;[36] to, finally, the mutilation of children who are told by adults that they need to "transition."[37] What's the next frontier? Many people predict legalized polygamy and polyandry. Many academic studies are also currently examining the desirability of societal acceptance of adults having a sexual interest in children. "Queer Theory does not have a bottom," exclaimed the mathematician James Lindsay, an expert on the Marxist dangers we deal with in this book.[38] "It has no limiting principle whatsoever."

The Chapters

AS ROBERT Reilly has written, "intellectual pedigree is important because wars begin in the minds of men well before the shooting starts."[39] We therefore begin in chapter 1 with the intellectual pedigree of the ideas on which NextGen Marxism is founded, a pedigree that includes most importantly Karl Marx and the utopian socialists who, inspired by the scientific and technological revolutions, rejected God and believed in the perfectibility of man. Chapter 1 explains how the Soviet Union's old, ham-fisted communist orthodoxy failed to convince Americans to give up their freedoms. American workers from the industrial Midwest to the West, East, and South refused to be swayed by the siren song of Bolshevism with American twangs. They did not want to destroy America; in fact, what they were demanding was a share in the American Dream, and they were intensely patriotic. No matter what the Kremlin and its fellow travelers tried in America, it failed. A quick swing through Marxism's efforts to sway American workers will, however, put what came later in starker relief.

In chapter 2, we trace the roots of Marxism's success in our century back to the 1920s and 1930s, when European Marxists came to recognize that the proletariat, too, was a very bad revolutionary. Those were the decades when the Frankfurt School came into being and Antonio Gramsci did his best writing from a fascist prison in Italy. It was not until the 1960s that their ideas germinated and sank deep roots. Gramsci's writings, particularly, began to move men and women in the 1970s, to the point that the Gramscian Paul Piccone writes that "if, in the history of Marxism, the period from the Erfurt program to 1914 can be characterized as the age of the Second International, from 1917 to the middle 1920s that of Leninism, from 1924 to the early 1950s that of Stalinism, and from the late 1950s to early 1970s that of Maoism, the 1980s are likely to usher in what may be called a new phase of 'Gramscism.'"[40] Without a doubt, the 2020s, too, belong to the Gramscian age of Marxism. Chapter 2, therefore, is devoted to understanding the fountainhead of these ideas. It also looks at the links between the Kremlin and the Italians and Germans. The Western Marxists, as they were called, did produce a cultural interpretation of Marxism that clashed with Stalin's views, but they were nurtured in the 1920s by Bolshevik intellectuals—many of whom, unsurprisingly, perished in Stalin's purges in the 1930s.

Chapter 3 then explains the blossoming of the ideas of Gramsci and the Frankfurt School scholars, particularly Herbert Marcuse, among the denizens of what came to be known as the "New Left" in America, Canada, Europe, and Japan from the early 1960s on. C. Wright Mills, Irving Howe, and others describe the New Left as the American acceptance that the worker would not revolt. Many explanations are given as to why the 1960s were a time of revolutionary fervor (particularly the years between 1964 and 1972), and they usually have to do with the confluence of the fight for civil rights, the Kennedy and Martin Luther King Jr. assassinations, the Vietnam War, and, overseas, decolonization. These were all strong forces that did unite to produce explosive social reaction. However, radical students also played a decisive role, first in stoking violence in the early 1960s, then in actual terrorism in the 1970s, and finally in capturing the institutions in the 1980s.

The year 1989 was an inflection point in the nation's history because the radical students of the 1960s, who had sought to emulate Fidel Castro, Che Guevara, and Ho Chi Minh by unleashing revolution in the United States, were beginning to find success in the mainstream. But they had not given up on their radical aspirations for the country.

One life best epitomizes this transition from 1960s radical to terrorist to professorship and then power broker—that of William Ayers. The life of this wealthy scion of America's industrial might, who became a radical at the University of Michigan at Ann Arbor, helped found the Weather Underground (identified by the FBI as a domestic terror group), and then discovered how to really change the country through academia, so epitomizes our story that we have devoted the entirety of chapter 4 to his metamorphosis. That chapter and the subsequent two chapters present how the groundwork of today was laid, and by whom. Khrushchev, Gramsci, and Mills are dead, but Ayers, Mann, and CRT's Kimberlé Crenshaw are very much still alive, so they represent the living present.

Thus chapter 5 is devoted to American offshoots of Horkheimer's critical theory, critical legal studies (CLS), and CRT. As Irving Howe explained, the New Left had devoted itself to the search for a "substitute proletariat," and the jury was out on whether the vanguard of the revolution would be led by students and intellectuals, on one hand, or blacks and other racial minorities on the other. The triumph of CRT over CLS heralded in a way the contention by Marxist ideologues that blacks would play the lead role in the revolutionary struggle. But the revolutionary organizing that Mann and others would use, with its single-minded pursuit of power accretion, was a new American phenomenon, one championed by the organizer emeritus Saul Alinsky, so we devote chapter 6 to understanding its intricacies.

Chapter 7 takes up the issue of the most disturbing and potentially most destructive aspect of NextGen Marxism: the sexualization of children and the attack on the family. To many, it may seem that the transgender cult and the appearance of pornographic books in school libraries are phenomena of the last several years. But in fact, attacks on sexual morality and the family have been part of the socialist project from the very beginning. Even more surprising is the theme of sexual deviancy among the socialist thinkers themselves. Part of the effort to protect America's children from this scourge requires that we better understand its sources and its true aims, which we explain in this chapter.

Chapter 8, one of the most important in the book in our view, lays out the infrastructure the international Left has created in the western hemisphere. The network building began in the 1980s, but it was the collapse of communism in Central and Eastern Europe in 1989 that set things on fire. Cuba's Castro, Brazil's Luiz Inácio Lula da Silva, and other Marxist leaders realized that they had to alter their approach. They met in Brazil in July 1990 and stated in the resulting document, "We assessed the crisis in Eastern Europe ... [and] reviewed the revolutionary strategies of the Left and the objectives that the international situation places on us."[41] Drawing heavily on Gramsci's ideas, they developed a strategy for exporting their revolution to the United States that would focus on changing the culture through an extensive network of organizations, rather than through a quick and violent revolution.

In chapter 8, we thus explore the plethora of networks—LeftRoots, Left Forum, the USSF, Freedom Road, and others—and their gatherings where Marxists congregate, strategize, and build momentum. As Garza, donning a Palestinian kaffiyeh, put it in a 2010 Social Forum meeting in Oakland, California, "the Social Forum is not a conference [something Garza asked those in her panel to repeat for emphasis] ... it's a movement-building process!"[42] It was these networks that prepared Garza and the other BLM founders for when the moment would come, and which, post 2013, helped them promote the BLM movement and its rioting online.

Chapter 9, finally, deals with *why* the United States must be saved and how that can be accomplished. America serves a fundamental purpose, which the authors believe is divinely inspired. One doesn't have to be a Christian, however, to agree that the United States brings together all the qualities, temperaments, advantages, and values that make Americans uniquely qualified to champion freedom. The United States has changed much since it led an international co-alition against Soviet communism from the end of the Second World War to 1990—but all the qualities of character that made her wage the struggle in the first place, and win it in the end, are still there. Chapter 9 explains that even though the entire world faces the same cultural Marxist threat that we do, the main battle is here. It is not just a moral imperative that would make us wage the battle against NextGen Marxism; it is also an existential responsibility.

The authors of this book approached their task fully understanding that this generation is not the first to fight Marxism. We stand on the shoulders of giants like Bill Buckley, Henry Regnery, Whittaker Chambers, James Burnham, Lee Edwards, Ed Feulner, and M. Stanton Evans, to name but a few. Others belong-ing to the political realm, such as Harry Truman, John F. Kennedy, Richard Nixon, Joe McCarthy (yes), and J. Edgar Hoover, may have been more con-troversial because of the actions they saw as necessary to take, but they none-theless join the intellectuals in leaving a rich legacy of ideas and actions from which to pick and choose. The polemics surrounding the latter group remind us, however, that the internal fight against infiltration requires deft handling far more than the external one against a foreign enemy, which attracts more summer soldiers and sunshine patriots. We thus begin our chapter on solutions by drawing on lessons from the past, both its wins and some of its losses.

We then explore what individual Americans can do today to fight the new communist scourge of NextGen Marxism. We need the local fights to make sure woke school practices are exposed, to make sure that the struggle sessions of the workplace do not go unchallenged, and to ensure that the adults expos-ing young children to perversities behind such practices such as drag queen story hour are not allowed to break the law with impunity.

Citizen warriors can do only so much, however, so we also look at how government policies can work to break the grip that NextGen Marxists have on institutions. The name of Florida governor Ron DeSantis comes up a lot, because the governor has done a great deal to keep the NextGen Marxists in check in the Sunshine State. But his policies are not the only ones highlighted. West Virginia's state treasurer Riley Moore and others also come in for praise for their forthright approach.

Our purpose with this book is to sound a clarion call on what is happening, connect dots between superficially separate phenomena, and then offer a way out. This will not be easy. The authors know all too well that to fight NextGen Marxism is not the most popular stand to take, particularly when those spreading these ideas hide behind such lofty-sounding campaigns as racial and social justice, sexual equality, love, and saving the planet. It is far easier to look away and pretend nothing is happening or that what is there is good. This is not the path we've taken, and with this book, we enjoin you to face up to the threat of NextGen Marxism as well.

1
BACKGROUND OF THE PRESENT CRISIS

MARXISM IS AT the heart of the current effort to destroy the American experiment in ordered liberty. We know that is so because the leaders of this effort have said it. Even when they try to conceal it, or leave it unsaid, we can recognize the essential characteristics of Marxism in their worldview, their tactics, and their goals. But the phenomenon we see today is not entirely synonymous with the original Marxism, and so we distinguish it by calling it NextGen Marxism, the latest iteration of the cultural Marxism birthed in the last century. Our mission is both to understand and explain NextGen Marxism. It is baffling to many that an ideology with such a proven track record of failure, leaving such a wake of human destruction, can still have any appeal at all. But somehow, against all reason, it does. Our goal is to understand *why*, in order to protect our liberties and our lives against it and, ultimately, to defeat it.

To accomplish this, we must start with the original Marxism. Where did it come from? How did Marxism differ from other revolutionary movements, such as the anarchists? Why did it not initially find fertile soil in Europe or the United States? What changes allowed for its eventual success? What is its appeal? Understanding the answers to these questions is essential to our current fight against NextGen Marxism.

To understand fully Marxism's trajectory in time, particularly its enduring appeal despite its acknowledged failures, one has to recognize not only what is unique to Marxism but also what is not. Because for all else that it might be, Marxism is also just one more in an age-old litany of voices that claim that man can create an ideal society here on earth, that discord and deprivation can be eradicated, that wealth inequality can be erased, and that all of this can be achieved by sublimating the interests of the individual to the interests of the community.

Arguments for a communal utopia begin with Plato, who suggested that although the ideal society did not exist, it could be formed. In Plato's ideal city, under the leadership of elite, well-educated philosopher-kings, there would be no more war, no poverty or hunger, no enmity. Individual families would be abolished, and some form of proto-communism would prevail—at least among the upper classes. Of course, today, logical people find it easy to disparage this type of utopian vision because we know all too well from the Soviet Union, China, Cuba, Venezuela, North Korea, and North Vietnam—to name just a few examples—that tyranny is the inevitable outcome of utopian aspiration.

This is not to say that debates over the purpose of life, the nature of justice, and how humans can best live together in community in a well-ordered society should not be ongoing and far-ranging. Indeed, not to seek to do better, to improve the world we live in, to achieve greater happiness and prosperity for more people, would be both inhuman and *un*human. Not to seek betterment would reflect a lack of charity and concern for others, and it would also go against those very fundamental impulses of humans to have more and to do more, to do better. One can even argue that exploring utopia is a necessary part of that conversation, because it allows one to debate what better looks like and to ruminate over an imagined ideal society. This process goes astray when it leaves the realm of rumination and enters the realm of implementation, when utopia is no longer the subject of abstract speculation but the object of determined idealists. Whether they push their vision by persuasion or by force, it yields a devastating impact on its victims and often on its perpetrators as well.

Marxism, as implemented by Vladimir Lenin in the Bolshevik Revolution of 1917, is the proof of this par excellence. In just the first few years of the revolution, *hundreds of thousands* of adversaries, class enemies, rebellious workers, peasants, kulaks (landowning farmers), and Cossacks were murdered, including many of those who had themselves been supporters and instigators of the revolution. To understand the depth of the cruelty inspired by Russia's Marxist revolutionary fervor, one has only to read a telegram of Lenin's, sent on August 10, 1918:

> *Comrades! The kulak uprising in your five districts must be crushed without pity. The interests of the whole revolution demand such actions, for the final struggle with the kulaks has now begun. You must make an example of these people. (1) Hang (I mean hang publicly, so that people see it) at least 100 kulaks, rich bastards, and known blood-suckers. (2) Publish their names. (3) Seize all their grain. (4) Single out the hostages per my instructions in yesterday's telegram. Do all this so that for miles around people see it all, understand it, tremble, and tell themselves that we are killing the bloodthirsty*

kulaks and that we will continue to do so. Reply saying you have received
and carried out these instructions. Yours, Lenin.
  P.S. *Find tougher people.*[1]

BETWEEN 1917 and the Soviet Union's dissolution, revolution and its promised
utopia were used to justify the deaths of twenty million souls—a conservative
estimate.[2] But well before that bloody epoch, the Jacobins of France demonstrated both the cruelty and futility of trying to create an ideal society through
revolution. It was the French Revolution, that proto-communist revolution,
that first manifested the modern revolutionary spirit: the urge to create an
imagined, ideal society by thoroughly eradicating the old.

How did we move from the abstract utopian speculations of Plato and
Thomas More to the guillotine of France and the gulags of Bolshevik Russia?
The answer begins partly with the Scientific Revolution of Galileo (1564–1642)
and Isaac Newton (1643–1727) and then moves to the thinkers of the Enlightenment. That path brought about profound changes in thinking about man's relationship to the world around him, which in turn paved the way for revolution
itself. As James Billington explains, "first came the slow growth of the *idea* of
secular revolution in early modern Europe. Then came the *fact* of a totally new
kind of upheaval within the largest city of the mightiest power in Europe."[3] The
emphasis here on the importance of the *idea of secular revolution* as a necessary
prerequisite for revolution itself reveals the central role that intellectuals will
play throughout this drama.

The Death of God and the Perfectibility of Man

THE IDEA of secular revolution begins with the Italian astronomer and inventor
Galileo Galilei. With his many innovations and discoveries, Galileo launched
the Scientific Revolution. This was not merely a matter of new methods of inquiry and new tools for scientific investigation but in fact a marker of a radical
shift in how the world was ordered. In the fight between Galileo and the Church
over the nature of truth (a theme you will find throughout this book) and how
we know whether something is true, Galileo lost in the short term—he lost his
trial before the Roman Inquisition for arguing that Earth moved around the
sun—but he was vindicated in the long term as scientific knowledge spread and
proved the Church wrong. In that battle, the inviolability of the Church was

eroded, and the belief that science could answer all questions and cure all ills began to take the place of belief in the sacred. Galileo's most important contribution may have been a simple telescope, but that was enough to reveal whole new possibilities for mankind, including a future in which God no longer stood on a pedestal but was displaced by man.

Galileo had demonstrated that through the use of reason and observation, human beings could better understand the natural world. This is an idea with which today's NextGen Marxists, deconstructionists that they are, are at war. At the same time, the British politician Francis Bacon (1561–1626) put forth the idea that human beings could use their reason and observation also to understand better and improve their own lives, indeed, the idea that they could improve their world to the point of perfection. His belief in the potential for human knowledge to create a perfect world was most clearly conveyed in an incomplete fantasy work he wrote around 1623 titled *New Atlantis*. In this fragment of a story, European sailors have discovered an island somewhere west of Peru called Bensalem, where human knowledge has been elevated to the highest pursuit: "The end of our foundation is the knowledge of causes, and secret motions of things; and the enlarging of the bounds of human empire, to the effecting of all things possible."[4] In other words, he is suggesting that everything can be known, and then anything is possible. For example, as a result of the power of knowledge, all human vice has been eradicated: "You shall understand that there is not under the heavens so chaste a nation as this of Bensalem; nor so free from all pollution or foulness. It is the virgin of the world."[5]

Bacon's utopia was a far cry from the classless, communist utopia that Marx and Engels would later envision, not least because Bacon's Christian faith was everywhere apparent: his work fully acknowledged the importance of divine salvation and intervention; he advocated the use of science to serve religion, not to displace it; he supported the importance of marriage and family; and he believed in the value of tradition, especially the handing down of wisdom through the ages. But Bacon also believed in the power of science to solve all ills, an idea conveyed in *New Atlantis*, which laid the foundation for Enlightenment thinkers such as Jean-Jacques Rousseau, the Baron de Montesquieu, and John Locke to develop the idea that societies could be improved *to the point of perfection* through the exercise of reason.

Reform versus Revolution

CONSENT OF the governed was one of the key Enlightenment concepts to emerge from this new situation in which man could improve and even perfect his world. The idea was advocated by Locke, Montesquieu, and Rousseau, and yet the three understood it in diametrically opposed ways. One can best see that distinction in the differences between the American and French Revolutions, which occurred at nearly the same time. The American Founders, shaped more by Locke and Montesquieu and informed by a deep knowledge of and respect for history and the natural law tradition, believed they could develop a system that could achieve the consent of *all* the governed, both majorities and minorities. One can see this nascent form of an inclusive social contract from the very first moments of the American experiment with the Mayflower Compact, which was in essence America's first constitution:

> *Having undertaken, for the Glory of God, and advancements of the Christian faith, and the honor of our King and Country, a voyage to plant the first colony in the Northern parts of Virginia; do by these presents, solemnly and mutually, in the presence of God, and one another; covenant and combine ourselves together into a civil body politic; for our better ordering and preservation, and furtherance of the ends aforesaid: and by virtue hereof do enact, constitute, and frame, such just and equal laws, ordinances, acts, constitutions, and offices, from time to time, as shall be thought most meet and convenient for the general good of the colony, unto which we promise all due submission and obedience.*

AMONG THE 102 passengers were both Pilgrims—fervent Christian believers who sought to create a community free from moral corruption—and "Strangers": craftsmen, merchants, and indentured servants whose purposes were primarily economic. To survive in the new world, they needed each other. They would therefore need a set of laws on which they could all agree, laws that would of necessity allow for different views and values. This nascent social contract later came to fruition in the US Constitution, the First Amendment of which not only guaranteed freedom of religion but, importantly, guaranteed the right to dissent:

> *Congress shall make no law respecting an establishment of religion, or*

prohibiting the free exercise thereof; or abridging the freedom of speech, or of the press; or the right of the people peaceably to assemble, and to petition the Government for a redress of grievances.

THE AMERICAN constitutional process was one of deliberation and compromise. It was also an organic process of trial and error, one that had been going on since the signing of the Mayflower Compact. The constitutional process was far from perfect: compromise with the Southern states meant that slavery was not abolished, as many of the Northern participants had wanted. But the Declaration of Independence and the Constitution did provide what Martin Luther King Jr. referred to two centuries later as a promissory note: "a promise that all men, yes, Black men as well as White men, would be guaranteed the unalienable rights of life, liberty, and the pursuit of happiness." The system developed by the Founders was thus inclusive to its deepest core: individual rights were sacrosanct because they were grounded in Nature and Nature's God. Moreover, because it was believed that every individual was created in the image of God, the misuse of another person was not only a grievous offense but a sin against God.

In the century and a half that spanned the signing of the Mayflower Compact and the formal creation of the United States in the Declaration of Independence and the Constitution, the American people were able fully to put behind them the practices, institutions, and beliefs of medieval Europe and to embrace the modern system of capitalism, understood here as "a system based on private property rights, freedom of exchange and a government under law ... a process within which individuals voluntarily interact in the pursuit of their own private ends and, in doing so, create an order."[6] One might argue that it was possible for the American settlers to achieve this only because they did not have an established landed aristocracy or monarchy with which to contend (acknowledging that they did face a sort of "landed class" in the native populations). But the fact of a blank slate alone would not have necessarily led to the outcome it did. They had an advantage in coming to the new world, to be sure, where they could make a fresh beginning, but adding to this very important colonial experience, they were also very much shaped by the ancient ideas of Greece and Rome, by Enlightenment thinkers such as John Locke, and above all by their Christian faith. John Adams wrote to Thomas Jefferson that it was "the general principles of Christianity" on which independence had been achieved.

Christianity provided the foundation for certain presuppositions commonly held by the American people. Robert Reilly described these presuppositions: "the immutability of human nature; the constancy of the universe; the basic goodness of creation; the existence of a benevolent God; the indispensability of Christian morals and the eternal destiny of man in the transcendent, along with their implied limitations on the role of politics in man's life."[7] Thus the American Revolution is better thought of not as a revolution but as what Ellis Sandoz describes as "an antimodernist recovery and rearticulation of Western and English constitutionalism"[8] or what Peter Drucker simply calls "the Conservative Counter-Revolution of 1776."[9]

The French Revolution, on the other hand, inspired by the utopian ideas of Rousseau, was the very opposite: it instituted a complete rejection of the past, of tradition, and of Christianity. Although Rousseau was not the sole inspiration for the French Revolution, it likely would never have taken the shape that it did without his radical conceptions of freedom, civil society, and the state. Rousseau began his famous work *The Social Contract*, published in 1762, with the most famous and yet most nonsensical words he ever wrote: "Men are born free, yet everywhere are in chains." What did this even mean? He believed in a mythical state of nature in which man was born free but becomes enchained by his own passions and faults and by the judgment of others around him. Rousseau believed that an individual could reach his liberation, and then perfection, only under an all-powerful state and with the dissolution of all classes and civil institutions, including the Church. Under such an all-powerful state, man would be "freed" from his own selfish and destructive passions as well as from the oppression of others around him. But this would, of course, require "an absolute surrender of the individual, with all of his rights and all of his powers, to the community as a whole."[10]

Rousseau posited a fantasy world, not drawn from history but existing only in his imagination, in which everyone miraculously knows and agrees upon "the common good"—a fantasy construction in itself—a world in which peasants hang out under an oak tree; always act wisely; and rule the world with peace, unity, and equality:

> As long as several men in assembly regard themselves as a single body, they
> have only a single will which is concerned with their common preservation
> and general well-being. In this case, all the springs of the State are vigorous

and simple and its rules clear and luminous; there are no embroilments or conflicts of interests; the common good is everywhere clearly apparent, and only good sense is needed to perceive it. Peace, unity and equality are the enemies of political subtleties. Men who are upright and simple are difficult to deceive because of their simplicity; lures and ingenious pretexts fail to impose upon them, and they are not even subtle enough to be dupes. When, among the happiest people in the world, bands of peasants are seen regulating affairs of State under an oak, and always acting wisely, can we help scorning the ingenious methods of other nations, which make themselves illustrious and wretched with so much art and mystery?[11]

WHEN, IN history, has one ever seen several men in assembly having a single will? When have the rules of the state ever been clear and luminous? When have relations between people ever not been tinted by conflicts of interest? Rousseau, perhaps more than anyone other than Marx, brings to mind Cicero's famous dictum: "There is nothing so absurd that some philosopher has not said it."

Yet for all his absurdity, Rousseau has had a devastating impact on any number of countries by inspiring their utopian revolutions, first in France, then in Russia, and today, in the equity revolution that is sweeping through the United States. One must not underestimate its seriousness. As Thomas Carlyle quipped, "there once was a man called Rousseau, who wrote a book containing nothing but ideas, the second edition was bound in the skins of those who laughed at the first."[12] A number of the ideas Rousseau brought into the world have reverberated with destructive force down through the ages, not least among them his distorted conception of freedom, which is the very opposite of what Americans think of as freedom. As Robert Nisbet explained, "freedom for Rousseau is the synchronization of all social existence to the will of the state, the replacement of cultural diversity by a mechanical equalitarianism."[13] The collectivist ideal that the NextGen Marxist holds close to his heart is Rousseauian.

With this Rousseau provided the justification for a dual tyranny: an all-powerful state, on one hand, and the destruction of the institutions and forms of cooperation between people that would have protected them from an all-powerful state on the other. As Alexis de Tocqueville had pointed out in observing the importance of civil society as a protection against tyranny, "it is clear that if each citizen, as he becomes individually weaker and consequently more incapable in isolation of preserving his freedom, does not learn the art of uniting with those like him to defend it, tyranny will necessarily grow with equality."[14] Rousseau's attack on social institutions was a direct attack on the ability of individuals to unite with others. Robert Nisbet explains that an essential characteristic of totalitarianism is not merely that it is an all-powerful state but also that it comprises an atomized people: "Totalitarianism involves the demolishment of the social ties among a people, such as are represented by the family, church, or university, and the replacement of these by the unitary connection of citizen to citizen. It is the reduction of social man into political man, and involves the substitution of the state alone for the myriad relationships which compose traditional society."[15] Thus, with Rousseau's dual tyrannies, the age of utopian experiments as well as the totalitarian state were born. In bringing together the promise of the perfectibility of the individual with the idea that such perfection could be achieved only by sublimating the interests of the individual to the "common good" (whatever that might be) under an all-powerful state, one can see the impetus that not only brought utopian experiments from the realm of the purely speculative to the realm of action but that also ensured it would happen in a profoundly destructive way.

Rousseau's vision came to fruition in 1789 with the French Revolution. Less than one year after the US Constitution was ratified, France's revolutionaries started killing off their past—the Church, the monarchy, the aristocracy, their history—and trying to craft a political future based on pure reason, with all power vested in the state. Abbé Sieyès, who had helped draft France's new Declaration of the Rights of Man and of the Citizen, explained, "The nation is prior to everything. It is the source of everything. Its will is always…the supreme law."[16] On July 14, 1789, revolutionaries stormed the Bastille, a fortress, armory, political prison, and symbol of the corrupt monarchy of France. In the frenzy that followed, the governor of the Bastille was beheaded with a knife and his head mounted on a pike. Whereas the American Founders sought to establish a form of republican government in which all citizens are equal (making, to be sure, concessions to Southern states on slavery, which the Founders expected to wither away soon), Rousseau had argued that consent of the governed could be achieved only by eradicating those who did not consent, thus providing the intellectual justification for the French revolutionaries' wholesale slaughter of political adversaries. It occurred both in Paris as well as in the countryside. Peasants across the country rose up against their landlords, destroying manor houses. All told, in what is referred to as the Reign of Terror (1793–94), an estimated forty thousand people were executed or murdered, including priests, noblemen, and political adversaries, and another three hundred thousand were arrested. It was a starkly different approach to political change from the American experience. It is little wonder that decades of instability and violence followed.

Intellectuals and the Culture of Revolution

AS A result of the different examples set by the American and French Revolutions, by the early 1800s, the world was changing rapidly. The continued rapid pace of scientific discovery, innovation, and industrialization was also having its impact. The old ways of despotic monarchies, feudal landlords, and serfdom were no longer satisfactory or sustainable. But as large numbers moved from farms into mills and factories, new problems arose: difficult working conditions, overcrowding and urban squalor, and large-scale unemployment when economies turned downward. All of these factors gave rise to grievances—and it was grievances that drove the urban dwellers and peasants in the French Revolution in 1789, that drove European industrial workers in the revolutions of 1848, and that drove Russian workers and peasants in 1905. The grievances might have been addressed through reform of the existing system, but thanks to a professional class of intellectuals, a culture of revolution had emerged, building on the utopian, rationalist thinking of the seventeenth and eighteenth centuries. Any number of radical thinkers were willing to address these grievances with promises of communal ownership, government by local council rather than representative democracy, and even earthly paradise. As the historian Richard Pipes explains, "it is radical intellectuals who translate these concrete complaints into an all-consuming destructive force. They desire not reforms but a complete obliteration of the present in order to create a world order that has never existed except in a mythical Golden Age.... The existence of popular grievances is thus a necessary but not sufficient explanation of revolutions, which require the infusion of radical ideas."[17] Lenin himself acknowledged the essential role of intellectuals—belying the very concept of spontaneous proletarian revolution championed by Marx—when he wrote, "Without revolutionary theory there can be no revolutionary movement."[18]

The pioneer socialist Henri de Saint-Simon, for example, inspired a movement in which "missionaries" went around Europe calling for central planning of economic resources and condemning worker exploitation and private property. One of the Saint-Simonians captured well the confusion and despair that infected this period and, not surprisingly, the enormous gap left by the destruction of the Church:

> What man will come to give new life to this debris? Oh! The times are pressing and propitious. The veil of the temple is torn; the sanctuary is empty; the oracles are mute; and the throne is broken; the kings have left; the heroes are dead; and the earth silently awaits a savior.[19]

THE WRITERS and thinkers of the Enlightenment had inspired efforts to remake European society, but those efforts led to chaos and disorder. They had been effective in overturning the old monarchic, Christian order, but they had not delivered a new harmonious society free from want or discord. As Edmund Wilson has written,

> the first years of the nineteenth century were a highly confused epoch.... The rationalistic philosophy of the eighteenth century, upon which the French Revolution had been based, was still the background to most people's thinking... but this rationalistic philosophy, which had been expected to solve all the problems, had failed to rescue society from either despotism or poverty.[20]

THIS WAS the world into which Karl Marx was born in 1818, in Trier, Germany, to a prosperous family. Marx grew into a young man who was egomaniacal, profligate, even demonic. He showed the very darkest side of what it means to displace God with man. In a poem titled "Human Pride," Marx wrote, "Then I will wander godlike and victorious through the ruins of the world, and giving my words an active force, I will feel equal to the creator." In a collection of poems titled *Savage Songs*, he wrote these lines:

> It is a dark form from Trier,
> An unleashed monster,
> with self-assured step
> he hammers the ground with his heels,
> And raises his arms in all fury to heaven
> As though he wished to seize the celestial vault
> And lower it to earth.

In rage he continually deals with his redoubtable fist,
As if a thousand devils were gripping his hair.

MARX ENTERED the University of Berlin, where the philosopher G.W. F. He-gel had been the most prominent and illustrious professor. Though Hegel had died just a few years before Marx arrived, his influence was still keenly felt, especially through a group known as the Young Hegelians, who were deeply critical both of Christianity and of the prevailing political system. After a short career as a journalist, in 1843 Marx and his wife moved to Paris, where he be-gan to meet radical thinkers who included Heinrich Heine, Mikhail Bakunin, Pierre-Joseph Proudhon, and Friedrich Engels. The latter friendship eventually developed into a lifelong collaboration.

Their first publication together was "The Holy Family," referring not to what most would think of as the Holy Family of Christianity but to the Young Hege-lians, the group of which Marx had once been a part but which he now tore apart. Marx and Engels here began developing their radical ideology. As one paper of the time wrote, "every line preaches revolt . . . against the state, the church, the family, legality, religion and property. . . . Prominence is given to the most radical and the most open communism, and this is all the more dangerous as Mr. Marx cannot be denied either extremely broad knowledge or the ability to make use of the polemical arsenal of Hegel's logic, what is customarily called 'iron logic.'"[21]

Various strands of revolutionary ideas continued during this time to wind their way through Europe. Many were utopian or communistic; some held on to the Christian faith, whereas others rejected it; some called for a radical break with the past, whereas others argued for more gradual change. There was little agreement, even among revolutionaries, on what revolution should entail, until Marx commandeered a position of leadership through trickery, bullying, and egotism. One of the revolutionary groups of the time, the League of the Just, was planning to switch its name to the Communist League. In drawing up its manifesto, one of the members shared his draft with Engels, who said to Marx, "Just between ourselves I played a hellish trick on Mosi." Engels explained that he had substituted their own program for the draft that had been shared with them.[22] Thus, in a backhanded way, Marx and Engels made themselves the voice of communism. As the Marx biographer Robert Payne wrote, when Marx first met with the League of the Just in London in 1847, he "did not know, and could not have guessed, that the League would become the parent body of all communist parties which have proliferated throughout the world."[23]

With the publication of *The Communist Manifesto* in 1848, Marx and Engels described a world defined by class struggles—struggles between oppressor and oppressed.[24] As Marx and Engels saw it, with the rise in trade and manufacturing, feudal society had given way to bourgeois society, and the contending forces were reduced to two: the bourgeoisie and the proletariat. Marx and Engels claimed that the bourgeoisie acted out of cold self-interest and were to blame for the death of religion and the feudal order, which they had replaced with "naked, shameless, direct, brutal exploitation."[25] They described a world of laborers crammed into factories for dull, backbreaking work—slaves both to the bourgeois class and to the alienating machines themselves. Even the family had been reduced to a mere monetary relationship in this dark view of the world. History is an inexorable force, according to Marx and Engels, governed by "laws" of human conduct and social development, laws which make inevitable the conquest of the bourgeoisie by the proletariat. Private property would be abolished. The family would disappear. Marriage between one man and one woman would be replaced by an openly legalized "community of women."[26] Nation-states would be abolished.

It was the darkest of all the revolutionary programs. Many others had taken note of poor working conditions in factories and mills, of poor living conditions in the cities, and others had offered various solutions to address these ills, but Marx and Engels took the revolutionary impetus in a direction that allowed it to be both more virulent and more violent. They stood apart in calling for the "forcible overthrow of all existing social conditions."[27]

The radicalism of their proposal elicited the ire and condemnation of other revolutionaries. Proudhon, for example, himself an anarchist and socialist who had declared that "property is theft!" tried to rein Marx in: "because we are at the head of a movement let us not make ourselves the chiefs of a new intolerance, let us not pose as the apostles of a new religion, even if it should be the religion of logic and reason."[28] But Marx ignored the plea and did exactly what Proudhon begged him not to do—he made himself not merely the apostle but the god of his new, destructive religion.

Marx declared, "The philosophers hitherto have only interpreted the world in various ways: the thing is, however, to change it."[29] Where did Marx find the hubris or sheer egotism to believe both that it was his mission to change the world and that he understood it sufficiently to execute that mission? He and Engels believed that they had discovered the laws that guide human nature and shape social evolution, primarily the labor theory of value (which to Marx meant different things than it had to Adam Smith or David Ricardo—these earlier, liberal economists saw the price of a good or service as the number of labor hours it would take a purchaser to obtain it, whereas to Marx, it was the value of the number of hours it would take a worker to produce it) and historic materialism. They believed that man was nothing more than a material being and that all history was defined by the exploitation of one group by another. On the basis of these flawed beliefs, they asserted that revolution was both imminent and inevitable. They were wrong on all counts. They were wrong about the labor theory of value, and about historic materialism, and therefore they were wrong that revolution was inevitable. If left to its own devices, if allowed freely to compete in the marketplace of ideas, Marxism would certainly have failed. Indeed, it did fail repeatedly. Where it has found success, it was only eventually through subterfuge or force.

The revolutions and upheavals that swept through Europe in the 1900s were not the revolutions Marx and Engels had predicted. The question is why not. To begin with, as stated earlier, Marx and Engels were simply wrong about the so-called laws guiding history and human interactions. They greatly oversimplified class relations and even oversimplified the complexity of human beings by reducing them to their class. Similarly, advocates of CRT, one of the primary strands of today's cultural Marxism, greatly oversimplify human beings by reducing them to the pigmentation of their skin, their sexual orientation, or their national origin. It is entirely inaccurate today to equate darker skin with poverty or poor performance in school or the inability to get a driver's license to vote, and yet those are the assertions of CRT. Similarly, it was inaccurate for Marx and Engels to have assumed that the working class, the "proletariat," had no attachment to tradition and no hope for a better future within the current constructs. In fact, the Industrial Revolution brought great advances in poverty reduction. Marx and Engels also failed to recognize an inherent resistance to radical change, which one could argue is a trait almost universally shared. "Society as a whole is more and more splitting up into two great hostile camps, into two great classes directly facing each other—Bourgeoisie and Proletariat," declared Marx and Engels in

The Communist Manifesto. But it was not so. Many workers no doubt wanted improvements to their working conditions, but never did a majority of workers support the idea of revolution. We will see in the next chapter how this dynamic played out in Italy and Germany between 1918 and 1921.

As inaccurate as Marx and Engels were in their assumptions about the working class, they were equally wrong about their so-called bourgeoisie. It was true that with the rise of industrialization and capitalism, virtually all Western countries were seeing a decline of the landed classes—aristocracy whose wealth and power were based on large landholdings—and a rise in the new middle class. But it was inaccurate of Marx and Engels to assert that there was a monolithic group one might broadly identify as the middle class, what they termed the bourgeoisie, and it was equally inaccurate of them to assert that those in the middle classes were hostile to those in the working classes. Without question, working and living conditions were notoriously bad in places, but a steady stream of reforms and laws were increasingly being enacted to protect workers. At the same time, the very nature of the capitalist system demanded a certain responsibility among business owners toward their employees, who were neither slave laborers nor indentured servants. These were free men and women who had the freedom to leave one job for another—if not always the wherewithal. Without a doubt, owners wanted to generate profits, but above all, they wanted their businesses to survive, and surviving meant striking a balance between keeping costs low while maintaining peace and stability in the workforce.

Thus, as Richard Eberling explains, "Marx not only misinterpreted capitalism's 'birth pangs' for its 'death rattle,' but he totally misread how capitalism has actually evolved, considering that as an economic system it was just emerging when Marx wrote, and was not ending."[30] Capitalism did not deepen the divisions between owners and workers, as Marx had predicted, but rather weakened those divisions, and it eroded barriers based on class, education, or opportunity that had previously prevented social or economic mobility. As Eberling concludes, "rather than capital accumulation leading to a concentration of wealth and income, it has worked to disperse ownership and wealth among the members of industrial society."[31]

Marx and Engels had based their ideas on a false anthropology, a misreading of history, and a misunderstanding of economics. Therefore the outcomes they predicted—a spontaneous uprising of workers against the middle class, a withering away of the state, and so on—did not occur. But Marx was able to exert his influence in other ways that helped spread his ideas. The wave of upheavals that spread through Europe in 1848 brought about some reforms but did not upend the existing systems and, indeed, engendered a resistance to revolution, much as the French Revolution had after the Reign of Terror. This brought a period of calm and economic growth to Europe. But the American Civil War breathed new life into the workers' movement. The dramatic decline in cotton exports from the United States that occurred because of the Civil War caused widespread unemployment among English and French textile workers. But the American war over slavery impacted Europe's workers in another way as well. As Marx explained in the introduction to *Das Kapital*, "as in the eighteenth century, the American War of Independence sounded the tocsin for the European middle class, so in the nineteenth century, the American Civil War has sounded it for the European working class."[32] Indeed, in 1864, Marx drafted a letter congratulating Abraham Lincoln on his reelection, stating, "The workingmen of Europe feel sure that, as the American War of Independence initiated a new era of ascendancy for the middle class, so the American Antislavery War will do for the working classes."[33]

Thus, inspired by the American Civil War and driven by the resulting economic hardships in Europe, an international meeting of workers was convened in London in 1864. This led to the founding of the International Working Men's Association, better known as the First International, and for a time created something of an international workers' movement. Marx's ideas gained some traction there, but a number of different revolutionary ideas were competing for primacy, from reformist socialism to radical Marxist socialism to anarchism. But none won out, and again, the predicted revolution failed to materialize. For a brief moment, in 1871, in the disarray following the Franco-Prussian War, communists managed to gain and hold power for the two and half months of the Paris Commune. But that movement quickly faltered, and its instigators were executed, imprisoned, or exiled. In 1889 the Second International brought together labor and socialist parties again in an organization that lasted until 1916, but it, too, only highlighted the ongoing conflict between the revolutionary Marxists, on one side, and the more reform-minded social democrats, on the other.

Revolution Comes Out of the Wilderness

IT WAS only in 1917, with the Bolshevik Revolution in Russia, that Marxism finally won out over other labor movements and reform programs and entered the mainstream with its radical vision for revolutionary change. As James Billington wrote, November 1917 finally "brought the revolutionary tradition out of the wilderness and into power."[34] What allowed the Marxist vision finally to succeed in Russia where previously it had resulted only in failure? At its simplest, it succeeded primarily by virtue of the force and personality of Lenin. He had what E. H. Carr described in a more positive light as "clear-headed genius, confident persistence and polemical temperament."[35] A contemporary of Lenin's, Peter Struve, provided a darker explanation for Lenin's political success:

> [Marx's] doctrine of class war, relentless and thoroughgoing, aiming at the final destruction and extermination of the enemy, proved congenial to Lenin's emotional attitude to surrounding reality. He hated not only the existing autocracy (the Tsar) and the bureaucracy, not only lawlessness and arbitrary rule of the police, but also their antipodes—the "liberals" and the "bourgeoisie." That hatred had something repulsive and terrible in it; for being rooted in the concrete, I should say even animal, emotions and repulsions, it was at the same time abstract and cold like Lenin's whole being.[36]

THIS DARK side of Lenin's personality brought an exclusionary, scorched-earth approach to politics that allowed Marxism finally to prevail. As Richard Pipes has written, Lenin treated all politics as warfare: everyone was defined as either friend or enemy, which in turn meant there was no room for compromise or dissent.[37] These remained the defining characteristics of Soviet communism for the next seventy years, and they persist in a somewhat diluted form in NextGen Marxism.

Thus the success of Marxism in Soviet Russia can be largely attributed to the personality of Lenin himself. But Lenin also made important changes to Marxism, addressing some of its weaknesses, which was essential to its transition from theory to practice. To begin with, Marxism had never been able to win in the open marketplace of ideas. It was always competing with other revolutionary or reformist ideologies, sometimes pulling ahead, other times lagging behind. This was as true in prerevolutionary Russia as it had been in

Europe throughout the 1800s. Lenin forced the adoption of his version of despotic Marxism in his program, which would entail a "revolutionary democratic dictatorship of the proletariat and the peasantry." To the extent that others challenged the supremacy of the Marxist–Leninist program, as they certainly did, he did not simply reject their ideas; he killed them off. During the so-called Red Terror, from December 1917 to February 1922, an estimated one hundred thousand political opponents were executed.[38] It was only this strategy of force and exclusion that finally allowed Marxism to dominate. It was a pattern that was to be repeated in China, Vietnam, North Korea, Cuba, and Laos.

Prior to the Bolshevik Revolution, Marxism had also failed because capitalism did not, as Marx had posited, spontaneously collapse from its own inherent contradictions and give birth to a dictatorship of the proletariat. As even the Frankfurt School socialist Herbert Marcuse acknowledged decades later, "growing productivity, a rising standard of living, and the concentration of economic and political power worked together to reconcile a large part of the laboring classes to the established society."[39] In other words, developments in the nineteenth century had demonstrated that capitalism worked. It lifted people out of poverty. At the same time, industrializing societies saw significant reforms that helped protect workers and gradually improve working conditions. The dilemma, then, for Marxists, was that workers in industrial societies were not inclined to revolt against capitalism, and certainly not to dismantle it. It also helped, as we will see later, that their civil-society institutions were too strong for revolution to succeed. To the extent that workers did revolt, they generally wanted reforms, not full-scale revolution. Russia was different. Russia was still a predominantly agrarian society under the autocratic rule of the Romanov dynasty. These and other factors in Russia's circumstances made it fertile ground for takeover by a small band of iron-willed revolutionaries.

This points to another factor that had kept Marxism from succeeding in its first seventy years: a lack of organized leadership structure. This was apparent in the fractured leadership of the International Working Men's Association, during the Paris Commune of 1871, in the Second International from 1889 to 1916, and in Russia following the February Revolution of 1917, before Lenin took over eight months later. Lenin made clear, once he and his small band of Bolsheviks took power in the October Coup, that communism could succeed only with dictatorial leadership. Because it is a top-down, superimposed form of government, rather than a representative form of government that rules with the consent of the governed, it can survive only with a clearly defined leader who holds absolute power. This was the role that Lenin took on for himself and then modeled for other dictatorial leaders around the globe.

Lenin also made an important tactical change to Marx's original vision. In his 1902 publication *What Is to Be Done?*, Lenin argued that "an organization of revolutionaries" is "an essential factor in 'making' the political revolution" and that this organization must be tightly restricted to professional revolutionaries. Thus Lenin identified the Party as the agent of revolutionary change, rather than the working man or the factory, neighborhood, and barrack councils that had emerged in 1905 and were later tried in Italy and Germany (*soviet* is the Russian word for "council"). This Party would serve as a vanguard that would bring a socialist consciousness to the workers.[40] When Marxism was finally instituted as a comprehensive national program in Bolshevik Russia, it did so not as the bottom-up revolution that Marx so confidently predicted but rather as a top-down imposition by an elite, using extreme instruments of force, violence, and social control. This explains how Marxism was finally implemented after seventy years in the wilderness, first in Russia, then in China, Cuba, North Korea, and Vietnam. These were all underdeveloped, agrarian societies with weak and corrupt leadership. Marxism was imposed by iron-willed, ruthless leaders who used a combination of authoritarian controls and extensive cultural indoctrination to impose their revolutionary, socialist consciousness onto their subjects.

The Bolsheviks' International Aspirations

MARXISM, IDEOLOGICALLY, was never just a call for local or national revolution; it was always a call for global revolution. Marx had ended *The Communist Manifesto* with a call to arms: "Let the ruling classes tremble at a Communistic revolution. The proletarians have nothing to lose but their chains. They have a world to win. Workers of the world unite!" Lenin and his Marxist confreres embraced this aspect of Marxism, and from the very beginning, they expressed aspirations to bring the revolution of the working class to all industrial societies. In March 1919, the Third or Communist International was formed, more commonly known as the Comintern, the purpose of which was to promote revolution abroad—as well as to control communists abroad—and to defend Soviet Russia from attacks by the capitalist countries.[41]

At the Second World Congress of the Communist International in July 1920, Lenin presented a strategy for global communist victory that would build on a crisis of colonized people. Lenin argued that World War I had been fought to decide which of the two groups of great powers—the English or the German— would have the right "to pillage, enslave and exploit the whole world."[42] The result of victory by the English bloc, Lenin argued, was that 1.2 billion of the world's population were now "subjected to the colonial yoke, to the exploitation of a brutal capitalism."[43] This created an "exceptional revolutionary crisis." The path to victory, Lenin argued, lay in demonstrating to the oppressed of the world that they had sufficient consciousness and organization for a "successful and victorious revolution." This, again, was Lenin's model for success: he would not wait for workers to initiate a spontaneous revolution (which would likely never come about), but the Party would serve as the intellectual vanguard, in- stilling in workers a revolutionary consciousness. Thirty-three different coun- tries were represented at the Second International, including the United States, where Marxism already had a long history.

German immigrants had first brought the ideas of Karl Marx to the United States following the failed European revolutions of 1848. According to Theo- dore Draper, "the German immigrants brought with them a degree of trade- union and political consciousness then unknown in the United States."[44] But as in Europe, Marxism in the United States found itself competing with other revolutionary and reformist ideologies, including the social democracy of Ferdinand Lassalle and the anarchism of Bakunin. Again, as in Europe, sharp divisions emerged over whether laborers should seek gradual improvements of their working conditions within the capitalist system or should overthrow cap- italism altogether. Histories of socialism in the United States, not unlike Marx himself, paint the relationship between workers and owners in a very simplistic way. Draper, for example, in his seminal history of the communist movement in America, wrote of the late 1800s,

> *The relations between labor and capital were largely undefined and uncon-*
> *trollable except by sheer force on both sides. Employers fought labor organi-*
> *zations by every possible means. Strikes were ruthlessly crushed by armed*
> *guards, police, sheriffs, militia, and federal troops. Court injunctions tied*
> *the hands of unions on the mere threat of a strike. Working conditions often*
> *ranged from the primitive to the abominable.*[45]

BUT IN fact, relations between owners and workers were far more nuanced than Draper would have us believe, and indeed, radical labor organizers were often the instigators of violence, against which owners had to defend themselves and other workers.

To take just one example, following labor unrest in the 1880s and 1890s, a group of business leaders in New York formed the Get-Together Club. Its purpose was "to entertain men of thought and action who have really done something in the world, and to encourage efforts along the lines of improving the welfare of the human race, especially the workingman."[46] They held regular meetings and published a monthly magazine "devoted to improving the conditions of the employed."[47] That is not the image of employers fighting labor organizations by every possible means that Draper paints. The picture on the labor side is also not so simple. It was not the innocent, downtrodden victim portrayed by the Left. Indeed, much of the violence was organized not for the betterment of the workers but for the benefit of individual organizers or companies. Samuel Parks, for example, a leading figure in New York City's labor unrest, had ordered an estimated two thousand strikes against New York building contractors in the early 1900s, and yet ultimately it was proven that this was merely a system of graft for self-enrichment: he would demand payment in exchange for calling off a strike, for which he ultimately went to prison. He was also working in partnership with a Chicago-based builder, the George C. Fuller Company, which was trying to break into the lucrative New York construction business.[48]

These more accurate depictions of labor relations help explain why Marxism—and even other less radical forms of socialism or social democracy—did not find greater success in the United States. Immigrants came to the United States to escape famine, poverty, conflict, or a lack of opportunity in their home countries. They believed in what America had to offer. They believed that if they worked hard, their children would have better opportunities than they had had. For the most part, they simply wanted to improve the system. They wanted an opportunity to succeed within the system, not to overthrow it. This helps explain why efforts to bring Marxist socialism to the United States met with as little success as they had in Europe.

But the success of the Bolshevik Revolution in Russia changed everything. Prior to that moment, socialists had not been able to gain power anywhere in the world. When the Marxists rose from obscurity to take power in Russia, it sent shockwaves through the socialist world:

> In May 1917, there were only 11,000 members of the Bolshevik party in all Russia. Yet five months later the Bolsheviks seized power.... The supreme lesson seemed to be that a small party could seize power if only it had enough revolutionary zeal and purity of doctrine.... Such was the infinitely optimistic horizon that the Bolshevik revolution appeared to open up. Small wonder that its first impact on politically starved and spiritually depressed revolutionary Socialists everywhere was so overpowering.[49]

YET EVEN with the inspiration of the Bolshevik success in Russia, Soviet communists still had to resort to underhanded tactics to win converts, a strategy they employed for nearly the full seventy years of their existence.[50]

Bringing the Bolshevik Revolution to the United States

ROBERT REILLY has written, "Intellectual pedigree is important because wars begin in the minds of men well before the shooting starts."[51] Men do not go to war, either literally or figuratively, without the idea of conflict having first developed. We have traced the intellectual pedigree of the Bolsheviks' scorched-earth revolutionary fervor from the Scientific Revolution through the Enlightenment to Rousseau, the French Revolution, Karl Marx, and, finally, Vladimir Lenin. The question is, how did it then come to the United States?

The first and most important way was through Marxists themselves, many of whom came to the United States and seeded their ideas in the culture, which we explore in fuller detail in chapter 6. But they alone would likely have had a limited impact on the broader culture. This was America, after all, a land of pioneers and patriots, individuals who fled their home countries in search of religious freedom or economic opportunity. Marxist ideas therefore met with a great deal of resistance. Both Lenin and Stalin understood this, and both understood the value of propaganda in reshaping attitudes. In what was likely their first major propaganda effort in the United States, they identified the murder trial of the two Italian anarchists Bartolomeo Vanzetti and Nicola Sacco as an opportunity to paint the United States as xenophobic and anti-immigrant.

The case of Sacco and Vanzetti would likely have remained a footnote in history if not for the Soviet propaganda machinery. The two men had languished in prison for five years as their various appeals failed. But in 1925, the Soviet Union's chief propagandist, Willi Münzenberg, created an organization called the International Labor Defense. Its initial mission was to turn the Sacco–Vanzetti case into a propaganda win for communism[52]—and it was enormously successful. In a short period of time, it was no longer Sacco and Vanzetti who were guilty but America. Soviet propagandists and their American supporters made a global cause célèbre of Sacco and Vanzetti. They did so through extensive publicity and fundraising campaigns and also, importantly, by winning over influential elites who then became effective advocates for the Soviet cause—even if they did so unwittingly. Dorothy Parker; Katherine Anne Porter; the Harvard law professor Felix Frankfurter, who later became a US Supreme Court justice; and the British author H. G. Wells were just a few of the elites who were successfully manipulated by the communists and became champions for the innocence of Sacco and Vanzetti. So effective was this campaign that it created what Stephen Koch describes as an "orchestrated multinational mass hysteria."[53] When Sacco and Vanzetti were, in the end, executed in August 1927, violent demonstrations broke out in capital cities across the globe, from Johannesburg to Berlin. Indeed, so effective was that campaign, and so absent any challenge to it, that the portrayal of the Sacco and Vanzetti case as one of pure anti-immigrant bigotry remains the dominant narrative today.[54]

Another line of effort to seed communist revolution in the United States was to exploit race relations and exacerbate the sense of grievance. As early as 1920, Lenin had suggested that "American Negroes" be included among the anticolonial and national-liberation movements that were a focus of the Communist Party, but it was not until 1928 that concrete steps were taken to do so. Following the Sixth Congress of the Communist International held in Moscow from July 17 to September 1, 1928, the Comintern issued its "Resolution on the Negro Question in the United States," describing its perception of the situation this way:

> The industrialization of the South, the concentration of a new Negro working class population in the big cities of the East and North and the entrance of the Negroes into the basic industries on a mass scale, create the possibility for the Negro workers, under the leadership of the Communist Party, to assume the hegemony of all Negro liberation movements, and to increase their importance and role in the revolutionary struggle of the American proletariat.

The Negro working class has reached a stage of development which enables it, if properly organized and well led, to fulfill successfully its double historical mission: (a) To play a considerable role in the class struggle against American imperialism as an important part of the American working class; and (b) To lead the movement of the oppressed masses of the Negro population.[55]

IN OUTLINING a strategy to achieve this objective, the Comintern's Resolution stated, "Special stress must be laid upon organizing active resistance against lynching, Jim Crowism, segregation and all other forms of oppression of the Negro population."[56] The Comintern issued a directive to the American Communist Party to increase sharply its attention to the "American Negro question."[57] Little progress was made over the next year and a half, but then American communists found a cause to latch on to when police arrested nine African American teens, aged thirteen to nineteen, on March 25, 1931. The teenagers were accused of rape aboard a train near Scottsboro, Alabama. One of the two white girls who claimed to have been raped later admitted having lied to avoid accusations of prostitution. The nine boys received hasty trials with all-white juries, and eight of the nine were sentenced to death. That this case was a true breach of justice has never been in question, nor has the legitimacy of the outrage it generated. Its relevance here is its exploitation by communists to fuel a revolution against capitalism.

James Allen, a member of the Communist Party USA and editor of the communist paper *Southern Worker*, was only sixty miles away, in Chattanooga, Tennessee, when he caught wind of the case. His first article, published on April 2, called for "mass protest meetings, resolutions and telegrams ... [to] save these workers from mass lynchings."[58] Allen's role was critical in publicizing the case. As one historian of the era has written, "we might never have heard of the Scottsboro case if Sol Auerbach, using his Party name, James S. Allen, had not arrived in Chattanooga, Tennessee, in mid-July 1930."[59] While it was Allen who brought the case to the attention of the Communist Party, it was the Party's propaganda apparatus that then helped spin the case into another cause for global protests against the United States.[60] Demonstrations on behalf of the Scottsboro Boys were orchestrated in Berlin, Budapest, Paris, Rio de Janeiro, Zurich, and Santiago. Bricks were thrown through the windows of American consulates.[61] The Communist Party also organized a speaking tour in Europe for Mrs. Ada

Wright, the mother of two of the boys. This tour helped drive support for communism and condemnation of "imperialism" and of the United States.

The narratives established by communist propagandists in both the Sacco and Vanzetti case and in the case of the Scottsboro Boys remain to this day the historical record on both cases—not an insignificant achievement. But in the grand scheme of things, the communist shaping of those narratives is a mere footnote in history. The more important takeaway is twofold. Despite their heavy-handed efforts, Lenin and other Soviet Marxists failed to bring about the workers' revolution in the United States for which they had hoped and plotted. The Communist Party in the United States never had more than one hundred thousand members at any one time, even at the height of its influence in the 1930s and 1940s. However, Marxism, particularly after Lenin brought it to power in the Soviet Union, exerted a deep influence in the United States, particularly through the culture and through intellectuals. It planted seeds that took a long time to sprout, but one could argue that without those seeds, today the United States would not be grappling with CRT; diversity, equity, and inclusion (DEI); and all of the other identity-based attacks on the American system.

Angela Davis, for example, who looms large as a major influence on today's younger Marxist activists, credits her mother's role as an activist defending the Scottsboro Nine as a major influence on her own early activism.[62] Davis also had a close relationship with her professor and ideological mentor Herbert Marcuse, who helped further guide her along the path of cultural Marxism, which later had far more success in the United States than Soviet Marxism. John Howard Lawson is another through whom those early propaganda efforts rippled deeply through the culture. A young playwright, he embraced communism in the 1920s and then headed up the Hollywood division of the Communist Party USA. He, too, had been influenced by both the Sacco and Vanzetti and Scottsboro Nine cases. He also believed culture should serve as an instrument of social change, an idea that the Soviet communists fully embraced and that the Italian communist Antonio Gramsci turned into a full-blown strategy for revolution. Lawson was uniquely positioned to implement that strategy in the United States: as the cofounder and first president of the Screenwriters Guild of America, he was able to exercise control over Hollywood's immensely influential storytelling. He is quoted as having instructed fellow writers,

As a writer try to get 5 minutes of the Communist doctrine, 5 minutes of the

party line in every script that you write…. It is your duty to further the class struggle by your performance…. If you are nothing more than an extra wearing white flannels on a country club veranda do your best to appear decadent, do your best to appear to be a snob; do your best to create class antagonism…. If you are an extra on a tenement street do your best to look downtrodden, do your best to look a victim of existing society.[63]

DAVIS AND Lawson are just two of the intellectual vanguard whose ideas have reverberated through American culture. The list of writers and artists who were seduced by socialism is a long one, and many of their works have become a permanent part of the American canon: Jack London's *The Call of the Wild* (1903); Upton Sinclair's *The Jungle* (1906); Sinclair Lewis's *Babbitt* (1922); John Steinbeck's *The Grapes of Wrath* (1939); and Arthur Miller's *Death of a Salesman* (1949) and *The Crucible* (1953).

Conclusion

UTOPIAN VISIONS for mankind are not new. Men have long dreamed of a world in which poverty, injustice, evil, and inequality are eradicated. The scientific discoveries of Galileo and Newton gave new life to utopian thinking because they created the false belief that science could lead to human perfection. Marxism was one strain among many utopian ideologies. What distinguished it from others was its vision of irreconcilable conflict between social sectors, the division of the world into oppressor and oppressed, and its scorched-earth approach to change. Marxism was always a call for violent revolution: Lenin breathed that vision into life and, in so doing, inspired revolutionaries around the globe. But despite the success of Lenin's example in the Bolshevik Revolution, communists failed to bring about a workers' revolution in industrialized countries. The unsubtle and violent exercise of power over a weak and disengaged population was possible in Russia and neighboring countries, and later in countries such as China, Cuba, and Vietnam. But it would take more to bring a revolutionary consciousness to functioning, prosperous democracies.

Lenin had already partially stumbled on the solution. In his 1902 publication *What Is to Be Done?*, he identified the importance of what he called "political exposure," by which he meant exposing workers to "all cases of tyranny, oppression, violence, and abuse" to create in workers a revolutionary consciousness.[64]

"These comprehensive political exposures are an essential and *fundamental* condition for training the masses in revolutionary activity," he wrote.[65] The new Marxist leadership in Russia, along with their fellow revolutionaries across the globe, broke new ground in using culture and information for political purposes. Although they did not bring about the worldwide workers' revolution that Marx had predicted, they did learn important lessons about how culture can be shaped, about the central role of ideas, and about the importance of a revolutionary vanguard that could propagate those ideas. Those ideas have changed and adapted in the centuries and decades since they were first brought to life, but in their essence, they lie at the heart of today's attacks by NextGen Marxists on the American system of ordered liberty.

2
THE CULTURAL AWAKENING

THE SPARK FOR what decades later became Marxism's winning strategy in the West sprang from the crashing defeat of two revolutions in 1919–20. These failures generated sudden bursts of thinking on political strategy simultaneously in Italy and Germany, the two countries that in a few short years would herald fascism in Europe. Factory-rich northern Italy and industrialized Germany had become hotbeds of revolution in 1919 after the senseless butchery of World War I groaned to an end. The bloodstained overthrow of the Russian tsar and the creation of the Soviet Union in 1917 inspired Marxists and anarchists the world over to dare to dream that they, too, could dispatch the bourgeoisie and establish workers' councils, or soviets. But revolts in both countries failed, and the fear of chaos quickly helped bring about national socialism. Following this fiasco, Marxist intellectuals began to ask about themselves: What went wrong? How could we have done things differently?

Italy

WE START with Italy because the prophet of its stillborn revolution, Antonio Gramsci, has become the unrivaled Marxist political theorist of the past half century. Born in 1891 to a literate, middle-class Italian father of Albanian origin and a Sardinian mother, Gramsci joined the Italian Socialist Party (PSI) in 1913 and soon became Italy's leading Marxist intellectual. From our perspective in the early twenty-first century, Gramsci is in line to become our era's Niccolò Machiavelli—and, indeed, the Renaissance political master strategist was somewhat of a hero for Gramsci, who often alluded to him in his writings. Rather than devoting his attention to how an unscrupulous prince, supposedly Ferdinand the Catholic of Aragon, could use cunning and deception to gain absolute power, as Machiavelli had done, Gramsci focused on how Marxism, the sworn enemy of God, the family, and private property, could gain hegemony and reshape society. The Marxist party that was able to transform the entire conceptual apparatus would be the new Prince, Gramsci wrote in his essay "The Modern Prince," which he penned between 1929 and 1934. "I have said that the protagonist of the new Prince in modern times cannot be an individual hero, but the political party, that is, that particular party which, at different times and in the different internal relations of the various nations, aims (and is rationally and historically founded for this end) to found a new type of State," he wrote.[1]

Though the New Left of the 1960s and its heirs, the NextGen Marxists of today, present Gramsci as an antiauthoritarian who found Stalin's methods repugnant, his entire strategy was focused on establishing undistilled communism. He was committed to the dictatorship of the proletariat, to a collectivist state and a centrally planned economy, and to the destruction of parliamentary democracy and the free market system. Gramsci excused Stalin's barbarism as necessary to the preservation of the Soviet Union. "Gramsci never really called into question the legitimacy of Stalin's role as heir to Lenin and as the political leader behind whom loyal communists throughout the world should align themselves in a solid and indestructible phalanx," wrote Duke University's Frank Rosengarten.[2]

Gramsci died in 1937 but remained virtually unknown outside Italy until the 1960s, when his works began to be translated in full into other languages and he became a focus of serious academic inquiry. He is best known for the *Prison Notebooks* he put together behind bars, where he spent the last decade of his life after 1926 (and which contains the preceding passage). The eminent British Marxist scholar Eric Hobsbawm notes that Gramsci was only able to tackle such subjects as political strategy and the nature of socialist society because he was in prison. Had he been free, communism's suppressive nature would have seen Gramsci end in Stalin's gulag. Ironically, prison protected Gramsci and ensured he was "writing not for the present but for the future."[3]

Three well-defined stages influence Gramsci's development as a political master-strategist—the aborted industrial revolt of 1919–20; his year and a half in Moscow from 1923 to 1924 (and his return for a few weeks in 1925); and the last decade of his life from 1926 to 1937, spent in a fascist prison in southern Italy.

The Biennio Rosso

MANY OF Gramsci's political epiphanies were forged in the central role he played in the industrial uprisings that shook Italy's north in 1919 and 1920, and especially the manufacturing hub of Turin, where he lived. Those two years are known as the *Biennio Rosso*, the two red years, and for a moment it looked to many like labor was about to trounce capital. That this did not happen compelled Gramsci to grope for a systematic political theory that would explain failure and adumbrate future success.

The Biennio was birthed with 1,663 strikes across Italy in 1919.[4] Soon, all of the north was caught in a wave of strikes and factory occupations that involved hundreds of thousands of workers, while peasants occupied land in the Mezzogiorno. In Turin, workers began forming factory councils, which explicitly echoed the workers' councils, or soviets, that had started in Russia in 1905 and culminated in the revolution. The first council was set up in September 1919 at the Fiat-Brevetti plant, in which every work unit elected a workshop commissar.

At twenty-eight already the head of the left-wing faction within the PSI, Gramsci founded in 1919 a Marxist newspaper, *L'Ordine Nuovo* (The New Order). It immediately started to advocate for the councils. As Gwyn Alfred Williams says, the Turin workers "unleashed and rode a mighty surge of working-class revolt and aspiration which drew in anarchists, syndicalists, libertarians and the hitherto apathetic.... It was *L'Ordine Nuovo* and Antonio Gramsci in particular who gave it form and public style."[5] Gramsci's hope was that the councils would perform the same function in Italy as they had in the tsarist empire. "In Russia, where the workers' council first appeared, a system of workers' councils shared power with the Provisional Government—the 'dual power' situation—from February to October 1917, after which the Bolsheviks seized power," write Andreas Møller Mulvad and Benjamin Ask Popp-Madsen, Danish socialist academics who have researched the councils.[6] Another Marxist academic and Gramscian, the United Kingdom's Megan Trudell, writes that Gramsci was interested in "organizations in the Italian working class that could potentially play the role of embryonic soviets or workers' councils."[7]

Gramsci had hoped that the councils would get all the power in the end and not share governance with parliament. Marxists to our day preach this form of "direct democracy," or "participatory democracy," in preference to the representative democracy of the West. Gramsci believed what the Bolsheviks had promised—that it should be "all power to the soviets." Communists, of course, needed to play the ideological role and "influence the decisions of the factory councils, and transform the rebellious impulses sparked off by the conditions that capitalism has created for the working class into a revolutionary consciousness and creativity."[8] (Lenin resolved the tension between which entity would have real power, the councils or the party, decidedly in favor of the latter.)

Gramsci chided reformists who vainly hoped to change the Italian economic apparatus through parliamentary procedures. Continued faith in capitalist
democracy would leave the system unchanged, he said. For reformers like the
socialist leader Filippo Turati, Gramsci wrote, "parliament stands in relation
to the soviet like the city to the barbarian horde."[9] Gramsci believed that "the
socialist state cannot be embodied in the institutions of the capitalist state."[10]

Indeed—and this is a key point—communists should only agree to participate in elections "strictly in order to create the conditions for the triumph of
the proletariat... embodied in the system of councils, outside and against parliament."[11] We see this thinking continue to the present, where today's Marxists
feign interest in the political process only as a stratagem to gain power.

A problem, however, was that, as Trudell puts it, Gramsci became "convinced
that such councils had to be in place before a revolutionary situation arose, that
they were key components of the revolution, not just structures for organizing
production in a postrevolutionary society."[12] And that clearly hadn't happened.
The PSI had not prepared the worker for revolution, had not molded a revolutionary consciousness. The Socialist Party had not been able to bridge the differences between the industrial north and the rural south, between proletarians
and peasants, the two potential agents of change. And that led to its eventual
inability to produce a Union of Italian Soviet Republics.

The revolutionary industrial activity, and the workers' councils, had advanced by fits and starts through 1919 and 1920 until they came to a head in
September, when factory occupations expanded outside of Turin. "Between 1
and 4 September, the occupations rolled forward through Italy, not only in the
industrial heartland around Milan, Turin and Genoa, but in Rome, Florence,
Naples, Palermo, in a forest of red and black flags and a fanfare of workers'
bands," wrote Williams.[13] Peasants south of Naples seized land.

And it was at that moment that the leaders of the PSI went for the option
Gramsci despised, choosing reformation of the existing system over its complete overhaul, so they abandoned the revolutionaries. The Party chose to nego-
tiate for workplace reforms rather than attempt to establish the dictatorship of
the proletariat, following a close vote by about one million union workers, who,
by a small margin, went for the side of the reformers.

Italy thus came this close to ruin in late 1920 but escaped the drabness and
downright horrors of Russia, and later Eastern Europe. Marxists to this day

are, of course, despondent over this and blame the PSI for not having indoctrinated the working class into revolutionary consciousness. The writers at WorkersControl.net say, for example, that by September 1920, the workers had achieved, "without question, the most widespread working class movement in Italian history, and one of the most significant in the history of the world working class, yet this tremendous movement would find itself without any leadership, any organized body capable of directing it towards a conquest of power beyond the factory walls."[14]

As Trudell wrote, to Gramsci, the PSI had "failed to understand the real processes and was incapable of connecting and directing the various struggles."[15] Gramsci himself wrote that "the Socialist Party watches the course of events like a spectator; it never has an opinion of its own to express, based on the revolutionary theses of Marxism and the Communist International; it never launches slogans that can be adopted by the masses, lay down a general line and unify or concentrate revolutionary action."[16]

The Communist International, the body the Bolsheviks had set up in Moscow to export revolution worldwide, followed events in Italy closely. In August, its executive committee sent the PSI a stern letter signed by Lenin, Nikolai Bukharin, and Grigory Zinoviev, which read, in part, "In Italy there are at hand all the most important conditions for a genuinely popular, great proletarian revolution.... Every day brings news of disturbances. All eye-witnesses—including the Italian delegates—assert and reiterate that the situation in Italy is profoundly revolutionary. Nevertheless in many cases the party stands aside, without attempting to generalize the movement, to give it slogans ... to turn it into a decisive offensive against the bourgeois state."[17]

Gramsci understood the primary lesson of this historic defeat: there was a need for painstaking indoctrination of the people years, perhaps decades, *before* complete transformation was attempted again. Before the people could be dispossessed of their private property—which is what Marxism seeks at bottom, after all—they had to be shorn of their belief in the system. They had to be deprogrammed, in other words. Then their consciousness could be raised, so that they might attain a new "revolutionary consciousness"; they had to be reprogrammed with a new cultural software. And it was only through the actions of the Communist Party, he wrote years later, that the working class could achieve revolutionary consciousness. The councils' bitter defeat had also taught

Gramsci "that a party was necessary for a revolution, and that councils alone could not make the revolution."[18]

But this lay ahead. In the immediate, Gramsci and other leaders broke off from the PSI within four months of the debacle and founded a party that they hoped would take up the historic revolutionary role they envisioned, the Italian Communist Party (PCI), in Livorno on January 21, 1921. In June 1922, Gramsci traveled to Moscow as a representative of the brand-new PCI. In October, Benito Mussolini and some thirty thousand of his Black Shirts marched on Rome, and King Victor Emmanuel appointed him prime minister. The fascist government swore a warrant for Gramsci's arrest.

Gramsci and the Soviets

GRAMSCI'S HOPE that the Turin factory councils would lead to a collectivist state with a planned economy was born of his careful study of the Bolshevik experiment—just as his later epiphany that the Party had to play the leading ideological role came from his reading of Lenin. This close attention to events in Russia in fact had led him to early breaks with Marxist orthodoxy. In an article for the PSI organ *Avanti!*, written in December 1917, Gramsci expressed an early refutation of Marx himself. Russia was an agricultural backwater that was only very partially industrialized. The Russian Revolution therefore had proved wrong Marx's maxim that a bourgeois capitalist phase had to precede the triumph of revolution. From this, Gramsci also adduced that economic relations were not the be-all and end-all, breaking with Marxist orthodoxy.

The Bolsheviks, he wrote, "are not 'Marxists,' that's what it comes down to: they have not used the Master's works to draw up a superficial interpretation, dictatorial statements which cannot be disputed." The Bolsheviks did "live out Marxist thought" of revolution, which Gramsci hastened to add was "one which will never die." But their revolution was living proof that economics did not guide man's actions. "The main determinant of history is not lifeless economics, but man; societies made up of men, men who have something in common, who get along together, and because of this (civility) they develop a collective social will."[19] It was societal relations that imbue meaning into things—*culture*, in other words, regulates man's actions.

Gramsci was somewhat besotted with Lenin, who paid more attention to political strategy—the focus of Gramsci's attention—than Marx or Engels ever had. "The Russian communists are a leading caste of the first order. Lenin has shown himself, testify all who have approached him, to be the greatest statesman in contemporary Europe; the man who freed the prestige, which inflames and disciplines peoples; the man who manages, in his vast brain, to dominate all the social energies of the world which can be turned to the service of the revolution; who holds in check and beats the most refined and vulpine statesmen of the bourgeois routine," Gramsci wrote in 1919.[20]

Lenin took note of the young Sardinian, whether because of this flattery or the strength of Gramsci's analysis. Gramsci arrived in Moscow in June 1922 as a delegate to the Executive Committee of the Third International, the governing body of the Communist International, or Comintern, and intended to stay only until December for the Fourth World Congress of the Comintern, where communist parties across the world sent delegates and which that year was held in Moscow and St. Petersburg (renamed Petrograd by the godless Bolsheviks). Soon after arrival, he fell ill and had to spend some months at a sanatorium outside of Moscow. There he met his eventual wife, Julia Schucht, and shared a cottage with the German communist leader Clara Zetkin, of whom we will read again later in this chapter. A stay that was intended to last from May to December turned into twenty months, as Mussolini's fascists, now ensconced in government, pledged to throw Gramsci in prison upon his return.

That meant that Gramsci was able to use the next two years to observe up close the making of the Soviet Union, a historic process that he had hitherto studied only from afar, and to meet heroes such as Lenin and Leon Trotsky. "In direct contact with the makers of the Russian Revolution, with members of the various foreign delegations to the Comintern, and, through Julia and other Russian friends, with the numerous cultural and literary groups that enjoyed an all too brief flowering in the early years of the Revolution, Gramsci was a witness to and a participant in a period of intense political and intellectual ferment in the Soviet Union," writes Rosengarten.[21] He accumulated a great deal of prestige, being elected to the Comintern's Executive Committee at the Fourth Congress.

The meeting with Lenin took place on October 25, 1922, and lasted two hours, though there are few official details of what was discussed. According to a letter released decades later, Lenin inquired about the reunification of the Italian Communist and Socialist Parties.

Marxist thinkers have made much of the evolution of both men, especially regarding the question of where they place the stress of the development of revolutionary conscious and the overthrow of the state. Is it on the shopfloor experience of the workers' councils, or the guiding role of the Communist Party? After the failure of the revolt in Russia in 1905, Lenin had emphasized the soviets, but the 1917 coup made him stress the Party. "The majority of the soldiers sympathized with the Bolsheviks, voted for them, elected them, but also expected them to decide things," Alastair Davidson quotes Lenin as saying. But Lenin also said, "The history of the Russian revolution has shown precisely that no argument can convince the great masses of the working class, the peasants, the small employees, if they are not convinced by their own experience."[22] Gramsci, for his part, had started out underscoring the primacy of councils, only to be convinced by the events of 1920 that the Party alone had the coordinating power to overthrow the bourgeois state. But Gramsci's thinking continued to evolve, and he settled on emphasizing the reorganization of social life as the way to create class and revolutionary consciousness. Davidson draws a picture of Lenin passing the baton to Gramsci: "the image of men in a relay race comes to mind."[23]

Lenin had much to teach Gramsci. Lenin, for instance, spoke and wrote a lot about hegemony, one of the concepts for which Gramsci is best known. But as the intellectual historian Paul Piccone points out, Gramsci's notion of hegemony differed from Lenin's. For the Soviet founder, hegemony was primarily a theory of domination—how the workers exercised class domination through the Party.[24] For Gramsci, it was a far richer theory about the controlling narrative of society, about how to take it apart and replace it with a counternarrative.

Trotsky likely had a direct impact on Gramsci's cultural thinking, even if Trotsky's imperious manner evidently rubbed Gramsci the wrong way, and his independent streak made Gramsci fear that he would splinter Russia's Communist Party—and therefore led Gramsci to excuse Stalin's behavior. Rosengarten, among others, makes a very good case when he writes that "the seed of an idea that was to germinate in Gramsci's mind in 1923 and 1924, and come to full fruition in his reflections in the *Prison Notebooks*—the idea that the conquest of power by the proletariat in the countries of Western Europe would require a strategy significantly different from the one followed by the Russian Bolsheviks"[25]—was to be found in speeches that Trotsky made in 1922 and later.

Speaking at the Fourth Congress in November 1922, Trotsky explained that in

Russia, the civil war had begun after the Bolshevik coup in October 1917. "Why did events follow this course? The explanation must be sought in the political backwardness of a country that had just cast off Czarist barbarism.... In countries that are older in the capitalist sense, and with a higher culture, the situation will, without doubt, differ profoundly," Trotsky told the delegates. "In these countries the popular masses will enter the revolution far more fully formed in political re-spects.... What does this mean? This means that it will hardly be possible to catch the European bourgeoisie by surprise as we caught the Russian bourgeoisie."[26]

All these seeds, and others Gramsci gathered during the *Biennio*, were to germinate later in his capacious brain. In December 1923, Gramsci finally left Moscow for Vienna, where he took up clandestine work on behalf of Italy's communists and where he was to stay until May 12, 1924. On that date, Gram-sci returned to Italy after having been elected to the Chamber of Deputies in the elections held on April 6—in which Mussolini's coalition also won a governing majority. Gramsci returned to Moscow in 1925 for sessions of the Fifth Enlarged Executive of the Comintern, from March 21 to April 6. "At these meetings Gramsci became more integrated than ever in the administrative and political structure of the Comintern," writes Rosengarten. "During the three weeks he spent in Moscow, he met Stalin and spoke at some length with him."[27] But Gramsci's days of freedom were numbered. In 1926, Mussolini outlawed the Communist Party, stripping Gramsci of his immunity, and Gramsci was arrested. At his trial in 1928, the fascist prosecutor Michele Isgro said, "We must stop his brain from working for twenty years,"[28] and Gramsci was duly sentenced to twenty years in prison. He was not released until April 1937, just a few days before he died. But the prosecutor was tragically wrong: brains don't stop working in prison.

Prison Years

GRAMSCI WAS sent to prison in Turi di Bari, in Italy's southern heel, in early 1929 and permitted to write. During the five years he was there, he read, thought, and wrote, read, thought, and wrote. The result was the *Prison Notebooks*, some thirty volumes containing three thousand pages, which were whisked out of his cell by comrades. What Gramsci wrote in the *Notebooks* forms the basis on which much of today's NextGen Marxism is built. At the time of this writing, most of Latin America is governed by Marxists who are openly Gramscians, including culturally and militarily significant nations such as Brazil, Colombia, Chile, and Venezuela. Europe's leftist parties, in or out of government, are also Gramscian. As Hobsbawm puts it, Gramsci is the "communist thinker who provided a Marxist strategy for countries in which the October Revolution might have been an inspiration, but could not be a model, that is to say for socialist movements in non-revolutionary environments and situations."[29] Those, first and foremost, include the United States, where the founders of BLM, the organizations that have turned everyone's lives upside down, were instructed in Gramscianism. And Gramscianism was distilled in the *Prison Notebooks*.

In prison, shorn of his leadership activities in Italy and in the Comintern, Gramsci had time to reckon with the world as it was. As David Forgacs, the editor of *The Gramsci Reader*, puts it, "the reality in which Gramsci found himself after 1926 was one in which socialist revolutions had either been defeated or had failed to take place in the West, where capitalism had managed to survive the post-war economic crisis and stabilize itself, where parliamentary regimes had stood firm or had been replaced with authoritarian ones."[30] The situation demanded that which was lacking: Marxist political analysis.

They also demanded a new strategy, one which would be different from that which had worked in Russia in 1917. It is the basis of such an analysis and strategy that Gramsci sought to develop in the prison notebooks. One important strand of this work was theoretical. The Marxist tradition in which he had matured as a political militant was strong on general predictions about the course of capitalist development and about connections between economic crises and political transformation. But it was weak on detailed analyses of the forms of political power, the concrete relations between social classes and political representation and the cultural and ideological forms in which social antagonisms are fought out or regulated and dissipated. There was no adequate Marxist theory of the state or of what Gramsci called the 'sphere of the complex superstructures': political, legal, cultural.

TO DO THAT, Gramsci conceived new terms and concepts and borrowed and adapted others. These are the guiding ideas that drive many political changes today. The main ideas, most of which are strongly interrelated, contained in the *Prison Notebooks* are the following.

The Theory of Hegemony

THIS IS perhaps the best-known Gramscian idea and the one that has had the most lasting impact. It means that the wealthy and powerful, in their pursuit of maintaining their money and power, no longer have to use force or threaten it to coerce the proletariat, the peasants, and so on into doing their bidding. This subordinate class has imbibed the cultural ideas of the ruling class—its *egemonia culturale*, its cultural hegemony, that is, its love of the family, God, native soil—and collaborates in its own oppression. Thus a conceptual superstructure, the way all of society is interpreted, keeps man down. Hegemony was at fault for "the 'spontaneous' consent given by the great masses of the population to the general direction imposed on social life by the dominant fundamental group; this consent is 'historically' caused by the prestige (and consequent confidence) which the dominant group enjoys because of its position and function in the world of production," Gramsci wrote in *The Formation of the Intellectuals*.[31]

The revolutionary had to dismantle old ways of thinking and put in its place a Marxist counternarrative. The object of Gramsci's lifework was to transfer hegemony from the capitalist, the parliamentary democrat, and the faithful to the worker, the participant in workers', neighborhood, or soldiers' councils, and those who believed in men, not God. Socialist hegemony was the goal. This requires patient and painstaking work. "What we can do, for the moment, is to fix two major superstructural 'levels': the one that can be called 'civil society,' that is the ensemble of organisms commonly called 'private,' and that of 'political society' or 'the State.' These two levels correspond on the one hand to the function of 'hegemony' which the dominant group exercises throughout society and on the other hand to that of 'direct domination' or command exercised through the State and 'juridical' government," Gramsci wrote.[32]

The hegemony of the oppressor class would not wither by itself, so to throw off old ways of thinking, revolutionaries had to take decisive action, part of which was to indoctrinate the population. This was similar to the role of agitation, as Lenin described it, in creating a revolutionary mindset among otherwise apathetic workers. Agitation was necessary to help workers understand the degree to which they were oppressed and thereby engender in them the fervor for revolution. But Gramsci took this concept to new depths. He called for periods of intense criticism, exhorting the resistant to recognize their own oppression and agreeing to overthrow the system. Thus struggle sessions were born. "Meetings held inside the factory, together with ceaseless propaganda and persuasion by the most conscious elements, should effect a radical transformation of the worker's mentality, should make the masses better equipped to exercise power, and finally should diffuse a consciousness of the rights and obligations of comrade and worker," wrote Gramsci in 1919.[33] This would be a "collective discussion, which sympathetically alters men's consciousness."[34] These struggle sessions are obvious direct forebears of the "antiracism" training sessions that American workers are forced to undergo today, which are engineered to effect the overthrow of what NextGen Marxists see as America's hegemonic narrative: "white supremacy."

That Marx had been wrong when he predicted constant revolutions by the proletariat, and that the culture of the dominant group needed to be dismantled through criticism, appears to have been an idée fixe of Gramsci's from very early on. A long paragraph in an essay he wrote the year prior to the Bolshevik Revolution, in 1916, for the socialist weekly *Il Grido del Popolo* already shows his preoccupation with the role culture plays in the struggle between the oppressed and his oppressor. Culture, he wrote, "is organization, discipline of one's inner self, a coming to terms with one's own personality; it is the attainment of a higher awareness, with the aid of which one succeeds in understanding one's own historical value, one's own function in life, one's own rights and obligations."[35] He then adds,

> But none of this can come about through spontaneous evolution, through a series of actions and reactions which are independent of one's own will—as is the case in the animal and vegetable kingdoms where every unit is selected and specifies its own organs unconsciously, through a fatalistic law of things. Above all, man is mind, i.e. he is a product of history, not nature. Otherwise how could one explain the fact, given that there have always been exploiters and exploited, creators of wealth and its selfish consumers, that socialism has not yet come into being? The fact is that only by degrees, one stage at a time, has humanity acquired consciousness of its own value and won for itself the right to throw off the patterns of organization imposed on it by minorities at a previous period in history. And this consciousness was formed not under the brutal goad of physiological necessity, but as a result of intelligent reflection, at first by just a few people and later by a whole class,

on why certain conditions exist and how best to convert the facts of vassalage into the signals of rebellion and social reconstruction. This means that every revolution has been preceded by an intense labor of criticism, by the diffusion of culture and the spread of ideas amongst masses of men who are at first resistant, and think only of solving their own immediate economic and political problems for themselves, who have no ties of solidarity with others in the same condition.

THE RAMIFICATIONS that hegemony has for concepts as basic as objective reality, let alone eternal truths, are immense, as Gramsci himself recognized. "In order to understand exactly the possible significance of the problem of the reality of the external world, it may be useful to develop the example of the notions of 'East' and 'West' which do not stop being 'objectively real' even if on analysis they prove to be nothing but conventions, i.e. 'historico-cultural constructions,'" he wrote in "The Modern Prince."[36] These mind-bending approaches were among his many links with the Frankfurt School, to which we will turn later in this chapter, and to postmodernism as well.

Mulvad and Popp-Madsen write that the concept of hegemony was what made Gramsci the Marxist superstar that he is:

Gramsci's concept of hegemony pointed to the ongoing "superstructural" function of ideology in maintaining capitalist relations of production. Such a reorientation had lasting influence on Western Marxism, as thinkers associated with the first generation of the Frankfurt School as well as thinkers like Louis Althusser repeatedly analyzed how bourgeois culture and the "ideological state apparatuses" contributed to the ongoing hegemonic renewal of the capitalist status quo. The success of Gramsci's concept of hegemony positioned him throughout the twentieth century as something resembling a master strategist for Western communist parties, which fought for communism in the distinct condition of capitalist, bourgeois cultural and ideological hegemony.[37]

THE DRIVE to make the subordinate group transcend its vassalage and become hegemonic creates a need for one of the hardest of Gramscian concepts: a historic bloc.

The Historic Bloc

IN HIS useful glossary of Gramscian terms at the end of *The Gramsci Reader*, Forgacs says, "This is a concept used by Gramsci to designate the dialectical unity of base and superstructure, of theory and practice, of intellectuals and masses (and not, as is sometimes mistakenly asserted, simply an alliance of social forces)."[38] This is true as far as what Gramsci says in his own very turgid writings. Many Gramscians today do, however, interpret it to mean the uncoerced union of disparate forces vying politically to overthrow the hegemony of the bourgeoisie.

The historic bloc is a key concept for the intellectuals behind BLM and other NextGen Marxists. Harmony Goldberg, the Gramscian scholar who founded the neighborhood organizing outfit where BLM cofounder Alicia Garza was trained as a Marxist cadre, writes that "the historic bloc is not a flat alliance of different classes. In every historic bloc, there is a single class that plays a leading role and serves as a cohering force. This role is not determined arbitrarily but reflects that in every society, there is a class whose position in society gives it the interest, consciousness and capacity to lead the rest of society in a transformative movement."[39] Eric Mann, the communist who trained another BLM cofounder, Patrisse Cullors, speaks of the "building of a Black/Latinx/Third World united front with an agreed upon Black priority."[40]

Today, just as Gramsci envisioned, the historic coalition would have to work through the two components that, as we have seen, Gramsci thought controlled the masses: civil society and the state. And because in the West the civil society part was too strong, revolution here required a different approach. This brings us to the next important Gramscian innovation.

The War of Positions and The War of Maneuvers

IN RUSSIA, the state apparatus of oppression was strong, whereas civil society was weak; in the West, it was the opposite. Thus, while in Russia the Bolsheviks were able to overthrow the state with a rapid coup d'état in October 1917, in the West civil society would not allow such a revolution, and in fact did not in Italy, Germany, and other countries. Given this, in countries such as Russia, only very partially industrialized and lacking strong civil institutions, revolutionaries could have a violent "war of maneuvers" and win. In the West, where societal institutions were more tightly knit, a protracted "war of positions" was required, one during which revolutionaries would infiltrate the institutions, indoctrinate members of the revolutionary bloc, and slowly undermine the hegemonic narrative.

This concept was a reflection of Gramsci's view that the oppressor could force the subordinate to comply with his wishes either with force or with cultural hegemony—writ large for the nation-state. As we have seen, the notion was probably at least partly the result of the seed planted by Trotsky in his 1923 speech. In prison, it blossomed into full flower. The example of Russia was strong, in any case. "In the East the State was everything, civil society was primordial and gelatinous," Gramsci wrote. "In the West, there was a proper relation between State and civil society, and when the State trembled a sturdy structure of civil society was at once revealed. The State was only an outer ditch, behind which there stood a powerful system of fortresses and earthworks: more or less numerous from one State to the next, it goes without saying—but this precisely necessitated an accurate reconnaissance of each individual country."[41] It was a mistake, said Gramsci, to think of the state solely as a creature of government and the apparatus of violent repression. The state was "an equilibrium between political society and civil society (or hegemony of a social group over the entire national society exercised through the so-called private organizations, like the Church, the trade unions, the schools, etc.)."[42]

The war of positions, incidentally, was not the result of a predilection for peace over violence but merely an expedient. The war of maneuver—that is, violence—could interrupt the war of positions, and should have, any time a propitious crisis came along—provided that the organic intellectual had done his job of convincing the worker that he had no stake in prolonging capitalism. "Even those military experts whose minds are now fixed on the war of position, just as they were previously on that of maneuver, naturally do not maintain that the latter should be considered as expunged from military science. They merely maintain that, in wars among the more industrially and socially advanced States, the war of maneuver must be considered as reduced to more of a tactical than a strategic function," wrote Gramsci.[43] "The superstructures of civil society are like the trench systems of modern warfare"[44] and would protect the citadel of bourgeois capitalism. The intellectuals had to do their job beforehand. "A crisis cannot give the attacking forces the ability to organize with lightning speed."[45]

As Hobsbawm put it, "granted that in Italy and most of the West there was not going to be an October revolution from the early 1920s on—and there was no realistic prospect of one—he obviously had to consider a strategy of the long haul. But he did not in fact commit himself in principle to any particular outcome of the lengthy 'war of position' which he predicted and recommended. It might lead directly into a transition to socialism, or into another phase of the war of maneuver and attack, or to some other strategic phase. What would happen must depend on the changes in the concrete situation."

As with the previous concepts we have discussed, the repercussions of the war of maneuvers/war of positions for today are enormous. The New Left and the student radicals of the 1960s eventually settled on this latter approach, after a failed stint of violence and terrorism, as the one best suited to overthrowing the American hegemonic narrative. A West German radical named Rudi Dutschke, a disciple of the Frankfurt School's Herbert Marcuse, termed the new war of positions the "Long March through the Institutions," a term that stuck and is now much better known than Marcuse's own term (which is mistakenly often attributed to Gramsci). Marcuse, as we will see in the next section, gave the approach his blessing.

In 2020, today's NextGen Marxists manufactured a crisis over George Floyd's death and halted the war of positions that had been in place, replacing it with a war of maneuvers in the form of generalized street mayhem. This was understood all too well by those who gave the BLM founders their political start in life. "If progressive forces have not adequately prepared for these moments of crisis, they are likely to be outstripped by the well-resourced and practiced ruling class who can 'reabsorb the control that was slipping from its grasp,'" wrote Harmony Goldberg. "Thus, the preparation of progressive forces in the periods preceding a crisis is potentially even more decisive than the political decisions made in the moment of crisis itself."[46]

Other Ideas

GRAMSCI IS also known for many other concepts that require a briefer treatment but still have application today. As we have seen, Gramsci believed that revolutionaries should take part in parliamentary democracy, but only to create the conditions to transfer political power to the councils, which would then work to abolish parliamentary democracy. The mission of the socialist state was to be a "transitional State" that would deliver communism. "This mission cannot be accomplished by parliamentary democracy," so the goal was "the replacement of the democratic-parliamentary State by a new type of State," one "embodied in a system of workers', peasants' and soldiers' councils," wrote Gramsci in 1919.[47]

We see this approach repeated constantly in Latin America, where Marxists run for president not on their long record of Marxism but as reformists and populists, only then to call for constituent assemblies that rewrite constitutions and erode the checks and balances of representative democracy in favor of what they call participatory democracy (which is praised by BLM). These Latin American Marxist leaders are on record as being Marxists. On January 22, 2022, on the anniversary of Gramsci's birth, Venezuela's Nicolás Maduro tweeted praise for Gramsci as "one of the main promoters of the Marxist cultural revolution of the XX Century. The works and thoughts of Gramsci guide us to undertake the changes that humanity requires."[48]

Another important theory was the philosophy of praxis. Praxis goes back to Aristotle and other Greek philosophers who juxtaposed *theoria* (theory undertaken for the sake of truth discovery) and *praxis* (practice, or activity undertaken for its own sake). As Joseph Gravina of the University of Malta puts it, "Gramsci's Philosophy of Praxis was an attempt to present Marxism as a political philosophy promoting the inter-definable relation between theory and practice. No practice without theory; every man was a philosopher."[49] Such a duality of thought and action fits perfectly a man who was both a philosopher and the founder and leader of a party. This interpretation in turn goes back to Marx's own position that "the philosophers have only interpreted the world, in various ways; the point is to change it," expressed in his 1845 "Theses on Feuerbach," which Gramsci quotes often.[50] A great proponent of praxis in our day is Derrick Bell, the recognized "godfather" of CRT, who wrote in 1995, "As I see it, Critical Race Theory recognizes that revolutionizing a culture begins with the radical assessment of it. It is our hope that scholarly resistance will lay the groundwork for wide-scale resistance. We believe that standards and institutions created by and fortifying white power ought to be resisted."[51] Praxis can also be seen in the intellectuals and academics who have become Europe's best-known hard-leftist leaders, such as many of the Syriza MPs who rose to power in Greece in the 2010s, who drew their inspiration from Gramsci and his later disciple, Louis Althusser, and Spain's Pablo Iglesias and many of his colleagues in the Marxist party Podemos.

Gramsci was, as Hobsbawm puts it so well, the communist strategist for countries where revolutions were not possible. In this sense, he was the first truly Western Marxist. He so refined the idea of a conceptual superstructure that shaped reality that we can think of it as his main innovation. Gramsci requires a granular understanding because his ideas reign today and are changing society. He influenced the thinking of every major American Marxist theorist in the second half of the twentieth century and is quoted by practically all the architects of CLS and CRT. Garza, cofounder of BLM, praises Gramsci in her 2020 book on power, writing, "We can apply an understanding of hegemony to almost any social dynamic—racism, homophobia, heterosexism, sexism, ableism."[52] But Gramsci never abandoned the worker as the leading class that would play the cohering role in the revolution, whose agency was necessary to overthrow capitalism because his lived experience taught him capitalism's alienation. That innovation belongs to the thinkers of the Frankfurt School, and it is to them and their roots in Germany that we now turn.

Germany

GERMANY'S OWN revolution came a few months before the Turin troubles started, and it, too, failed to produce a German soviet state. The revolution did end the rule of Kaiser Wilhelm II, who abdicated on November 9, 1918; later that day, Germany was declared a republic, and the armistice was signed two days later. But parliamentary democracy and capitalism survived a near-death experience, albeit to be guided by the inflationary and decadent Weimar Republic and to be overthrown by the Nazis in fourteen years.

Tumult concentrated the minds of German communists, much as it had Gramsci's brain, and they, too, looked inward for answers. The ones they found paralleled Gramsci's lifework but had their own innovations. Both camps shared an emphasis on the conceptual superstructure as a filter of natural reality and truth and as the keeper of the old order. Both also sought to undermine this hegemonic apparatus to achieve complete transformation. Both greatly influenced the American New Left and its radicals in the 1960s and, through them, the NextGen Marxists of our day. Herbert Marcuse of the Frankfurt School did so directly because he had moved to the United States, and because of his longevity (born only seven years after Gramsci, the German died in 1979, outliving the Italian by forty-two years). One key difference is that the German thinkers eventually gave up on the worker as the agent of revolution, something Gramsci never did.

An open question is whether the German Marxists set out to look at the culture for the origins of failure on their own or, as was the case with Gramsci, were given a helpful shove by Soviet leaders who were as intent on promoting communism internationally as they were on controlling all global manifestations of Marxism.

Either way, councils of workers, sailors, soldiers, peasants, and even intellectuals sprouted all over Germany during the armistice negotiations with the Allied powers, "forcing an end to the war at any price," according to the historian Gerhard Bassler.[53]

The first council was elected days earlier by thousands of protestors who answered the call for a street rally in the Baltic port city of Kiel on November 3, 1918, where sailors had started mutinying on October 28. Two rally leaders were revolutionaries, Karl Artelt and Lothar Popp, both shipyard workers who were members of the Independent Social Democratic Party (USPD), a leftist breakaway faction of the Social Democratic Party (SPD).

In a 1978 interview, a ninety-one-year-old Popp, by then an American citizen, described scenes that have the feel of the October Revolution in St. Petersburg, Russia. "At five o'clock in the afternoon of November 3rd, approximately ten thousand marines and some thousand workers gathered," he said. The revolutionaries then went over to where fellow sailors who had mutinied were being held prisoner and freed them. "A considerable number armed themselves" and began to have armed clashes with soldiers, though many of the latter joined the sailors. "The movement could not be intercepted any longer. More and more units joined in. *Soldatenräte* (soldiers' councils) were established. In each of the barracks revolution was made separately, also on each ship. From one ship they came to call me." Popp went on a ship called the *Bayern*. "I made a speech, they hoisted the Red Flag and that was that."[54]

The councils formed a Supreme Soldiers Council in Kiel, of which Popp was elected chairman, to be succeeded weeks later by Artelt (who, three months later, became one of the founding members of the German Communist Party, the KPD). The same experience multiplied throughout Germany, as everywhere that sailors from Kiel traveled, councils of soldiers, sailors, or neighbors were formed. The American Marxist scholar Murray Bookchin wrote, "The Kiel mutiny triggered a series of events that were far too numerous and consequential for the government to moderate. In the next few days, bands of armed sailors left Kiel and moved from city to city, spreading news of the mutiny and inspiring more radical locals to follow suit. On November 4–8, inspired by the example of the Russian soviets, workers and soldiers throughout Germany formed thousands of councils in virtually bloodless uprisings."[55]

The nationwide councils filled the vacuum "created by the paralysis and disintegration of the armed forces, the old organs of government, and most political parties and interest groups."[56] They essentially took over all the institutions for the next few weeks, though they kept the bureaucrats in place to take orders from the assemblies. Within days, councils or even council republics were formed in Hamburg, Dresden, Leipzig, Württemberg, and many other cities, even in Munich, the capital of conservative Bavaria. Many of the councils called for the nationalization of the means of production and opposed "the principle of the separation of powers, and the principle of indirect representation," according to Bassler.[57]

The red uprising seemed even about to engulf Berlin, the capital of the empire, but there the SPD—which sought the introduction of socialism through parliamentary means, but not Bolshevism—had the upper hand and prevented things from getting too far.

Days earlier, a general amnesty had seen the release from prison of the Marxist leader Karl Liebknecht, who was received by the Soviet ambassador and the revolutionary leader Bukharin, "both of whom shared Lenin's optimistic expectation that Germany would soon see a revolution comparable to October 1917 in Russia," according to Bookchin.[58] Bukharin told another Marxist leader and colleague of Liebknecht, Karl Radek, that Liebknecht was in complete agreement with the Bolsheviks.

On November 9, the day of the kaiser's abdication and the collapse of the government, members of the Marxist Spartacus League seized the offices of a Berlin newspaper and renamed it *Die Rote Fahne* (The Red Flag), a party organ for the revolution. Its new editor was the legendary communist Rosa Luxemburg, another Spartacus founder who had also just been released from prison. The insurgents also had guns, having raided a police station. At 4:00 PM that day, Liebknecht entered the palace in Berlin, from which the kaiser's

Hohenzollern dynasty had ruled, and announced from a balcony, "The day of the revolution has come.... The old order is no more. The reign of the Hohenzollerns, who lived in this palace for centuries, is finished. We now proclaim the free socialist republic of Germany."[59]

It was at that moment that the SPD leadership, fearing that Germany was on the brink of Bolshevism, hastily put together on November 10 a new government that would prevent Liebknecht's republic from going into effect. They gave their cabinet a Bolshevik name, the Council of the People's Commissars, but only to placate the communists. "All six of the new cabinet members professed to be Marxists, yet they did nothing to heed Marx's stern warning that the old state machinery had to be smashed," wrote Bookchin.[60] In a further blow to the Spartacus leadership and their allies, and to the hope for the creation of a German soviet republic, the German proletariat trusted and supported the SPD and its plan to introduce workplace reforms, also government ownership of the means of production (mines, steelworks, transportation, etc.), but without abandoning representative democracy. "The job of the SPD was to *use* the state, not to *replace* it structurally, as Marx had insisted," wrote Bookchin.[61]

The Spartacists and their allies, however, began to agitate for revolution. They demanded that a vote for a constituent assembly be delayed, to gain time to raise the workers' consciousness and turn them against parliamentary democracy and free markets. What they wanted was a council republic and socialism. The SPD leaders, wrote Luxemburg caustically in *Die Rote Fahne,*

> *want to spare themselves the revolution, the use of force, the civil war with all its horrors. Petit-bourgeois illusions! When the capitalist class sees that it is in the minority, it, as a well-disciplined parliamentary party, will declare with a sigh, There's nothing we can do! We see that we are outvoted. All right, we shall submit and hand over all our lands, factories, mines, all our fire-proof safes and our handsome profits to the workers.... These profound Marxists have forgotten the ABC of socialism. They have forgotten that the bourgeoisie is not a parliamentary party, but a ruling class in possession of all the means of economic and social power."[62]*

LUXEMBURG'S ALLY Clara Zetkin, writing in 1922, the year she shared a cabin with Gramsci outside Moscow, made clear what Luxemburg and the other communist leaders sought: "All power to the Councils! No National Assembly! Not bourgeois, but proletarian democracy! Dictatorship of the proletariat! Social revolution! These are the slogans which the 'Rote Fahne' carried to the masses of the working people."[63] The Spartacists eventually split off and formed a new party, the Communist Party of Germany (KPD), founded on December 30, with Luxemburg and Liebknecht among the handful of leaders. Zetkin was to be one of the first two communists to be elected to the Reichstag the following year.

Meanwhile, political and social tensions mounted, and blood began to be shed. On Christmas Eve, troops bombarded the palace, killing thirty insurgent sailors inside. Fear that communist violence would lead to a civil war, as it had in Russia under the Bolsheviks, led one officer, General Georg von Maercker, to form an elite paramilitary group that became known as the Freikorps—a group of young men from whom the Nazis would later recruit. The stage was set for violent revolution. On January 5, 1919, buoyed by a turnout in the hundreds of thousands of workers at a rally a day earlier, the newly constituted KPD and its allies voted for insurrection against the SPD government and formed a Revolutionary Committee.

The next day, an even larger group of communist supporters turned to the streets, and armed bands of workers seized some newspaper offices, train stations, and government printing offices. But the revolt fizzled out. The Revolutionary Committee provided no action plan, and no leadership, just as communist leaders had provided little indoctrination of the proletariat in the preceding years. The comparison with the Turin experience is stark.

The SPD-led government did act swiftly, by contrast, and marched on Berlin with Freikorps battalions, which proceeded to chase the revolutionaries out of offices they had occupied and started to hunt for Liebknecht and Luxemburg. As Bookchin writes vividly, "the two Spartacus leaders eluded the police for several days by moving from one apartment to another, but on the evening of January 15 a 'citizen guard' patrol found them in an apartment in the Wilmersdorf neighborhood. They were taken to the Eden Hotel—headquarters of the Horse Guards Division of the Freikorps—where they were questioned separately and physically abused."[64] Later that day, after inflicting more physical torture on them, the Freikorps shot dead the two communist leaders. Luxemburg's body was dumped in the Landwehr Canal, and her body was not recovered until the following spring. This was no doubt a cruel and ignominious end to one of the century's best-known Marxist thinkers, but Germany avoided revolution, and both parliamentary democracy and capitalism got to live for another dozen years. The last council government, the Munich Soviet Republic, was dismantled by the Freikorps in May. Street fighting continued for some time, until the Weimar Constitution was signed in August, and the economically unstable and dissolute Weimar Republic lived on until 1933.

Today, BLM leaders and other NextGen Marxists are regular guests of the Luxemburg Foundation in Berlin a century after her torture and assassination. The foundation, associated with Die Linke, the party of the hard Left in Germany, was founded in 1990 to continue Luxemburg's mission and, according to its website, "seeks to represent democratic socialism with an unwavering internationalist focus."[65]

What Went Wrong?

THE LESSONS of this other European revolutionary fiasco were not hard to deduce. In words that explain what happened, Bookchin writes,

> Marxist doctrine held that Germany's working class should have been highly committed to revolutionary socialist ideas. In fact, notwithstanding the size of the SPD and the Free Trade Unions, the very opposite proved to be the case. Modern industry had created a proletariat that was not only large but also relatively domesticated, subservient to labor bureaucrats and reformist political parties. For the most part German industrial workers accepted their rationalized, hierarchical, and orderly methods of work with a large measure of pride. Obedience to authority, where it was not too heavy-handed, was actually admired as evidence of discipline. This ethos of obedience and discipline extended from the factory into the unions and parties, and ultimately into everyday life as well.[66]

IT IS at this point that we turn to the intellectual soul-searching and ferment that for decades followed the events that transpired at breakneck speed between late October in Kiel and January 15 in Berlin. The men and women who took part in this contemplation eventually formed a think tank they named the Institute for Social Research, which was housed at the Goethe University Frankfurt. It is colloquially known as the Frankfurt School, and its best-known product is critical theory, a concept with strong intellectual connections to Gramsci's ideas about cultural hegemony, the war of positions, and so on. These men were not mere intellectuals, though; they either participated in the council movement themselves or were directly associated with the Soviet Union. They included some of the most important names in twentieth-century Marxist philosophy, including Hungary's Georg Lukács and Germany's Karl Korsch and Herbert Marcuse. They also included the man who bankrolled the institute, Félix Weil. Their efforts are often presented as an esoteric body of knowledge produced by intellectuals of a leftist bend of mind, but that ignores their background and minimizes their lifework. They were engaged not just in *theoria* but in *praxis*. Like Gramsci, these men were committed Marxists who supported the Soviet Union even after Stalin turned on its allies inside Russia and who sought to bring to the West, and then the world, collectivism, central planning, and the suppression of freedoms. Their experience of the councils animated the radicals of the 1960s, and it continues to resonate to our day, a full century later. As its name suggests, critical theory is the forebear of our own CRT, the doctrine of NextGen Marxists.

Félix Weil

FÉLIX JOSÉ Weil was born in Argentina in 1898 and lived there until age nine, when he was sent to Frankfurt to attend school. His father, Hermann Weil, had moved to that then up-and-coming South American country in 1890 as an employee of a Dutch grain company. Hermann then started his own business and became the world's largest grain trader—and fabulously wealthy. He became a political adviser to the kaiser, but young Félix went in the opposite direction.

In Frankfurt, Félix showed an interest in Marxism early on. In the heady days of November 1918, he joined the Frankfurt council government and participated in its occupation of the Frankfurter Hof. "He had put himself, in full uniform, at the disposal of the Frankfurt Workers' and Soldiers' Council during the November Revolution," writes Rolf Wiggershaus.[67] In February 1919, Félix Weil moved to Tübingen to study socialism under Robert Wilbrandt and often visited Zetkin, whom he met that year, in nearby Stuttgart. In April, he met Karl Korsch, Wilbrandt's assistant, and the two communists struck up a lifelong friendship. "Studying Marx in greater depth in Tübingen, and the discussions I had with Clara Zetkin radicalized me," Weil wrote in his unfinished memoirs.[68] As an Argentine, he was limited in what he could do politically. He simply became a deep-pocketed supporter of the Left, a "salon Bolshevik," as he described himself.[69]

The relationship between the communist matron and the young Marxist dilettante grew close, despite their forty-year difference in age. Zetkin didn't just radicalize Weil but impacted his personal life, introducing him to his future wife, Katherina Bachert, the daughter of a veteran socialist. But Zetkin owed Weil even more. Weil's Argentine biographer Mario Rapoport writes that in 1919, Weil was awakened in the middle of the night by a comrade from a socialist group. He told Weil that he had been sitting in a bar and overhead young nationalists swilling beer at a nearby table loudly plotting Zetkin's assassination that night. The two then ran over to Zetkin's house and whisked her out, taking her to the residence of a cousin, Silvia Weil Stern, where she stayed for several days. When the two students walked by Zetkin's house later that night, they found all her windows broken, and from that point on, Zetkin was surrounded by armed communists day and night. She took to calling Weil her "savior."[70] Soon her son Konstantin, the late Rosa Luxemburg's lover, became, too, fast friends with the wealthy Weil.

It was with Konstantin Zetkin ("Kostja" to his friends) that Weil first met Max Horkheimer and Friedrich Pollock sometime in November 1919, after they had moved back to Frankfurt. Before the year was over, the group had conceived of an institute to study why Marxism was not succeeding.[71] John Abromeit writes that in the time following the encounter with Weil, Horkheimer "deepened his knowledge of socialist theory and engaged in numerous lengthy discussions with Friedrich Pollock and Felix Weil on how best to institutionalize a more general theoretical discussion of socialism in Germany. These discussions would lead to the founding of the Institute for Social Research in 1923."[72]

Max Horkheimer

LIKE WEIL, Horkheimer was the son of a Jewish millionaire industrialist in Frankfurt, Moritz Horkheimer, who also aided the kaiser's war effort, in his case through his textile holdings. Like so many Marxists—starting with Marx himself—Max had "daddy issues," and he derided his father as a *Kriegsprofiteur*, or war profiteer. He even married an older woman from a lower-class background to spite Moritz. From early on, he formed views on the parasitical nature of the bourgeoisie. "Many will recognize that those on top in this society are horrible," he wrote.[73] He was deemed unfit to serve in the army and was actually at a sanatorium in Munich during the November Revolution, observing the Munich Soviet Republic from afar. He did defend it in a letter to his girl-friend, writing, "Don't believe the lies about Munich.... Madness and injustice are not the order of the day."[74]

He didn't think, however, that street violence would succeed. There were two types of revolution, he wrote. "There was a revolution in the streets, and it was inspiring, but the streets now mean death. All the great leaders are dead—Rosa Luxemburg, Karl Liebknecht, Kurt Eisner, etc.," but the bourgeoisie was too strong, he wrote in 1919.[75] Then he sketched out his version of the war of positions: "The second way of making revolution consists of entering into the government and sabotaging it. This type of revolution is not bad and can in the long run be better."

Horkheimer also wrote early on about the conceptual superstructure that underpinned and maintained the domination of the oppressor class. "The cultural superstructure" may change here and there, he wrote, "yet certain principal elements persist without significant modification." The parts of the culture that the oppressor class would not allow to be changed, that were "taboo," he wrote, were "those ideas which are an important component in the apparatus of domination of the ruling class."[76] The market rewarded not activities that were useful to the whole of society but those that have "specific usefulness in the act of exploitation." Therefore, "in this perverse state of things, the scale of rewards corresponds less to the real value an achievement may have for the existence of mankind, more to its importance for the survival of the old system.... This applies not only to leading positions in the actual apparatus of suppression and the large-scale ideological institutions such as the military, the police, the church, philosophy and economics, but even to mere attitudes and beliefs"[77]—in other words, Gramsci's cultural hegemony, north of the Alps. We can also see the antecedent of NextGen Marxism's call for the abolition of police departments and courts as mere "apparatuses of suppression." Not for nothing, Abromeit tells us that Horkheimer "was instrumental in the planning of the Institute from the very beginning, a fact that is often overlooked due to his lack of direct involvement in the Institute's affairs under its first director, Carl Grunberg."[78]

But first, the institute where all this would be curated needed to be set up. Weil spent 1921 living in Argentina with his wife, working as a spy for the Soviet Union. Upon his return, he got the ball rolling. Ian Gardner writes,

"Documentary evidence confirms that Weil approached Frankfurt University and the Ministry of Culture in August 1922 to seek their approval to establish the Institute as an adjunct to the University in Frankfurt. In November 1922 the legal body overseeing Weil's financial endowment was created and the Institute was formally established in early February 1923."[79] It was in May that year that our Marxist intellectuals met in a hotel in the countryside in Thuringia to determine the course of the institute.

Which brings us to the two men whose work was ostensibly to be discussed that week, Korsch and Lukács, two giants of twentieth-century Western Marxism, along with Gramsci and Horkheimer. The first three were to have the most direct impact on the New Left, and thus on NextGen Marxism.

Karl Korsch

OF THE four, Korsch is probably the least known, but his influence should not be underestimated. It was Korsch, says Abromeit, who suggested to Weil that he hold a Marxist Workweek—"the first extensive meeting of some of the most important younger critical Marxist theorists in Germany at the time."[80] Horkheimer was not in attendance, "for unknown reasons, but he was certainly well informed by Weil and Pollock about the discussions that took place there."

Born of peasant stock in Lower Saxony in 1886 (he lived a long life, dying in 1961 in Cambridge, Massachusetts), Korsch became a Fabian socialist in London, where he spent the years 1912–14. He went back to Germany for the War in 1914, and participated, though as a pacifist; he never carried a gun and was wounded three times. Korsch then became one of the leading theoreticians of the revolutionary soldiers' council of Berlin in 1918–19. His main takeaway from the Revolution was that the workers lacked the proper ideological indoctrination. Korsch joined the KPD in 1921 and became a communist member of the Thuringia State Diet, a position he held during the Marxist Workweek in May 1923. One of his main functions as a communist was to be primarily engaged in the Educational Section, "preparing and teaching courses for workers in the fundamentals of Marxism," according to Paul Breines.[81] Later that year, in October, Korsch became the "justice minister" of the short-lived KPD government in Thuringia. He was also editor of the party organ *Die Internationale* and wrote for or edited other communist journals. After being kicked out of the KPD for his far-leftist tendencies, he lectured at the university, where he taught Marxism to the dramatist Bertolt Brecht, who became a lifelong friend. A year after Korsch's death, Paul Mattick wrote that Korsch had "an understanding of Marxian theory superior to that of the most prominent party theoreticians."[82]

Korsch was thus the personification of the intellectual in constant praxis, a deep thinker who played a leading role in party politics and in the effort to educate the proletariat, as Gramsci had. It is to Korsch that posterity owes the popularization—if not the actual creation—of such interrelated terms as *vulgar Marxism* and *critical* as a Marxist modifier.[83] The first was the idea that Marxism had been vulgarized in the second half of the nineteenth century into making material determinism the reason for why man acted. "Many vulgar-Marxists to this day have never, even in theory, admitted that intellectual life and forms of social consciousness are comparable realities," wrote Korsch in a book published in 1923. To the California state historian Tom Meisenhelder, this makes Korsch, along with Lukács and Gramsci, "one of the founders of critical Marxism."[84]

The second, obviously related, term, *critical*, has come to mean an emphasis on society's ideological superstructure and how to undermine it through critiques—and its echoes are still felt to this day, fully a century later. "From beginning to end, [the Marxian theory] is a theoretical as well as a practical critique of existing society," Korsch wrote in *Three Essays on Marxism*.[85] Just before Hitler's ascension to power in 1933, Korsch directed a "study circle for critical Marxism" in Berlin, which was attended by Lukács and Brecht, among others. "For Korsch as for Antonio Gramsci, revolutionary change was as much about ideological struggle as it was about material conditions, and orthodox Marxism had simply failed to address this issue with any stringency or sensitivity," writes New Mexico University's David Craven.[86] The book that was ostensibly the subject of discussion at the 1923 Marxist Workweek was his *Marxism and Philosophy*, in which he criticized at length what he termed "vulgar Marxism." The other book, *History and Class Consciousness*, was by the Hungarian philosopher Lukács.

Georg Lukács

LUKÁCS WAS another intellectual who took a direct hand in government. In 1919, he took part in the one council revolution that succeeded in Europe (albeit for only 133 days!). That was in his native Hungary, where communists on March 31 set up the Socialist Federative Republic of Councils under their leader, Béla Kun, which history also knows as the Hungarian Soviet Republic. During the short-lived communist experiment, Lukács rose from deputy commissar to commissar of public education and culture, during which time he put some of his theories to work.

One of these Lukács had committed to paper that same year in his essay "Tactics and Ethics." It boiled down to the old communist maxim that the ends justify the means. "Tactics," wrote Lukács, "assume the form of Realpolitik." Because the communist sought a total transformation of the old order, "tactics free themselves in this way from the normal limits imposed by the legal order." Ethical self-awareness "makes it quite clear that there are situations—tragic situations—in which it is impossible to act without burdening oneself with guilt." Lukács then finished his essay by quoting from a novel by the leader of a Russian terrorist group, Boris Savinkov, who wrote, "Murder is not allowed, it is an absolute and unpardonable sin; it 'may' not, but yet it 'must' be committed."[87]

Such thinking allowed Lukács to marry a Russian terrorist himself, Jelena Grabenko, in 1914, and do other things along the way. As culture and education commissar, Lukács realized that the best way to destroy society—so communists could implement the change they lusted after—was to destroy the family. He therefore ordered that young schoolchildren in the new Hungary be taught sexual perversions. According to his biographer,

> special lectures were organized in schools and literature printed and distributed to "instruct" children about free love, about the nature of sexual intercourse, about the archaic nature of bourgeois family codes, about the outdatedness of monogamy, and the irrelevance of religion, which deprives man of all pleasure. Children were urged thus to reject and deride paternal authority and the authority of the church, and to ignore precepts of morality.[88]

THIS TYPE of attack on the family was continued later on American soil by the Frankfurt School's Marcuse, as we will see in the next chapter. As with many other of these ideas, we see echoes of this approach in our day, with drag queen story hour and the insistence that schoolchildren be instructed in sexual practices from a very young age or that parents be kept in the dark about what sex their children have "chosen."

Lukács became a commissar in the Fifth Division of the Hungarian Red Army in the short war that ensued when Hungarians overthrew the unpopular Kun council government. Lukács ordered the execution of eight of his own soldiers in a public square, telling an interviewer that they were a runaway bat-talion and he had to restore order. Again, the ends justified the means. After the collapse of the Kun government, Lukács fled to Vienna and somehow kept evading extradition to Hungary.

His 1923 book *History and Class Consciousness* was the other manuscript to be discussed at the Marxist Workweek.[89] In it, Lukács postulates many of the same theories that Gramsci had about the transformation of false conscious-ness into revolutionary consciousness. Accused of ultra-leftism by Stalinists, Lukács had to recant the views expressed in the book after the Soviet Commu-nist Party summoned him to Moscow in 1930. He continued to support Stalin until the dictator's death in 1953 and became one of the lodestars of Western Marxism in the twentieth century.

The Frankfurt School

OTHER ACTIVE communists attended the Marxist Workweek. Richard Sorge, a debonair German Russian Soviet intelligence agent, may have been the model for James Bond. Ian Fleming described Sorge as the "most formidable spy in history."[90] Sorge recruited Hede Massing as a Soviet agent, and she attended the Workweek along with her husband, Julian Gumperz, who supervised publish-ing KPD material and, according to the House Un-American Activities Report of 1956, was a member of the Comintern.[91] Karl Wittfogel and Karl Schmuckle were members of the KPD as well. In 1951, as a former communist, Wittfogel willingly testified before a US Senate committee, implicating others as mem-bers of the Communist Party.[92]

As Wiggershaus tells us, "in fact, the meeting was clearly the 'first seminar on theory' held by the Institute of Social Research."[93] Wiggershaus adds that "Weil's heartfelt wish was still to create a foundation similar to the Marx–Engels Institute in Moscow—equipped with a staff of professors and students, with libraries and archives—and one day to present it to a German Soviet Republic."[94]

Let's not forget that in the months prior to his late 1919 brainstorming ses-sions with Horkheimer, Weil had met Zetkin, Korsch, Pollock, and, according to Gardner, also the Soviet radical Karl Radek, the German communist propa-gandist Willi Münzenberg, and Heinrich Susskind, the editor of *Die Rote Fahne*. The young Weil, in other words, must have been a sponge for the communist wisdom being dispensed by the radicals he was encountering, who clearly saw in the young German Argentine a very deep-pocketed benefactor.

It was the communist leader Zetkin who advised Weil to open the Frank-furt School, according to a young Yugoslav who was an early member of the school.[95] Even if that is exaggerated, Zetkin's close relationship with Weil from 1919 onward, and that of her son Konstantin (who did take part in the Marxist Workweek), is significant, given the leading role she played in creating the So-viet policy of an international "united front" in 1921, which Lenin and Trotsky supported. A friend of Engels, Zetkin had held leadership positions in world communism since the 1880s and, from 1921 on, in the Comintern. A united front of all Marxist parties—in Germany's case, the communist KPD and the social democrat SPD—was necessary because the worker supported the SPD at higher rates than he did the KPD. The proletariat had "false consciousness." The workers, she said, were "almost desperate" yet "unwilling to struggle."[96] As Zetkin said, many among the proletariat supported the burgeoning fascist movement, which, she added, could not be defeated through military means alone. There was a need to bring the workers into the communist fold, and not just those who worked with their hands. "All those whose labor, be it with hand or brain, increases the material and cultural heritage of humankind," needed to be indoctrinated.[97] And it just so happens that remedying false consciousness was to be job number 1 for the Frankfurt School then being created.

Comintern support of Zetkin's united-front strategy ebbed over time, espe-cially after Lenin's death in 1924, and Stalin in time buried the concept. But it is hard to believe that early Soviet leaders were not, too, behind the founding of the Frankfurt School. Not only was Zetkin in constant contact with Lenin and Trotsky, but Weil, too, met in Germany in 1920 with Zinoviev, the all-important head of the Comintern. There is also the fact that the Frankfurt School was to be an adjunct of the Marx–Engels Institute back in Moscow. Wittfogel, who was at the Marxist Workweek, was a full-time associate of the institute.

The Frankfurt School's task of spreading Marxism was laid out from the start. Weil said that "at the opening ceremony for the Institute on 22 June 1924 in the presence of the representative of the Minister of Science, Art and Edu-cation … and in the presence of the Mayor and other leaders of the state and district authorities, I myself and Professor Grünberg [head of the Frankfurt School] in particular in his speech, publicly and programmatically laid down the Marxist character of the Institute."[98]

But the founders then opted for concealing its Marxism. The original name was the Institut für Marxismus (Institute for Marxism). Weil wrote later, however, that being so forward "would incite too much resistance.... The title of the Institute had to be clothed in Aesopian terms."[99]

It should hardly surprise, then, that the products of the school attempted to subvert society and create the conditions for the installment of a Marxist alternative to capitalism and representative government. Horkheimer, who replaced Grünberg as the school's director in 1930, was the originator of critical theory, the school's best-known product and one of its more impactful down to our day. Horkheimer had still not given up on the Soviet Union. Just a few years before he became director, Horkheimer had written an essay that made clear how he felt, even for Stalin's Soviet Union: "He who has eyes for the meaningless injustice of the imperialist world, which in no way is to be explained by technical impotence, will regard the events in Russia as the progressive, painful attempt to overcome this injustice."[100]

In a 1937 essay, "Traditional and Critical Theory," Horkheimer introduced the world to his brainchild. Traditional theory, he wrote, was traditional philosophy—a body of thought that underpinned the current power arrangement. "The scholar and his science are incorporated in the apparatus of society; his achievements are a factor in the conservation and continuous renewal of the existing state of affairs," he wrote.[101] Critical theory, alternatively, was a revolutionizing attempt at overthrowing that order. It was "not just a research hypothesis.... It is an essential element in the historical effort to create a world which satisfies the needs and powers of men."[102] The men and women of the age were trapped in a box they could not break out of, processing the natural world through instrumental rationality, which benefited the status quo. Because it catalogued and categorized all natural phenomena, reason itself was now working against the liberation of the individual. The Industrial Revolution had suggested automation into everything, from entertainment to genocide. The Enlightenment had failed.

Unremitting criticism would make people doubt the old verities and, in time, abandon them. Capitalism and parliamentary democracy were the results of the Enlightenment and the Industrial Revolution it had made possible. "The technological advances of the bourgeois period are inseparably linked to this function of the pursuit of science," he wrote.[103] Critical theory would be "wholly distrustful of the rules of conduct with which society as presently constituted provides each of its members."[104] Critical theory "urges a transformation of society."[105]

Critical theory was, therefore, the ultimate "red pill" in the world created by the 1999 science fiction cult classic *The Matrix*. In the movie, the protagonist, Neo (Keanu Reeves), is given a choice between a blue pill and a red pill. If he takes the blue one, then Neo will go back to his prior existence not knowing that the reality of his own servitude is being concealed from him—he will keep his false consciousness. If he takes the red pill, however—and we must pause to consider that this is an interesting choice of color—Neo will become aware that the social structures of oppression are pervasive. In one of the flick's most dramatic scenes, Neo and the resistance leader Morpheus (Laurence Fishburne), who becomes mentor to Neo, sit in a dark, spartan room, with thunder rolling outside, and discuss the matter:

> MORPHEUS: Do you want to know what it is? [*long dramatic pause*] The Matrix is everywhere. It is all around us. Even now in this very room. You can see it when you look out your window, or when you turn on your television. You can feel it when you go to work, when you go to church, when you pay your taxes. It is the world that has been pulled over your eyes to blind you from the truth.
>
> NEO: What truth?
>
> MORPHEUS: That you are a slave, Neo. Like everyone else you were born into bondage, born into a prison that you cannot smell or taste or touch. A prison, for your mind. Unfortunately, no one can be told what the Matrix is. You have to see it for yourself. This is your last chance. After this there is no turning back. You take the blue pill, the story ends, you wake up in your bed and believe whatever you want to believe. You take the red pill, you stay in Wonderland, and I show you how deep the rabbit hole goes. Remember. All I'm offering is the truth. Nothing more.

Then, after Neo takes the red pill, MORPHEUS *adds*: Follow me.[106]

THE FALSE consciousness permitted by taking the stupefying blue pill, and the sudden awareness of society's oppressive structure awakened by swallowing the red pill, plus the fact that Morpheus is enticing Neo to struggle against this conceptual hegemony, has led others to point out the similarities between the critically acclaimed first film of the Matrix series (the sequels did not reach the same acclaim) and the writings of the critical theorists in one or two academic papers and essays.

Without the red pill of critical theory, by which Horkheimer means a dialectical approach to everything, the bourgeois "believe they are acting according to personal determinations, whereas in fact even in their most complicated calculations they but exemplify the working of an incalculable social mechanism," Horkheimer writes in his foundational essay.[107] The "whole perceptible world ... is seen by the perceiver as sum total of facts; it is there and must be accepted."[108] Only critical theory, the red pill, can awaken the individual from his stupor. And that was because critical theory showed the supposed devastation and inequalities created by capitalism. "The theory shows how an exchange economy, given the condition of men (which, of course, changes under the very influence of such an economy), must necessarily lead to a heightening of those social tensions which in the present historical era lead in turn to wars and revolutions," he wrote.[109]

"The aim of this activity [critical theory] is not simply to eliminate one or other abuse, for it regards such abuses as necessarily connected with the way in which the social structure is organized. Although it itself emerges from the social structure, its purpose is not ... the better functioning of any element in the structure. On the contrary, it is suspicious of the very categories of better, useful, appropriate, productive, and valuable, as these are understood in the present order, and refuses to take them as nonscientific presuppositions about which one can do nothing," added Horkheimer. "The critical attitude of which we are speaking is wholly distrustful of the rules of conduct with which society as presently constituted provides each of its members."[110] The aim of the theory is to "strive for a state of affairs in which there will be no exploitation or oppression, in which an all-embracing subject, namely self-aware mankind, exists," though success is not guaranteed, as it was not to Neo, because "the idea of a transformed society, however, does not have the advantage of widespread acceptance, as long as the idea has not yet had its real possibility tested."[111]

It is not hard to see how we get from all this to Nikole Hannah-Jones, whose 1619 Project is a self-conscious effort to make Americans see that they, too, are slaves like Neo. "I like to say the 1619 Project is the red pill in *The Matrix*. You read this book and suddenly you start to question your reality and you realize all of this was created. And then you try to subvert it. I want y'all to do that," she

NEXTGEN MARXISM | 87

said at an appearance in Fairfax, Virginia, on February 19, 2023.[112]

But before the critical theorists could achieve this transformation, their own society was turned upside down, though not in the way they wanted. When German president Paul von Hindenburg appointed Adolf Hitler as chancellor in 1933, the scholars of the Frankfurt School had to flee Germany. The Nazis closed the institute as soon as they came into power, so the scholars first went to Geneva, in neutral Switzerland. Then, in 1934, Columbia University in New York generously offered offices at Teachers College, so Horkheimer, Theodor Adorno, Leo Löwenthal, Wittfogel, Weil, Korsch, Horkheimer's assistant, Marcuse, and others reconstituted the Frankfurt School in Morningside Heights. Later still, in 1940, some of them went to California. They were "cultural Marxists," after all, and America's mass culture, their nemesis, was directed from Hollywood to a semihypnotized public, so they had to be in situ to see it.

The impact they were to have on us, starting in the 1960s, reverberates to our day and is the subject of our next chapter.

3
THE [OLD] NEW LEFT

To HERBERT MARCUSE, then a twenty-year-old soldier in the kaiser's army, the spontaneous street politics and council eruptions breaking out across Germany in late 1918 had been a shot of fresh Baltic air, an exciting and needed response to a savage, unpopular war. "My [political] experience began in 1918 with the German Revolution," said Marcuse in 1972, also giving the credit to Rosa Luxemburg, whom he said he "greatly admired."[1] Marcuse had joined the newly formed soldiers' council in Berlin, which elected him as its representative, and he prepared to participate in bringing about a new dawn. "He attended meetings, rallies, and street demonstrations (some called by the Spartacists), and as part of the security force mobilized to defend against the incipient counter-revolution, was assigned to stand with a rifle in the Berlin Alexanderplatz and return the fire of snipers," writes the Marcuse biographer Barry M. Katz.[2]

Disillusionment soon set in, however, when he perceived the council movement as growing stale. The German Revolution had been pregnant with possibilities to establish a true people's power and bring an end to bourgeois ideas about capitalism and parliamentary democracy, but all that had been aborted by workers too cautious to support revolutionaries and who placed their trust, instead, in social democrats promising only to reform the status quo, not to overthrow it. "I left this Soldiers Council when they began to elect former officers as a matter of course," Marcuse would later write.[3]

Fast-forward half a century. When confronted with similar circumstances in the United States of 1968, the now seventy-year-old Marcuse resolved not to let fate cheat him twice. Marcuse had joined the Frankfurt School in 1932, the year he resigned his position as Martin Heidegger's assistant because the philosopher was finally becoming a member of the Nazi Party. Soon, he became Horkheimer's assistant. Having come to America when the Frankfurt School went into exile in New York in 1934, Marcuse stayed on in America after the defeat of the Nazis, and by the late 1960s, he had become a tenured professor who was highly influential among the new rebels. *The New York Times* had labeled him the "Guru of the New Left," and the pope denounced him by name, a rare distinction in the two-thousand-year history of the papacy. Marcuse's 1964 *One Dimensional Man*, wrote the Marcuse biographer Douglas Kellner, had "emerged as an important influence on the young radicals who formed the New Left," just as his 1954 *Eros and Civilization* had led to the polyamoric sexual experimentation of the 1960s (for Marcuse was also the "Guru of the Sexual Revolution").[4] Understanding that the end of his mortal coil could not be very far, Marcuse told a meeting of the radical newspaper *The Guardian* in 1968, "I certainly cannot wait. And not only because of my age. I don't think we have to wait. And even I, I don't have any choice. Because I literally couldn't stand it any longer if nothing would change. Even I am suffocating."[5] The time for action was now, and Marcuse resolved to help the New Left until he could no longer.

He sensed the similarities between the council movement of his Berlin youth and the radical students and black activists in the urban America of the 1960s. In both milieux, change was coming from below; there was the same whiff of "people power." The New Left of the 1960s was grassroots, spontaneous, and totalizing in its approach to change. The movement was independent of political parties or representative government; indeed, it was disdainful of them. Marcuse grasped, too, what ideological and practical changes needed to be made to make the revolution of the 1960s succeed where the one of the 1910s had failed.

The abortive end of the German Revolution (which Max Weber described as the "enormous collapse which is customarily called the Revolution") had been a multifaceted calamity for Marxists. Not only had a golden opportunity been thrown away in Germany, but to Marcuse and others—including the thinker Hannah Arendt, also influential among the New Left despite her hostility to Marxism—the revolution's failure had been a historic and global turning point. The miscarriage of revolution had, first, made clear the need to drop class as the attribute with which to divide society. "Arendt and Marcuse both suggest that it was at this point in Western history that class lost its pivotal role in social organization," writes the Arendt scholar Caroline Ashcroft of Queen Mary University of London. And with that, because the proletariat was an artifact of class division, came an even more significant change by the New Left: "the question of who constituted the revolutionary actor was burst open."[6] The worker was no longer to play the leading role in revolution, and Moscow's model of revolution was no longer the touchpoint. Under the influence of the

German and Italian Marxists, particularly those who were affiliated with the Frankfurt School, the New Left was born.

The New Left

THE TERM the *New Left* first appeared in France and Great Britain in the 1950s, but for the American audience, it was popularized by the Marxist sociologist C. Wright Mills, who spent most of his career at Columbia University. Mills had already begun to shape the zeitgeist of the 1960s counterculture with his 1956 book *The Power Elite*. Mills described what he saw as a power elite comprising three entities: several hundred powerful corporations, the federal government, and the military—or to use Mills's more colorful terms, the corporate chieftains, political directorate, and the professional warlords—and, needless to say, they were all white men. This triumvirate of elites runs the country, he alleged. The problem is that his analysis was not based only on what he believed was happening in the United States; it was also very much a response to what had happened with the Nazi takeover in Germany. Mills had been influenced by German sociologist Franz Leopold Neumann, whose 1942 book *Behemoth: The Structure and Practice of National Socialism* proposed an explanation for how Hitler's national socialism came about. Neumann himself was a socialist and was also affiliated with the Frankfurt School, and so unsurprisingly, he saw the world strictly in Marxist terms of power structures locked in irreconcilable differences. Perhaps that was not such a great leap to make after what happened in Nazi Germany, but for Mills to have used the same analysis for the United States was something of an absurdity.

Yet Mills's argument that the white, male elite not only held all of the power of the United States but held it to the detriment of everyone else became one of the foundational ideas of 1960s radicalism. The so-called power elite were the enemy, and revolutionary change was the only solution. These ideas of Mills's lay at the heart of the student movement's constitution: the Port Huron Statement. Its author, Tom Hayden, referred to the "triangular relations of the business, military, and political arenas." Indeed, because of them, he wrote, America was no longer democratic: "The American political system is not the democratic model of which its glorifiers speak. In actuality it frustrates democracy by confusing the individual citizen, paralyzing policy discussion, and consolidating the irresponsible power of military and business interests."[7]

Thus, while Mills helped to lay a foundation for attacking American democracy, he made his most important contribution to the upheaval of the 1960s in identifying a new agent for revolutionary change. In using the term *New Left*, Mills rejected the worker as a locus of revolutionary change; he dismissed that idea as outdated Victorian Marxism. Instead, he argued that intellectuals might be the agents of revolutionary change, particularly young intellectuals. In spring 1960, when he published his "Letter to the New Left," he wrote that it was an idea whose time had come.[8] He pointed to recent uprisings of young people in Turkey, Taiwan, Japan, Great Britain, and, of course, Cuba, where the thirty-two-year-old Fidel Castro had just months before grabbed the reins of power.

In fact, Castro was a major influence in shaping the New Left. Fresh from law school and surrounded by a band of youthful revolutionaries, Castro had successfully ousted Cuban dictator Fulgencio Batista in January 1959. In case any of America's elite youth had missed that fact, Harvard's chief academic officer, McGeorge Bundy (later to be President John F. Kennedy's national security adviser and, later still, president of the Ford Foundation), welcomed Castro to Harvard in April 1959. So many students were interested in seeing Castro that the event had to be moved from an auditorium to the football stadium. Capturing that shift in focus from the worker to the student, Castro explained that he agreed to speak at Harvard because "that is where you find the real 'military spirit': in students, not in the barracks."[9] With that model to look to, the New Left abandoned the idea, once and for all, that workers would be the agents of revolutionary change.

The New Left was, moreover, a phenomenon principally in the industrialized countries: the United States, Canada, Germany, France, and Japan. And, as Marcuse saw it, the New Left had revolutionary potential such as hadn't been seen in half a century—precisely because of its similarities with the revolutionary Germany of 1918–19.

"The strength of the New Left may well reside in precisely these small contesting and competing groups, active at many points at the same time, a kind of political guerrilla force in peace or so-called peace," Marcuse told his *Guardian* listeners in 1968. "But, and this is, I think, the most important point, small groups, concentrated on the level of local activities, thereby foreshadowing what may in all likelihood be the basic organization of libertarian socialism, *namely councils of manual and intellectual workers, soviets,* if one can still use the term and does not think of what actually happened to the soviets, some kind of what I would like to call, and I mean it seriously, organized spontaneity."[10]

Add to that that the worker wanted nothing to do with the New Left. The workers had formed Hard Hats for Nixon: some four hundred New York City construction workers joined approximately eight hundred policemen in attacking a thousand students protesting the Vietnam War in 1970. The worker had let the revolution down in 1919 in Germany, and everywhere else ever since.

The new fighter was—and this is a phrase to which Marcuse returns again and again—the "ghetto population." Thus "what we can envisage is not, as I said, this large centralized and coordinated movement, but local and regional political action against specific grievances—riots, ghetto rebellions and so on, that is to say, certainly mass movements which in large part are lacking political consciousness and which will depend more than before on political guidance and direction by militant leading minorities."[11] He added toward the end of *One Dimensional Man*,

> *Underneath the conservative popular base is the substratum of the outcasts and outsiders, the exploited and persecuted of other races and other colors, the unemployed and the unemployable. They exist outside the democratic process; their life is the most immediate and the most real need for ending intolerable conditions and institutions.*[12]

HOWARD ZINN, a transitional figure between the Old and New Left, identifies the same problem and proposes the same solution four years later. "Certainly in the United States, the traditional idea that the agent of social change will be the proletariat needs reexamination inasmuch as the best-organized workers are bribed into silence with TV and automobiles and are drugged into complacency by entertainment," Zinn wrote in 1968 in *The New Left*. "Recent experience suggests that Negroes, especially those in the ghetto, may be the most powerful single force for social change in the United States. Marx saw the industrial proletariat as the revolutionary force because it was motivated by exploitation and was organized by the factory. Black people in the United States, who also are exploited, are concentrated in the ghetto."[13]

Both men took a hand in creating the new revolutionary force. Marcuse didn't just leave it to chance that those "of other races and other colors" might be inspired one day to become militants and fight to change the system. As we will see in chapter 5, he worked actively to make the emerging discipline of ethnic studies a factory of revolution.

In Marcuse's new revolutionary world, political parties and parliamentary democracy would also be pushed aside. "Now, last, to the organization of the New Left. I already mentioned the obsolescence of traditional forms of organization, for example a parliamentary party. No party whatsoever I can envisage today which would not within a very short time fall victim to the general and totalitarian political corruption which characterizes the political universe," said Marcuse. "As against these forms, what seems to be shaping up is an entirely overt organization, diffused, concentrated in small groups and around local activities, small groups which are highly flexible and autonomous."[14] This was as much a call for community organizing as anything else, and we will explore its role in chapter 6.

But Marcuse left no doubt in *The Guardian*'s newsroom that day that the New Left contained the hope of a revolutionary future. "I believe that the New Left today is the only hope we have. Its task—to prepare itself and others, not to wait or to prepare today, yesterday and tomorrow, in thought and in action, morally and politically, for the time when the aggravating conflicts of corporate capitalism dissolve its repressive cohesion and open a space where the real work for libertarian socialism can begin.... The prospects for the New Left are good if the New Left can only sustain its present activity," Marcuse told his avid journalist listeners. The men and women of the New Left were the "true historical heirs of the great socialist tradition." They "contain the human beings, men and women, black and white, who are sufficiently free from the aggressive and repressive inhuman needs and aspirations of the exploitative society, sufficiently free from them to be free for the work of preparing a society without exploitation." Then he added his closing comment: "I would like to continue working together with them as long as I can."[15]

Different groups came under the umbrella term of the New Left: the radical students of Students for a Democratic Society (SDS), which later metastasized into the terrorists of the Weather Underground (who were, too, part of the New Left); the Student Nonviolent Coordinating Committee (SNCC, pronounced "snick"), the black liberation militants; and the hippies, the radical feminists, and so on.

SDS has often been called the "flagship organization of the New Left"—a student organization that included Marxists and other idealists who sought to change America's establishment through social revolution.[16] The opening line of its 1962 manifesto, the Port Huron Statement, captures SDS's essence: "We are people of this generation, bred in at least modest comfort, housed now in universities, looking uncomfortably to the world we inherit."[17]

Zinn identified three main elements of the New Left: SDS, SNCC, "and that assorted group of intellectuals, civil rights workers, and draft-card burners who have actively opposed the war in Vietnam."[18] SDS was set up at the University of Michigan by middle- and upper-middle-class students and was overwhelmingly white. Overall, SDS students tended to come from northern universities, observed Zinn, while SNCC was peopled more with students from historically black colleges in the South.

New Left figures included SDS members such as Bill Ayers, his then girlfriend and now wife Bernadine Dohrn (both of whom went on to found the Weather Underground), and the seven radicals who were arrested in Chicago for rioting and fighting with the police in 1968: Rennie Davis, David Dellinger, John Froines, Tom Hayden, Abbie Hoffman, Jerry Rubin, and Lee Weiner. An eighth person who had been charged in Chicago, but whose case was later declared a mistrial, was the Black Panther leader Bobby Seale, also an icon of the New Left.

Angela Davis, a Panther member of great influence over BLM's architects and other NextGen Marxists in our present day, can also be considered part of the New Left. Her inclusion here shows, however, the great heterogeneity of the New Left, which to many denotes a break with the Soviets. Davis, who, in the 1980s, twice ran as vice president on the Communist Party ticket, was as supportive of Castro's Cuba as she was of Erich Honecker's East Germany and Leonid Brezhnev's Soviet Union. In 1979, the Soviet Union gave her the Lenin Peace Prize and feted her. Before boarding the plane in Moscow, Davis turned around and exclaimed, "Long live the science of Marxism–Leninism." Such slavish commitment to communist "science" was not emblematic of all New Leftists, who were praised for following more the spirit of Marxism than the letter. But Davis also internalized the lessons of cultural Marxism, which she got directly from the lips of Marcuse, who taught philosophy to Davis—as well as to Abbie Hoffman—at Brandeis University in Boston.

Students such as Hoffman, Dohrn, Ayers, and Davis either studied Marcuse's philosophical poison straight from him or read other critical theorists or postmodernists. They thus were able to supply many in the larger media-influenced student body around them with the cause that was famously missing in the 1955 hit *Rebel without a Cause*. America's youth were primed to be discontent, to disparage the prosperity that had given them their safety and ease and lives of comfort of which others around the world could only dream—and disparage it they did.

One has only to think of the seminal, if self-absorbed, Port Huron Statement, which continues:

> *We are people of this generation, bred in at least modest comfort, housed now in universities, looking uncomfortably to the world we inherit…. Some would have us believe that Americans feel contentment amidst prosperity— but might it not better be called a glaze above deeply felt anxieties about their role in the new world?*[19]

IT SHOULD come as no surprise that within three years of Castro's visit, Harvard's chapter of SDS would have six hundred dues-paying members and the mission of "shaking America to its roots."[20]

For the New Left rejected both Moscow and Washington, DC, but it embraced Cuba, North Vietnam, Algeria, and Mao's China with passion, even as (or perhaps because) the latter was undergoing its vicious 1966–76 Cultural Revolution. In this they echoed Marcuse, who praised Mao and said of Castro's Cuba, "I would say the society which comes closest to what Marx had in mind today is perhaps Cuba, where an effort is made to build up socialism not in an authoritarian, bureaucratic way but really from below; that is to say, not on the back of the people but with the active participation of the people."[21] Castro was, of course, sending his opponents to the firing squad by the thousands while Marcuse waxed poetic about him. One of Castro's ministers declared 1961 to be the "Year of the Firing Squad."[22] But this fascination with Cuba and Mao's Cultural Revolution reverberates to this day, when NextGen Marxists continue to lionize the Cuban revolution and reproduce Mao's struggle sessions as "antiracist trainings."

Mills himself traveled to Cuba in 1960, breathlessly talking to every *revolucionario* whom his minders put in front of him. The result was a political pamphlet titled *Listen, Yankee*, a gushing view of Cuba's revolution that glossed over the killing of dissidents and cultural genocide. Even the socialist magazine *Jacobin* panned it: "Reading through the interview transcripts, anyone who has conducted research in Cuba will have the vaguely familiar impression of being shepherded toward approved spokesmen," wrote Pace University's Michelle Chace.[23]

One of the telling aspects of this flattering portrayal of a communist dictatorship is that Mills exclusively interviews middle- or upper-class revolutionaries, drawing from that a romanticized picture of intellectuals becoming revolutionaries and taking to the mountains. He also celebrates the cultural destruction and swallows whole the revolution's fabrication that prior to 1959, Cuba was backward (something easily discounted by United Nations statistics).[24] Thus, he writes, in the voice of a Cuban, "we are building, at breakneck speed, an entirely new society, and we didn't inherit much to build it with from the old order in Cuba."[25] The Cuban revolutionaries, Mills surmised, were doing Marxism right; Cuba was uniting *theoria* with *praxis*—unlike the Soviet Union, which 1960s radicals found stodgy: "While the Old Left embraced Soviet Marxism and the Soviet Union, the New Left combined forms of critical Marxism with radical democracy and openness to a broad array of ideas and political alliances," Kellner, a supporter, wrote in 1968.

"*Whereas the Old Left was doctrinaire and puritanical, the New Left was pluralistic and engaged emergent cultural forms and social movements. While the Old Left, with some exceptions, tended to impose doctrinal conformity and cut itself off from 'liberal' groups, the New Left embraced a wide range of social movements around the issues of class, gender, race, sexuality, the environment, peace, and other issues.… It embodied the best features of previous socialist and anarchist traditions that it concretized in social struggles such as the antiwar, feminist, ecological, communal, and countercultural movements.*"[26]

"For Marcuse," added Kellner, "it was the demand for total change that distinguished the New Left and its championing of freedom, social justice, and democracy in every sphere of life. Marcuse embodied many of these defining political impulses of the New Left in his own thought and politics."[27]

The New Left, said Marcuse, represented "a total protest, not only against specific evils and against specific short-comings, but at the same time, a protest against the entire system of values, against the entire system of objectives, against the entire system of performances required and practiced in the established society. In other words, it is a refusal to continue to accept and abide by the culture of the established society. They reject not only the economic conditions, not only the political institutions, but the entire system of values which they feel is rotten to the core."[28] How he did not envisage that this total transformation, this demand that the totality of life be politicized, would not have to end in totalitarianism should boggle the mind—or perhaps Marcuse was all too aware.

In fact, he added for good measure, "And in this sense I think one can indeed speak of a cultural revolution in the sense that the protest is directed against the entire cultural establishment, including the morality of the existing society." This was what the students of the time were drinking from the firehose, before they became the professors that Barringer began to notice in 1989.

These points are all key to what was distinct about the New Left. The New Left didn't just abandon the Soviet line (which it was more or less forced to do, following Stalin's death in 1953, Moscow's cruel treatment of Hungary in 1956, and the de-Stalinization process begun by Khrushchev); more importantly, the New Left absorbed the grand lesson of the councils and finally abandoned the worker. "Almost everyone on the left, but the Marxist remnants especially, was fervently on the hunt for a 'substitute proletariat'—some agency that might yet undertake the historical mission assigned to the workers by Marxism," wrote Irving Howe in 1982 for *The New York Times Magazine*.[29]

By doing this, it shifted the categories on which to divide society from the mutable and (especially in America) ever-shifting socioeconomic ones to the immutable ones of race and sex. Gone were the days of associating the Left just or even primarily with better working conditions on the factory floor or a minimum wage. Issues such as environmentalism, the Vietnam War, and racial justice became fronts in an ideological war for total transformation of the country. This brings to mind once again David Horowitz's adage of "the issue is never the issue. The issue is always the revolution. In other words the cause—whether inner city blacks or women—is never the real cause, but only an occasion to advance the real cause which is the accumulation of power to make the revolution."[30]

For that was undoubtedly what excited people like Marcuse about the New Left. It demanded total change, not piecemeal reform. And it demanded "popular democracy," just as Luxemburg and Liebknecht had rejected the SPD's idea of a national assembly and demanded "a political system in which all power was in the hands of the soldiers' and workers' councils."[31]

In his 1969 "Essay on Liberation," Marcuse praised most of these aspects of the New Left. He lauded how "the 'unorthodox' character of this opposition, which does not have the traditional class basis, and which is at the same time a political, instinctual, and moral rebellion, shapes the strategy and scope of the rebellion. It extends to the entire organization of the existing liberal-parliamentary democracy. Among the New Left, a strong revulsion against traditional politics prevails, against that whole network of parties, committees, and pressure groups on all levels; against working within this network and with its methods."[32]

As to why the worker had to be jettisoned from his pole position as the main agent of revolution, the reasons were many. Gramsci had seen the worker join the ranks of Mussolini's fascists, but he blamed the leftist parties and intellectuals for insufficient education of the worker. The Germans were more unforgiving: the proletariat hadn't just gone right-wing by joining first the Freikorps, then the Nazis, but had supported the leftist, SPD alternative to the Spartacists and the KPD. In Turin, the unions and the Socialist Party betrayed the worker. Many of the German thinkers drew the opposite conclusion from their experience: the worker had never quite bought in to the communists' promise of a people's democracy. The worker had betrayed the revolution.

The Frankfurt School's explanation for the failure wasn't just a "hegemonic narrative" to be punctured but an entire conceptual superstructure that, through reason, ordered the world for the benefit of the bourgeois. Escape, for scholars such as Horkheimer and Pollock, was well-nigh impossible. Marcuse was much more optimistic. He instantly saw the revolutionary potential of his New Left disciples. An exchange between Marcuse and his fellow Frankfurt scholar Theodor Adorno is illustrative.

As head of the reconstituted institute, now back in Frankfurt, Adorno in 1969 had called the police to clear away student demonstrators who had gathered at the premises. He then protested in a television interview that "even though I had established a theoretical model, I could not have foreseen that people would try to implement it with Molotov cocktails."[33] He also told Der Spiegel, "If I were to give practical advice, as Herbert Marcuse has done to a certain degree, it would detract from my productivity" as a philosopher. This prompted back-and-forth letters with Marcuse, who, as we have seen, had remained in the United States and thrown himself headlong into pushing the New Left in its new direction. "Our (old) theory has an inner political content, an inner political dynamic, which today more than ever pushes toward a concrete political position," wrote Marcuse. Molotov cocktails were the point of philosophy.

Mills, in his famous letter to the *New Left Review*, had already advised the new revolutionary agents not to "cling so mightily to the 'the working class' of the advanced capitalist societies as the historic agency, or even as the most important agency, in the face of the really historical evidence that now stands against this expectation." That was "a legacy of Victorian Marxism that is now quite unrealistic," added Mills.[34]

Another reason for the New Left to jettison the worker was the acceptance—common to most of the Frankfurt scholars by the 1960s—that capitalism was, in fact, much better at supplying material goods, something that made the conceptual superstructure more of a locked box. "Independence of thought, autonomy, and the right to political opposition are being deprived of their basic critical function in a society which seems increasingly capable of satisfying the needs of the individuals through the way in which it is organized," wrote an exasperated Marcuse in *One Dimensional Man*, which, as we know, was widely read by his young disciples.[35]

Marcuse's former boss, Max Horkheimer, admitted this, too, in an interview he gave in 1969, four years before his death, in which he also acknowledged, to boot, that the implication was that "justice" required a less free society. Marx, said Horkheimer, had erred in believing that

> *capitalist society would necessarily be overcome by the solidarity of the workers due to their increasing impoverishment. This idea is false. The society in which we live doesn't impoverish workers, but helps them toward a better life. And moreover, Marx didn't see at all that freedom and justice are dialectical concepts: The more freedom, the less justice, and the more justice, the less freedom.*[36]

IF HORKHEIMER was right about the inverse relationship between liberty and justice, then the only logical conclusion for those who desired justice was to restrict liberty, something which, as it turns out, the Marxist Left never has any compunction about. Marcuse was a leader in this camp, writing in a 1969 essay—interestingly titled "Repressive Tolerance"—that conservative views would have to be censored once the Left gained power. In the essay, he supported

> *the practice of discriminating tolerance in an inverse direction, as a means of shifting the balance between Right and Left by restraining the liberty of*

the Right, thus counteracting the pervasive inequality of freedom (unequal opportunity of access to the means of democratic persuasion) and strengthening the oppressed against the oppressor. Tolerance would be restricted with respect to movements of a demonstrably aggressive or destructive character (destructive of the prospects for peace, justice, and freedom for all). Such discrimination would also be applied to movements opposing the extension of social legislation to the poor, weak, disabled.[37]

SPEECH THAT slowed the march to central planning was to be restricted—for make no mistake, that's what Marcuse, Horkheimer, and the New Left wanted. Freedom to make economic decisions was too wasteful. "Today, the opposition to central planning in the name of a liberal democracy which is denied in reality serves as an ideological prop for repressive interests," wrote Marcuse. "The goal of authentic self-determination by the individuals depends on effective social control over the production and distribution of the necessities. Here, technological rationality, stripped of its exploitative features, is the sole standard and guide in planning and developing the available resources for all. Self-determination in the production and distribution of vital goods and services would be wasteful. The job is a technical one, and as a truly technical job, it makes for the reduction of physical and mental toil. In this realm, centralized control is rational if it establishes the preconditions for meaningful self-determination."[38] Self-determination required central planning—get it?

In an interview a decade later with Bill Moyers, President Johnson's former press secretary, Marcuse made clear that to him, Marxism was the right alternative to wasteful free markets.

Well, you know that I'm labeled as a Marxist philosopher—though controversial Marxist philosopher—and I never protested against this label. I, indeed, still retain the basic concepts of a Marxian analysis, which means: for any length of time this system couldn't work, no matter what happens, either in a pre-fascist or in a fascist form. The alternative is still socialism, but not the socialism we have today in the Soviet Union, but the socialism Marx really conceived of: that is to say a socialization, of course, of the means of production, and their control and distribution by what he called freely associated individuals. That is to say, men and women themselves, who do the work in a producing society, would have the responsibility for their work, and would determine what to produce, how to produce, and how to distribute the product. What may have appeared as utopia at the time Marx wrote, is today a very real possibility, because we have all the resources to do it. And that is precisely why the entire establishment is mobilized against it.[39]

MARCUSE ACTUALLY thought that this central planning could finally be brought about because capitalism had finally achieved the end of scarcity. Human beings, he told Moyer, had been made instruments of alienating labor "in order to overcome the scarcity that existed on earth. I believe it is less and less necessary now." Curiously, he never associated the end of scarcity with the capitalist system he wanted to tear down, or socialism with the re-creation of such scarcity.

Reason also would itself need to be kept in check, as it was just a tool of the hermetically sealed conceptual apparatus. "The more rational, productive, technical, and total the repressive administration of society becomes, the more unimaginable the means and ways by which the administered individuals might break their servitude and seize their own liberation," wrote Marcuse. "All liberation depends on the consciousness of servitude," he added in one of his most famous lines. Liberation depended on taking the red pill of recognizing "that you're a slave, Neo!"

The problem was that the material satisfaction of needs that is the abundant hallmark of capitalism kept man's servitude hidden from himself. Capitalism's material plenitude was the blue pill that prevented men from seeing reality. Surrounded with all of the creature comforts that capitalism produced, man was blind to his own enslavement. "The emergence of this consciousness is always hampered by the predominance of needs and satisfactions which, to a great extent, have become the individual's own." The solution? Change the entire mental contraption. "The optimal goal is the replacement of false needs by true ones, the abandonment of repressive satisfaction."[40] Though they may not know they have been influenced by Marcuse, these are thoughts pulsating through the brains of today's NextGen Marxists.

Toward the end of *One Dimensional Man*, Marcuse makes clear that as a body of work, critical theory would help the soldiers of the New Left and those in the "ghetto population." Of the latter, he adds, "Their opposition is revolutionary even if their consciousness is not." This was why intellectuals such as he were needed at this (he hoped) historical turning point. He lamented that the "critical theory of society possesses no concepts which could bridge the gap between the present and its future; holding no promise and showing no success, it remains negative." But even in what was a desperate struggle to make man understand that he was surrounded by a material abundance that made him a slave, critical theory (by which he meant himself as its embodiment) would do all it could. "It wants to remain loyal to those who, without hope, have given and give their life to the Great Refusal."[41]

Marcuse then abruptly brings the book to an end by quoting his dead Frankfurt School colleague Walter Benjamin (who was himself quoting a novel by Goethe) with the line "it is only for the sake of those without hope that hope is given to us." This should lead us to wonder if "hope" here is the thing the revolutionary must hang on to in his fight against a conceptual system that is almost impossible to penetrate and dismantle *or* if "hope" is actually the enemy of liberation, for any man who harbors it will refuse to see his own servitude, and thus all hope must be abandoned before man decides to tear the whole system down!

Ideas Have Consequences

THIS WAS heady stuff for the children of the New Left, the college students who had spent their childhoods in the placid years of the Eisenhower America of the 1950s and were now coming into intellectual contact with subversive ideas. It must be added that the new nihilism didn't just emerge as spontaneous combustion in 1960; the ground had been well prepared. And Marcuse himself played a part. As the "Guru of the Sexual Revolution," he had advised women to "liberate" their bodies and become serial adulteresses. His target, of course, was society and its key institution, the family. In his 1955 bestseller, *Eros and Civilization*, Marcuse made clear that changing "the value and scope of libidinal relations would lead to a disintegration of the institutions in which the private interpersonal relations have been organized, particularly the monogamic and patriarchal family"[42]—an obvious echo of Lukács's own attempts to destroy society by sinking the family first.

For the intellectuals, the students, the marchers, and practically everyone associated with the New Left, the critical theory apple didn't roll away from the trunk but fell with a thud and stayed there. Marcuse's works, said Moyers, "had a profound influence on a generation of discontented young people who talked about, and sometimes acted upon, his ideas, even when they hadn't read them."[43] And, obviously, this thinking also reverberates down to our day.

The reason the New Left had abandoned the Soviet Union was not ideological but strictly Marcusian: Stalinism had introduced an insufferable degree of bureaucratization in the Soviet Union. When asked in an interview why he objected to the way the Soviet Union operated, Marcuse answered, "The objection I have, or let me put it this way, the way in which socialism in the Soviet Union deviates decisively from the Marxist concept is in the authoritarian and bureaucratic construction of Soviet society in which the regime is imposed upon the people instead of the people actually determining the development of their own society."[44] In other words, poor Marcuse was still pining for the councils.

And it is bureaucratization that the thinkers of the New Left, again, opposed in the Soviet Union. "The student movements of the 1960s in the United States, West Europe and Japan share certain common concerns," wrote, in 1969, Staughton Lynd, an author-activist and enthusiastic supporter who, in the 1960s, drew close to such New Left figures as Hayden, Zinn, and Dellinger. The first of these, he wrote, was a "rejection both of capitalism and of the bureaucratic communism exemplified by the Soviet Union."[45]

Though it probably wouldn't have been a motivating factor, there is also the irony of history that so many of the people surrounding the Frankfurt School, the Marxist Workweek, and the Marx–Engels Institute (on which the Frankfurt School was based) were killed in Stalin's purges or by his agents overseas. David Riazanov, who founded, in 1921, the Marx–Engels Institute in Moscow, dedicated to the study and publication of the works of communism's two founders, was executed in 1938 at the height of Stalin's Great Terror, known as the Yezhovshchina, accused variously of being a Menshevik or a Trotskyite. Zinoviev, the head of the Comintern who sent Weil to Argentina; Béla Kun; Willi Münzenberg; Karl Radek; Heinrich Susskind, and others, including, of course, Trotsky himself, all met similar ends. Zinoviev begged his executioners for mercy, clinging to their boots, when he faced his death in 1936, a scene apparently recreated for entertainment at Stalin's dacha.

New Lefties such as Mills and Zinn also took a dim view of academic pursuits that did not have an ideological goal. The latter, of course, was a member of both the New and the Old Left, as FBI files confirm that in the 1940s and 1950s, Zinn was a member of the pro-Soviet Communist Party USA.[46] However, in the 1960s, Zinn, then in his forties, obviously sensed the greater revolutionary potential of the New Left and became one of its leading proponents. In a 1968 essay, "Marxism and the New Left," Zinn warned his younger colleagues to remember that Marxism dictated that the meaning of things was constantly changing. "It tries to avoid scholasticism, which dutifully pretends to record in full, to describe accurately—forgetting that mere description is the same as circumscription," Zinn wrote.[47] In this we get a strong whiff of the Frankfurt School's rejection of reason for altering the natural world in the act of cataloguing. In fact, Zinn quotes the guru himself: "the pretense of 'passive' description is what Herbert Marcuse calls 'operationalism.'"

Zinn also warned them not to get too caught up in the Marxian theory but to concentrate on the societal-change aspect—the praxis, or action. "If the New Left is wise, it will take from Marxism not all the exact propositions about the world Marx and Engels lived in," he wrote, in an echo of Mills's essay of eight years earlier, about the emphasis on the worker being a fetishism of the Victorian era. Rather, Zinn said, the New Leftists should emphasize Marx's approach: "this approach demands a constant redefinition of history in light of immediate reality, and an insistence on action."[48] In other words, again, the point of philosophy is Molotov cocktails!

This was a matter that Marcuse stressed to young Angela Davis back when she attended his graduate seminar on Immanuel Kant at Brandeis. In a letter to Davis published in 1970 as "Dear Angela," Marcuse recalls wondering what the German experience had to teach those fighting for black liberation in the United States, and he adds, "Then, however, I took out the prospectus you wrote for your thesis, and I read the following sentence: 'The notion (in Kant) that force provides the link between the theory and practice of freedom leads back to Rousseau.'"[49] Davis agreed that it was her mentor who had taught her to unite theory and practice. "Herbert Marcuse taught me that it was possible to be an academic, an activist, a scholar, and a revolutionary," Davis famously once said in a televised interview.[50]

For action needed ideological direction. Of the two main New Left organizations, Zinn found SDS the more ideologically aware. SDS, he said, has "more white, more middle-class, and more intellectual people than SNCC, and thus they have read more Marx." This "refreshing lack of pompous intellectuality" among the members of SNCC did, however, have "an unfortunate side: the lack of analysis of alternative tactics, systems and institutions."[51] The mostly black members of SNCC were not as aware of Marxist solutions to their problems. This lacuna Zinn tried to fill when he become the group's only white adviser.

The ideological sherpas of the students and black militants were, however, well pleased with the rejection of representative democracy by their young charges, especially when compared to the Old Left of the 1930s and 1940s, whose "suspicion of parliamentary democracy did not seem to be very penetrating," according to Zinn. By comparison, "the militants of today...have always had a basic mistrust of politics. The vote, these New Left people know, is only an occasional flicker of democracy in an otherwise elitist system. The voice of the people, therefore, must be manifested in other ways: by day-to-day activity, by demonstrations, by a politics of constant protest rather than by the traditional politics of the ballot."[52]

The replacement of the bureaucratic Soviet Union as their ideological lodestar with even crazier communist governments in the Third World; the rejection of rationality, or "scholasticism"; and the skepticism toward democracy and embrace of a street-level, neighborhood-organizing "people's democracy" are all strands that start with Luxemburg and run through Korsch, Horkheimer, and Marcuse, then through Hayden, Ayers, Mann, Hoffman, Rubin, Davis, and Mills and down to our day to the founders of BLM, their mentor Goldberg, and the 1619 Project architect Hannah-Jones.

The rejection of property is, of course, the top unifying factor for anyone who calls himself a Marxist, so it is a feature that united both the Old and the New Left. Thus one has Abbie Hoffman bellowing, "I believe in the redistribution of wealth and power in the world"[53] or "we must become Castros." Jerry Rubin, for his part, expressed the nihilistic idea that "all money represents theft. To steal from the rich is a sacred and religious act. To take what you need is an act of self-love, self-liberation. While looting, a man to his own self is true!"[54] This is, of course, the descendant of Marx's call for the abolishment of individual private property and the direct ancestor of today's insistence that looting, burning, and rampaging are forms of reparation and not violence at all if no individual is physically attacked, an assertion made by BLM and Hannah-Jones and then absurdly repeated by members of a fawning press.

This growing nonchalant attitude to violence, combined with the disdain for private property and the skepticism toward the democratic process, plus the constant emphasis on action, action, action, was too potent a cocktail not to self-combust and turn into something far uglier than the self-regarding Port Huron Statement. The movement went from flower power to fire power. The pent-up social tension exploded, and the country quickly veered from 1967 being the Year of Love to 1968 being one of the bloodiest of the century. After the assassinations of Martin Luther King Jr. and Bobby Kennedy in 1968, urban riots broke out in more than 120 cities, leaving thirty-nine people dead and twenty-six hundred wounded. The murder rate that year went up a whopping 12.7 percent, which stood as the nation's largest jump until the equally politically charged year of 2020, when it shot up 30 percent.[55] The aforementioned Chicago battle between SDS members and cops took place in Chicago's Grant Park that year, too, another harbinger of craziness to come.

It should hardly surprise, then, that those advocating armed struggle and other types of violence got the upper hand within SDS. In his book *Days of Rage*, Brian Burrough quotes the SDS member Dotson Rader, capturing the growing zeitgeist: "The meaninglessness of 'democratic' methods was becoming clear to us in the spring of 1967. The Civil Rights Movement was dead. Pacifism was dead."[56] The infatuation with Cuba began to take on a different tone. No longer was the nearby Caribbean island a place to watch a lawyer and a medical doctor—Fidel Castro and Che Guevara—unite theory and practice and violently overthrow the system; they became role models to emulate. The French communist intellectual Regis Debray was also popular among the New Left. Like Mills, Debray had gone to Havana, from where he wrote that "small, fast-moving guerrilla groups ... could inspire a grassroots rebellion, even in the United States," and the idea took hold.[57]

The final breakup came a year later at the SDS Convention in 1969, when Ayers and eleven other sociopaths who had created an SDS faction called the Third World Marxists finally declared their independence from the rest of the organization, which was helpless to arrest the slide into violence. The twelve founded the Weather Underground, which right out of the gate proclaimed that it was dedicated to the violent overthrow of the United States and declared war on its government. Its opening manifesto, tellingly named "You Don't Need a Weatherman to Know Which Way the Wind Blows" (whence the group's name) after a line from a Bob Dylan song, "Subterranean Homesick Blues," was very unlike the more wistful Port Huron Statement. It declared that the twelve signatories were dedicated to the "destruction of US imperialism and the achievement of a classless world: world communism."[58] The statement identified the United States as a "monster" and the West as "US imperialism and its lackeys," which it said were locked in conflict with the national liberation struggles of Asia, Africa, and Latin America. The document, more than thirteen thousand words, was beyond parody in its excesses. It started and ended by quoting a famous slogan of Lin Piao, long Mao's defense minister and a man so radical that he was blamed for some of the worst excesses of the Cultural Revolution: "Long Live the Victory of People's War!"

Unsurprisingly, the Underground embarked on a campaign of bombings, many of which were botched, and the FBI officially listed the group for what it was, a domestic terrorist association. Hoffman's 1971 revolutionary oeuvre, *Steal This Book*, was a how-to of revolution, or as he himself put it delicately in the introduction, the book's purpose was "not to fuck the system, but destroy it." It included sections on bomb-making, breaking out of prison, and how to survive in the underground.[59] The years 1968–69 became a perfect parallel to the German Revolution exactly fifty years earlier, right down to the fact that the campaign of violence was also to be aborted.

The American New Left's terror stage lasted only a few years, carried out sporadically by the Weathermen, the Panthers, and other assorted groups that sprung up around the same era, such as the Symbionese Liberation Army and the Puerto Rican Fuerzas Armadas de Liberación Nacional (Armed Forces of National Liberation). The reasons the revolution went nowhere were the same as a half century earlier: ordinary folks, least of all the workers, were not at all interested in following the Weather Underground, the Black Panthers, and the others into Days of Rage. Ayers, Dohrn, and the others were rich kids who carried more white guilt than street savvy and had little understanding of what everyday Americans wanted or were about. Those amateurish terrorists who were not caught by the law and sent away for long prison sentences went underground or overseas to places like Cuba or Algeria.

In their failure, the Weathermen and the other groups thus showed in stark form the futility of violent revolution in the West, especially if it was not preceded by cultural indoctrination. Most of the terrorist groups that emerged in the late 1960s and early 1970s had disintegrated by the early 1980s. The Weathermen themselves dissolved in 1977, with a rump group forming another communist terror group, the May 19th Communist Organization, named for Ho Chi Minh's birthday and the date of the Weathermen's bombing of the Pentagon in 1972.

Luckily for them, London's *New Left Review* had started translating Gramsci in the late 1960s, as we saw in an earlier chapter. Hobsbawm put it best when he said that since, "in Italy and most of the West there was not going to be an October revolution from the early 1920s on—and there was no realistic prospect of one—he [Gramsci] obviously had to consider a strategy of the long haul." And that is what happened in the 1970s.

Rudi Dutschke, a West German radical who was a disciple of Marcuse, soon outlined the Gramscian strategy for the new age, which he called the "Long March through the Institutions" (a communist nod to Mao's Long March in China of the 1930s). By this, of course, he meant infiltrating society's institutions and acculturating everyday Americans (or Japanese, or Germans, or Canadians) to such Marxist ideas as abolishing the family, property, the nation-state, God, and so on. This became the philosophy that guided how the Marxist penetration of American society and her institutions would be implemented.

Marcuse couldn't have been more proud of his pupil. "Let me tell you this," he wrote to his disciple in 1971, "that I regard your notion of 'the long march through the institutions' as the only effective way, now more than ever."[60] A year later, Marcuse described Dutschke's strategy as "working against the established institutions while working with them. But not simply by 'boring from within,' rather by 'doing the job,' learning (how to program and read computers, how to teach at all levels of education, how to use the mass media, how to organize production, how to recognize and eschew planned obsolescence, how to design, etc.), and at the same time preserving one's consciousness while working with others."[61] The takeover of the universities, and everything else, that we saw in the 1980s was being hatched.

Their new, Gramscian understanding of the war of positions soothed the New Left's (now getting long in the tooth) disappointment of having to accept that an outright war of maneuvers—that is, revolution—was futile, or at least not immediately in the offing. They would have to burrow in. If violence came at all—as Marx had written that it must—it would be more as a final, paroxysmal outburst that would act as a coup de grâce, after the institutions had been taken over. As we saw in the preceding chapter, Gramsci himself had not abjured violence. The war of maneuver could interrupt the war of positions at any moment. Whether BLM intended 2020 to be this paroxysm is a question, of course, that will never be answered definitively but should be part of the conversation.

Revolution Now

FROM THE comfortable confines of his plush home, Marcuse, of course, blamed the workers for the failures of 1968–69 and the violence that followed. The workers had been blinded to their own servitude by capitalist abundance and, just like the German workers of his youth, were fearful of the Soviet example.

He told Moyers in 1974, when it was clear that violence would fail to bring change, that the conditions for revolution were "not yet ripe," then added, "You cannot expect the majority of the working class, today, to entertain any, let's say, radical or revolutionary projects, as long as their situation, their living conditions, are what they are today. Compared with their parents and grandparents, they are much, much, much better off. And socialism, to them, is mainly what they have in the Soviet Union, and that, to them, is no attractive alternative."[62]

Marcuse protested to Moyers that he had never prescribed a change in revolutionary agency. "By the way, I never said the students, as a group, would replace the working class as the vehicle of change. I always considered the student movement as a preparatory movement in the development of consciousness."[63] It was just that, as we see, the conditions were not ripe.

Again, Marcuse was speaking to Moyers when it was finally becoming clear that violence would not succeed. The Weathermen were grinding to a halt and dissolved three years later. By the time of his interview with Moyers, Marcuse had already embraced Dutschke's march.

But did Marcuse have a hand in the turn to violence? Douglas Kellner says that post-1965, Marcuse in his writings "sought forces of revolution that would make such change possible, as well as a revolutionary strategy that they could follow. Since the industrial working class was, in his view, integrated into advanced capitalism, Marcuse sought new radical political agency, successively, in non-integrated outsiders and minorities, in students and intellectuals, in a 'new sensibility,' and in 'catalyst groups.'" Significantly, adds Kellner, "Marcuse supported strategies of militant confrontation politics from about 1965 to 1970."

It was only then, writes Kellner, that Marcuse "shifted to the advocacy of political education and the formation of small oppositional groups modeled on workers' councils; during the 1970s he called for a 'United Front' politics and the long march through the institutions." However, whether the militant revolutionary of the late 1960s or the Machiavellian strategizer of the Gramscian-style March through the Institutions, Marcuse did not veer from his view that society had to be subverted and the system replaced. "Throughout, Marcuse remained faithful to a Marxist tradition of revolutionary socialism represented by Marx, Luxemburg and Korsch," adds Kellner.

The New Left was, too, learning the lesson that revolution would not work. Marcuse told Moyers in 1974, "The best of them have learned that what was lacking in 1968, 1969, was a suitable form of organization, and an adequate, theoretical foundation for their action—for their political practice. Both they are trying to find now."

The following exchange between the two men is instructive:

MOYERS: But you don't have the resources of tradition. You're asking the American people to turn away from 200 and more years of experience, and walk into an unknown area.

MARCUSE: I'm sorry, that, I think, is no problem whatsoever to me, because that has always happened in history.... What is different in this country is that you don't have a militant worker movement tradition. Whatever there was has been, really, in a violent and a bloody way, suppressed. That you don't have. And that has to be built up gradually and painfully and patiently. But it can be built up.

THAT WOULD be the job of the "best of them," the ones who had realized that what was lacking was a suitable form of organization and a theoretical foundation for political practice.

Ultimately the New Left is considered something of a failure. It survived only for that one decade of the 1960s and never managed to take hold of political power. But Marcuse was right that the members of the New Left were the "true historical heirs of the great socialist tradition." As such, they played a vital generational role in handing down a new version of the socialism of old to a new generation of academics, intellectuals, and community organizers who in turn would seed the values and ideas of socialism deep into American culture. Indeed, the New Left did not take political power in the 1960 or 1970s, but one can make a strong case that it did in 2008 with the election of Barack Obama to the presidency; that it did in Bernie Sanders's and the Far Left's hold over the Left; that it did with the radical ideas that have now taken over American media, boardrooms, and culture. The New Left was born in the early 1960s, turned terroristic in the Days of Rage at the end of the decade, and then fully metamorphized in the 1980s into the intellectual vanguard that would indoctrinate a nation. One life personified this transformation, to which we devote the next chapter.

4

THE METAMORPHOSIS

NO FIGURE SO perfectly personifies the metamorphosis from 1960s radicalism to armed revolution to terrorism to chief Long Marcher through the Institutions than William Ayers. To his friends, he was simply Bill, or even Billy, and they ranged from his merry band of SDS *compañeros* to those who became Weather Underground terrorists to Columbia professors to the Venezuelan Marxist dictator Hugo Chávez and President Obama, whom Ayers introduced to the political world of Chicago in the 1990s. As of this writing, the seventy-eight-year-old, with his earrings and jeans, his baseball cap and his T-shirts, acts up like that loveable scamp who never grew up, part Peter Pan, part Huck Finn. Probe further and you find that Bill Ayers is more Pol Pot with a dash of Charles Manson. His story, intertwined with those whose lives he affected, especially that of his former girlfriend Diana Oughton and his wife, Bernardine Dohrn, tells the tale of the progression that takes us from Eisenhower-era normalcy to the regime politics we are currently experiencing.

Chronologically, the evolution takes him from suburban bourgeois placidity to the merchant marine, student politics, conversion to Marxism, then actual terrorism, to a decade as a fugitive, finally emerging from hiding and getting by with a slap on the wrist, then getting an Ivy League graduate degree in education, becoming Chicago's citizen of the year in 1997, and being called "a school reformer" by such figures as Tom Brokaw, and, finally, kingmaker.[1]

Ayers started his long life in Glen Ellyn, a leafy suburb of Chicago, as the privileged son of the well-connected Thomas Ayers, who went on to become CEO of Commonwealth Edison. Young Bill played football, wrestled, and ran track at the private academy where he spent his last three years of high school. Ayers then moved on to Ann Arbor in 1963 to attend the University of Michigan, where he was a double legacy, and joined the jock fraternity Beta Theta Pi. His roommate was Jim Detwiler, the Wolverines' star halfback. "Bill was the best friend I had in school," said Detwiler to an interviewer in 1990. "In those days, he considered himself a jock."[2] Dad got him a summer job at the advertising firm Leo Burnett, and Bill's corporate life seemed about to start.

It didn't take long for Ayers to undergo his first remake. According to a profile in the *Chicago Reader*, Bill dropped out of college the following year, "hitchhiked to New Orleans, and joined the merchant marines. He worked two four-hour shifts a day painting, cleaning, and watching the deck of a grain ship that docked in Marseilles, Athens, and 'all the sleazy port cities of Europe.'" "I didn't know what I was going to do with myself," Ayers was quoted as saying. "Then I had this moment of clarity. I was sitting in Constitution Square in Athens reading a newspaper and I read about the war in Vietnam. Vietnam was blowing up and I felt I had to do something."[3]

Most of the action was in college, so in 1965, Ayers headed back to the United States and Ann Arbor. Only "this time he didn't hang out with jocks. He ran with the civil rights crowd—the veterans of voter registration campaigns in the south who were the heart and soul of the fledgling anti-war movement." He was promptly arrested for the first time at an anti-war rally at the Ann Arbor draft board and spent ten days in prison. When he got out, he joined SDS. Then he moved back and forth between Ann Arbor and Cleveland, where, in 1967, he took part in an SDS project that had members live in the inner city, as the mostly white student-radical group tried to shimmy up to racial minorities.

Lest we forget, just three years earlier, Herbert Marcuse had made his observation about the revolutionary base shifting to "the substratum of the outcasts and outsiders, the exploited and persecuted of other races and other colors riots, ghetto rebellions and so on," but which lacked revolutionary consciousness yet and needed ideological programming. As pointed out above, Zinn agreed. The black revolutionaries, Zinn lamented, did not have Marxist solutions at their fingertips. As Zinn wrote, "spontaneous uprisings in the ghetto are alarm signals but they do not produce change. Perhaps it will take systematic, persistent organizing and education, in the ghettos and in the universities."[4]

The moment for action had come. Cleveland predictably exploded into race riots in 1967, and the mayor set an 8:00 pm curfew. After breaking curfew one night, Ayers at one point came face-to-face with national guardsmen. His callous reaction to fellow young Americans serving in the Guard was soaked with social condescension and an early harbinger of his disregard for the lives of anyone in uniform: "I remember they were so young. They looked like twerps. One day they were pumping gas, and now they were holding M-16s." After that summer, Ayers went back to Ann Arbor and moved into a small house with his then-girlfriend Diana Oughton, a tragic figure of whom we will hear more.

The year 1968 proved as pivotal for Ayers as it had been for the New Left. The Tet Offensive in January, when the Viet Cong and the North Vietnamese launched a vicious attack on US installations and the US Embassy at Saigon, left a mark on Ayers, as it did on the nation—Lyndon Johnson announced two months later that he would not run for reelection. Then later that year, Ayers joined others at SDS and headed to the Democratic National Convention in Chicago.

"Ayers emerged from the convention disorders convinced that the powerful force he and his friends confronted would concede nothing without violent struggle.... This was no time for peaceful protest," the *Chicago Reader* profile continued, quoting Ayers as saying, "Everything was coming together in 1968. There was the student uprising in Paris and the takeover at Columbia University; people believed anything was possible. It was a time of war; thousands of people were being killed. The cities were in flames. It was time to put your life on the line. We thought we were winning. We thought the government was toppling. We felt Johnson's resignation was a major victory."

The final breakup of the SDS came at its convention in June 1969, when Ayers and eleven other members of the SDS faction called the Third World Marxists declared their independence from the collapsing SDS and founded the Weather Underground, which dedicated itself to the violent overthrow of its own nation through all-out revolution. Its manifesto was very unlike the more wistful Port Huron Statement, declaring that the twelve signatories were dedicated to the "destruction of US imperialism and the achievement of a classless world: world communism."[5] The very next month, the top Weatherman leader Bernardine Dohrn, who in a few months would become Ayers's new girlfriend, and is today his wife, led a large Weathermen delegation to Cuba to learn directly from revolutionary leaders from the communist island, and from Vietnam, Mao's China, and North Korea, how to bring the revolution home. According to Lucinda Franks, writing in *The New York Times Magazine*, they met "with representatives of the Vietnamese National Liberation Front, who advised them to build a street-fighting guerrilla force."[6] Burrough writes that "the Cubans treated Dohrn like visiting royalty, featuring her in government magazines and introducing her to dignitaries from throughout the revolutionary world." Ayers himself personally "enjoyed contacts with Cuban diplomats that would endure for years to come."[7] The Cuban consulate in New York became a liaison office for the terrorist group.

The Weathermen called for a large-scale three days of mayhem in Chicago, dubbed "Days of Rage," starting on October 8. It was the result of a resolution which read, "The Elections Don't Mean Shit—Vote Where the Power Is—Our Power Is in the Street," which loudly proclaimed to what extent the New Left had abandoned the democratic process and civil disobedience and was veering into open violence.[8] As they prepared for the event, Ayers advised, "We're not urging anybody to shoot from a crowd. But we're also going to make it clear that when a pig gets iced, that's a good thing, and that everyone who considers himself a revolutionary should be armed."[9]

As the Days of Rage approached, Ayers went around saying that the Weathermen's Cuban and Viet Cong advisers were advocating guerrilla warfare in Chicago, but the evidence is strong that Ayers lied. The historian Arthur M. Eckstein writes that at their meeting in Havana, the Cubans and the Vietnamese advised Dohrn and the others "to do everything they could to reproduce the massive and aboveground antiwar demonstrations that had shaken the American administration in 1967,"[10] no doubt understanding that outright violence would abort revolution, as it had done in Germany and Italy. Eckstein cites Dohrn's own notes from the meetings in Havana, which were taken by the FBI in a 1970 raid on a Chicago Weatherman safehouse. Dohrn has confirmed this, as have other Weathermen who were in Havana. As has Ayers himself, in his 2001 book *Fugitive Days*, though, typically, he blames John Jacobs for the distortion, insisting that he was just a bystander.

Further evidence shows that Ayers and Jacobs met those returning from Havana in Nova Scotia, and they leaned on them to say publicly that Havana and Hanoi wanted a confrontation with police in Chicago. Under pressure, Dohrn remembered that a Viet Cong official had said to her, "When you go into a city, look for the person who fights the hardest against the cops. That's the person to talk to all night.... Look for the one who fights."[11] Ayers seized on what was a statement about tactics and distorted it into Cuban and Vietnamese support for violence in Chicago.

When the day finally came, Ayers, Dohrn, and others in leadership gathered around a bonfire at Lincoln Park, alongside some two hundred Weathermen. Wearing helmets and goggles, the group then fanned out through the city's streets, throwing bricks through windows, but within hours, they were all arrested and charged with crimes. The "thousands and thousands" that the leadership had promised would come to Chicago never showed up. Instead, angry citizens of the Windy City threw ashtrays and other projectiles from their windows and balconies at the rioters below. Indeed, allies in the New Left, including the Black Panther leader Fred Hampton, had warned the Weathermen that the Days of Rage were ill planned and would fail. But rather than take the message that the country was not with them, Ayers and the rest of the leadership doubled down on revolution. "You know, we didn't step back and take a sober view of it," the Weather leader Jon Lerner is quoted by Burrough as saying. "We took a reactive view, which was 'Well, if we're the only people who will do this, it's us against the world.' And after that, it was."[12]

In a country reeling from riots; the assassinations of President John F. Kennedy, his brother, the attorney general Robert Kennedy, and Martin Luther King Jr.; as well as that summer's gruesome Manson murders, Ayers became frothier and frothier. He summed up the group's nihilism with a bone-chilling message: "Kill all the rich people. Break up their cars and apartments. Bring the revolution home, kill your parents—that's where it's really at."[13]

The Mansonian Moment

THE FASCINATION with Charles Manson by all the Weathermen, but especially Ayers's sweetheart Dohrn, is both puzzling and instructive at the same time. Manson, the son of a sixteen-year-old prostitute who had spent most of his childhood in the streets, had become by the late 1960s the handsome and charismatic leader of a small cult that imbibed deeply from the hellish brew of 1960s phenomenology: group sex, psychedelic drugs, and heavy metal—all things they shared with the Weathermen. The cult, known as the "Family," also believed in the need to start a race war and that if they could "set forth chaos in the white man's world by causing murder and mayhem, the establishment as we know it would fall."[14] These considerations aside, Ayers's and Dohrn's enthrallment with Manson appeared to have owed at least equally to his nihilism, methods, and complete lack of sympathy for the Family's victims—stances they shared.

On August 9–10, 1969, Manson directed the Family to massacre five people at the Hollywood home of film director Roman Polanski, including his eight-months-pregnant wife, the actress Sharon Tate. The gruesome murder spree was a capstone to a psychedelic decade and haunts America to this day. The first victim that night was eighteen-year-old Steven Parent, who had been visiting the caretaker of the Polanski home and whom members of the Family shot in the face four times as he drove out. Once inside the Polanski home, the members of the Family herded Tate, the writer Wojciech Frykowski, the heiress Abigail Folger, and the celebrity hair stylist Jay Sebring into the kitchen and tied them up.

According to a short biography of Manson, "Sebring was shot and brutally kicked as he tried to defend Tate. During the terrifying murder spree, both Frykowski and Folger managed to escape from the house but were chased and stabbed to death." Tate, wearing a negligee, pleaded for her life and that of her unborn child, but her tormentors responded by stabbing her repeatedly in the belly, including with a fork. "Look, bitch, I have no mercy for you. You're going to die, and you'd better get used to it," one of Manson's cult followers, Susan Atkins, spat at Tate as the actress expired her last.[15] The next day, the Family killed two more people, Leno and Rosemary LaBianca, by stabbing them several times, including with a carving fork they left in Leno's stomach.

On December 14, in prison and having agreed to testify, Atkins wrote that "what had happened had served its purpose. That was to instill fear in Man himself. Man, the establishment. That's what it was done for. To instill fear—to cause paranoia. To also show the black man how to go about taking over white man."[16]

Just a few days later, for five days between Christmas and New Year's Day, some four hundred members of the newly convened Weather Underground gathered in Flint, Michigan, for a convention they called a "War Council," and which Burrough described as "the pep rally from hell, a five-day orgy of violent rhetoric intended to set the stage for the underground revolution."[17] According to the always sage Daniel Patrick Moynihan, at the Flint convention, "Charles Manson's photograph was everywhere. He and his band of psychotics were the cultural heroes of the occasion."[18] On one wall of the convention, the Weathermen displayed their revolutionary heroes: Karl Marx, Fidel Castro, Ho Chi Minh, and Vladimir Lenin. On the other side were their enemies: President Nixon, FBI director J. Edgar Hoover … and Sharon Tate.

One of the things that most scandalized Moynihan was Dohrn's "rhapsodizing to the convention on the murders in Los Angeles." At one point, Dohrn took the stage and rejoiced about what had happened four months earlier, saying, "Dig it. First they killed those pigs, then they ate dinner in the same room with

NEXTGEN MARXISM | 119

them, then they even shoved a fork into a victim's stomach! Wild!" Peter Collier, who remembers Dohrn saying this at the War Council, added that "then she held up three fingers in a Manson fork salute."[19]

Today, Dohrn—remade as a professor of child education at Northwestern University, of all things—offers a totally implausible explanation as to why she celebrated one of the most grisly murder sprees in American history: "I'd love to forget it and I wish I hadn't said it. But it was completely ripped out of context. What I was trying to say, of course, was that Americans love to read about violence."[20] Ayers, likewise, defends her as having been "ironic," or speaking "partly as a joke."

No one doubts that Dohrn now wishes she had not so publicly delighted in the satanic behavior of the Manson Family, or that she would love to forget about it, but in no way can her words be interpreted as wry commentary about Americans' love of violence. Also, those who were at the Flint convention confirm that she was dead serious and that the sympathy for the nihilistic pursuit of chaos by the Manson Family was thick on the ground.

Mark Rudd, another Weatherman leader, would later write, "There were crazy discussions at Flint over whether killing white babies was inherently revolutionary, since all white people are the enemy. Out of this bizarre thinking came Bernardine's infamous speech praising Charles Manson and his gang's murder of actress Sharon Tate, her unborn child, and the LaBiancas.… We instantly adopted as Weather's salute four fingers held up in the air, invoking the fork left in Sharon Tate's belly. The message was that we shit on all your conventional values, you murderers of black revolutionaries and Vietnamese babies. There were no limits now to our politics of transgression."[21]

Grove City College professor Paul Kengor also quotes the former 1960s radical David Horowitz as writing, "In 1980, I taped interviews with thirty members of the Weather Underground who were present at the Flint War Council, including most of its leadership. Not one of them thought Dohrn was anything but deadly serious."[22] Moreover, Eckstein says that the "Weather Bureau"—their version of the Politburo—had approved the Manson remarks beforehand, as it had approved the picture of Sharon Tate on the enemy wall.

The Weathermen put Sharon Tate on their enemy list because she represented for them, as she had for Manson, the civilization they wanted to incinerate. "Scrawled in Sharon's blood on the outside of the front door was the word 'pig.'

An obvious reference to the white establishment that Charles Manson clearly thought was represented by Sharon Tate," wrote Frank Wilkins.[23] The Weathermen hated the Man as much as Susan Atkins, and had as much mercy for the establishment, including white babies, as she had shown a begging Sharon Tate. "All white babies are pigs!" shouted someone from the crowd during the War Council.[24] Not for nothing did Dohrn also scream in Flint, "We're about being crazy motherfuckers, and scaring the shit out of honky America!"[25] Added Jerry Rubin, "I fell in love with Charlie Manson the first time I saw his cherub face and sparkling eyes on TV. His words and courage inspired us."

As Kevin D. Williamson commented in *National Review*, "That cherub face later had a swastika carved into it."[26]

Like Moynihan, who said that there was "an element of psychopathology in all this,"[27] Kengor writes that some sort of line was crossed that night in Flint, some sort of cosmic transgression that would exact a heavy toll on the nation. It was "the first steps into a dark world. From the high altar of Rev. Dohrn's four-finger salute flowed domestic terror cells, gunpowder, and bomb-making units."[28]

The delight expressed in Flint at the orgiastic slaughter of that summer in Hollywood would have its consequences. Kengor quotes Rudd as saying that a "new decade now dawned. The New Red Army marched out from Flint, exhilarated and terrified." Kengor adds that the members of this New Red Army "would spend the next decade literally plotting the violent overthrow of the United States of America, which (quoting their hero, Che Guevara) they declared 'the Great Enemy of Mankind.'"

America's New Red Dawn

AYERS AND his friends soon began putting words into action. In January, they raided the offices of SDS and burned its records. "Protest was dead. SDS was no more," writes Eckstein.[29] The New Red Army—as they called themselves—fanned out to several cities in collectives of between ten and twenty people. Franks wrote that "one Weatherman would later tell me that in order to rid the members of their bourgeois habits, the collectives forced couples to separate, required homosexuality, drugtaking and round-the-clock sessions of self-criticism. One time, they skinned and ate an alley cat."[30] As with all communist endeavors, a purge quickly followed Flint, and Ayers himself started it in Cincinnati when he arrived on January 2 to examine its collective. Burrough says that about one hundred Weathermen ended up being purged. Through it all, Ayers displayed a trademark callousness about the lives that would be lost. When Larry Grathwold, an FBI informant placed inside the Weathermen, warned Ayers that innocent bystanders might get killed in a particular bombing, he said that Ayers responded, "We can't protect all the innocent people in the world. Some will get killed. Some of us will get killed. We have to accept that fact."[31]

The Weathermen also ventured into group sex to completely break down any lingering inhibitions, which echoes Lukács's and Marcuse's use of the powerful sexual urge to undermine society. Burrough says that Ayers took the lead at the fist mass orgy, in Columbus, Ohio, in 1970, when he took the hand of the girl he was dancing with, shouted, "It's time to do it!" and led her upstairs to the attic, where mattresses had been arrayed.[32] In their less randy moments, they read Mao, Che, Malcolm X, and Frantz Fanon. The last one, a Martinican revolutionary, became the writer of choice for the entire New Left. He popularized the phrase first written by Jean-Paul Sartre, "by any means necessary," which epitomized Marxists' dictum that the ends justify the means. In the United States, it was propagated by Malcolm X. Fanon gave expression to the relativism of the New Left when he wrote, "Truth is that which hurries on the break-up of the colonialist regime; it is that which promotes the emergence of the nation; it is all that protects the natives, and ruins the foreigners."[33]

A March 6, 1970, bomb explosion in a West Village townhouse was a miserable milestone in the history of Ayers and the Weathermen group he led. It killed three people, all Weathermen, and led to two federal indictments against Ayers.[34] More importantly, among the dead was Diana Oughton, Ayers's girlfriend, and Terry Robbins, Ayers's best friend, who had been assembling the bomb in the basement when it accidentally went off. Neither knew anything about explosives or even elementary principles of electricity. The third killed was Ted Gold, who was crushed by a wall. The blast also nearly killed another Ayers friend who figures prominently in his life story, Kathy Boudin.

As Franks put it, "[top Weatherman leader] Cathlyn Wilkerson and Kathy Boudin, on the floors above, scrambled out of the townhouse that was collapsing around them. They were practically naked; their clothes blasted to shreds. They ran down the street to the house of a neighbor, who let them wash and change."[35] The two fifty-pound cases of dynamite with roofing nails packed around them had been intended to blow up Fort Dix, New Jersey, where officers were to hold a dance with their sweethearts, and different parts of Columbia University. Instead, parts of Diana's body were found stuffed with roofing nails four days later as cranes sifted through the rubble: an arm with no hand, a leg with no foot, a set of buttocks, and so on. Her head was never found. Had they not blown themselves to pieces and carried out their plan, the outcome would likely have been mass murder. Ayers had visited the townhouse just before the bombing and was likely involved in the preparation of a crime that, after all, involved his girlfriend and best friend.

After the townhouse bombing, Ayers became a fugitive. Others dispersed around the country. The leadership spread the rumor that it was the police who had murdered the three terrorists, leading Eckstein to observe that "even after March 6, devotion to lethal violence remained strong in some Weatherman groups."[36] No one dared question the strategy of continuing a violent revolution, he added. Ayers headed to upstate New York to practice shooting and then had a secret meeting with the Buffalo Weatherman collective. Eckstein quotes Grathwold, the FBI informant inside the Weathermen, as saying that Ayers harangued the East Coast people, negatively comparing them to the West Coast terrorists, who had just successfully bombed a police station in California (it is not clear if Ayers was referring to bombings in San Francisco or in Berkeley). He praised Dohrn for her leadership in that operation. Ayers, according to Grathwold, declared that "Weatherman had to be one hundred percent Marxist–Leninist indoctrinated," and he also preached on the "ill-effects of monogamy and male chauvinism to operate at the highest level of violence."[37] Grathwold testified under oath that Ayers had credited Dohrn, who around this time was becoming his sweetheart, for the St. Valentine's Day bombing of a San Francisco police department, which killed a policeman.

There is no mention that Ayers brought up his dead girlfriend Diana in Buffalo as he pointed to the Village disaster as an example of the deficiencies of the East Coast collective. Indeed, according to Burrough, in May, Weatherman leader Jeff Jones had to take Ayers on a walk in Mendocino, California, at a safehouse where many in the leadership were temporarily staying, and tell him, "Bill, your best friend just killed your girlfriend and it's okay for you to be angry about that and mourn."[38] In fact, Ayers would later write that he thought it was "heresy" for Weathermen at that Mendocino retreat to speak of catching their breath after the townhouse killing.

But it was at Mendocino that the Weather Bureau finally decided to reject lethal bombing, with Dohrn and Jones convincing the reluctant Ayers that they had to stop trying to kill people. When they did, the three emerged as the leaders of the Weathermen, sidelining Rudd and expelling Jacobs. "It was a coup d'etat not unlike the one engineered at the SDS convention in Chicago a year before," writes Eckstein.[39] From that point on, they would continue bombing, but targeting property instead of people and phoning ahead to prevent fatalities. Tom Hayden, the former SDS leader who had promoted violence in Newark but who now had taken a more conciliatory approach, warned the Weathermen to stop celebrating bloodshed, reminding them that that was not where the country was.

Ayers continued setting off explosives, participating in the June 1970 bombing of New York City's police headquarters; of the US Capitol in March 1971, which caused $300,000 in damage; and of the Pentagon on May 19, 1972, Ho Chi Minh's birthday, among others. Ayers was in the middle of it all. As the writer Deroy Murdock put it, "as a top Weatherman, Ayers inspired, instructed and directed a domestic-terrorist network that bombed no fewer than 18 locations."[40]

Eventually, though, Ayers and Dohrn settled for domestic underground chic for about a decade. The legend the couple has built around themselves, which has it that they lived in poverty, moving in and out of "working class hideouts," has been shown to be just that—a legend. Burrough says that "nor, contrary to myth, did Weatherman leaders, especially its best-known alumni, Bernardine Dohrn and Bill Ayers, operate from grinding poverty or ghetto anonymity: For much of their time underground, Dohrn and Ayers lived in a cozy California beach bungalow, while the group's East Coast leaders lived in a comfortable vacation rental in New York's Catskills mountains," writes Burrough,[41] who, forty years later, found Cathy Wilkerson still upset about the dichotomy between the opulence in which Ayers and Dohrn lived and the meagerness of the rank and file. "In time, the difference between the top and the bottom became really gross. Offensive," Burrough quotes Wilkerson as saying.[42] Franks said that after coming out of hiding in 1974, Jane Alpert "told me of her travels underground and of how Weathermen fugitives lived joyless, determined lives, existing on yogurt and endless political debate, spending the night here and there in sleeping bags."[43]

Death of the Weathermen

SLOWLY IT began to dawn on Ayers and the other leaders that the revolution was not coming home, that staying underground had produced zero results, and that it wasn't just the country that was moving on—the remnants of the New Left were also passing them by. By 1974, the Weathermen had become the worst of all things to a revolutionary: irrelevant. Staying underground, said Ayers, had become "an increasingly high-cost fantasy"[44] and cut them off from the movement. Because the FBI had executed warrantless break-ins of supporters of the group, mostly to tap phones, the law increasingly turned on law enforcement rather than the terrorists, and two FBI officers were indicted. That meant that most of the fugitives could come out from hiding. Ayers and the others then decided on a bizarre plot: to create an aboveground political movement that would in short time bring in different strands of the Far Left under the leadership of Ayers, Dohrn, and the others. It was as manipulative as it was brazen. The name of the movement would be the Prairie Fire Distribution Committee, named after a pamphlet called *Prairie Fire*, cowritten by Ayers and Dohrn (and dedicated to Bobby Kennedy's assassin, Sirhan Sirhan). The new manifesto was a rejection of the Weatherman Manifesto, repudiating street violence and extending an olive branch to the working class, whom the original manifesto had derided as racist pigs.

At a July 1975 convention in Boston, the group created a permanent organization, the Prairie Fire Organizing Committee (PFOC), and the secret plan was that Ayers and the others, once they emerged from hiding and took care of their legal troubles, would take over the PFOC. Yet another conference was planned for January 1976 at the University of Illinois Chicago (UIC) campus. That conference, which would gather members from groups across the Left, was a "kind of a Hail Mary pass for Weather's leadership, their last shot at regaining all they had thrown away," quipped Burrough.[45]

At the conference in Chicago, the tension over the cynical attempt to return to working-class concerns and the then-emergent identity politics broke out in the open. Black and Feminist Caucuses were created, and they aired their anger over PFOC's attempt to return to "vulgar Marxism." The arguments became so intense that it became clear there would be no PFOC coalition. Eventually, the man who had been brought to run the organization, an aging communist by the name of Clayton Van Lydegraf, made leaders such as Dohrn and Ayers submit to self-criticism sessions, during which they admitted to "counterrevolutionary" crimes. Van Lydegraf accused Ayers, Dohrn, and the others of abandoning the black cause and "attempting to 'destroy' feminists, gays and lesbians in Weather's ranks. Dohrn, Bill Ayers and all the others were summarily expelled. Van Lydegraf ordered that no one could have any contact with them," wrote Burrough, who quotes someone describing it as a Stalinist purge—with "everything but the bullets."[46]

At the end, Dohrn issued a chilling taped statement that was more redolent of the Cultural Revolution then finally coming to an exhaustive end in Maoist China. "This is Bernardine Dohrn," it began, according to a contemporary report from a revolutionary magazine. "I am making this tape to acknowledge, repudiate and denounce the counterrevolutionary politics, and direction of the Weather Underground Organization [WUO].... We led the entire organization to abandon the principles of anti-imperialism, liquidated the Black nation and the leading role of national liberation struggles, and heightened our attacks on the women's movement. I repudiate and denounce, the Central Committee of the WUO, myself included, who bear particular responsibility for the criminal consequences of having led the WUO into full blown opportunism."[47] Dohrn named Ayers and others and accused them all, including herself, of "white supremacy, white superiority and chauvinist arrogance." Thus her own internal revolutionary devils had consumed the young, miniskirt-wearing revolutionary who a scant seven years earlier had stood on a stage in Flint and celebrated the fork left in Sharon Tate's pregnant belly.

Van Lydegraf tried to resurrect the Weathermen, but the black and women's groups would have none of it. The Weather Underground, which had begun so ominously seven years earlier by declaring war on the United States in the name of world communism, met an ignominious end by simply petering out. According to Burrough, as their terrorist world crumbled around them, the women in the organization's leadership decided to do that most bourgeois, human thing: to get pregnant. Dohrn, Wilkerson, and Eleanor Stein gave birth in 1977 and 1978. In 1980, Kathy Boudin had a son with David Gilbert, also a Weatherman. In 1982, Ayers and Dohrn tied the knot.

On December 3, 1979, charges having been dropped against both of them, Ayers and Dohrn walked into a Chicago courthouse with their lawyer. The evening before, they'd had a splendid dinner with friends, consuming gourmet food and "first-growth Bordeaux," according to Burrough. Eventually, Dohrn paid a fine of $1,500 and was given three years' probation. Instead, Jimmy Carter's Justice Department went after the FBI for the warrantless break-ins, indicting two top agents (who were later pardoned by Ronald Reagan). Nixon had thought that the Weathermen's involvement with foreign enemies mooted the question of constitutional protections. Carter's Justice Department disagreed, but even if it was right, one must still wonder how people who had rebelled against their own government, and inflicted violence against their society, could be expected to enjoy the constitutional protections of such a state.

Ayers, at least, seemed to acknowledge that he got away with something. "Guilty as hell, free as a bird—America is a great country," is how he put it in typical, unrepentant fashion in an interview with David Horowitz and Peter Collier, two former leaders of the New Left in the 1960s who later became disillusioned with it and turned against it.[48] In fact, Ayers has never expressed any remorse for what he did. "I don't regret setting bombs. I feel we didn't do enough," Ayers was quoted as saying by *The New York Times* in 2001. As for his call to "kill all the rich people. Kill your parents," it was "a joke about the distribution of wealth," he said in an interview that, providentially, appeared on September 11, 2001.[49]

But the murders weren't quite done yet. Some bitter-enders who wanted the violence to continue formed the May 19th Communist Organization (again, Ho Chi Minh's birthday). Kathy Boudin, the Italian-born communist Silvia Baraldini, and other ex-Weathermen, such as Judy Clark, Susan Rosenberg (of whom we will hear again), Marilyn Buck, and about ten other women, formed the core, though David Gilbert was also associated. On October 20, 1981, Gilbert, Boudin, Clark, Baraldini, and Buck joined members of the Black Liberation Army to rob a Brink's armored truck in the sleepy New York State community of Nyack. They made off with $1.6 million but killed two policemen and a bank guard. Boudin and Gilbert, who were in charge of the getaway car, were nabbed by the police. In 1983, Gilbert was sentenced to seventy-five years in prison, while Boudin got a twenty-year sentence the following year. They had to do something with their four-year-old son Chesa, named after the cop killer Joanne Chesimard, who lives as a fugitive in Havana, so they gave him to Ayers and Dohrn to raise. Chesa Boudin also, unfortunately, figures prominently later in this book.

Writing in *The New York Times Magazine*, Franks describes the Boudin arrest in this manner: "An off-duty corrections officer named Michael Koch drove into the midst of a gun battle between police and the assailants fleeing from the Nyack robbery. He jumped from his car and went off in pursuit of a woman who turned out to be Kathy Boudin. 'It was a firefight, like I was back in Vietnam,' Koch said. He struggled to subdue Kathy Boudin and as he did so, the Weatherwoman looked back at her fleeing B.L.A. accomplices and, in childlike indignation, screamed: 'I didn't shoot him! He did!'"[50] Franks, who was the wife of the legendary Robert Morgenthau, the longest-serving district attorney in the history of the state of New York, understood women like Boudin and Oughton intrinsically. Like them, she had gone to an exclusive school, they to Bryn Mawr and she to Vassar, and like them, she, too, had hated the war. But the comparisons ended there, and Franks showed no sympathy for, as she put it, "the children of the rich killing the less privileged in the name of revolution."

Long Marcher

AYERS, DOHRN, and the others did not resurface chastened and ready to work through the democratic process to reform society; rather, they sought to undermine it through stealth, because they had been unable to do so through violence. As we have seen, SDS members like Ayers had abandoned democracy and civil disobedience to turn to terrorism, but we should examine further what facilitated this switch for them. Their rejection of representative democracy and their amorphous belief that they could replace it with "participatory," or "direct," democracy was likely their gateway drug.

Decried as "bourgeois democracy," representative democracy had always been no more than an expedient, if that, to Marxists, starting with Marx himself. We have seen how, to Gramsci, the mission of attaining communism "cannot be accomplished by parliamentary democracy." Writing in the *Claremont Review of Books* in 2011,[51] William Voegeli makes a good case that to turn-of-the-century progressives and Marxists like Herbert Croly and John Dewey, parliamentary democracy and political rights were of no intrinsic value, and no more than means to an ultimate end, which was to fashion a new individual and form of human association.

It is no coincidence that it was after leaving the Underground that Ayers became a Gramscian and started to cite the Marxist Machiavelli. It is also no coincidence that Ayers brought up Gramsci in a 2011 speech in connection with the supposed failures of representative democracy and the imagined superiority of the participatory kind. Part of the hegemony, he said, was the belief that a class of elected representatives could rule over the rest of us.

In his talk, Ayers blamed what he saw as President Obama's failures (e.g., to stop "police torture in Chicago" or "wildfires in the west") with regard to the continued use of representative democracy itself. "Authentic democracy is direct democracy," said Ayers to the Ohio Valley Philosophy of Education Society. He cited Gramsci's theory of hegemony and explained how the people needed to remove the class of elected representatives as deciders. "In order to become truly liberated and free, people need to overcome their belief that it's a normal and natural state of affairs for a ruling class to rule or a political class to govern."[52]

Voegeli quotes Paul Berman, who came from among the SDS ranks but later wrote trenchantly about their shortcomings, as saying that it was their embrace of direct democracy that led to SDS's "degeneration into violence and irrationality."

To SDS and the rest of the New Left, direct democracy meant achieving unanimous consent because they thought majority rule was undemocratic. It produced, at best, mediocre results. All over the world, whether in Paris, Tokyo, or Mexico City, the New Left pined for councils rather than endure what they thought was the mediocrity produced by representative democracy. As Voegeli put it, "the idea, such as it was, held that the elected representatives, set apart from the citizen-electors by virtue of being elected, ceased to be representative. True democracy could not withstand the attenuation caused by delegating authority, and needed to be kept close to the citizens trying to determine the contours of their lives and communities." The New Left did not think of "direct democracy" as a corollary to representative democracy, as a civic-minded approach that made the citizen more engaged with his representatives or participate more in the democratic process; they thought of it as a rival model directly opposed to the representative, parliamentary kind, a replacement. Conservatives today rightly want to take power away from the elites, but the elites in question are the bureaucrats of Washington, DC's, permanent state, and what conservatives want to do is give the legislative power back to their elected representatives. Not so those who pine for participatory democracy—they want to replace the legislators.

A problem that becomes clear from the start is that participatory democracy, whether at SDS or with Marxists abroad in Cuba, Vietnam, the old East

Germany, or wherever communism has been foisted on a population, leads to interminable meetings. In a book, Berman quotes an SDS member from Newark as writing in a report, "Although many of us regard voting as undemocratic, there is a real question about whether we can afford to take eight hours to attain consensus on every issue." Berman also comically cites how members of an SDS organizing project in Cleveland "once held a twenty-four-hour meeting to decide whether to take a day off and go to the beach."[53]

Another problem is that direct democracy disposes of the checks and balances and the separation of powers that are so important to keeping tyranny at bay and which, for this reason, America's Founders worked so hard to build into the founding documents. Out of the miasma always rises a Napoleonic or Lenin-like figure. As Berman put it, "over time participatory democracy, by dispensing with the formalities and organizational dynamics of representative democracy, became a formula for demagoguery and chaos."[54] At the end, there was the "final embrace of totalitarian doctrines."[55]

Because endless meetings at the local factory council cannot determine decisions on war and peace, a national budget, or anything larger than the local waterworks, a Napoleonic figure must rise, just as Lenin threw over the soviets and set up the dictatorship of the proletariat through the vanguard of the Communist Party. Irving Howe confronted Tom Hayden at a public meeting in New York in May 1965 and challenged him on precisely this point: "Tom, you talk about participatory democracy, and criticize America for its absence; would you also criticize the so-called socialist countries for the same lack?"[56]

Sometimes these incipient tyrants try to hide their leadership, or lust for power, by pretending self-effacement, and even literally taking a back seat in the room where "direct democracy" is ostensibly happening. A 2002 book describes how the leftist American political theorist Michael Walzer, later to become editor of the journal *Dissent*, himself came reluctantly to the conclusion that his friend Hayden was just such as figure. Walzer in 1965 accepted Hayden's invitation to attend a meeting of the Newark Community Union Project and "to 'test' Tom's claim that the movement was being led by community people. But it was 'perfectly clear' to Walzer that Hayden had, in fact, 'run the meeting from the back of the room. Nothing was done without Tom's approval, and everyone got a crick in the neck from turning around to look at him sitting in that last row.' "[57] Howe ended up describing Hayden as a "Bolshevik type" and a "future commissar." Hayden, if we recall, went on to marry the actress activist Jane Fonda, who in 1972 became "Hanoi Jane" by visiting North Vietnam and justifying the torture of American prisoners of war.

This was Ayers's intellectual milieu as he underwent his third metamorphosis —the first having been from Eisenhower-era jock to campus activist, then to underground terrorist, and now to academic Long Marcher, his last incarnation (thus far—he told *The New York Times* in 2001 that one must "hold out the possibility of endless reinventions"),[58] a progression that mirrors how the country has gone from Happy Days to BLM. But this progression conceded nothing in terms of goals pursued. As Voegeli so well put it, Ayers and the others who emerged from hiding (and the NextGen Marxists that the New Left engendered from the 1980s onward) continued to believe that "constitutional limitations could be legitimately defied." The only difference was that "this defiance should be carried out shrewdly rather than valiantly."

Thus the new Ayers continued to labor for central economic planning, public rather than private property, and, of course, participatory democracy. As he said in his speech in the Ohio Valley, the end goal was still "a commons characterized by shared ownership of community property" and "a society that is actually self-governing, with a revolving cast of people taking responsibility for the functions of government." But the new way was through indoctrination of the young—starting with one-year-olds—and Dutschke's march through the institutions.

In 1982 we find Ayers as a pre-K teacher at a day care in the West Side of Chicago, instructing children as young as one year old on the wisdom of the murderous Chairman Mao. B. J.'s Kids enrolled children aged one through four, and Ayers found employment there soon after coming out of hiding. It was the perfect start to his new venture. The center tutored the little tykes on how to fight sexism, racism, and imperialism; discouraged competitive activities; and introduced the young charges to "restorative justice." Today this approach is one of the foundations of the new order that organizations like BLM want to introduce, and one of the things it does is put the criminal and the victim on the same moral plane. "The biter is just as hurt as the person who's been bitten," the founder of the center, B. J. Richards, told *New York* magazine in 1982.[59] These ideas would later be implemented in real life in the San Francisco of the twenty-first century, by Ayers's adopted son and the city's district attorney,

Chesa Boudin. The results were so predictably malign that Boudin was recalled in a special election even by that city's famously liberal voters.

Two years later, Ayers earned a graduate degree from Bank Street College of Education. He then enrolled at Columbia University, where he received a doctorate in education in 1987 from the university's notoriously leftist Teachers College (TC). TC's most iconic figure was the socialist John Dewey, who championed participatory democracy, and it was the college that offered Horkheimer and his Frankfurt School a home in 1933. While at TC, Ayers studied under Maxine Greene, who urged teachers to lecture their students about the evils of capitalism.[60] The writer Sol Stern said that Ayers had an epiphany while studying under Greene: the revolution could start at colleges of education. "As Ayers wrote later, he took fire from Greene's lectures on how the 'oppressive hegemony' of the capitalist social order 'reproduces' itself through the traditional practice of public schooling—critical pedagogy's fancy way of saying that the evil corporations exercise thought control through the schools. It hadn't occurred to Ayers that an ed-school professor could speak or write as an authentic American radical."[61]

After he graduated, Ayers landed a job as an education professor at UIC, and he and Dohrn moved back to the Windy City in 1987.[62] Thus Ayers was finally becoming a college professor two years before *The New York Times's* Felicity Barringer took note of communists taking over American universities.

At UIC, and in other hats he wore, Ayers focused on exactly the areas one would if one were burrowing in and indoctrinating for the future: elementary-school education, teacher training, taking over school boards, and curriculum writing. At his new position, he trained dozens of new teachers a year, and over the years, he published regularly in academic journals. His many books centered on how to change society through teaching. He also created an alternative teacher certification program called Golden Apple Teacher Education, the goal of which was "to overcome societal factors that contribute to oppressive teaching and learning conditions," according to a letter written in 2008 by one of his colleagues, William H. Schubert, the chairman of UIC's Department of Curriculum, who came to Ayers's aid when he was being attacked by the McCain campaign (for reasons to be discussed anon).[63]

The 1990 *Chicago Reader* profile cited earlier said that Ayers had championed Chicago's school reform act of 1988, which gave locally elected councils control over budget, curriculum, and the hiring of principals. "School reform isn't perfect, but it's a beginning," Ayers told the *Reader*. "It gives people some control, which is important; people have to take control of their lives. OK, the schools stink. They're designed to separate people by class and race and then control them. Now what? Change them! Get involved in your school council. You've got some power, use it. Don't tolerate lousy schools. Rebel! Be empowered! Take a risk!"[64] These are words that obviously betray his predilection for participatory democracy, but also words that conservatives should follow as they try to fight the success that Ayers and his ilk have had.

To his credit, the writer of the profile, Ben Joravsky, did not do just the puff piece so many others do but asked himself hard questions. Ayers, Joravsky wrote, had been "worse than dumb. He was arrogant, dogmatic, and unbearably self-righteous. He scorned his parents and turned on his friends. He was cruel. And the question that's bugging me—especially now, as I watch him effortlessly work his magic on these students—is when (or if) the old Bill Ayers ended and the new one began."

UIC made Ayers associate professor in 1992 and eventually granted him the title of "distinguished professor of education and senior university scholar." Ayers's clout advanced even further when, in 1990, Richard Daley Jr. was elected mayor of Chicago. The new mayor's father, Richard Daley, had been mayor both during the police street fight with SDS during the 1968 Democratic National Convention and during the Days of Rage the following year, but things were now peaceful and very different, and the new mayor didn't seem to care that Ayers was trying to dismantle society by stealth.

Daley Jr. had a good relationship with Ayers's wealthy and well-connected father, Thomas Ayers, who had added the chairmanships of Northwestern University and the Chicago Symphony to his former helmsmanship of Commonwealth Edison. Unsurprisingly, shortly after the election, Ayers received a job offer from Chicago Public Schools to train teachers.[65] Mayor Daley even made Ayers assistant deputy mayor for education, also in 1990 (or just a few months after Barringer started noticing how communists were taking over academia).

In 1997 the mayor presented Ayers with the Chicago Citizen of the Year Award for his work in founding the Small Schools Workshop, which used private donations to create "more relevant curriculum and teaching" and ended up opening about a hundred elementary and secondary schools. These positions allowed Ayers to publicly push his far-left education "reform" throughout the entire city and country. In the mid-1990s, Ayers was able to secure $50 million from the Annenberg Foundation to spend on a radical new proposal to transfer all hiring authority to local school councils, and then spent lots of money selecting and training the people who would be members of such councils.

Ayers's work was not relegated to etching the contours of Marxism on the young minds of primary and secondary schoolchildren. In his own college classes, he also worked to impose a new hegemony. According to the author Mary Grabar, the syllabi for his classes are reed-thin polemics that include mostly books Ayers has written, cowritten, or edited, which often are simply justifications for going to war with the United States over Vietnam or racism. The course description for his class Urban Education, for example, says, "We need to look beyond our isolated situations, to define our problems globally. We cannot be child advocates … in Chicago or New York and ignore the web that links us with the children of India or Palestine."[66] As Sol Stern put it, "the readings Mr. Ayers assigns to his university students are as intellectually diverse as a political commissar's indoctrination session in one of his favorite communist tyrannies."[67]

His senior-level course Improving Learning Environments did make an exception by promoting a writer other than himself. Ayers required students to read *Pedagogy of the Oppressed*, often referred to as the bible of critical pedagogy, by the Brazilian Maoist Paulo Freire.[68] Freire took a Marxist approach to education, dividing the world into oppressors and oppressed, and believed that the traditional system of education was designed to keep the poor submerged in a culture of silence. As the radical theologian Richard Shaull writes in the foreword to *Pedagogy of the Oppressed*,

> In this country, we are gradually becoming aware of the work of Paulo Freire, but thus far we have thought of it primarily in terms of its contribution to the education of illiterate adults in the Third World. If, however, we take a closer look, we may discover that his methodology as well as his educational philosophy are as important for us as for the dispossessed in Latin America. Their struggle to become free Subjects and to participate in the transformation of their society is similar, in many ways, to the struggle not only of blacks and Mexican-Americans but also of middle-class young people in this country.[69]

SHAULL GOES on to say, "The young...realize that the educational system today—from kindergarten to university—is their enemy."[70] After Freire was forced to leave his home country of Brazil, he ended up as a consultant to Harvard University's School of Education and to the World Council of Churches. According to Lisa Kolpe, from the University of San Francisco School of Education, "his work has inspired a movement of educators and activists to use teaching as a means to confront all forms of oppression, and seek avenues for liberatory movements that helped heal from racism, colonialism, and sexism."[71] Ayers was by no means the only professor preaching from Freire's epistle; as Barringer attests, there were many other Ayerses throughout the country at the time. Today, *Pedagogy of the Oppressed* is the third-most-cited resource in the social sciences[72] and is among the top-five resources used in graduate schools of education.[73]

Ayers's career in the academy was shaped by beliefs he never abandoned throughout all his many incarnations (except perhaps when he was a teenage jock in the 1950s). Throughout, he never lied about his intentions or goals. In his 1974 pamphlet *Prairie Fire*, he and his three coauthors stated, "We are communist women and men, underground in the United States for more than four years.... Our intention is to disrupt the empire...to incapacitate it, put pressure on the cracks, to make it hard to carry out its bloody functioning against the people of the world, to join the world struggle, to attack it from the inside."[74] And in an interview in 1995, he hadn't changed at all. "I am a radical, Leftist, small 'c' communist," he told an interviewer in 1995, in an admission peppered with laughter. "Maybe I'm the last communist who is willing to admit it. We have always been small 'c' communists in the sense that we were never in the Communist party and never Stalinists. The ethics of communism still appeal to me."[75] Two decades later, he was still trying to attack America from the inside, only he was no longer doing so with bombs; rather, he was using the ideological shrapnel of education.

As Grabar puts it, it is clear that Ayers intends teachers to be the sparks of revolution, as one of his syllabi says: "Teachers might not change the world in dramatic fashion, but we certainly change the people who will change the world.... This single spark could be that long-anticipated catalyst."[76]

At TC, Ayers had learned that education was "the motor-force of revolution." It is instructive that Ayers employed this aphorism while speaking before Hugo

Chávez, praising the Venezuelan dictator's use of education to indoctrinate young children into socialism.[77] Specifically, speaking at an education forum in Caracas in 2006, Ayers hailed "the profound educational reforms underway here in Venezuela under the leadership of President Chávez. We share the belief that education is the motor-force of revolution." Ayers added that he looked forward to seeing how "all of you continue to overcome the failings of capitalist education."[78]

This much Ayers tried to do with all the opportunities that UIC and Mayor Daley gave him, indoctrinating unsuspecting students to create in the United States what Chávez was to create years later in Venezuela.

Kingmaker!

AS HE continued to insinuate himself into the city's powerful educational institutions, using them to dismantle society from within, Ayers also became one of three writers for a grant proposal that secured $49.2 million from an educational initiative by Ambassador Walter Annenberg. That created an entity called the Chicago Annenberg Challenge (CAC). Matching private funds turned that into a $160 million kitty that over the years Ayers and others distributed to "community organizers and radical education activists."[79] In early 1995 a young community organizer who had just graduated from Harvard Law School and was making his way in the Windy City, and who had no prior experience in educational efforts or fundraising, was appointed the first chairman of the board of the CAC. His name was Barack Obama.

In fact, it was the terrorist-turned-educator who had introduced Obama to Chicago's political world by hosting at his home a reception that launched his first campaign for the Illinois Senate.[80] The occasion was a party at which state senator Alice Palmer, nominally a Democrat but in reality a communist and Soviet apologist who was preparing to run for a seat in the US House of Representatives, was introducing to the world of leftist Chicago politics her chosen successor: the thirty-three-year-old Obama, then a Chicago city councilman. The scene was at the apartment that Dohrn and Ayers owned in Hyde Park, Chicago's radical-chic neighborhood.

Several witnesses who were at the party attest to the hopes that Ayers and Dohrn obviously had for their young visitor. "When I first met Barack Obama, he was giving a standard, innocuous little talk in the living room of those two legends-in-their-own-minds, Bill Ayers and Bernardine Dohrn," *Politico*'s Ben Smith quoted the leftist blogger Maria Warren as writing in 2005. "They were launching him—introducing him to the Hyde Park community as the best thing since sliced bread."[81]

How or why Ayers and Dohrn glommed on to Obama is more of a matter of conjecture. Obama's mentor when he was growing up in Honolulu was a card-carrying member of the Communist Party by the name of Frank Marshall Davis. Teenage Obama was enthralled with Davis and mentioned him in double-digit numbers in both of his biographies (though only as "Frank"— Obama is, if anything, smart). Davis was an embittered enemy of the United States (with apparent reason to feel bitterness, according to Paul Kengor. No liberal, Davis was almost lynched in Kansas as a mere child). But Davis was also a shill not just for the Soviet Union but for the murderous Stalin too, and the US government kept a file on him, believing him to be a spy. The most important thing about Davis, in this context, is that he was from Chicago, though. Thus Frank Marshall Davis swam in the same Chicago waters as his fellow communists Ayers, Dohrn, and Palmer.

The last had served on the executive board of the US Peace Council, which was created by the Communist Party USA (CPUSA) and was, like the party itself, a front for Soviet interests. Palmer jetted around the Eastern Bloc and the Soviet Union well into the 1980s, defending Soviet policy—even predicting, less than a handful of years before its collapse, that the Soviet economy would soon surpass that of the United States. "The key to their system is the focus on groups, not individuals. They say it is the people together—not leading, privileged individuals—who make the nation happen. It will be up to worker teams to carry out the plan at their workplaces," Palmer had told the CPUSA organ *People's Daily World* after attending the twenty-seventh Congress of the Communist Party of the Soviet Union in 1986. She moreover showed herself to be a believer in the superiority of the factory workers' council. Failure to meet the factory quota, the party organ quoted her as saying, "will result in discussion with planners, managers and workers. These talks will determine whether the quotas were unrealistic, whether the machinery was poor or the workers poorly trained. After this evaluation, peer pressure and group pressure to do better will be focused on factories or worker teams."[82]

As for Obama, "Frank" had done his job. He was, too, a Marxist revolutionary when he attended Occidental College, according to writers such as Kengor and Stanley Kurtz.

Now, many people looking at all this may see a conspiracy in which Davis, having spotted a politically attuned, fatherless young man who hung on his every word, sent him to Chicago with letters of introduction, assured of greater things to come. That conspiracy could very well be true—or it could be that all these people simply run in the same circles. No document at the Obama Presidential Library will ever shed light on this; the media didn't choose to vet in 2008, and it will certainly not vet now.

What is *not* a matter of conjecture is that Obama knew Ayers and Dohrn very well by the time he ran for president in 2008. The former terrorists had not just introduced him to the political world of Hyde Park as "the best thing since sliced bread." Obama worked with Ayers on the CAC for seven years—the former as chairman and the latter as the head of the project's implementation arm—and the two also served together at Woods Fund Chicago, another charitable fund that the Left appropriated to funnel real money into its own organizations (the Annenberg Challenge board, for example, gave hundreds of thousands of dollars to one of Ayers's pet school projects, while the Woods Fund gave grants to Jeremiah Wright's church, which Obama attended, and to the center where Dohrn worked, according to CNN).[83] Obama even wrote a blurb for a book that Ayers wrote in 1996, *A Kind and Just Parent: The Children of Juvenile Court*. It was just another compilation of Ayers's nutty ideas on the criminal-justice system, but Obama found it to be "a searing and timely account of the juvenile court system, and the courageous individuals who rescue hope from despair." And Obama and Ayers teamed up to speak together—on the criminal-justice system—on at least one occasion in November 1997.

So, no, when Obama, under pressure to explain his relationship with an unapologetic terrorist, first by Hillary Clinton in the primary, then by John McCain in the general election, characterized his relationship with Ayers as "a guy who lives in my neighborhood" and "somebody who worked on education issues in Chicago that I know,"[84] he was less than forthcoming with the truth. Ditto with the idea, pushed by Obama and his spokespersons, that Obama was a young child. "Sen. Obama strongly condemns the violent actions of the Weathermen group, as he does all acts of violence," Obama's press secretary Bill Burton told *Politico*'s Ben Smith. "But he was an 8-year-old child when

Ayers and the Weathermen were active, and any attempt to connect Obama with events of almost 40 years ago is ridiculous."[85] Obama was born on August 4, 1961, and was thus eighteen when Ayers and Dohrn walked into a police station to much fanfare, and twenty when Boudin and Gilbert participated in the murders in Nyack, New York. He was forty years old when Ayers said, "I don't regret setting bombs. I feel we didn't do enough."

In the second half of 2008, as the election heated up, many of Ayers's colleagues, and others who simply sought to help the suddenly vulnerable Obama, rushed to Ayers's defense, calling him a model citizen, waiving away his terrorism as mere youthful indiscretion, or affirming that his work since resurfacing had atoned for his past violence (it hadn't, of course—as we have seen, Ayers was simply continuing by stealth and in Gramscian fashion what he couldn't achieve through force). In this vein, Tom Brokaw, to many the dean of American journalism, and speaking a few days before he was to moderate the next presidential debate, referred to Ayers as "a school reformer." This prompted Sol Stern to quip, "Calling Bill Ayers a school reformer is a bit like calling Joseph Stalin an agricultural reformer."[86] One could perhaps add that Ayers may have agreed that it was a fair and flattering comparison.

Why Ayers?

AYERS HAS always been coy about which bombings he carried out, though it is likely that he was involved in the botched townhouse explosion. The reason to go into such great detail of his life is that his personal odyssey from rich high-school jock to SDS dilletante to terrorist to fugitive to graduate student to college employment to "distinguished professor" influencing young minds to establishment figure doling out tens of millions of dollars in grant money to kingmaker neatly brings together all the elements of the Marxist takeover of America's sense-making institutions, and thereby American society. His life makes manifest the transformation from New Left to NextGen Marxism. His accession to the academic profession in 1987 came less than two years before Barringer's article appeared and in precisely the same year that Allan Bloom, another Chicagoan, published his *The Closing of the American Mind: How Higher Education Has Failed Democracy and Impoverished the Souls of Today's Students*, a warning about what Bloom was witnessing happening around him in academia.

There was another thing: Ayers, like Oughton, Boudine, and others, was a child of Greatest Generation parents (in these three cases, at least, all liberals) who perhaps spared the rod too much. Once again, Franks's commentary is trenchant:

> *Having suffered the hardships of war and depression themselves, parents in the 1960s catered to their children's every whim. This indulgence the Weathermen treated with contempt and wanted to obliterate in their quest to become true revolutionaries. Ironically, it may have been the one thing that allowed them to continue being revolutionaries long after there was any possibility of revolution. They lacked a good healthy fear of life, having received few of its blows. Sheltered and protected for so long, they felt invincible. Even when they went underground, as much as they liked to deny it, they felt they could always go back.*[87]

AND THE next generation, which Ayers was to influence directly and indirectly, took the revolution further, as we will see.

5
THE TAKEOVER

RIGHT AROUND THE time that Bill Ayers and his teacher Maxine Greene, and so many others of their ilk, were intellectually storming the barricades of the schools of education in the mid- to late 1980s, the law faculties, too, were being reshaped. As for ethnic-studies departments, they were already in the hands of a revolutionary Left intent on subverting America, largely because they were created precisely with that purpose in mind. It is only in the present era, however, that ethnic studies are becoming pervasive in universities and increasingly in K–12 and that the worldview of ethnic studies (to mount "a resistance against Western epistemology,"[1] in the words of one of its founders) has begun to permeate other disciplines. These were the disciplines that were falling to Marxists, as Felicity Barringer had observed in her 1989 article. Had Marxists cared about actual physical infrastructure, they would have infiltrated schools of engineering. But because they cared about the *cultural* infrastructure of society, they captured the faculties of education, law, and ethnic studies. They didn't want to poison the water supply; they wanted to poison as many minds as they could.

In both new theaters of the present Gramscian war of position—education and law—they were as successful in establishing beachheads, and then gaining ground, as they had been with ethnic studies. A study of 2013 data "found that only 11% of law school professors were Republicans, compared to 82% who were Democrats."[2] Meanwhile, a 2019 study by the Martin Center that analyzed 290 syllabi from three leading schools of education found that the vast majority of the authors assigned to those who would be teachers one day were radicals who adhered to multiculturalism or critical pedagogy. The textbook most often used was Paolo Freire's *Pedagogy of the Oppressed*—the one rare book not by himself that Ayers used in his classes—which preaches this new pedagogy as an instrument against the hegemony of the dominant elite and as a way to liberate people who were not yet aware of their own subjugation. "Even at a first glance, when perusing education school websites, faculty biographies, syllabi, research titles, and texts, one sees the words 'critical,' 'multicultural,' and 'equity' with alarming frequency. They are the revealing buzzwords of radical politicization."[3]

These buzzwords came from somewhere. These terms—*dismantle, centering, disrupt, problematize, interrogate,* all existing words with new revolutionary twists that made up a veritable new dialect—were furnished by a coterie of legal academics who took over an important corner of the law faculty, the area of civil rights. From the late 1960s into the 1980s, these legal academics called their work "critical legal studies" (CLS). Then, from 1989 on, a new generation of scholars emerged. They were mostly black, but some were also of Japanese or Mexican origin, and many were female. They rejected the domination of CLS by white, male academics. This new generation of academics began to call their work "critical race theory," or CRT.

But because the way had been paved for them in the late 1960s and especially the 1970s by the ethnic-studies revolution, it is best to discuss what happened there before we move into the law faculty lounge.

Ethnic Studies

ETHNIC STUDIES irrupted onto the scene in 1968–69. In a dynamic that the country would see repeated again and again in other walks of life, middle-aged members of the elite and in positions of power at first tried to resist, then panicked, and finally gave way to activists with ulterior motives. With ethnic studies, this sequence happened with the utmost drama, including long strikes and acrimonious break-ins. The revolutionary beginning befits the explicitly revolutionary goal of ethnic studies. It was not and was never meant to be "area studies," but its opposite. "Area studies programs arose out of American imperialism in the Third World, and bear names such as African studies, Asian studies, and Latin American studies. These programs were designed to focus on US/Third World relations and to train specialists to uphold US hegemony in regions in which the US had heavy economic and political investments," wrote Evelyn Hu-DeHart, director of the Center for the Study of Race and Ethnicity in America at Brown University. "Ethnic studies programs, which grew out of student and community grassroots movements, challenge the prevailing academic power structure and the Eurocentric curricula of our colleges and universities. These insurgent programs had a subversive agenda from the outset." In short, the field of ethnic studies "challenges Western imperialism and Eurocentrism, along with their claims to objectivity and universalism."[4]

Ethnic studies, therefore, emerges from the intellectual primordial ooze of the

1960s, from which we get the frontal ideological attack on eternal truths, such as the reality of the natural world, which the proponents of ethnic studies—as all Marxists everywhere see everything—regard as just one existing worldview among rival narratives. Ethnic studies is therefore the on-the-ground product of critical theory, the theory of hegemony, of postcolonial liberation, all with a dash of postmodernism. It focuses solely on the new minority groups officialized by the government through the census and other surveys—Hispanic, Native American, Asian American, and so on—whose marginalization is assumed by analogizing the unique suffering of black Americans.[5] "European immigrants have dominated America and defined the national identity as white and Western. Groups of color have a shared history of having been viewed as distinct from the European immigrants and their descendants. They are the 'un-meltable ethnics,' or ethnics without options regarding whether to invoke their ethnicity," writes Hu-DeHart, then quoting an unpublished paper that asserted, "It is both practically and theoretically incorrect to use the experience of white ethnics as a guide to comprehend those of nonwhite, or so-called 'racial' minorities."[6]

Thus, among other things, just as the government had officialized the new minority groups by creating them and giving them pride of place in government documents, the field of ethnic studies did the same in the academy. The emergence of these disciplines was, as well, another key step in the transferal of revolutionary agency from socioeconomic classes to races and ethnic groups. It cemented the idea that new groups of immigrants were to be treated differently from prior groups: "Hispanics" and "Asian Americans," especially, would not be permitted to embark on the same trajectory as the Sicilians, Syrians, Armenians, and Eastern European Jews of the Ellis Island era. They were to be the shock troops of the marginalized categories, and the Ellis Islanders and Irish, Germans, Scandinavians, and so on of the mid-1800s were to join the descendants of the Founding Fathers as the oppressor class. Ethnic studies was meant to curate the history of grievances for each group, with the resulting resentment milked to subvert the American system from within. Thus we have *black* studies, *Hispanic* studies, *Native American* studies, and so on, each cataloguing and curating every instance of real or perceived cruelty, preparing the now aggrieved minorities for the helot revolution.

The creation story of ethnic studies itself bespeaks of this revolutionary fervor. In the late 1960s, student protests arose to demand ethnic studies at San

Francisco State University (SFSU) specially, but also on a few other campuses, including the Berkeley and Santa Barbara campuses of the University of California (UC) system. In fall 1968, a radical coalition that included the Black Panthers, the Student Nonviolent Coordinating Committee, the Afro American Student Union, the Black Student Union, the Asian American Political Alliance, and others formed the Third World Liberation Front (TWLF) to agitate for ethnic studies. Soon, this new organization was organizing what became a five-month strike at SFSU, and it presented a list of fifteen demands.[7]

It called for the creation of a black-studies department, not just a program or discipline. That way, ethnic-studies professors would not have to go hat in hand to the heads of the social-sciences department, or any other department, to ask for "permission to teach, which clearly shows that the power lies with the other departments and administrators."[8] The TWLF also demanded a bachelor's degree in black studies and that all black-studies courses be concentrated under the umbrella of the black-studies department. The group also insisted that students be given the authority to hire the staff of the new department and that all black students who wished to be admitted be granted admission.

The SFSU president Robert Smith, a liberal, at first held firm. A month after the strike had begun, he closed the university, but California governor Ronald Reagan insisted that he reopen it, so Smith resigned in December. He was replaced by a faculty member, Samuel Ichiye Hayakawa (known as SI, and a maverick who switched party affiliations from Democrat to Republican in 1973 and then served the state as a US senator between 1977 and 1983). But he, too, had to compromise with the striking students and professors. On March 20, 1969, Hayakawa agreed to establish the first College of Ethnic Studies in the country, with its classes designed for people of color. The department was fully operational by fall 1969, with Hayakawa leaving it to the striking students to create the courses. The college was composed of a black-studies department and another two departments devoted to "La Raza" and Asian American studies. An American Indian studies department came along later. Women's studies came along around the same time, and for the same reasons.

The Marxist ideological content of ethnic studies was apparent from the start. In a 2018 interview with *Socialist Worker*, Jason Ferreira, today the chair of the Department of Race and Resistance Studies (the name could not be more explicit) at SFSU's College of Ethnic Studies, explained the history of that first coalition that had agitated for ethnic studies back in 1968: "The TWLF was formed based on the political principle of Third World solidarity, which is animating Cuba, Algeria, Tanzania and Vietnam. So it's no coincidence that they called themselves the TWLF—like the National Liberation Front in Vietnam." The list of fifteen demands was strategically aimed at specific issues related to creating the department, but that wasn't for lack of a greater vision. "It wasn't 'we want global revolution' or anything like that. This was intentional because the students wanted to be able to struggle over something concrete and be able to win a base for later," said Ferreira.[9]

The effects were felt city- and nationwide. "The politicization at [San Francisco] State led to their deeper involvement in Chinatown politics, developing the voice of Chinatown youth and connecting with those people in the community who had been silenced—like the Communists who had a history going back to the 1930s in Chinatown, but who had been silenced and purged because of McCarthyism and the right-wing leadership," added Ferreira. It was only a few years later that the communist paramilitary group I Wor Kuen created the Chinese Progressive Association of San Francisco, a pro-Maoist China group with which Ferreira is associated and which proved essential in sustaining BLM, as we will see in chapter 8.

Stokely Carmichael was also explicit about the end goal of ethnic studies. He said that Black Power was "a movement that will smash everything Western civilization has created" and that it was "precisely the job of the black educator to train his people how to dismantle America, how to destroy it."[10]

By this point, it shouldn't surprise anyone that, given how key ethnic studies is to the takeover of the institutions and the imposition of a rival worldview, Herbert Marcuse was not far from the fray. Just a couple of months after Hayakawa caved, Marcuse, then in the midst of his more revolutionary stage in the late 1960s, led a march of students, who occupied the registrar's office at UC San Diego, where he was a professor at the time. The May 1969 protest was held by radical students demanding that the school devote its third college, then in the planning, to "people of color" and Third World studies. The demand, in other words, perfectly paralleled those at SFSU. The name they wanted for the school was "Lumumba–Zapata," after the lionized Congolese communist leader Patrice Lumumba and the Mexican revolutionary Emiliano Zapata, whom the Left had appropriated.

The two groups pushing this agenda were the Black Student Caucus and the separatist Movimiento Estudiantil Chicano de Aztlan, which was being advised at the time by the literature professor Carlos Blanco, a Basque communist. Marcuse and Blanco teamed up to stir the trouble, and Marcuse was the first person to occupy the registrar's office, leading a mob into the premises after breaking down the door. When the university's chancellor demanded that someone pay for the damage, Marcuse sent a money order for the full amount. Angela Davis, who had followed Marcuse to UC San Diego, and who also was a protest leader, said later in an interview regarding the events there, "Herbert Marcuse taught me that it was possible to be an academic, an activist, a scholar, and a revolutionary."[11]

From these revolutionary beginnings, ethnic studies has done nothing but expand. Within twenty years, there were some seven hundred ethnic-studies programs and departments in the nation, and in the 2020s, this number grew to close to nineteen hundred. According to College Factual, in 2023, the top ten programs, in order, were Stanford, Yale, Wellesley, Brown, Columbia, Georgetown, Dartmouth, UC Los Angeles, UC Berkley, and UC Davis. In other words, ethnic studies has gone mainstream, and all the top universities and colleges offer degrees in it.[12] Graduates of these programs can earn up to $50,000 a year, according to College Factual. But earning potential isn't the point. As Angela Davis told a large crowd of students at California State University Los Angeles in 2016, black studies is "the intellectual arm of the revolution." That came minutes after her introduction, when she declared to rapturous applause, "I have always been a communist."[13]

In the 2020s, ethnic-studies received a second wind after the 2020 BLM revolt. On August 17, 2020, following months of costly and deadly riots organized by BLM, California governor Gavin Newsom signed a bill making it mandatory for students at all twenty-three campuses of the California State University system to take a three-unit ethnic-studies course. BLM had a direct impact on the governor's decision: the BLM cofounder Melina Abdullah, head of BLM's Los Angeles chapter and a former professor of pan-African studies at Cal State Los Angeles, lobbied Newsom hard to sign the ethnic-studies bill into law, traveling to Sacramento frequently for two and a half years.

Many other colleges and systems also moved to adopt ethnic studies in 2020. In New York, the state approved a requirement that all students graduating from the state university system take ethnic studies. A typical experience was that of Kayla Corbin, who, with four other graduate students, established in 2020 the Africana Studies Faculty Learning Community at the University of Richmond. Its purpose was to work on a proposal for an "Africana Studies Program,"[14] and it makes clear how ethnic studies remains the offspring of the marriage of the collectivism and oppositional struggles of the Marxist tradition with postmodernism's search for rival "epistemes."

Quoting liberally from Cedric Robinson's 2000 book *Black Marxism: The Making of the Black Radical Tradition*, Corbin speaks of "the development of a collective consciousness that interrogates systems of white supremacy."[15] One of the most insidious things about the "Western order of knowledge," she writes, is that "knowledge is defined by white people, specifically wealthy or propertied white men." That's why there was a need for "an alternative order of knowledge."[16] In late 2020, after months of riots petrified leaders at many of our elite institutions into submission, the faculty of the University of Richmond voted overwhelmingly to create not an outright department but a degree-granting Africana studies program at the School of Arts and Sciences. "The Program's interrogations begin not with race as an assumed concept but as a site of profound epistemological and ontological meaning-making that must be considered in relation to gender, class, nation, ethnicity, religion, and sexuality," says the university.[17]

Many states, particularly blue ones, also rushed in post-2020 to make it a requirement to take ethnic studies for those wishing to graduate from high school. Maine passed a law requiring schools to offer courses on black studies and the history of genocide; Connecticut, too, requires schools to offer black and Latino studies; in nearby Rhode Island, the state house passed a bill on African American studies in 2021, and as of this writing, Minnesota, too, looks set to pass one as of November 2023. After vetoing an earlier version, Governor Newsom signed a high-school bill in October 2021, thus making the Golden State the first one to require ethnic studies in high schools.

It was in reference to the bill that Newsom vetoed in 2020 that *The New York Times* columnist Bret Stephens wrote a definitive definition. "What is 'ethnic studies'?" asked Stephens. "Contrary to first impressions, it is not multiculturalism. It is not a way of exploring, much less celebrating, America's pluralistic society. It is an assault on it.... Ethnic studies is less an academic discipline than it is the recruiting arm of a radical ideological movement masquerading as mainstream pedagogy." Then quoting from the bill, Stephens added, "From the opening pages of the model curriculum, students are expected not just to 'challenge racist, bigoted, discriminatory, imperialist/colonial beliefs,' but to 'critique empire-building in history' and 'connect ourselves to past and contemporary social movements that struggle for social justice.'"[18]

That would be fine, wrote Stephens, if it appeared in *The Nation* magazine. It would be fine, too, he added, "if students were exposed to critical race theory the way they might be exposed to Marxist philosophy or some other ideology— as a subject to be examined, not a lens through which to do the examining. The former is education. The latter is indoctrination. The ethnic studies curriculum conceals the difference." Stephens was also on to something when he called ethnic studies "an older relative to critical race theory." Ethnic studies did precede CRT and greatly influenced it, so it is to the leftist corruption of our legal institutions that we turn now.

Critical Law

ON DECEMBER 5, 1985, *The Harvard Crimson* decried that polarization was so tearing apart Harvard Law that good professors were leaving, and the school was having great difficulty replacing them. The reason was that a new discipline had been sweeping law faculties for less than a decade: CLS, an American derivative of critical theory that also drew inspiration from Parisian postmodernism. "The reason so many law professors are dissatisfied with their positions at Harvard is not merely opposition to the trend toward radical legal scholarship exemplified by Critical Legal Studies," read the unsigned editorial at the *Crimson*. "What many object to is the polarization of the Law School faculty that has accompanied the growing popularity of CLS."[19]

Whoever wrote the editorial was clearly sympathetic to CLS. The debate it had sparked over the future of legal education was "one of the most exciting and positive developments in the school's recent history," the editorial read, and it fretted that half a dozen senior professors threatening to leave over it would threaten not just this development but the school itself:

> *The political infighting has led to bitterness among both conservatives and the liberal-CLS camp and has all but destroyed the tenure process. Neither side deserves all the blame for what at times has been bitter fighting, but the*

*result of their unrestrained battle has been unfortunate. The Law School
has been unable to tenure faculty from other schools since 1981 and has had
routinely to promote junior faculty to fill teaching positions. With several
liberal junior faculty members coming up for tenure this spring, many of the
moderates and conservatives fear a leftist coup which might permanently
divide the faculty. The result could be an unfortunate migration of some of
Harvard's most prized legal experts.*

THE COUP did happen, and Harvard, like other top law schools, became irredeemably leftist. By 2015, the *Crimson* was reporting that 98 percent of political
donations by Harvard Law School professors went to Democrats, just shy of
the 100 percent achieved by the Schools of Education and Design.[20] The 1980s
takeover of Harvard Law, and of other law faculties, did not start with the CLS
ascendancy, however, but went back to the late 1960s, a recurring pattern in
our tale. The result is that, today, the legal profession plays an active, probably
leading role in challenging the legitimacy of the United States, its sovereignty,
and its way of life.

This is nationally unsustainable. The law is one of the main bonds holding
society together. America is the country that it is because it has the rule of law.
All one has to do to prove that assertion is to live in a society ruled by men and
not laws. But for the rule of law to prevail, everyone, or a substantial majority,
must agree to the abstract idea that is law. Once respect for the law disappears,
society falls apart, and we see many examples of this around the world, starting
with Latin America right next door to us.

This is a problem that accelerates when it is the legal profession itself that is
undermining that respect. And if there was one idea that united the different
trends nipping at the legal profession starting in the 1960s, it was that law lacked
objectivity and, well, legality—that there was no exterior authority, neither de-
ity nor nature, from which the law emanated. Legal scholars concluded that
"no external, universally accepted normative source exists to resolve conflicts
of value," as the CRT pioneer Mari Matsuda wrote in 1987.[21] The legal system
that we had was simply concocted by the rich and powerful to remain rich
and powerful. The law was detached, malleable, and to be used strategically for
purely political reasons. Everything became a power dynamic.

The Left, including the large philanthropic organizations and elements of the legal profession, then naturally decided to use the law instrumentally to achieve its ends, just as it imagined that the rich and powerful had done to create an oppressive system. And it was up front about seeking power to create complete transformation, the two pillars of the Marxist Left. That became the hallmark of something new: public interest law.

Public-Interest Law

R. S. RADFORD, at the Pacific Legal Foundation, defines public interest law as "a term that was coined around 1970, essentially to provide cover for left-wing foundations to channel tax-free dollars to activists who would use the courts to advance a radical social agenda."[22] The activist firms grew in an upswell in a few short years. The always astute political commentator Walter Olson records that most of the institutions that dominate the field of public-interest law were created between 1966 and 1969. This phenomenon, as Olson explains in a 2013 paper for the Capital Research Center, "dates back to what has been called the rights revolution, in the Sixties and early Seventies, in which courts regularly agreed to create wholly new rights at the request of what were called public interest lawyers—themselves a newly fledged variety of lawyer conceived of as serving (in effect) as lobbyists" for what we today would call members of the marginalized categories.[23] The legal campaigns were "managed from within the law schools, as professors coordinated strategy with outside litigators, legal services programs, funders, sympathetic journalists, and other players. Law schools directly housed many key legal action centers that supported landmark suits."

Public-interest law was thus a concrete manifestation of the idea that law was indeterminate, had no inherent wellspring, and should be used to achieve societal change. It produced real victories for the Left, as litigators worked to gain power to achieve societal transformation and enshrine the Left's agenda. Strategic landmark suits and US Supreme Court decisions changed policy, and therefore society and culture. Among the institutions launched between 1966 and 1969, with the aid of philanthropic organizations like the Ford, Carnegie, and MacArthur Foundations, Olson counts progressive behemoths that are around to this day: "in civil rights law, the Lawyers Committee for Civil Rights under Law, Mexican American Legal Defense and Education Fund (MALDEF), Puerto Rican Legal Defense Fund, and Native American Rights Fund; in women's rights law, the ACLU Women's Rights Project and National Women's Law

Center; in environmental law, the Environmental Defense Fund, Sierra Club Legal Defense Fund (later EarthJustice), and Natural Resources Defense Council; and comparable groups in many other areas, including organizations devoted to welfare rights and school finance equalization. Ford also funded major expansions of existing groups such as the American Civil Liberties Union and NAACP Legal Defense Fund."[24] These networks then worked with sympathetic journalists, because, as Olson points out, "public interest litigation tends to be complicated, and reporters depend on relatively few sources who are in a position to analyze its detail."

All of this seeped into the law schools. In fact, the law schools were ahead, as they had already pioneered the clinical legal movement in the 1950s, with the help of the Ford Foundation, which was spending its money to change curricula. As Michelle Fabio put it, "a legal clinic (also called a law school clinic or law clinic) is a program organized through law school that allows students to receive law school credit as they work part-time in real (not simulated) legal service atmospheres."[25] The students perform all the tasks of real lawyers; they research, draft briefs, and interview clients. Importantly, the clinical movement was all about societal transformation, and all in a leftist direction, tied at the hip with public-interest law, sharing with it a desire for "social justice."

"Spurred by the civil rights movement, young people flocked to law school hoping to work for social change and were discouraged to find a calcified curriculum having little to do with their aspirations," wrote Minna Kotkin for Harvard Law's Center on the Legal Profession.[26] It didn't hurt that Lyndon Johnson's "War on Poverty" was funding civil legal work. "These fledging enterprises, staffed by idealistic and overworked young lawyers, began to look to law students as a means of leveraging their impact. Clinical education began with students volunteering at local legal services offices, where they were thrown into the thick of poverty law practice without much guidance from the only marginally more experienced staff attorneys," adds Kotkin. It was at these public-interest practices that students' consciousnesses were raised. It also didn't hurt that Ford, in 1968, created the Council on Legal Education for Professional Responsibility to promote legal clinics and, again, invested large amounts in this effort.

Public-interest law continues to plague us to this day; all these organizations have, if anything, gained in power. To be sure, some organizations on the Right, such as the Pacific Legal Foundation, have emerged. Radford reminds us that "what is never addressed, of course, is exactly how or why a Leftist slant on social and political issues, as opposed to any conflicting viewpoint, equates to 'the public interest.'"[27] But conservative organizations fight a rearguard battle. An often untold shift in the late 1960s, most pronounced among the philanthropic organizations, is that needs-based philanthropic help ceased being the goal; *change* became the goal, and not just change, but systemic, and progressive, change. Again, Olson: "Effective philanthropy (it was argued) required changing the unjust social conditions that permitted poverty, ill health, and deprivation to arise in the first place. That required politically aware giving to organizers and activists who could best challenge old institutions. The old programmatic service ethic of direct help to the needy was passé—'merely ameliorative,' in the telling phrase of one new-style grantmaker."[28] Indeed, Paul Ylvisaker, head of the Public Affairs Program at the very powerful and wealthy Ford Foundation during the 1950s and 1960s, was fond of calling philanthropy the "passing gear of social change."[29] He was right.

Dramatic change is what can make the Left so much more appealing, and dangerous, because conservatives advocate for reform or evolutionary change, whereas the Left works for sexier revolutionary change. It wants to tear down and rebuild from scratch, which history has proven to be a very destructive and destabilizing course of action. But evolutionary change, while less destructive, is also less dramatic. In but one example, in 1968, Ylvisaker invested $2.2 million of the Ford Foundation's money into creating MALDEF. Returns on investment (if societal change is what was intended) were almost immediate. MALDEF itself explains how, in 1974, its Washington, DC, counsel Al I. Perez decided to seek changes to the Voting Rights Act (VRA) to require that ballots and election material be printed also in Spanish, and also to expand preclearance provisions to areas with significant Mexican American populations. Perez recruited two lawyers from the massive Washington, DC, firm Hogan and Hartson, which had a public-interest practice. "Together the three formulated a legal, legislative, media and community outreach strategy of proposed amendments to the VRA's pre-clearance provisions," boasts MALDEF.[30] In 1975, Representative Ed Roybal, who used to work for the radical community organizer Saul Alinsky, and who was elected to Congress in 1962 with the help of communists, introduced a bill requiring bilingual ballots and making Texas subject to the Justice Department's preclearance. The bill passed, and the nation took yet another step into the balkanization of distinct ethnic groupings that was to be used by NextGen Marxists for decades to come.

All this change can and must be undone, but it won't be easy. Yes, a Supreme Court that is sympathetic to undoing the changes of the Left has produced the *Dobbs* and *Students for Fair Admissions* decisions and may undo the Chevron deference principle that allows the permanent bureaucracy to legislate. But the Left is not letting up. Writing in 2018 in *The Yale Law Journal*, the Marxist Yale Law alum Charles Du argued for public-interest law to refocus "on a commitment to developing left political power: the capacity to effectuate the fundamental structural transformations of society necessary to achieve justice and equality for all."[31]

The idea that the law was unmoored from any neutral and objective truth, let alone from transcendental truth, or God's law, also led to a more abstract attack on the law, which was no less damaging for its abstraction. That was the very same CLS (or critical legal theory—both terms are used, though CLS is used most frequently) that the writers of the *Crimson* editorial found so beguiling in 1985 but that, as they admitted, was causing such polarization at Harvard Law and elsewhere. Apart from a belief in the indeterminacy of the law, CLS also shared with public-interest law the belief that law was "necessarily intertwined with social issues" (as Cornell Law puts it in its entry on critical legal theory).[32] This was not as much a contradiction as we may think at first; if the law was being used by the rich and powerful to keep their privileges, it could also be used to tip the scales the other way. As its name betrays, CLS was a direct descendant of critical theory.

Critical Legal Studies (or Theory)

PUBLIC-INTEREST LAW led to CLS, or at least chronologically preceded it, because the law firms and university clinics seeking class-action suits that would lead to societally changing judicial decisions believed that they were battling an oppressive legal system. These activist-lawyers and students saw the "public interest" as being in direct conflict with the American legal system. Corporate law, in particular, was the ultimate way to keep the rich rich. Critical legal theorists agreed. However, whereas public-interest law sought societal change through landmark judicial decisions, CLS practitioners saw their task as undermining the system through intense criticism and by sowing doubt on its very legitimacy. They held that the law was never neutral—that its intent was inherently political, in fact. There is never any "rule of law," they held; it is always "rule by men." They were at war with an idea dear to the Founders: that the law must be based on natural law. The Founders quoted numerous times the English jurist William Blackstone, who had written that "no human laws are of any validity if contrary" to the laws of nature.[33] The CLS prescribers weren't saying that American law had violated natural law; they were saying that there was no such thing as fundamental or transcendental truth upon which the law could be based.

Another distinction was that CLS was the self-declared American offspring of Horkheimer's criticalist approach. Horkheimer, along with Adorno, thought that not just law but reason itself was instrumentalized and political (and they weren't necessarily wrong, in an environment in which reason becomes unmoored from transcendental truth). Critical legal theory had the same aims as critical theory: to revolutionize society, though in CLS's case, the focus was limited to the law and did not apply to all sensory experience. "A central project of the CLS movement is to unmask the ideological nature of the law" is how a writer for the academic content platform of Cambridge University Press put it.[34]

Landmark suits do change society, issue by issue: bilingual ballots, the racial preferences of affirmative action, the reinterpretation of the VRA that gave us race-majority electoral districts. But CLS is even more corrosive. Successfully chipping away at the legitimacy of the law, one of the foundations of civilization, would in time bring the entire edifice down. Because, to the "crits" (the term they used for themselves), law was an instrument of oppression, undermining the law meant destabilizing, and ultimately eliminating, the courts, the prison system, and the police, who are after all the armed men and women who ultimately enforce the laws passed by legislators. It should hardly surprise us that today these are the avowed goals of the Marxists who founded BLM and of their mentors, such as the Communist Party leader Angela Davis.

Besides, to hear Harvard Law's Duncan Kennedy tell it, in the 1970s and 1980s, the courts were no longer friends of change, which necessitated the shift from public-interest activism to the nihilism of CLS. Kennedy, the godfather of the CLS movement and its most important voice, wrote in 2002 that "by the 1970s and 1980s, there were no longer 'popular movements' aggressively raising rights claims, there were no longer federal courts willing to invalidate legislation and regulations in the interests of oppressed groups."[35]

None of this is coincidental, as CLS's debt to Marxism is direct. As the Cornell entry explains, "although CLS has been largely contained within the United States, it was influenced to a great extent by European philosophers, such as Karl Marx, Max Weber, Max Horkheimer, Antonio Gramsci, and Michel Foucault.... Many in the CLS movement want to overturn the hierarchical structures of modern society[,] and they focus on the law as a tool in achieving this goal."[36] As Duncan Kennedy defined it himself, CLS was "the emergence of a new left intelligentsia committed at once to theory and to practice, and creating a radical left world view in an area where once there were only variations on the theme of legitimation of the status quo."[37]

The status quo—the American system—had to be delegitimized by exposing the legal system as a sham. Allan Hutchinson and Patrick Monahan call it "a full frontal assault on the edifice of jurisprudential writing and thought."[38] Like its German forebear, critical theory, CLS rejects the very presuppositions upon which jurisprudence must rest. Private property, victims, aggressors, tort—these are all conventions created by men who want to oppress other men. "It is not merely the truth of nature that is at stake, but the nature of truth itself. The Critical scholars seek to reformulate the ground rules, to revise the criteria for valid legal theory," wrote Hutchinson and Monahan at the height of the movement in 1984.[39]

CLS is also partial heir to the legal realist movement of the first half of the twentieth century, which held that concrete social reality was ill translated into legal abstractions. Legal realists believed that the main problem was with language, however, and were much less interested in the political project of the legal system. Not so with critical legal theorists, for whom the politics of the legal concoction was the main thing. CLS, then, was a kind of legal realism in the hands of the New Left.

CLS writing and analysis started gathering pace in the 1970s, and it became a cohesive movement in 1977, when its practitioners held the Conference on Critical Legal Studies at the University of Wisconsin at Madison. It grew in universities at a rapid pace. According to Hutchison and Monahan, the sixth annual CLS conference, held at Harvard in 1982, attracted almost one thousand people. Duncan Kennedy at Harvard was the best-known crit, probably the godfather of the movement, but another well-known proponent was Roberto Mangabeira Unger, a Brazilian philosopher who also taught at Harvard Law, and, to a lesser extent, Robert W. Gordon at Stanford Law. All three are alive in their eighties at the time of this writing.

Kennedy, the main critical legal theorist, wrote in an essay in 2002 that CLS "operates at the uneasy juncture" of two traditions, leftist thought and postmodernism, whose aims do not differ greatly. "Leftism aims to transform existing social structures on the basis of a critique of their injustice, and, specifically at the injustices of racist, capitalist patriarchy. The goal is to replace the system, piece by piece or in medium or large-sized blocs, with a better system," wrote Kennedy. Postmodernism, meanwhile, "aims at liberation from inner and outer experiences of constraint by reason."[40]

Most critical legal theorists were at war with the concept of individual rights, especially property rights. Unger calls for "disaggregation of the consolidated property rights"[41] and recognizes only four rights, which are communal, and didn't shy from passing this on to his students. Kennedy recognizes that this aversion draws from "Marx's critique of rights as individualist rather than communist, and specifically the Marcusian critique of 'repressive tolerance.' There is an undeniable genealogical connection between this critical strand and the communist practice of denying any legal enforcement of rights against the state, in the name of the revolutionary truth that 'bourgeois civil liberties' were a reactionary or counterrevolutionary mystification."[42]

In a 2012 interview with James R. Hackney Jr., who a few years later became dean of Northwestern Law School, Kennedy said that he was "very influenced from the beginning" by two Continental leftist ideas. The first was "the critical theory, Western Marxist, and post-Marxist strand (which would include Herbert Marcuse and Jean-Paul Sartre)." The second was the "structuralist strand," a twentieth-century intellectual movement that analyzes all human actions as a set of relations that construct a conceptual structure that is made up by humans and not natural—once again, a denial of the existence of absolute truth. Kennedy added that he came to these views because "I was just a child of the zeitgeist. These ideas were very much in fashion with the intellectual left beginning in the late sixties through the seventies."[43]

Kennedy wasn't influenced only by Marcuse but also by Gramsci. His name, wrote Kennedy in 1982, "is a battle cry for people who are repelled or antagonized by the variants of Marxism which place no importance whatever on what people think." Kennedy then identified two of the Gramscian themes we discussed in chapter 2: "if you don't like the variants of Marxism where all the emphasis is on economic structure, or in the instrumental use of violence to achieve the goals of particular groups, then you tend to wave Gramsci as a flag." Kennedy singles out Lukács and Korsch as two other twentieth-century intellectual figures who were also key to Western Marxism, "but their status within the communist movement was so much more problematic" than Gramsci's, which leaves the Italian communist leader as the lodestar for new Marxists.[44]

Gramsci, thought Kennedy, provided a blueprint for crits seeking to undo the oppressive legal system. "Gramsci's work is very suggestive about our situation as radicals involved in the legal profession," wrote Kennedy. "In Gramscian terms, the legal system is a complicated bloc, that is, it involves on the one hand an element of the use of force, of violence, of direct coercion and unmediated oppression by people against other people."[45]

That would be the police, of course, and Kennedy, like all good Marxists, is particularly troubled by law enforcement protecting private property: "The legal system helps organize the deployment of guns to prevent people from socializing the means of production." But the legal system is also the writing of laws. "It's part of the life of people who have enormous political power mainly as an instrument. They can use it and they see it as an instrument of the exercise of direct domination."[46]

And of course, Kennedy charges the law with the worst accusation of all: "The legal system maintains the social structure of the capitalist state.... It's a picture of the universe, of life, if you are a worker, in which you are constantly being told by people who are frightening but also authoritative that you can't have it because it's illegal. That's really it." In other words, by stopping theft, the legal system prevents wealth redistribution. But Gramsci offers a way for legal radicals. "The Gramscian analysis would end by saying that what one can know as a radical is that that is all pure nonsense." Radical lawyers can try to help the poor facing exploitation, yes, but beyond that, "there is a function for radical lawyers which goes beyond just helping the direct victims of the system," and that would be "simply to try to systematically demystify legal reasoning as something that somehow can be used as argument for or against doing anything."[47]

The problem is that all this demystification, all this delegitimizing, had a corrosive impact on society. This may have been a feature, not a bug, to the crits, but to those who wanted the preservation of society, it was frightening. Paul M. Bator fled from Harvard in 1987, going to the University of Chicago's Law School, but not before opining that the impact of CLS on Harvard had been "absolutely disastrous."[48] Three years earlier, Paul D. Carrington, the dean of Duke University Law School, warned that if law is seen as nothing more than deception "by which the powerful weaken the resistance of the powerless...enforcement and even obedience may be morally degenerate."[49] Carrington added that "such disbelief threatens competence," because competence depends on having the "needed confidence that law matters.... A lawyer who succumbs to legal nihilism faces a far greater danger.... He must contemplate the dreadful reality of government by cunning and a society in which the only right is might."

But while busying themselves in ravaging the foundation of American society, the crits had overlooked a factor then gaining salience and that, forty years later, has reached fever pitch: the importance of race. In their midst, at their conference and in their faculties, CLS was raising up adherents who were, like themselves, Marxist, anti–private property, and equally pining for society to be undermined, deconstructed, and tossed aside. The only difference was that they weren't white, or male, in many instances, and they thought that their "lived experiences" gave them a legitimacy and a voice that white men like Kennedy lacked. "This movement is attractive to minority scholars, because its central descriptive message—that legal ideals are manipulable and that law serves to legitimate existing maldistributions of wealth and power—rings true for anyone who has experienced life in non-white America," writes Mari Matsuda, a professor at the University of Hawai'i's School of Law. The nonwhite CLS members were attracted by the ideas that "fundamental change is required to attain a just society, and by a utopian conception of a world more communal and less hierarchical than the one we know now," writes Matsuda, of Okinawan ancestry. The problem was that white men could not write in the abstract about the experiences of an oppression that few, if any, of them had ever felt. "The imagination of the academic philosopher cannot recreate the experience of life on the bottom." So, what was the answer? "Instead," wrote Matsuda, "we must look to what Gramsci called 'organic intellectuals,' grass roots philosophers who are uniquely able to relate theory to the concrete experience of oppression."[50]

Black Americans became the organic Gramscian intellectuals of the late twentieth and early twenty-first centuries. In 1989—again, that pivotal year—Matsuda, together with Derrick Bell, Kimberlé Crenshaw, Richard Delgado, Neil Gotanda, Gary Peller, Charles Lawrence, and others, went on to found a separate subgroup of CLS that they called critical *race* theory. It quickly became dominant in the field of civil rights. Kennedy managed to survive and thrive, but other white men had to leave the field. CRT has provided the language and, therefore, the thinking of what we know today as woke, which in fact is far too benign a term for what it truly entails, which is obliteration of anyone who dares to dissent from the new intellectual orthodoxy.

Critical Race Theory

THE CRITS of color had already been meeting on the margins of the CLS annual conferences, and then, from the mid-1980s on, more formally as a caucus. But eventually the differences between the white crits and their nonwhite counterparts grew too difficult to manage. The 1987 paper by Matsuda represented one of the last attempts to bridge the gap. The race crits found a lot of good in CLS, especially the promise that it would "lead to the transformation and ultimate achievement of the utopian vision," wrote Matsuda. But CLS was too woolly, not sufficiently hands-on and results oriented, they thought.

"Within CLS little consensus exists as to what good social organizing looks like, or whether traditional left organizing, as opposed to post-left dis-organizing, is the key to ending oppression," wrote Matsuda. "Exactly what will a just and joyous world look like? We are not told. How will we get there? Again, silence."[51] (We can't at this point but pause and observe the sublime irony of Matsuda grousing about the crits' lack of forthrightness on their proposed alternatives. She couldn't or wouldn't bring herself to write the word "Marxist" or "communist" but instead reached for such euphemisms as "a utopian conception of a world more communal and less hierarchical.") For Crenshaw, the main issue was race: "our dissatisfaction with CLS stemmed from its failure to come to terms with the particularity of race, and with the specifically racial character of 'social interests' in the racialized state," she wrote in the collection of essays that is the foundational text of CRT, 1996's *Critical Race Theory: The Key Writings That Formed the Movement.*[52]

The "key formative event," as the authors of the book call it, was a conference by crits of color held at a convent outside Madison, Wisconsin, in the fateful year of 1989. Crits of black, Japanese, and, in one case, Mexican ancestry, thirty-five in all, gathered for a few days of discussion. They had to name their group something, so Crenshaw, Lawrence, Matsuda, and a few others named the conference "New Developments in Critical Race Theory," and the term stuck.

Years later, at another conference with Matsuda, Crenshaw recalled, "Only she [Matsuda], Neil Gotanda, Chuck Lawrence and maybe a handful of others knew that there were no new developments in critical race theory because CRT didn't have any old ones. It didn't exist! It was made up as a name. Sometimes you have to fake until you make it."[53] Delgado's recollections are also worth noting. He said in an interview years later, "So we gathered at that convent for two and a half days, around a table in an austere room with stained glass windows and crucifixes here and there—an odd place for a bunch of Marxists—and worked out a set of principles."[54]

One of their first tasks was to convince whites, especially white men, to leave the field of legal civil-rights writing and teaching. This was not difficult, as they used the white guilt already harbored by their white colleagues to evict them from the field. Delgado, the son of a Mexican American sharecropper who taught at the University of Alabama Law School—and who was therefore proof of the viability of the American promise—was singularly trenchant about the need for whites to go elsewhere. "The time has come for white liberal authors who write in the field of civil rights to redirect their efforts and to encourage their colleagues to do so as well. There are many other important subjects that could, and should, engage their formidable talents," he wrote.[55] The triumph of CRT over CLS was thus complete and thereby resolved one of the questions that Marcuse and others had left outstanding since the 1960s—to wit, who would lead the revolution, black Americans or white intellectuals.

As to Matsuda's question, "How will we get there?" CRT had a response—it was to be much more openly revolutionizing than its American father, CLS, and its German grandfather, critical theory. CLS introduced the idea that the law schools would serve as "organizing sites for political resistance."[56] But CRT also took organizing to a new level. "Adherents of Critical Race Theory must act in formally organized ways and also informal ways," wrote John O. Calmore. "Our community relations must be broadened and deepened."[57]

CRT wasn't just going to lawyer. It was created to sabotage capitalism, representative democracy, and practically all liberal values. But it aimed to start, as the other critical schools had, with the legal culture. "As I see it, Critical

Race Theory recognizes that revolutionizing a culture begins with the radical assessment of it," wrote Harvard Law's Derrick Bell, the recognized eminence grise of the movement, in 1995.[58] "It is our hope that scholarly resistance will lay the groundwork for wide-scale resistance. We believe that standards and institutions created by and fortifying white power ought to be resisted."

In other words, by revolution, Bell meant a complete societal change, and what it would introduce was an alternative to capitalism, which he despised. "Those in the academy, in cooperation with their judicial and practitioner counterparts, have performed yeoman service in protecting and furthering the capitalist system which has held sway in the nation since its earliest days. Its guiding principle is that free and robust competition will bring deserved rewards to those who, through innovation, perseverance, and hard work prevail in the marketplace; but it will bless all the land with the benefits of efficiency and productivity. Perhaps this theory was once believable, but the record of capitalism is that its efficiency and productivity come at a very high price. Its essence is exploitation, which is based on the ability of some to require many to sell their labor for less than the value of what they produce." Bell then decried those in the academy (there were some pro-capitalist professors in his day, before CRTers went to work) who defended free markets as a "valuable form of social reform, replacing as it did the nation's earlier reliance on human slavery. Historians advise us that even this boast belittles the role of slavery in American history. In actual fact, the nation's earliest wealth was based on slavery. The Revolutionary War, fought with slogans of freedom and equality, was funded by the economic power slavery made possible."[59]

Bell wrote this passage in 1986, fully thirty-three years before the mendacious 1619 Project regurgitated these falsehoods about free markets, and we now can see whence they emanate. And this is the same Derrick Bell whose work the newest member of the US Supreme Court, Ketanji Brown Jackson, constantly praises. Bell's work, Brown said in a 2020 speech at the University of Michigan Law School, is "a pioneering contribution to critical race theory scholarship, and it remains urgent and essential reading on the problem of racism in America." Of Bell's 1993 *Faces at the Bottom of the Well*, Jackson said, "My parents had this book on their coffee table for many years, and I remember staring at the image on the cover when I was growing up."[60]

In *Faces*, Bell quoted one of his favorite "educators," the Brazilian Maoist

Paulo Freire (scare quotes must be used, as the discipline that Frere pioneered, critical pedagogy, and his best-known work, *Pedagogy of the Oppressed*, are not at all about teaching but about how to organize revolution in the classroom). And the quote was a doozy: "Freedom is acquired by conquest, not by gift. It must be pursued constantly and responsibly."[61] And just like Freire, that's how Bell saw his task. Bell used his Harvard classroom and his considerable clout to spread his ideas. And Bell was by no means the only critical race theorist to make clear that replacing capitalism with Marxism by using Gramsci's technique was the right approach for CRT adherents.

Crenshaw, second only to Bell as a foundational architect of CRT, wrote that the struggle for CRT was "to create a new status quo through the ideological and political tools that are available. Gramsci called this struggle a 'War of Position' and he regarded it as the most appropriate strategy for change in Western societies. According to Gramsci, direct challenges to the dominant class accomplish little if ideology plays such a central role in establishing authority that the legitimacy of the dominant regime is not challenged." The capitalist hegemony in modern societies like America "is highly institutionalized and widely internalized," she wrote, quoting Joseph Femia. "Consequently," added Crenshaw, "the challenge in such societies is to create a counter-hegemony by maneuvering within and expanding the dominant ideology to embrace the potential for change."[62]

Duncan Kennedy was ecstatic about its new militantism and revolutionary potential. He had grown weary of the failure of CLS to change society. Roger Severino, the Heritage Foundation vice president who studied under him at Harvard Law, said at one time, "Duncan Kennedy was a defeated Marxist. There was a moment when he thought that they had lost."[63] Then CLS came along and offered a reprieve. Kennedy understood that, from CRT's emergence onward, an ideological Left intent on carrying out the Gramscian and Marcusian strategies had displaced the merely liberal. He wrote in 2002,

Perhaps the biggest change from the 1950s and early 1960s was that the white male working class no longer played a significant role in left thinking. White male left liberals and radicals saw themselves as deserted or betrayed by that class, had lost their faith in it, or had never identified with it. For most left political activists, the straight white male working class was, at worst, the core of the enemy camp and, at best, the necessary object of conversion.... The remaining left intelligentsia was rid of the radicals who had made their lives miserable throughout the 1960s and freed of the worrisome problem of the white male working class. The left liberals were now the left. They could, sometimes, institutionalize themselves and develop all kinds of more or less oppositional or collaborative attitudes toward the mainstream.[64]

TRANSLATION: WITH the terrorists out of the way, and the reactionary white working man also disposed of, the Long March through the Institutions could truly begin.

Conclusion

THE OCCUPATION of the faculties of education, law, and ethnic studies, starting in the 1980s has given the Marxist Left an incredible advantage in its campaign to change minds. It is what has produced today's woke mindset. All of the founders of BLM took some of form of ethnic studies in high school or college; Patrisse Cullors credits her high school social-justice magnet program for initiating her into Marxism and, specifically, the study of Chinese communism. Alicia Garza has a master's degree in ethnic studies from SFSU, while Melina Abdullah teaches pan-African studies at California State's Los Angeles campus. Meanwhile, the concept that the legal system itself is corrupt, that it is merely the handmaiden of white supremacy, leads directly and inexorably to the call by BLM and all the other NextGen Marxist offshoots to abolish the entire legal structure and leave society defenseless. When Cullors says that "abolition is getting rid of police, prisons, jails, surveillance and the current court system as we know it,"[65] she's spouting the creed of Ayers, Duncan, Kennedy, and Bell.

An important pillar of this thinking is the denial of truth, the pretense that what has existed until now has been a hegemonic conceptual apparatus that had to be torn down and replaced with a counternarrative, through a process of consciousness raising—in other words, the application of the ideas first incubated in Western Europe in the 1920s, as we saw in chapter 2. Writing in 1963, at the dawn of the 1960s tumult that propitiated the 1980s takeover, Yale's Willmoore Kendall, one of the foremost conservative philosophers of the twentieth century, said, "For he who would destroy a society must first destroy the public truth it conceives itself as embodying.... Justice, the principles of right and wrong and the law are not artificial and man-made, but rather are discovered by man through the exercise of reason."[66]

Once Marxists could unmoor man, or at least some men and women, from fundamental truth, they could try to turn them into foot soldiers who could be organized, networked, and sprung on society. This is the subject of the next two chapters.

6
ORGANIZING FOR REVOLUTION

OMMUNITY ORGANIZING IS one of the key strategies of NextGen Marxism. As we have seen repeatedly, the biggest dilemma confronting socialists has been that workers wanted reform, not the wholesale destruction of their world. They wanted better conditions, better pay, and better hours, within the context of keeping their jobs, their families, and their countries. It should therefore come as no surprise that the spontaneous revolutions Marx predicted never came about in the West. Workers had revolted, but never in sufficient numbers to overthrow the societies in which they lived. The answer to this dilemma was organizing—creating neighborhood or local organizations that would inflame people's grievances and resentments, first focusing on a specific local issue, then building coalitions and scaling up to gain more and more power until societal change was achieved.

In America, the man who devised the community-organizing strategy that applied to US conditions and circumstances was Saul Alinsky, one of the most significant American socialists of the twentieth century. Alinsky was one of the first Marxists to start organizing on the basis of race and ethnicity, pioneering a campaign to unite Mexican Americans in Los Angeles in the late 1940s. Cesar Chavez, the Mexican American farm union leader, was an Alinsky creation. As we will see, Alinsky was Machiavellian about getting power, openly creating conflict and stoking resentment. He dedicated his groundbreaking 1971 book *Rules for Radicals* to Lucifer, "the first radical known to man who rebelled against the establishment and did it so effectively that he at least won his own kingdom."[1] Alinsky was, in other words, so enthralled with a successful revolt that he forgot that what the devil produced was literally *hell*, as all other such revolutions produce. But leftists who lust after sweeping societal transformation worship Alinsky. A young Hillary Rodham wrote her 1969 thesis for Wellesley on Alinsky, in which she praised what she called the "Alinsky method"— organizing for power based on a "technique of confrontation," "fanning latent hostilities" and "resentments," because "conflict is the route to power," and being unapologetic about pursuing "self-interest."[2] In her thesis, which remained hidden for many years until it emerged online in 2007, the precocious Rodham wrote that "Saul Alinsky is more than a man who has created a particular approach to community organizing, he is the articulate proponent of what many consider to be a dangerous socio-political philosophy."[3] That is modern-day American community organizing.

But Alinsky borrowed much from Lenin. In Russia, by the start of the twentieth century, socialist ideas had been rising in popularity, but not enough to spark a regime-changing revolution. In response, Lenin wrote one of his most important strategic documents in 1902, titled *What Is to Be Done?* Lenin expressed his frustration with the fact that the workers did not have a *revolutionary consciousness.* He recognized early that the worker needed to be *organized.* He saw evidence of unrest among workers regarding their conditions; he even saw outbursts of "desperation and vengeance." But the occasional strikes and other forms of revolt he dismissed merely as the resistance of the oppressed. He wrote, "They marked the awakening antagonisms between workers and employers; but the workers, were not, and could not be, conscious of the irreconcilable antagonism of their interests to the whole of the modern political and social system."[4] It was the belief that the relationship between workers and employers could never be reconciled, and the subsequent desire for all-out revolution, that Lenin sought to instill. Lenin, who died early in 1924 and was focused on the Soviet state he founded, did not quite produce a formula for instilling that antagonism, especially in the West. That task was left to the Western Marxists, and later to Alinsky. One of their innovations, as we have seen, was removing "all-out revolution" as a primary goal. But Lenin's ideological and tactical seed was important.

Lenin proposed that the Party itself serve as the agent of revolutionary change, removing the councils from their pole position and rendering moot the slogan "All power to the soviets." Professional revolutionaries would have to bring a socialist consciousness to the workers. This model—professionals or elites working to change the attitude of their targeted agents of revolutionary change—became the go-to method for revolutionaries throughout the twentieth century and into the twenty-first.

This has reverberated down to our day, from Alinsky to Students for a Democratic Society to ACORN, Eric Mann, and BLM. They all developed techniques for making people unhappy and angry enough to revolt. Lenin did it through what he called agitation: "It is not enough to explain to the workers that they are politically oppressed.... Agitation must be conducted with regard to every concrete example of this oppression."[5] Agitation was needed to show the workers all the ways in which they were oppressed or ill treated, and then to call the workers to revolutionary action.[6] One big difference with Alinsky is that he pursued community organizing with the local community council in mind. He agreed with all of the Party's central tenets, and he believed in centralized decision-making within the council. But his dream was a familiar one to readers by now: that of "citizen participation" in council meetings, if not actual direct, "participatory democracy." Indeed, one of the first organizations he founded was the Back of the Yards Neighborhood Council in 1939, in the meatpacking district of his native Chicago (Alinksy was born on the South Side to Jewish immigrant parents in 1909). Its motto was "We the People will work out our own destiny."[7]

Lenin effectively got rid of the councils after he dissolved the Constituent Assembly in January 1918. The Party would provide organizing, leadership, *and* agitation. "We must 'go among all classes of the population' as theoreticians, as propagandists, as agitators, and as organizers," Lenin said.[8]

With this strategy, Lenin was breaking new ground. He sought, as Professor Arto Artinian wrote, to "redraw the geography of ideological space," and he understood that he would need a complex organizational structure to do so. Artinian wrote,[9]

> *Lenin's view of the party was not simply (and only) one of a centralized hierarchy arranged along military lines. His approach also contained an understanding of the party as a network, which presupposed decentralization and autonomy in its daily functioning.... The Bolshevik Party was a party of a new type, a new form of revolutionary organization: the armed party, or put slightly differently, the party-army.*[10]

LENIN'S DUAL use of organization became a model for American organizers decades later.

In *Rules for Radicals*, Alinsky quotes Trotsky's summary of Lenin's April Thesis, in which the Soviet founder is quoted as saying, "We are in the minority. In these circumstances there can be no talk of violence on our side. We must teach the masses not to trust the compromisers and defensists. 'We must patiently explain!' "[11]

Marxist-Leninist Organizing Comes to the United States

SOCIALISM FACED the same obstacles in the United States that it had in other industrial countries: workers wanted better conditions, more opportunity, and more prosperity, but they wanted those improvements through reform—they did not reject private property and representative democracy but indeed wanted greater access to both. Many had fled Europe for the United States to escape the poverty of their home countries; the last thing most wanted was to destroy the American system. Yes, radical individuals and ideas coming out of Russia tried to change that. Alexandra Kollontai, Nikolai Bukharin, and Leon Trotsky were among the most prominent of the radical Russians who traveled to the United States to advocate for socialist revolution. But they met with limited success.

On January 14, 1917, just ten months before the Bolshevik Revolution in Russia, a handful of socialists gathered in Brooklyn, including Kollontai, Bukharin, and Trotsky, for the purpose of "organizing the radical forces in the American Socialist movement."[12] Trotsky was to lead the coming socialist revolution in the United States. But just one month later, Tzar Nicholas II abdicated, opening the way for the Bolshevik Revolution in Russia. The Russian exiles quickly left the United States and returned to Russia, where, within a matter of months, they found themselves in charge of their country.

With the Russians fully absorbed in their own revolution, American leftists again floundered. The leading American communist of the time, Louis Fraina, believed that socialism would come about in the United States through mass action, what he described as the "instinctive action of the proletariat."[13] This was strikingly similar to Marx's original belief in the spontaneous uprising of the proletariat and their overthrow of the capitalist system. But that had never happened in Europe, and it was looking highly unlikely in the United States. The success of the Bolshevik Revolution in Russia inspired enthusiasm and support from a number of American leftists. However, it did not bring a socialist revolution in America any closer: American socialists remained weak and fractured throughout the 1920s. This was, again, due to an absence of revolutionary consciousness among the workers.

The Declaration of the Comintern's Sixth Congress, held in Moscow in 1928, three years into Stalin's rule, expressed deep frustration with the world's working class, which it described as "incapable of adopting sustained and scientifical-ly planned strategy and tactics or of carrying on the struggle in an organized manner on the basis of the stern discipline that is characteristic of the proletar-iat."[14] The declaration described how that stern discipline would be achieved. It begins with the Communist Party itself: "a revolutionary organization, bound by an iron discipline and strict revolutionary rules of democratic centralism."[15] This was Lenin's strategy, but now enforced by Stalin's all-controlling discipline. "The Communist Party must extend its influence over the masses of the urban and rural poor, over the lower strata of the intelligentsia, and over the so-called 'small man,' i.e., the petty-bourgeois strata generally. It is particularly important that work be carried on for the purpose of extending the Party's influence over the peasantry."[16]

From Communism to Community Organizing

THIS STRATEGY was later to be distilled in America, through Alinsky, Mann, and the others. But we must be clear here that the Lenin–Alinsky strategy of community organizing should not be confused with the type of civic commu-nity outreach that has long existed here.[17] Starting as early as the mid-1800s community organizing served as a bridge between charities and recipients to address social problems. Indeed, from their foundings, American com-munities have worked together to address social problems. The vibrancy of American self-government is itself grounded in civil society, not on exploiting resentments to organize for power. As Tocqueville observed during his travels through the United States in 1831–32,

> Americans of all ages, conditions and all dispositions constantly unite to-gether.... To hold fetes, found seminaries, build inns, construct churches, distribute books, dispatch missionaries to the antipodes. They establish hos-pitals, prisons, schools by the same method. Finally, if they wish to highlight a truth or develop an opinion by the encouragement of a great example, they form an association.

THIS DESCRIPTION of civil society depicts Americans who freely come together for a shared purpose. They might hold very different religious or even political beliefs, but they are able to cooperate for a common end.

But that was not at all that we know as "organizing" today. The Communist organizational model is diametrically opposed to American civil society. The Communists' layers of organization were there both to control and also to indoctrinate members into revolutionary thinking and thus bring about radical social change. They used whatever local grievances would capture a person's attention and bring him into the Communist orbit. It was deceitful, manipulative, and exploitive, and those characteristics have only become more deeply entrenched as "community organizing" has become the predominant strategy for NextGen Marxists.

A 1952 study for the RAND Corporation on Bolshevik strategy and tactics underscores the sharp difference between American voluntary organizations and Leninist revolutionary organizing. The study describes voluntary associations in the United States as

> skeletal in the sense that they are manned by a small core of individuals—the administration, the local subleaders, a few faithful meeting-goers—around whom there fluctuates a loosely bound mass of dues-payers. This type of membership has, on the whole, only a very limited relation to the organization; its agreement with it may be of the vaguest sort; it may give little or no time to the organization nor be guided by its pronouncements save, as in unions and professional groups, on very narrow issues; in short, the power implications of membership are minimal.[18]

THE MARXIST–LENINIST revolutionaries who exercised control from Russia and those Americans who embraced that program introduced a set of tools to the United States that ran directly counter to the American ethos of a self-governing nation of individuals living in ordered liberty. The tools they brought were grounded in Marxism's zero-sum view of the world, in its view of irreparable divisions and antagonisms, in the idea advocated by Rousseau that one manages dissenters by killing them off. The tools they used were honed by Lenin and Stalin, who believed in iron-fisted control from on high, that the ends justify any means, and that there is no place for anyone in a dictatorship of the proletariat except for the proletariat, with the vanguard of the Party in control.

Yet, in the end, Soviet communism eventually lost whatever grip it had on America's radical leftists. Despite the impressive organizational structure it had established in the United States, it never had more than one hundred thousand members. Once Kruschev denounced Stalin at the twentieth Congress of the

Soviet Union in 1956, Soviet Communism's hold over America's radical Left was all but over. That enthrallment had been slowly dying for years, and with that key turning point in April 1956, it was largely finished. But the lessons learned over the previous four decades around organizing and indoctrinating had by then been deeply instilled in the culture of the Left. They may have abandoned Soviet communism, but they held on to much of Marx and Lenin. Lenin's strategy for an organization of revolutionaries to instill a socialist or revolutionary mind-set and thereby accrue power was deployed repeatedly in the decades ahead, by Alinsky, Tom Hayden and Students for a Democratic Society (SDS), the Midwest Academy, Mann's Labor Community Strategy Center, and BLM.

Sowing Seeds of Revolution: Saul Alinsky

IT WAS the Communist Party USA that first built out the Marxist–Leninist organizational strategy in the United States, but it was Alinsky who translated it into a uniquely American idiom starting in the late 1930s. So effectively did he do so that his 1972 book *Rules for Radicals* remains one of the definitive playbooks, and he was a singular influence not just on Hillary Rodham Clinton but also on other prominent leftists, such as Barack Obama. Alinsky always pointed out that he was never a member of the Communist Party, but he admitted to working closely with them and learning from them.[19] Just before his death in 1972, Alinsky told *Playboy* in an interview, regarding his decades of organizing, "Anybody who tells you he was active in progressive causes in those days and never worked with the Reds is a goddamn liar."[20]

As Stanley Kurtz writes,

> *Alinsky … worked closely for years with Chicago's Communist Party and did everything in his power to advance its program. Most of his innovations were patterned on Communist Party organizing tactics…. Alinsky supported the central Marxist tenet of public ownership of the means of production. Unlike the New Left, however, Alinsky had no expectation of reaching that end through swift or violent revolution. He meant to approach the ultimate goal slowly, piecemeal, perhaps over generations, through patient organizing efforts at the local level.*[21]

LIKE ALL radicals who claim to want justice or equality for *all* people, Alinsky in fact was unrepentant about seeking power for an elite few. Starting with his first book, *Reveille for Radicals*, published in 1946, and thereafter, he divides the world along Marxist lines: the oppressed from the oppressors. He seeks power for the marginalized, but not so that they can improve their lot in society. "A radical is one who advocates sweeping changes in the existing laws and methods of government. These proposed changes are aimed at the roots of political problems which in Marxian terms are the attitudes and the behaviors of men. *Radicals are not interested in ameliorating the symptoms of decay*," Rodham writes in her thesis.[22] It was not truly justice Alinsky was after but power, and he understood that only the slow, steady work of organizing would get him the power he desired.

In the introduction to his second book, Alinsky wrote, "*The Prince* was written by Machiavelli for the Haves on how to hold power. *Rules for Radicals* is written for the Have-Nots on how to take it away. In this book we are concerned with how to create mass organizations to seize power and give it to the people."[23] Except, of course, that this "people power" always ends up in centralized power because, as Lenin discovered in 1918, large questions of state cannot be decided by neighborhood councils.

Alinsky himself was not allergic to centralized power. His "organization of organizations" model was to identify the organizations that already existed in a neighborhood and create a supreme body that brought together their leaders. "First, the neighborhood contained within it a number of vital organizations, even though they were not 'organized' to act as a unit," writes John Kretzman. "Four basic kinds of associations were particularly important: churches, ethnic groups, political organizations, and labor unions. The organizer's task was to forge a coalition of leaders from these groups. Their constituencies would then follow as the 'organization of organizations' model took shape. Because of this existing pattern of associations, organizers could concentrate on pulling together their leaders, a very small percentage of the neighborhood's residents, and could plausibly claim representative community status for their new neighborhood group."[24]

In fact, for Alinsky, and for those schooled by Alinsky, organizing is about constantly scaling up the power that has been attained until control is achieved over the whole system, nation, country, and globe. Organizers thus may start first by getting residents, public park users, public transportation riders, or members of a "victimized" category to focus on a specific problem of which they were not aware, by getting them to feel aggrieved (in Gramscian language, dropping their false consciousness) and then convincing them to sign a petition, attend a meeting, or join a protest, sit-in, or rally.

Once the initial goal has been met—say, the organizers have pressured local government officials to agree to switch procurement decisions from corporate chain stores to local mom-and-pops, especially minority-owned ones, or to fund some local project—then the organizers move on to a larger issue. "Remember," wrote Alinsky, "once you organize people around something as commonly agreed upon as pollution, then an organized people is on the move. From there it's a short and natural step to political pollution, to Pentagon pollution."[25]

Mann, of whom we will speak more below, put it in this fashion when speaking at a workshop in 2010:

> When I'm knocking door to door in Newark, it may be that the first conversation I have with the woman is that the apartment is so cold, that the heat has been turned off. I don't say, "can we discuss freeing Cuba," you know? I say, "it's cold in here. How are we going to get this damn heat on? Are we going to develop a campaign for the landlords to turn on the heat?" but, in the process of getting to know her, hanging around in her home, getting to know her kids, something comes up on the TV, I'll comment on it.... if you're not going to get people better bus service, if you're not going to get people better housing, then you're going to have a problem.[26]

TO BE clear, the purpose of organizing for Alinsky, as for Mann, was gaining power. "In short, life without power is death; a world without power would be a ghostly wasteland, a dead planet!" Alinsky wrote.[27] To gain power, he was willing to work within the system. Alinsky wrote that his answer to a young radical who accused him of working within the system was that there were only three options: "Do one of three things. One, go find a wailing wall and feel sorry for yourselves. Two, go psycho and start bombing—but this will only swing people to the right. Three, learn a lesson. Go home, organize, build power and at the next convention, you be the delegates."[28]

But Alinsky was working within the American system only to destroy the system from within. "We will start with the system because there is no other place to start from except political lunacy. It is most important for those of us who want revolutionary change to understand that revolution must be preceded by reformation," he wrote.

To assume that a political revolution can survive without the supporting base of a popular reformation is to ask for the impossible in politics. Men don't like to step abruptly out of the security of familiar experience; they need a bridge to cross from their own experience to a new way. A revolutionary organizer must shake up the prevailing patterns of their lives—agitate, create disenchantment and discontent with the current values, to produce, if not a passion for change, at least a passive, affirmative, non-challenging climate.[29]

THE POOR, he understood, did not want revolution, so the organizer should not start his work by promising one.

Sanford D. Horwitt described a 1964 meeting between Alinsky and the SDS leaders Todd Gitlin, Hayden, and Lee Webb during which Alinsky scolded the young radicals, who itched to enter his field of organizing. Alinsky, recalled Horwitt, was adamant that "effective organizing had to begin with 'the world as it is'—and in the here and now, he told the young radicals sarcastically, what the poor want is a share of the so-called decadent, bourgeois, middle-class life that the SDS kids were so eager to reject."[30] The participatory democracy of SDS was "something akin to the old town-meeting democracy, where everybody speaks his piece, consensus is the goal, and leadership and hierarchy are resisted, while Alinsky's 'organization of organizations' approach put a premium on strong leadership, structure, and centralized decision-making," wrote Horwitt.[31]

Alinksy's scorched-earth approach was also a precursor to the cancel culture of today. He famously says, in *Rules for Radicals,* "Pick the target, freeze it, personalize it, and polarize it."[32] This approach, along with Marcuse's famous 1969 essay "Repressive Tolerance," paved the way for cancel culture: destroying those who do not share your worldview. Alinsky had a zero-sum view of the world, one irreconcilably divided between those who have power and those who do not. His use of organizing to build a power base and his use of agitation to stoke a sense of grievance are inspired by Lenin's playbook. That Alinsky did not embrace the sobriquet of Communist or Marxist or Leninist, or ever join the Party, can be described as deliberately deceptive window dressing. Perhaps better seen as a transitional figure between the Old Left and the New, like Zinn, Alinsky has earned his reputation as the "father of community organizing."

Sowing Seeds of Revolution in the Ghettoes: Students for a Democratic Society

AS WE saw in the meeting between Alinsky, Hayden, Webb, and Gitlin, SDS also tried to break into Alinsky's community organizing. We can gather from Alinsky's caustic remarks that he did not think much of what the callow youth called organizing, but it does bear some resemblance to what BLM has tried in our new century.

SDS, the premier organization of the New Left, was the end product of a long line of socialist organizations, shaped by earlier socialist writers and intellectuals. Jack London and Upton Sinclair were among those who first founded the Intercollegiate Socialist Society (ISS) in 1905, whose aim was to promote "an intelligent interest in Socialism among college men and women, graduate and undergraduate, through the formation of study clubs in the colleges and universities."[33] By 1917, ISS had chapters on more than seventy campuses across the country. But tensions over opposition to World War I divided the organization, and by 1921, it had to regroup under the name League for Industrial Democracy (LID). Its stated aim was "a new social order based on production for use and not for profit"—a discrete way of saying socialism.[34] In this iteration, the organization was focused more on socialist politics than on educating on college campuses. It concentrated much of its early efforts on the trade unions in the belief that it might yet be the workers who would bring about the revolution. But as that failed to materialize, in the 1930s, it turned its attention back to college students. Its student wing, the Student League for Industrial Democracy (SLID), was formed in 1934. It was not long-lived, but it had a long-term impact through some its members, a number of whom went on to play major leadership roles. As the group accurately described themselves, "the history of the Student League for Industrial Democracy is the record of the apprenticeship of the prophets and makers of socialism in the United States."[35]

One of its most notable members was Walter Reuther, who perhaps did more than any other single person to develop and implement progressive policies and programs in the United States. He had helped found a chapter of the SLID while a student at Wayne State University. At the time, Reuther was a member of the Socialist Party and had campaigned for the Socialist Party's candidate for president.[36] Eventually, Reuther disavowed both socialism and communism, but for the rest of his life, he advocated enthusiastically and effectively for social democratic policies.

Another member of the short-lived SLID who had long-lasting impact was Aryeh Neier. Neier was born to Polish Jewish parents in Berlin before he and his family moved to the United States. As a student at Cornell University in the 1950s, Neier joined SLID and hosted speakers such as John Gates, who had argued that it was time to establish an American communist party free from Soviet domination and who served as editor of the communist newspaper *Daily Worker*.[37] Neier ended up becoming president of SLID, and then, just a year out of college and only twenty-one years old, he became executive director of SLID's parent organization, the League for Industrial Democracy. From this position, he decided to revitalize the student division of the organization, SLID, and so in 1959, he renamed it Students for a Democratic Society.[38] In 1993, Neier became president of George Soros's Open Society Institute, where he helped to expand Soros's network of activist philanthropies and in that way directly impacted today's world of NextGen Marxists.

This is a brief overview of the organizational history of SDS, but what about the intellectual history that gave rise to SDS? The 1950s were a time of general peace and prosperity for the United States. What was behind the discontent among college students that made them ripe for organizing and then erupt into the violence of the 1960s? Many from the older generations who had been seduced by the false promises of socialism for a fairer and more equitable world had been sowing the seeds of discontent for years. Writers were a particularly potent force in tarnishing the image of the American middle class and the dream of a peaceful and prosperous life. Americans, and American students in particular, had been fed a steady stream of content critical of American power and prosperity, written mostly by socialists or inspired by socialist ideas—Jack London's *The Call of the Wild* (1903), Upton Sinclair's *The Jungle* (1905), Sinclair Lewis's *Babbitt* (1922), John Steinbeck's *The Grapes of Wrath* (1939), Arthur Miller's *Death of a Salesman* (1949) and *The Crucible* (1953), J. D. Salinger's *The Catcher in the Rye* (1951), Allen Ginsberg's *Howl* (1956), Jack Kerouac's *On the Road* (1957), and John Kenneth Galbraith's *The Affluent Society* (1958), to name just a few.[39]

These books, among many others, entered the mainstream and helped to shape an image of America's middle class as pathetically conformist, pawns of their own consumerism, superficial, spiritually dead, and unhappy—even though opinion polls and surveys indicated that Americans were by and large happy in the 1950s. The writer and satirist H. L. Mencken described them as the "booboisie."[40] These books also demonstrated how much easier it is to bring about change by influencing the culture than by trying to organize a violent revolution of workers—and it was not only books but all forms of culture. Gitlin wrote,

> The future New Left read David Riesman and C. Wright Mills and Albert Camus, and found in them warrants for estrangement, but nothing influenced me, or the baby-boom generation as a whole, as much as movies, music and comics did. On the big screen, on posters, and in popular magazines, America was mass-producing images of white youth on the move yet with nowhere to go. What moved the new sullen heroes was the famous rebellion without a cause.[41]

SDS STARTED looking for ways to bring about their vision. They were inspired by the activities of SNCC, which we described in chapter 3. In 1961, Hayden spent time in McComb, Mississippi, with the SNCC activist Bob Moses on their first voter registration project. The next summer, Hayden wrote the Port Huron Statement, and then in summer 1963, at a meeting of the National Student Association, the radical black leader Stokely Carmichael encouraged SDS to engage directly in communities.[42] According to Gitlin, who was then the president of SDS, in August 1963, "Stokely Carmichael of SNCC met with Tom Hayden and proposed that SDS organize poor whites to ally with SNCC's poor blacks in a class-based alliance—and SDS agreed to try."[43] So while around three hundred students from the north went south to Mississippi to help with SNCC's voter-registration efforts there, SDS sent more than a hundred students into the poor neighborhoods of major cities, including Newark, Philadelphia, Chicago, and Cleveland, under the auspices of what they called the Economic Research and Action Project (ERAP).[44] We encountered some of this activity in chapter 4.

The idea was to organize the urban poor into a coalition in support of civil rights. In summer 1963, members of SDS went into major American cities under the auspices of ERAP. But their tactics grew more and more extreme, with the ultimate aim of sparking violence. Hayden and his fellow SDS volunteers in Newark worked to "organize the ghetto" by—once again—elevating grievances.

They organized demonstrations, they picketed stores for allegedly mistreat-ing black shoppers, they staged a sit-in at the mayor's office to protest the slumlords.[45] The SDS spent three years exacerbating discontent, heightening already-existing tensions between black and white residents and demonizing police and local officials.[46] Hayden and others met with representatives of the pro-Castro Movement for Independence. They collaborated with representa-tives of North Vietnam—America's avowed enemies—and promised to bring the war home, which is exactly what Hayden did in Newark.[47] The SDS national secretary Gregory Calvert told a *New York Times* reporter, "We are working to build a guerilla force in an urban environment. We are actively organizing se-dition."[48] Hayden brought in Hassan Jeru Ahmen, a militant activist with a long criminal record, to form a battalion of "Black Beret" mercenaries in Newark.[49] They flooded Newark with anti-police propaganda and instructions for making Molotov cocktails, which included the directive "Light rag and throw at some white person or white person's property."[50]

On July 12, 1967, Hayden and his team achieved the desired result: Newark erupted in violence. By the time it was over, riots had spread to forty-three cities in the United States. The month after the riots had finally ended and the buildings had stopped smoldering, *The New York Times Review of Books* pub-lished an article by Hayden, in which he wrote,

> *The role of organized violence is now being carefully considered. During a riot, for instance, a conscious guerilla can participate in pulling police away from the path of people engaged in attacking stores. He can create disorder in new areas the police think are secure. He can carry the torch, if not all the people, to white neighborhoods and downtown business districts. If neces-sary, he can successfully shoot to kill.*[51]

THIS WAS Lenin's "armed party" at work. This was a group of students, mem-bers of the SDS as well as others, serving as agents of revolutionary change. This was disgruntled white kids going into a troubled urban area "as theoreticians, as propagandists, as agitators, and as organizers," to use Lenin's formulation. By exacerbating every grievance, and adding some guerrilla warfare training, they were able to spark a short-lived revolution. The sad part is that what SDS accomplished in Newark and other American cities was far more destructive to the populations they were ostensibly trying to serve. Their so-called revolution did not bring about the promised utopia but devastation. Robert Margo, a professor of economics at Boston University, and William Collins, of Vanderbilt University, concluded, "The riots were unambiguously negative. They reduced incomes of African Americans' employment, and they reduced housing values. In the case of housing values, it was broader; it actually affects overall housing values in cities, but the impact is primarily felt by African Americans."[52]

Unfortunately, the destructive impact of SDS's "community organizing" was whitewashed, and the lesson was lost. In spite of the fact that numerous investigations and court cases found similar patterns of deliberate instigation in riots across the United States—in Rochester, Cincinnati, Baltimore, San Jose, Toledo, Philadelphia, Watts, Detroit, and Chicago—the National Advisory Commission on Civil Disorders, appointed by President Johnson, concluded in what is known as the Kerner Report that racism was the primary cause of the riots. Although the members of the commission were not unanimous in their conclusions, it was the ideologues who won out. The Kerner Report described the riots "not as signs of oppressive poverty and social breakdown but as righteous political protests against racist institutions, in particular the police. The events in Watts, Detroit, and elsewhere were not riots … they were rebellions; instead of seeking to quell the outrage in the nation's inner cities, responsible government officials needed to awaken to the racism so deeply and systematically embedded in American life, and then attack it head-on."[53] Sound familiar?

This has become the dominant narrative today. It was a flawed conclusion, and yet it set the tone for what has become the front line in today's culture war. How did that happen? There was ample evidence to show that these elite, disgruntled white kids had exploited members of the poor, urban ghettoes to fuel their revolutionary dreams, at great cost to those inhabitants—and at no cost to the white kids. Hayden never spent a day in jail either for what he did in Newark or for starting the riots in Chicago to disrupt the Democratic National Convention, nor even for conspiring with America's enemies. Indeed, he became an American hero: he married Jane Fonda, moved to Santa Monica, California, and served in the California state assembly for eighteen years. The lesson of Hayden's life—in no small part because of the whitewashing of the Kerner Commission—is that Leninist organizing pays off.

Sowing Seeds of Revolution by Stealth: The Midwest Academy

BY 1969, SDS had divided over how to move forward. Some were frustrated with what they saw as the slow pace of progress in ending the Vietnam War and racial discrimination. But what they really wanted was to destroy the American free-market system and install socialism. One faction of the SDS chose Alinsky's second option of the three he gave: "go psycho and start bombing." They had worked successfully to incite violence, then they went fully militant. Ayers and Dohrn's Weather Underground had only approximately three hundred supporters, and probably far fewer who actually went underground and pursued their war against the United States.[54] That left nearly one hundred thousand other students who had been part of SDS who now had nowhere to go.

Some, as we discuss elsewhere, went to law school to pursue change through the legal system. Their efforts gave rise to critical legal studies, which in turn led to critical race theory. Another group believed that they could more successfully bring about socialism through stealth—using Alinsky's tools of community organizing to build a power base while keeping their radical agenda quiet. This was a faction shaped not just by Fidel Castro and the North Vietnamese but also by Michael Harrington, the influential socialist whose 1962 book *The Other America* did so much to ignite the War on Poverty. Harrington eventually formed the Democratic Socialists of America (DSA), where he developed a strategy of community organizing to bring about socialism in a gradual way. He did not believe that a radical socialist party could succeed; rather, he believed in building coalitions made up of civil-rights activists, intellectuals, workers and labor leaders, and others. Other members of the DSA also contributed to this strategy, including Frances Fox Piven, Barbara Ehrenreich, and Peter Dreier. Dreier promoted the idea of "transitional reforms" developed by the French Marxist André Gorz: "Create government programs that only seem to be 'reforms' of the capitalist system. Rightly understood, these supposed reforms are so incompatible with capitalism that they gradually precipitate the system's collapse."[55] In short, the idea was to expand entitlement programs and government spending to such a degree that the system eventually collapses. Dreier, it should be noted, served as an adviser for Obama's 2008 presidential campaign.

Alinsky ended up playing an important role in the stealth socialism movement. Kurtz points to a key moment on Labor Day 1969 when several former leaders of the SDS, including Paul and Heather Booth and Steve Max, gathered with Harry Boyte, a former senior adviser to Martin Luther King Jr. and a community organizer. The group published a pamphlet titled *Socialism and the Coming Decade*, in which they argued that because the United States was in a "non-revolutionary period," an organization of socialists should "found and guide community organizations among the working class."[56] This group around the Booths turned to Alinsky for training and tactics. Following their training with Alinsky, Heather Booth formed the Midwest Academy. Now fifty years old, the Midwest Institute's basic mission hasn't changed: "our training method is designed to give organizers the tools to turn their passion into actions that build power and result in progressive change."[57] And in the course of its fifty years, it has spawned many other organizations fighting for revolutionary change. More importantly, it helped shape the presidency of Barack Obama, who himself started his political career as a community organizer.

The bottom line is that this strand of *stealth socialism*—using community organizing tactics, keeping radical goals under wraps, and promoting transitional reforms as a pathway to wholesale systemic change—has been far more effective in the long run in moving the United States away from its free-market orientation and in radicalizing significant numbers of the population, even though it has received far less of the limelight than the militant wing of the SDS. Many organizations across the country have grown out of the network, not least of which has been BLM.

Sowing Seeds of Revolution among the Bus Riders: Eric Mann's Labor Community Strategy Center

MANN WAS among those who had started their radical careers embracing the violence of SDS: as an SDS volunteer, he had helped stoke violence in Newark, served two years in prison for firing a gun into the windows of the Cambridge Police Department, and then served as a leader of the Weather Underground. But when all of those strategies ultimately failed, he, too, embraced community organizing to bring about a radical new world. He helped popularize the term *transformative organizing*, which he defines as follows: "left-wing organizing as characterized by militant opposition to racism, war, and the abuses of Empire, strategized by people who self-identify as revolutionary, radical, liberal, and progressive."[58] He explicitly distinguished his transformative organizing from Alinsky's "pragmatic/realistic" approach, which he dismissed as nonideological and therefore too moderate in its goals.[59] Mann's goal, he says, is "to transform the power structures and policies of racism, patriarchy, and capitalism."[60] In short, he wants power, and he wants revolution, and whereas he once used violence as a means to achieve those ends, he now uses community organizing.

In 1975, Mann joined the Chicano Marxist–Leninist group August 29th, which in 1978 coalesced with the People's Republic of China paramilitary US front group I Wor Kuen and the Black Revolutionary Communist League to form the League of Revolutionary Struggle. The league's manifesto states, "Our unity signals a big advance in this struggle for Marxist–Leninist unity and for a single, unified, vanguard communist party."[61] Mann and his wife, Lian Hurst, left the league in 1984, and four years later, they founded the Labor Community Strategy Center in Los Angeles.

The center's purpose, Mann explained, is "to build an anti-racist, anti-imperialist, anti-fascist united front."[62] He refers to his creation as the "Harvard of Revolutionary graduate schools" or, in more inspired moments, "the University of Caracas Revolutionary Graduate School." Mann teaches organizing, while Hurst instructs the trainees on Marxist–Leninist–Maoist ideology. "People think they can join an organization, and go out, and change the most dictatorial country in the world by just showing up. We don't think so. Organizing is a skill, is a vocation," Mann said.[63]

One of the center's first activities was to create the Los Angeles Bus Riders Union (BRU). Why bus riders? Mann gives two main reasons. The first is that he identified the bus-riding population as more easily organizable than factory workers. "At a time when many workplaces have 25 to 50 employees, an overcrowded bus has 43 people sitting and from 25 to 43 people standing," he wrote in a 1996 essay.[64] "Ten organizers on ten different buses can reach 1,000 or more people in a single afternoon."

The second reason was more potent: whereas workers tend to be majority white, the bus riders are largely made up of minorities. "On most inner-city buslines the passengers are 100% people of color—black, Latino, and Asian," he wrote in the essay. The revolution would be led by the people of other races, as Marcuse had foreseen, and thus organizers had to recruit there. "Given the social formation of the US as a settler state based on virulent white supremacy, the racialization of all aspects of political life operates as a material force in itself," he wrote. "Thus, any effective Left movement must confront the major fault lines of the society…. In a racist, imperialist society, the only viable strategy for the left is to build a movement against racism and imperialism."

In addition to organizing bus riders, Mann's Labor Community Center was hard at work creating a new generation of radical operatives. One of its more notable recruits ("recruited" is the word Mann uses in his book *Playbook for Progressives*, the title of which is a clear take on Alinsky's *Rules for Radicals*)[65] was Patrice Cullors, one of the cofounders of BLM.

Sowing Seeds of Revolution in Ferguson: Black Lives Matter

THREE YEARS before Cullors made a national and global name for herself by founding BLM, Mann had already identified her as a gifted student in the art of organizing. Cullors was first recruited at the age of seventeen, when activists from Mann's Labor Community Center had gone to her high school to give a presentation. A 2006 case study followed Cullors and three or four other BRU trainees as they worked to convince students to demand that the Los Angeles Metropolitan Transportation Authority halve the cost of student passes, from twenty dollars a month to ten, and eliminate the application process altogether, which the center contended discouraged students' families from taking advantage of the pass. Overcrowding was also a problem that the organizing trainees identified as a potential rallying cry, as it forced the students to be late because full buses didn't stop for them. Cullors is quoted as saying, "We've heard stories of police waiting for students to get off the buses to give them truancy tickets," striking a strong anti-police tone that became the dominant narrative of BLM.[66]

At the same time that the center trained Cullors on organizing tactics, it gave Cullors a solid ideological grounding in radical, Marxist thinking. She took a six-month, intensive training program while she studied in a class taught by Hurst about the "problems of imperialism, women's studies, strategies and tactics."[67] In her memoir, *When They Call You a Terrorist*—the foreword to which was written by Angela Davis—Cullors wrote that at the center, "I read, I study, adding Mao, Marx, and Lenin to my knowledge of [bell] hooks, [Audre] Lorde and [Rebecca] Walker."[68] By the time Mann wrote his book, Cullors had been training at the center for a full decade, had helped found the center's Summer

Youth Organizing Academy "to recruit and train a new generation of high school youth," and was herself teaching "classes on political theory and organizing."[69]

Cullors wrote in her memoir that she "found a home at the Strategy Center, a place that will raise me and hold me for more than a decade." Mann, she wrote, took her "under his wing. Eric is older and wiser, and fearlessly anti-racist." But Mann always made clear that his ultimate aim was to form revolutionaries who would take down the entire system. Mann's strategy was to recruit BRU members for specific bus-related concerns but then to scale up quickly. He instructed his trainers to "go beyond narrow 'trade union' or 'bus' consciousness to build a movement based on a more transformative, internationalist consciousness" and create a "united front against US imperialism—rooted in the strategic alliance of the multi-racial, multi-national working class."[70]

Cullors delivered on that, along with the BLM cofounders Alicia Garza and Opal Tometi. Concretely, how did they do that? By organizing. Cullors scaled up from the Strategy Center, using it as a platform to position herself at the center of an intricate, self-reinforcing web of revolutionary groups. Some she had founded herself, such as Dignity and Power Now, an anti-prison organization she brought to life in 2012,[71] and others she had come alongside. This intricate web proved invaluable. Following the acquittal of neighborhood watchman George Zimmerman in 2013 for the killing of Trayvon Martin, Cullors and Garza saw an opportunity and founded BLM with Tometi.

All three women had been trained up in the ideology and tactics of Marxist organizing, with the end goal of revolutionary change—or what is now more discretely referred to as "systemic change." But to be clear, systemic change means to change the entire system—from free-market republicanism to centrally controlled socialism. While Cullors had trained at Mann's Labor Community Center, Alicia Garza had also been trained in community organizing at the Oakland, California–based School of Unity and Liberation (SOUL), which was described in one profile this way:

> Year-round, SOUL goes on the road to high schools, colleges, and community organizations with a series of educational programs that deconstruct the world system of capitalism in accord with a Political Education Workshop Manual that lays out detailed lesson plans on topics ranging from racism to homophobia to "why the rich get richer."[72]

THE SOUL website describes its work this way: "we are laying the groundwork for a strong social movement by developing a new generation of organizers with the skills and analysis necessary to build collective power and win systemic change."[73]

As important for the creation and growth of BLM was how a large web of Marxist groups helped to make BLM a national and global phenomenon the following year, in Ferguson, Missouri.

The Ferguson experience was thus the next iteration of community organizing; it was the Big Political Scale-Up in motion. Garza, then still little known to the public, told the publication *In These Times* that while the Ferguson riots were taking place, "organizations here were grappling with how to show up in a moment where most people are in motion—for the most part, spontaneous motion—and it doesn't look like our regular organizing work." Garza added that her work in Ferguson was to "make sure the organizations and activists on the ground had the capacity to really hold this moment and extend it into a movement."[74]

Ferguson was transforming the art of organizing. "We have to move out of our myopic understanding of local organizing and build a national and international movement that prioritizes all black life," Cullors and the activist Darnell Moore wrote in Britain's *Guardian* newspaper in September 2014. "We have a moment, inspired by those working on the ground in Ferguson, to transform black people's relationship to this country. The time is now."[75] In 2016, in an essay tellingly titled "We Didn't Start a Movement. We Started a Network," Cullors remembered,

> When it was time for us to leave, inspired by our friends in Ferguson, organizers from 18 different cities went back home and developed Black Lives Matter (BLM) chapters in their communities and towns—broadening the political will and movement building reach catalyzed by the #BlackLivesMatter project and the work on the ground in Ferguson. It became clear that there was a need to continue organizing and building Black power across the country. People were hungry to galvanize their communities to end state-sanctioned violence against Black people, the way Ferguson organizers and allies were doing. Soon after, Opal, Alicia, Darnell and I helped create the BLM network infrastructure. It is adaptive and decentralized with a set of guiding principles.[76]

THE UNIVERSITY of Illinois black-studies professor Barbara Ransby, one of the movement's historians, wrote, "The Ferguson uprising was a defining moment for the early twenty-first-century Black Freedom struggle." Ransby, who has had a long association with the Freedom Road Socialist Organization, continued, "Protestors defied state power and exposed what many outside the Black community would rather ignore—the violent underbelly of racial capitalism and systemic racism.... In the summer and fall of 2014, Ferguson became the epicenter of not only Black resistance but resistance to the neoliberal state and its violent tactics of suppression and control. It was evident that, while Brown's killing was the catalyst, the Black working class of Ferguson was angry about much more, and their anger resonated and reverberated around the country and beyond."[77]

The activists saw in this new iteration of organizing an opportunity to change the culture of the United States. Culture does not come in the DNA; it must be transmitted. As the historian Christopher Dawson said, culture is "an accumulated capital of knowledge and a community of folkways into which the individual has to be initiated."[78] One of the main goals of NextGen Marxists is to interfere in that transmission. It was therefore no coincidence that it was the National Domestic Workers Alliance (NDWA) that paid its "special projects" director Garza to go to Ferguson and stay there, networking after Brown's killing, and we will see in chapter 8 how the NDWA was formed at the behest of socialist leaders overseas. The George Soros–funded NDWA hired Garza right after she graduated from Harmony Goldberg's SOUL, another of the Marxist-organizing preparatories that groom would-be activists across this country. Garza was in Ferguson also as a member of LeftRoots, an important connector of left-wing activists that seeks to build what it calls "21st century socialism" with a type of central planning that it calls "democratically-planned production."[79]

Little wonder, then, that NDWA does not hide the fact that "for NDWA, a strategy focused on changing the beliefs and mental models that help people make meaning of the world is a goal in and of itself," as it said in a case study on how it uses Hollywood movies to change the culture.[80] NDWA is equally open about preying on people's emotions and playing loose with reality to effect the change it seeks: "NDWA's culture change strategy is built on the recognition that there are two types of truths, and both of them matter: what's factually true, and what's emotionally true." NDWA is therefore firmly committed to interfering with the transmission of the American creed and culture. It is also very clear about the power that it seeks: "NDWA seeks to build power on three intersecting fronts: 1. Political power—the ability to change policy, and to elect and remove policymakers. 2. Economic power—raising wages for workers and improving labor markets, as well as partnering with the private sector to create good jobs in the care industry, and to hold companies that are creating jobs accountable. 3. Narrative power—the ability to change the rules and norms that our society lives by."

For the NDWA, Ferguson was ground zero for organizing for power.

Conclusion

"IF ONE word could adequately sum up all that the Leninists have learned about the technology of mass manipulation in the 20th century, that word would be *organization*," concluded Eugene Methvin in his study of the 1960s riots and unrest in the United States.[81] Soviet communism itself had lost its grip on the American Left, but knowledge of its tools and its zero-sum view of the world were firmly planted among America's radicals. Once Marxism–Leninism died out, once Stalin was denounced, what remained behind was a vision of the world in which everyone thinks the same; where one can silence the voice of those who think differently, or do away with them altogether; a world in which one's discontent and bitterness will be washed away with the realization of the utopian dream. Even after Soviet communism proved its cruelty and bankruptcy, what remained behind were the tools it had once so effectively used: the exploitation of grievances, the changing of the narrative through propaganda, the manipulation of the population through grassroots organizing, and, ultimately, the use of violence in an attempt to bring about revolutionary change.

We have seen this vision brought to life in wave after wave: by Alinsky, by SDS, by the Weather Underground, by the critical race theorists, by ACORN, by BLM. These are the movements of NextGen Marxism. Their grievances, their revolutionary agents of change, and their utopia might have changed from the original Marxist–Leninist paradigm, but their overall intention remains the same: to dismantle Western society and grab hold of the reins of power—as BLM's Garza phrased it, "to keep dismantling the organizing principle of this society."[82]

Understanding and exposing this strategy are key to combating it. Philip

Selznick pointed out in his 1952 study of Bolshevik organizing that Leninists' use of mass participation for political purposes gave them a tactical advantage "in the struggle for power."[83] But he also made the critical point that reliance on organizational weapons is a sign of strategic weakness:[84]

> *Indeed, one of the general functions of organizational weapons is that of eluding the need to win consent as a condition for attaining or wielding power. When a power-oriented elite wishes to exercise authority beyond its ability to mobilize favorable opinion in its own right, organizational manipulation may be one method of doing so without the use of violence. The Leninists rely on organizational devices to gain power for a minority.*[85]

IN OUR final chapter, on how to defeat NextGen Marxism, we further explore how best to use these insights into the uses of organizational weapons, both their tactical advantages and also their intrinsic weaknesses.

7
SEXUALIZING CHILDREN
AND THE ATTACK ON THE FAMILY

O F ALL THE ways that NextGen Marxism is attacking the culture of the
United States, none is more disturbing—and ultimately more destructive—than the attack on the family and the sexualization of children. The
aggressive promotion of transgender ideology (as distinct from the effort to
promote tolerance, acceptance, and care of individuals with gender dysphoria)
has particularly spurred many parents to step into the culture wars. It should
be emphasized that the reason for parents' decision to act is the gravity of the
consequences: the promotion of the idea that a child is "born in the wrong
body" can lead to mutilation, sterilization, a lifelong dependence on medical
treatment and/or medication, and the inability to bear children or to fully experience sexual pleasure. Parents rightly want to protect children from these
catastrophic outcomes. There is also deep concern over the shortage of research
into the long-term physical and psychological consequences of "gender transition." But other issues around the sexualization of children are also spurring
many adults to engage in the cultural battle: graphic sex in books for children,
drag queen story hours, sexually explicit and age-inappropriate content in
school-sponsored sex education, and the breaking down of the walls of separation between boys and girls in restrooms and locker rooms. Moreover, parents
in a traditional male and female marriage understand that it is the model of the
family they embody that is under attack, along with their right to raise their
children according to their values.

To be clear, what threatens our society today is not the existence of adults
who choose to live outside the bounds of traditional marriage and morality.
Those who experience same-sex attraction, who do not marry, or who have sex
with multiple partners have always existed—with varying degrees of acceptance.
These behaviors may not be traditional, but they are not components of gender theory. Gender theory is something else altogether. It involves the denial of
biology and the deconstruction of reality and truth. Gender theory posits that
men can become women, and vice versa; that people can be born in the "wrong

body"; that sex is not assigned at birth and has nothing to do with biology; that children can consent to sex with adults; that children have the emotional maturity to make such life-changing decisions as the amputation of healthy body parts and the consumption of puberty blockers; that men and women must resist their instincts, whether to protect and provide or to procreate and start families; that men can compete with women in sports without affecting the outcome. It has been a theme of this book so far that NextGen Marxism and all cultural Marxisms engage in the deconstruction of truth, and in this sense, gender theory is the most radical of all the radical theories that compose NextGen Marxism.

So, whether it is latter-wave feminists railing against femininity, or the feminine urge to bear and rear children, or Marxists against "the patriarchy" as the source of individual private property, or male swimmers competing against females because they insist they are women, the commonalities are clear. The Hungarian historian and political theorist Gergely Szilvay put it this way in a 2022 book on the subject: "the great common point that unites the advocates and theorists of gender theory is the radical separation of body and soul, body and spirit, and body and personality." Whether it's a Marxist, a feminist, or an LGBTQ activist, "the point is the same—the ignoring of biological constraints and the denial of human nature, together with constructionism."[1] What makes today's gender theory a threat to our very civilization is the fact that its proponents do not merely want acceptance; they want supremacy and exclusion. As Carl Trueman points out,

> *The sexual revolution does not simply represent a growth in the routine transgression of traditional sexual codes or even a modest expansion of the boundaries of what is and is not acceptable social behavior; rather, it involves the abolition of such codes in their entirety. More than that, it has come in certain areas, such as that of homosexuality, to require the positive repudiation of traditional sexual mores to the point where belief in, or maintenance of, such traditional views has come to be seen as ridiculous and even a sign of serious or moral deficiency.*[2]

IN THE few years since Trueman published these words in 2020, those who hold traditional views have come to be viewed not merely as ridiculous but as dangerous, even fascistic, and a number of measures—from executive orders to laws, DEI rules, and hiring and acceptance preferences—are being increasingly deployed to exclude or punish those who hold traditional views. To many, it seems incomprehensible that we have arrived at such a place in our culture. But if one digs deeply into the ideology and the personalities of those driving revolution, it makes perfect sense that this is where we have arrived, because this is where the road was leading all along.

The purpose of this chapter is to reveal the deep flaws in the foundations on which the attacks on family and sexuality have been built. Why is this important? Because many people who support adolescent transgender surgery, for example, believe they are doing good. They believe this mutilation and other forms of "gender-affirming care" are in fact a kindness. Many who attack the traditional family thus believe they do so to make those who embrace nontraditional relationships feel more accepted. Many who try to reduce sex to nothing more than a physical act akin to sleeping or eating, or who would reduce a human embryo to a mere fetus, a clump of cells without humanity, believe they are enacting some kind of good. But beneath those beliefs—even if it is not always recognized as such—is an ideology of the human person, of sexuality, and of identity. The tragically deep flaws in that ideology must be exposed if we are to recover from the current state we are in.

Other analysts have already provided valuable insights, mapping some of the influences that have led us to where we are today. Andrew Klavan has talked about the importance of Rousseau and the Marquis de Sade. Carl Trueman discusses the influence of Nietzsche and Darwin. Chris Rufo connects the dots between gender theory and the NextGen Marxist project. These are all important threads in understanding the ideology that has culminated in today's sexual politics. A goal of this chapter is to build on that legacy by exposing two factors that have not been adequately recognized: the aberrant sexuality of the ideologues themselves and how their own deviancy or inconstancy drove them, at least in part, to attack the very institutions, such as monogamous, heterosexual sex and marriage, that they themselves rejected. Secondly, a goal is to demonstrate that while today's gender theory has its ideological roots in Rousseau, the Marquis de Sade, Marx, Nietzsche, and Freud, it was brought out of the realm of academia and theory and into the bedrooms of Americans by a generation of men who sought to use sexual politics to destroy one of the foundational institutional pillars of society—the family—and thus as a way to dismantle the nation-state.

The Trinity of the Most Monstrous Evils

When we look back at the history of Marxists and other socialists, we tend to focus on their efforts to overturn the economic order. Marx himself had reduced humans to their material or economic interests, and when we think of the major experiments in socialism—the Soviet Union, China, Cuba—we think of them first and foremost as economic experiments: efforts by the state to control the economy. The fact that every other aspect of life then required control as well was something of a by-product of economic control—the point that Friedrich Hayek made in his landmark book *The Road to Serfdom*.

Yet from the very beginning, utopian socialists have been every bit as focused on overturning the cultural and the moral order as well as the economic order. Indeed, nearly all have shared the view expressed by the utopian Robert Owen that private property, religion, and marriage constitute the "trinity of the most monstrous evils."[3] One can draw a straight line from the anti-family, anti-morality position of Owen and other utopians and socialists of the 1800s to BLM in 2020, which posted on its website (and subsequently removed following heavy criticism) the goal of destroying the nuclear family: "we disrupt the Western-prescribed nuclear-family-structure requirement by supporting each other as extended families and 'villages' that collectively care for one another."[4]

Tearing down the norms and traditions around sex and the family have been at the heart of the socialist, utopian project from the very beginning. But why? Why attack as bedrock and essential an institution such as the family, which is sought and cherished by nearly everyone? The question answers itself: because the family is the bedrock of society.

Michael Walsh explains the radical Left's attack on the family this way: "The family, in its most biological sense, represents everything that those who would wish 'fundamental change' … on society must first loathe. It is the cornerstone of society, the guarantor of future generations … , the building block of the state but superior to it, because the family is naturally ordained, whereas the state is not."[5] This is without a doubt a wonderful, but only partial explanation, because the attack on the family does not make sense as ideology alone. It makes sense only if one looks first to the personalities behind the ideology: virtually every leading revolutionary voice, from Rousseau to Marx and Reich and Marcuse, was a philanderer, if not an outright sexual deviant, who failed his own family. Rousseau lived with his partner for twenty-five years without marrying her, and then he abandoned all five of his children to orphanages. Marx cheated on his wife with the family's young nanny and allowed his family to live in squalid poverty, resulting in the death of his two sons. Later, two of his daughters committed suicide (though it is likely that one of them took part in a suicide pact with her husband, but he then didn't carry through his end of the bargain, desiring only to be rid of his wife—making it then closer to a murder).[6] Marx and Engels argued in *The Communist Manifesto* that in their communist utopia, private property would be abolished, the family would disappear, and marriage between one man and one woman would be replaced by a community of women to be shared among the men.[7] They closed *The Communist Manifesto* by calling for the "forcible overthrow of all existing social conditions."[8]

Owen, among the most famous of all nineteenth-century American utopians, was another early radical for whom socialism and an attack on sexual mores were tightly bound. A successful Scottish cotton-mill owner, Owen moved to the more tolerant environment of the United States to create a utopian socialist community. He promoted his ideas through lectures and books, and he even addressed the US Congress for three hours—not once, but twice—in 1825. He argued that Americans had achieved political but not mental liberty, and therefore a second revolution was required. He promised that in his new society, "all will become as rich as they desire"; just a few hours of work a day will create a full supply of everything a human could need; "nothing will be wasted or abused." Indeed, he would create a world of "palaces, gardens, and pleasure grounds."[9] All that was preventing this beautiful world from coming about was his trinity of evils: private property, religion, and marriage. Given that he left his wife behind in England and was never rejoined with her, one supposes it may have been his own negative experience with marriage that led him to disparage it so vehemently.

In 1882, Victoria Woodhull was the first to publish an American version of Marx and Engels' *Communist Manifesto* in her magazine, *Woodhull and Claflin's Weekly*.[10] She was an outspoken advocate for women's rights, including the right to vote, and she was also an avid supporter of socialism and sexual freedom. She also happened to be the first woman to run for president of the United States. But as with the other utopian socialists, was she advocating for sexual freedom because it was necessary to achieve socialism? Or did she find in socialism a justification for her own rule-defying sexual behavior? At age fifteen, she had married an alcoholic, whom she later divorced, and she became an outspoken advocate for "free love." "Yes, I am a Free Lover," she said in one speech. "I have an inalienable, constitutional right and natural right to love whom I may, to love as long or as short a period as I can; to change that love every day if I please."[11]

Individuals such as Owen and Woodhull were eccentrics; they were outliers. Their utopian experiments in sexual freedom failed, and their ideas gained little traction. Just as Marxism had failed to gain traction in the 1900s because workers did not want to overthrow the economic systems that held out the promise of prosperity, so the utopian socialists failed to overthrow the family and its sexual morality because the family remained the apogee of personal happiness and economic stability.

The true breach in the inviolability of the family was not struck until about the 1930s. It was a process helped along by Sigmund Freud but carried to completion by members of the Frankfurt School.

Freud, born in 1856 in the Austro-Hungarian Empire, developed theories around the human person that placed sexuality front and center as a driver of human behavior. He identified what he called the pleasure principle—a driving force in the human psyche that constantly seeks gratification.[12] He argued that happiness is derived first and foremost from pleasure, but the advance of civilization demands restrictions on man's sexual life. It seems Freud originally believed that this was a good thing: that restraining ourselves, especially our sexual appetites, has served us well. But then a breach appears—the conflagration of the First World War led him to suggest that perhaps our civilization is not so great after all: "in whatever way we may define the concept of civilization, it is a certain fact that all the things with which we seek to protect ourselves against the threats that emanate from the sources of suffering are part of that very civilization."[13] Indeed, he held civilization itself responsible for the nightmare of the war and the rise of Hitler: "what we call our civilization is largely responsible for our misery, and ... we should be much happier if we gave it up and returned to primitive conditions."[14] Like so many of his era who had lived through the horrors of world war, Freud developed a very dark view of mankind. He believed that the commandment to love one's neighbor as oneself was developed as an ideal because it was the very opposite of man's true nature. Man is a wolf to man, he wrote.[15]

But Freud was not an enemy of civilization. Unlike the Marxist revolutionaries, he believed that civilization could gradually be improved; he did not believe that it needed to be torn down and rebuilt. He also acknowledged that there may simply be aspects of mankind and civilization that cannot be reformed because of human nature itself—another important difference from the revolutionaries, who believed that human nature is malleable and that with enough shaping (coercion), man can be perfected and utopia attained.[16] Freud openly condemned communism's claim that it could deliver men from their evils. He said he could not judge whether abolishing private property would be more advantageous from an economic point of view, but the idea that common ownership would abate man's aggressive nature he called an untenable illusion.[17] Freud had opened a box of previously forbidden and even unthinkable topics: childhood sexuality, bisexuality, homosexuality, nonmonogamy, and gender fluidity (though he did not call it that), to name just a few. He had also suggested that the horrors of the early twentieth century were the result of sexual repression. Freud raised so many issues around the individual and civilization that had not previously been topics for discussion that despite his defense of the family, of bourgeois culture, of civilization, he in fact opened the door to their destruction.

One of the most significant people to walk through that door was Freud's student Wilhelm Reich. One can see in Reich that intertwining of personal experience and public philosophy that is so characteristic of many of the socialist revolutionaries. Born in 1897 in a part of today's Ukraine that was then still a part of the Austro-Hungarian Empire, Reich lost his home—a family farm— and everything he owned as a result of World War I, during which he served on the Italian front. At the end of the war, now homeless, he entered medical school in Vienna and became a member of Freud's inner circle. Reich himself was sex-obsessed and was drawn to Freud's theory that neuroses are caused by the social denial and frustration of sexual instincts.[18]

He reported having sex at the age of twelve with the family's chambermaid, had three marriages and many sexual partners, and raised his own children in what he called sexual freedom.[19] There was very definitely a darker side to this obsession: he had been witness to his mother's adultery with his tutor, and after he told his father about it, his mother committed suicide. As if that were not trauma enough, he also experienced firsthand the atrocities and violence of World War I.

Reich joined the Communist Party in 1928, and in 1929, he opened several sex-counseling centers under the auspices of the Socialist Society for Sexual Counseling and Sex-Research, supported by the Party, where he tried to advise workers about the centrality of sexuality in their lives. In 1932, he published *The Sexual Struggle of Youth*, which argued that young people should be allowed to have active sex lives, abortion should be legalized, and traditional marriage should be abolished. Most importantly for the understanding of today's Next-Gen Marxists and their attack on the family and sexualization of children, Reich found a way to integrate Freud's theories of sexual repression with Marx's theories of class conflict. Not unlike Freud, he wrote, "It is sexual energy which governs the structure of human feeling and thinking."[20] But he departed from Freud in embracing Marx's worldview of oppressors and oppressed. Reich wrote, "Perhaps the most important result of my political work for future sex-sociological investigations was the discovery that sexual suppression is one of the cardinal ideological means by which the ruling class subjugates the working population."[21]

As Austen Ruse explains, "Reich wanted to reconcile psychoanalysis with Marxism and believed that economic Marxism would fail because of the repressed sexuality of the proletariat."[22] But it was not merely the sexuality of the proletariat that was suppressed; it was specifically the sexuality of children. Reich wrote elsewhere that the "suppression of the love life of children and adolescents is the central mechanism for producing enslaved subordinates and economic serfs."[23] Sexualizing children required destroying the family, both because the family will protect a child and because the sustenance of healthy families requires sexual morality. Reich therefore attacked both the family and sexual morality, calling family life the "Achilles' heel of society."[24]

In 1939, with World War II looming, Reich fled Europe and brought his radical ideas to the United States. Reich ultimately left the Communist Party and rejected Marxism, but the work he had done ultimately served as a handing of the baton from Freud to Herbert Marcuse and other members of the Frankfurt School, and it was they who then carried on the race. Reich had laid the foundation for the belief that fundamental change in the way society was organized required the sexual liberation of the individual. Reich's book *The Sexual Revolution* gave the name to the cultural upheaval that would follow in the 1960s. Reich was mocked for his fixation on sexual pleasure and was considered too deviant even by the standards of the other members of the Frankfurt School, but his ideas nonetheless infused the theories of the Frankfurt School and in turn provided an ideological foundation—flawed as it was—for subsequent attacks on traditional relationships and sexuality.

War and Sex

WE HAVE made the argument that the sexualization of children and the attack on the traditional family, which are so central to the efforts of today's NextGen Marxists, are rooted not in any sound philosophical or moral argument but in the understanding that the family had to be dismantled if society was to be, and also partly on the sexual deviancy of a handful of thinkers. Owen, Marx, Woodhull, and Reich, among others, were unable to live within the confines of what constituted mainstream morality, and so they sought to destroy it with their "utopian" projects. They all identified humanity's problem as the triumvirate of private property, religion, and family, and they based their ideological prescriptions on the destruction of these institutions. The sexual behavior of these radical utopians strongly suggests that their ideology developed as it did not only to carry out their revolutionary ends but also to justify their own behavior, and it is important to recognize this flawed foundation in combating NextGen Marxism.

But another important factor shaping today's culture is equally deserving of attention: the epic crises of the twentieth century—the carnage of the two world wars, Hitler's Holocaust, Hitler's and Mussolini's fascism, and Lenin's and Stalin's brutal totalitarianism and the tens of millions of people killed. All were deeply traumatizing, and for those who survived, that pain had profound and far-reaching consequences. So many had lost family members, suffered deprivation and starvation, lost their homes and indeed everything they owned, and experienced persecution. These crises, which came in rapid succession, one after another, shattered belief in God, shattered belief in one's fellow man, and shattered hope. But most importantly, they shattered belief in society and civilization. This all fueled the deconstructionism of the postmoderns. Modernity, they thought, had failed. Winston Churchill presciently said, "Injuries were wrought to the structure of human society which a century will not efface, and which may conceivably prove fatal to the present civilization."[25] Some of the deepest injuries to the structure of human society wrought by those crises have been to our ideas around sex and the family.

So broken was society after the world wars that in the view of some radicals, the only solution was to destroy it altogether. Georg Lukács, the influential Hungarian communist, argued in 1926 that the one and only solution for what he called the "cultural contradictions of the epoch" was the revolutionary destruction of society.[26] He advocated for "a total break with every institution and mode of life stemming from the bourgeois world."[27] As we saw in chapter 2, Lukács did his best to achieve that as the education and culture commissar of the short-lived Hungarian soviet in 1919 by introducing the teaching of sexual depravity in elementary schools.

Reich, who did so much to set the ball spinning for the sexual revolution, argued that in the early twentieth century, "more misery was inflicted on humanity than in the preceding centuries."[28] He therefore believed that what had occurred brought every aspect of life, but particularly sexuality, up to that time into question:

> We may say that all concepts formulated by men to explain and shed light on their lives have been brought into question and have remained unresolved for two decades. Among those concepts none has collapsed so completely as that of compulsory sexual morality, which unshakably ruled human existence a mere thirty years ago. We are living through a true revolution of all values regarding sexual life. And among those values most seriously undermined are those relating to infant and adolescent sexuality.[29]

MAX HORKHEIMER and Theodor Adorno, two of the key members of the Frankfurt School and cofounders of critical theory, rejected the advances of the enlightenment and similarly embraced this destructive vision. "Enlightenment, understood in the widest sense as the advance of thought, has always aimed at liberating human beings from fear and installing them as masters. Yet the wholly enlightened earth is radiant with triumphant calamity."[30] They further wrote, "The affluent society has now demonstrated that it is a society of war."[31] Adorno called the family the "disastrous germ-cell of society."[32]

Marcuse, whom we met in depth in earlier chapters, had early concluded that the nature of civilization itself needed serious rethinking. He disagreed with Freud that for the sake of civilization, man must subjugate his instinctual drives; rather, Marcuse believed it was that very repression of instinctual drives that produced present-day society and its oppression. Freud's approach, thought Marcuse,

buttressed what he called the "'patricentric-acquisitive' culture."[33] He credited
Erich Fromm, a neo-Freudian member of the Frankfurt School, with attempting
"to free Freud's theory from its identification with present-day society."[34]

Libidinal wants and needs, wrote Marcuse, were shaped
to "cement" the given society. Thus, in what Fromm calls the "patricen-
tric-acquisitive" society (which, in this study, is defined in terms of the rule
of the performance principle), the libidinal impulses and their satisfaction
(and deflection) are coordinated with the interests of domination and there-
by become a stabilizing force which binds the majority to the ruling minority.
Anxiety, love, confidence, even the will to freedom and solidarity with the
group to which one belongs—all come to serve the economically structured
relationships of domination and subordination.[35]

MARCUSE WAS there to end this sexual repression and thereby liberate the minority from the sadistic ruling majority, and his book *Eros and Civilization* was
his tool.

In this 1955 bestseller, Marcuse argued that for civilization to advance to a
higher stage of freedom, a complete freeing of the instincts, particularly the
sexual instincts, was required. He advocated for "polymorphous sexuality" and
for making the human body "an instrument of pleasure rather than labor."[36] He
called for a revolution that would "eroticize previously tabooed zones, times,
and relations," *including childhood.* He wrote that "a twentieth-century revolution would require a different type of human being and ... such a revolution
would have to aim at, and, if successful, implement, an entirely new set of personal and sexual relationships, a new morality, a new sensibility and a total
reconstruction of the environment."[37]

Man's future freedom, according to Marcuse, indeed, his very survival, therefore depended on what he termed the decontrolling of the instinctual development to achieve a nonrepressive society. "Progress would depend completely
on the opportunity to activate repressed or arrested organic, biological needs,"
wrote Marcuse.[38] But just as Marx had been wrong in reducing man to his
economic impulses, Marcuse was wrong to reduce man to his sexual impulses.
Marx had wrongly blamed the poor working conditions of the early industrial
period on an innate and all-encompassing desire by one part of the population
(the bourgeoisie) to oppress another part (the proletariat). Similarly, Marcuse

wrongly believed that society was oppressive because man repressed his sexual desires. Both men were sufficiently arrogant to build entire worldviews around those false anthropologies, and the world has been paying the price ever since, not least because both men targeted the family—Marx in his *Manifesto*, in which he called for its abolition, and Marcuse in *Eros*, where he made clear that liberating the libido had one goal: eliminating the family. Changing the value and scope of libidinal relations would lead to a disintegration of the institutions in which the private interpersonal relations have been organized, particularly the monogamic and patriarchal family."[39]

Unlike the other members of the Frankfurt School who fled to the United States during World War II, Marcuse stayed on in the United States. He found a home in several American universities and in this way became one of the most important progenitors of ideas about sexual revolution. Many others played key roles in the evolution of the sexual revolution—Albert Kinsey, Karen Horney, and Gloria Steinem, to name just a few—but it was the German-speaking thinkers, Freud, Reich, Horkheimer, Adorno, Fromm, and Marcuse, whose ideas and writings provided much of the intellectual foundation for the destruction of sexual mores. Today's social dysfunctions, particularly the attacks on the traditional family and on sexual morality, are therefore the by-products of their desire to upend civilization. They then gave a patina of highbrow philosophy to others who wished to challenge the prevailing restraints on sexuality, gender identity, or traditional family structures.

Michael Foucault, a French postmodernist who became a leading attacker of both Western civilization and sexual mores, is one of those who used Freud and Reich as a jumping-off point to argue that "sexuality was not an 'essential' characteristic of human nature or gender, but a thoroughly social-historical construction."[40] Like so many of the radical revolutionaries who came before and after, he lived well outside the norms of accepted behavior—even by the loosening standards of the post-1960s world. He was a recklessly promiscuous pederast who was not merely having sex with young boys but, it came out later, would rape those who would refuse. Moreover, he maintained his promiscuity even after he was diagnosed with AIDS. But because he used the language of philosophy, and because he could draw on the ideas of others who had come before him, he had an air of legitimacy. Without the works of Freud, Reich, and Marcuse, in particular, Foucault would not have had the intellectual legitimacy to advocate for such outrageous violations of accepted morality. But theories around sexual satisfaction as an end in itself, and the roundly argued case that Western society's supposed oppression could be ascribed to suppression of sexual desire, led to a steady erosion of sexual mores as well as the traditional family.

Once Foucault argued that sexuality was a social construct, it was not a great leap to argue that gender itself was a social construct. Chris Rufo connects the dots between gender theory and the NextGen Marxist project. In a powerful video he released on July 11, 2023, the filmmaker, activist, and now Florida educator explains, "The transgender movement is inherently political, using the construction of personal identity to advance a collective political vision."[41] Rufo traces the history of how this movement veered hard left to—again—the same era when NextGen Marxists were taking over the institutions:

> In the late 1980s, a group of writers, including Judith Butler, Gail Rubin, Sandy Stone, and Susan Stryker, established the disciplines of queer theory and transgender studies. They argued that gender was a social construct, used to oppress racial and sexual minorities. They denounced the categories of man and woman as a false binary that upholds a system of hetero-normativity, the white male heterosexual power structure. These writers made the case that these systems must be ruthlessly deconstructed and turned to dust, and the most visceral, dramatic way to achieve this is transgenderism. If a man can become woman, if a woman can become man, they believed the entire structure of creation could be toppled.[42]

THIS EFFORT was rooted in Marxism, where the driver of revolution shifted yet one more time from Marx's working class to the students and intellectuals of the New Left to the transsexual NextGen Marxists. Now it is not merely capitalism that will be abolished but "heteronormativity"—that is, the biological reality of male and female as it has been recognized through millennia, along with what Michael Walsh describes as the "naturally primal force: the union of opposites into a harmonious, generative whole."[43]

The link with Marxism was clear, Rufo showed: "In a collection of essays titled *Transgender Marxism*, Rosa Lee argues that trans people can serve as the new vanguard of the proletariat promising to abolish hetero-normativity in the same way that Orthodox Marxism promised to abolish capitalism." Rufo then quoted Lee as writing,

In a different era, Marxists spoke of the construction of a new socialist man as a crucial task in the broader process of socialist construction. Today, in a time of both rising fascism and an emergent socialist movement, our challenge is transsexualizing our Marxism. We should think of the project of transition to communism in our time as including the transition to new communist selves, new ways of being and relating to one another. This is the great project of the transgender movement: to abolish the distinctions of man and woman, to transcend the limitations established by creation, to hitch the personal struggle of trans individuals to the political struggle of revolution. All of society must be reorganized to affirm their identities and more importantly, their politics.[44]

THE ASSOCIATION between sexual education and communism is also long and well established. The nation's oldest and most important sex-education association is actually named Sex Ed for Social Change (SIECUS). It was founded in 1964 by a handful of sex educators, including Isadore Rubin, its first treasurer. Rubin was the editor of the magazine *Sexology*, which ran from 1933 to 1983 and was described as pornographic or at best as "kinky and kooky," with articles devoted to "Extra Breasts in Women," "Can Humans Breed with Animals?," "Sexual Vampirism," and, yes, "Pregnant Men."[45] Rubin was also a communist. He was fired in 1950 as a New York City teacher by the Board of Education on suspicion of being a communist, a charge he refused to deny.[46] Five years later, in testimony before the House Un-American Activities Committee, a New York City detective said under oath that Rubin attended meetings of the Flatbush Club of the Communist Party, an association which Rubin, also under oath, later refused to refute.[47]

SIECUS pioneered sex education in the decades following its founding, fending off all criticism, and, as we noted in the introductory chapter, it is so powerful that it writes guidelines on comprehensive sex education for the Centers for Disease Control and Prevention (CDC).[48] It proudly asserts that its aim is to do much more than just educate about sex: "Sex education has the power to spark large-scale social change. SIECUS is not a single-issue organization because sex ed, as SIECUS envisions it, connects and addresses a variety of social issues. Sex ed sits at the nexus of many social justice movements—from LGBTQ rights and reproductive justice to the #MeToo movement and urgent conversations around consent and healthy relationships."[49] And SIECUS makes clear that it sees a clear link between racial and sexual oppression in an America that it believes wants to maintain both white and heterosexual supremacy. "Controlling the formation of sexual identities through racialized stereotypes and the reproduction of racial and ethnic minority groups is central to effective population controls," warned this CDC partner in 2020.[50]

This is the ideological framework on which adults today are justifying the mutilation and physical devastation of children.

Conclusion

ALEKSANDR SOLZHENITSYN, the writer who spent eight years in a Soviet gulag, came to understand that for humans to be capable of the depth of evil that he had witnessed and suffered, they needed to believe that they were in fact doing good. That required belief in an ideology. He wrote,

> Macbeth's self-justifications were feeble—and his conscience devoured him. Yes, even Iago was a little lamb too. The imagination and the spiritual strength of Shakespeare's evildoers stopped short at a dozen corpses. Because they had no ideology. Ideology—that is what gives evildoing its long-sought justification and gives the evildoer the necessary steadfastness and determination... the social theory which helps to make his acts seem good... in his own and others' eyes.[51]

MARX PROVIDED the ideology by which Lenin and Stalin and their many followers and enablers could justify the immeasurable evil they perpetrated in the Soviet Union. But although it worked—for a time—in the backwardness of the Soviet Union, it was an ideology that struggled to gain traction in Western, developed nations, where the demands of revolution failed to win out over the promise of opportunity and prosperity. But those who found in Marxism a justification for their greed, their envy, their resentments, their lust for power and control over others, or for their dismay with a world they saw as oppressive, were able to meld and adapt the ideology in ways that gave it traction in the West. Rather than grounding their call for revolution in economic disparities, they ground it in disparities around race, ethnicity, sexuality, and other aspects of identity.

They spent decades building an ideology of victimhood. In the 1960s, they also provided the physical tools for revolution—the Molotov cocktails, the bombs, the violent demonstrations. In the early 1970s, their promised revolution fizzled out, but only for a time. The ideological seeds had been planted: the purveyors of 1960s violent race-based revolution saw where they had failed, in part because the laws of the United States were against them, and so through the new ideology of critical legal studies, they sought to change law itself. Through their prominent positions in some of America's leading universities, they educated a new generation in their radical ideology. But then the generation raised up with critical legal studies rejected the white, male professors of critical legal studies as racist and sexist, as we saw in chapter 4. They amended the ideology yet again and called it critical race theory. For the past thirty-five years, they have been building out that ideology to justify identity-based revolution—and if one looks to the extent of the George Floyd protests and the prevalence today of diversity, equity, and inclusion training and administrators in nearly every public institution and major corporation, one could argue that they have done so quite successfully. As a result, NextGen Marxists are undoing much of the real progress of recent decades: they are redividing the country by race and ethnicity, reinstituting racial quotas and preferences, and reanimating resentments based on race, ethnicity, or gender. In short, everything they claim to despise from the past—the unequal power structures, the injustice, the inequalities—they have reinstituted, but with the tables turned. *They* want the power, *they* claim superiority—and their ideology tells them that they are justified in doing so.

The good news is that with their attack on children and the family, with their effort to fully rewrite the rules and norms around sexuality, the NextGen Marxists have finally gone too far, as we will see in chapter 9.

8
"IN THE BELLY OF THE BEAST"

THE REVOLUTIONARY STAGE of the Nextgen Marxist project was launched on US streets in 2013, when BLM was founded. On July 13 of that year, a Florida jury acquitted a neighborhood watchman named George Zimmerman of the killing of seventeen-year-old Trayvon Martin in Sanford, Florida. Later that day, the Oakland militant Alicia Garza posted to Facebook a message expressing her "deep sense of grief" over the acquittal. The post included the assertion that "Black Lives Matter," or, according to other accounts, the words "Our lives matter." Either way, her comrade Patrisse Cullors saw the post that night and created the hashtag #BlackLivesMatter, throwing it on Twitter. A third radical, Opal Tometi, told Garza two days later, "I've seen this emerging hashtag that Patrisse and you put online a day or two ago. I think we need to build a website and I think we need to elevate it and make sure that we're using it across our network and beyond."[1] That hashtag and the website became a global movement a year later in the burning streets of Ferguson, Missouri, after Garza descended on that city to organize leftists. The velocity of change then accelerated further after the protests and some 630 riots that followed the death of George Floyd in 2020.

That street chaos produced the roiling coup we see being attempted against the American constitutional order today. Americans confront it daily in the form of CRT notions in classrooms; "antiracism" trainings in the workplace; drag queen story hour; a multitude of diversity, equity, and inclusion administrators; environmental, social, and governance (ESG) measures in corporate life—all profound alterations to the way America is constituted, or has been until very recently. BLM's street chaos also led to the Biden adminsitration's pursuit of an untrammeled race-based approach throughout the federal government. Whether the coup utlimately succeeds, and we become a far different country, hangs in the balance.

The revolutionaries conspiring to overthrow America were ideologically schooled on Gramsci and Marcuse and organized along Alinsky lines, as we have painstakingly catalogued. They had drunk deeply from the CRT well and spoke the language of "systems of oppression," "white supremacy," and "dismantling and deconstructing." However, the time has come to shine a spotlight on a different source of America's troubles. When Tometi wrote Garza about sharing the emerging BLM messaging "across our network," she wasn't referring to friends and family. She had at her disposal an intricate lacework of far leftist groups to help amplify a unified message and to organize protests. These foreign Marxist networks helped spawn the street violence in the United States. They had urged the creation of cells inside "the belly of the beast," which is what they call our country. Their oft-stated goal was to weaken America and "realize Another World"—code for central planning and collectivism.

Let's briefly review how the revolution progressed. After BLM's founding in 2013, the revolt gathered force in 2014 following the police killing of Michael Brown in Ferguson, Missouri, where Marxists across the nation and the world converged to coordinate action going forward. The murder rate grew by 10 percent in cities and localities that experienced protests and riots in the seven years that followed, a phenomenon dubbed the "Ferguson effect."[2] Violence then reached a fever pitch in 2020, a year that saw more than six hundred riots; $2 billion in damages, the highest in US history; and more than twenty people dead.[3]

The cultural hit has been even more damaging. Administrators at leading institutions, this time not only cultural but across the landscape, from high-school principals to college presidents, museum directors and curators, editors of the country's leading newspapers and magazines, corporate CEOs, heads of sports leagues and athletes, clergy, political leaders, the federal permanent bureaucracy, theater directors, Hollywood studio bosses and actors, and PTA presidents—in a word, all of American life—surrendered and accepted, or at least paid lip service to, the falsehood that the country is racked with systemic racism and thus in urgent need of systemic change. This fabricated premise must be assented to by all if the project is to succeed.

The changes in our lives have been deep and wide. *The New York Times* columnist Bret Stephens has called it the "great American cultural revolution of the 2010s, in which traditional practices and beliefs—regarding same-sex marriage, sex-segregated bathrooms, personal pronouns, meritocratic ideals, race-blind rules, reverence for patriotic symbols, the rules of romance, the presumption of innocence and the distinction between equality of opportunity and outcome—became, more and more, not just passé, but taboo."[4]

The leaders of elite institutions swallowed whole another canard: that we were in the midst of a "racial reckoning," as the press likes to call it, unleashed by the killings of Martin in 2013, Brown in 2014, and Breonna Taylor and Floyd in 2020. The desperate attempts to eliminate all disparities immediately, by means of affecting outcomes only, and possibly pay trillions in reparations, depend on believing the "racial reckoning" narrative—that America is finally being confronted with her sins.

But this is all a deception crafted by the revolutionaries and repeated by the naive and the gullible, but especially by those who know better but share the revolutionaries' transformative goals. In reality, the founders of BLM, and more importantly, their mentors, had already been networking and plotting to bring mayhem to US soil for years before Martin ever, tragically, crossed paths with Zimmerman. They used interlocking national and international networks where they coordinated strategy with other radicals, including representatives and even leaders of foreign powers who sought to weaken or outright destroy the United States. Indeed, the US networks are sometimes created at the urging of these anti-American regimes.

As everyone ought to know by now, the Left is generally much better than the Right at organizing, the subject of a previous chapter; it is their métier to network and meticulously conspire to subvert society one neighborhood, one local theater group, one radio station at a time. While conservatives hold big national pep rallies where speakers take the main stage and give inspirational speeches to sympathetic audiences, leftists roll up their sleeves and go to work at national (or, as we will show here, international) gatherings that are chock-full of workshops, clinics, and training sessions. These sessions have been carefully planned in advance and calibrated to have the greatest impact going forward, to amplify a tightly controlled message that persuades journalists to use catchphrases of the Left, such as "racial reckoning" and "marginalized groups."

That is because the Left has a skein of global, reinforcing networks devoted to consciousness-raising and street protests. Among the most important revolutionary hubs figure Left Root, NetRoots, the World Social Forum (WSF), the US Social Forum (USSF), the Foro de São Paulo (the São Paulo Forum in Portuguese), and the Grupo de Puebla.

These are cross-fertilizing networks, and it's a chicken-and-egg question to ask where ideas first germinated, whether with academics in Boston, Paris, or Santiago de Chile (unless you want to go back to Gramsci, Lukács, or Marcuse). For example, the socialist US senator Bernie Sanders is in close telephone communication with the socialist president of Brazil, Luiz Inácio Lula da Silva, sources tell us. Who is giving whom ideas? And the cross-fertilizing doesn't happen only at the leadership level. Social media and the online culture have facilitated cross-border cross-fertilization. The same people who use social media to gin up violence in Lima, Peru, do the same with violence in Ferguson, Missouri. BLM's protests and riots find echoes in places with very different histories.

The WSF may not be known to many Americans, but it is exhibit A of how an international gathering can have—and has had—great impact on US national and local events. We are living in a tumultuous moment at least partly because the Marxist academic activists who run the WSF had decided by 2005 to create a US affiliate. Their stated reason for creating a US branch was to sabotage US policies from within—to wound the "beast" at home. This US outpost was duly created two years later in Atlanta, Georgia, at a massive gathering attended by fifteen thousand people and organized in part by the American Gramscians who were instructing the women who went on to found BLM six years later. These BLM architects and their Gramscian trainers openly proclaimed that they were creating the USSF to help foreign enemies of the United States. This is not conservative writers saying this; the people in question were unequivocal about their goals and how they would achieve them.

The World Social Forum

THE WSF itself was conceived in a short conversation among three Marxists in Paris in February 2000. One was the founder of an anti-capitalist and anti-globalization Paris-based organization, the Association for the Taxation of Financial Transactions and for Citizens Action (ATTAC), Bernard Cassen. The other two were Brazilians with ties to Brazil's Workers Party (Partido dos Trabalhadores, or PT), the socialist party that has been led for decades by Lula, president of Brazil at the time of this writing. The two, Chico Whitaker and Oded Grajew, were in the French capital to ask Cassen if it was possible to create an alternative to the World Economic Forum held in Davos, Switzerland, every year. What they objected to in Davos was not so much the rising globalization and erasure of borders that have made Davos a threat to individual freedom—*that* part they liked—but the free markets, or "neoliberalism" as Marxists term it, that they erroneously think Davos promotes. They wanted leftist groups and individuals to have an annual conference where they could network and prepare the way for a revolution, even a protracted Gramscian one. The two Brazilians asked the Frenchman to have ATTAC and *Le Monde diplomatique*, the far-left Parisian magazine he also runs, organize the alter-Davos gathering. Cassen suggested instead Porto Alegre, in Brazil's deep south.

"Two years before, I had written an article on the participatory budget of the PT administration and I knew the setting fairly well," wrote Cassen some time later, referring to the PT's use of local councils (councils again!) to set budgets in that city. Cassen then told his visitors, " 'We should call it the World Social Forum, to challenge the World Economic Forum, and hold it on the same day of the same month of the year.' It took all of three minutes. My friends said, you're right, let's do it in Brazil."[5] After that, Cassen met with Lula in Rio de Janeiro to explain the concept. Lula was not yet president of Brazil, but as head of the PT, he wielded considerable power in the PT-ruled state of Rio Grande do Sul. He greenlit the gathering. Though Cassen is always quick to insist that the PT has never been in control of the WSF, the heavy financial support of the PT government in Porto Alegre and Rio Grande do Sul was crucial.

The first forum was held in that city in January 2001, with some five thousand registered participants, though some accounts hold that as many as twenty thousand activists from 107 countries turned up. The motto for the event was "Another world is possible." The momentum came from the anti–World Trade Organization riots in Seattle in 1999, the Zapatista revolt in Chiapas, Mexico, in the mid-1990s, and other Marxist uprisings. But the sentiment there was the same as what Horkheimer had expressed in the 1937 essay in which he introduced critical theory: he wanted to be an instrument to overthrow the old order and "create a world which satisfies the needs and powers of men." Of course, we must again emphasize that though the purveyors of these utopias always promise a better world, they deliver exactly the opposite.

The WSF became an instant phenomenon. Forums were held annually after that, drawing leftist activists, academics, and politicians (sometimes all in the same person) from around the world to compare strategies on how to create that "other world." The first forum was heavily Franco-Brazilian, and for the first couple of years, the forums retained a strong European–Latin American flavor, with US participation noticeably scant. Then the organizers made a conscious decision to expand; the first outside Brazil was the forum held in Mumbai, India, in 2004, then others were held in Nairobi, Dakar, and Montreal. The Mumbai forum featured a veritable who's who from the socialist jet-setting world, including António Guterres from Portugal (today secretary-general of the United Nations); the socialist Elio Di Rupo, Belgium's prime minister from 2011 to 2014; and French socialist Kader Arif, former member of the European Parliament.

As early as 2003, the WSF main body, the International Council (IC), set its eyes on creating a US branch. It chose a far-left alliance whose members draw money from the coffers of the financier George Soros, the Grassroots Global Justice Alliance (GGJ), to oversee the first US gathering, which was to take place in Atlanta, Georgia. Ruben Solis Garcia, the founder of the Southwest Workers Union, which went on to be on the planning committee of the first USSF, wrote that "the US Social Forum (USSF) process started in 2003 in Miami at the Jobs With Justice gathering where a meeting of the International Council of the WSF was held and where Grassroots Global Justice first presented a proposal for a US Social Forum."[6] This demonstrates that efforts to establish a US beachhead came early. Solis also described the decision by the WSF to establish a subgroup that would focus on action items, the Social Movements Assembly. He paraphrased Marx's line about philosophers needing to move from ideas to practice in writing that the organizers "came together and decided it was not enough to interpret the world, it was also necessary to transform the world through collective action."

Four academics who were key organizers of the first US gathering said that the IC chose the GGJ because "it was strategic to hold a gathering of peoples and movements within the 'belly of the beast' that were against the ravages of globalization and neoliberal policies in the US and worldwide."[7] Opposing US policies and helping to sabotage them from within was the common theme. Project South, an Atlanta-based organization that trains activists, was also heavily involved in organizing the first US gathering and, going forward, the newly created US affiliate, the USSF.

Third World Led

THE ORGANIZERS did not mince words on why the USSF was urgently needed: "our government's current policies have a disproportionate and negative effect on the rest of the world. Thus our domestic movements—unified in a US solidarity economy coalition inspired by the WSF and solidarity economy movements—can offer the world solidarity in the global fight against our

government's current imperialistic and pro-corporate economic foreign policy."[8] As the USSF's Social Movements Assembly put it, it wasn't just another
world that was needed but "another US is near."[9]

Versions of this rationale for creating a social-forum beachhead in the United States are repeated by those associated with it: enemies of the United States
needed internal help. Speaking in front of three hundred people at the 2010
USSF, held in Detroit, Eric Mann was clear. He recalled that when he went
to work for the Black Panthers in the 1960s, "The black people with whom I
worked said, the United States is a racist, imperialist empire. The United States
stole Mexico, created the slave and the slave trade, killed the indigenous people.
We have to build a Third World movement, with third world people in this
country, in alliance with third world people, and overthrow imperialism."[10] This
"Black/Latinx/Third World united front with an agreed upon black priority" is
the Eric Mann version of the Gramscian "historic bloc," as we saw in chapter 2.

It is under the USSF umbrella that we first detect the future founders of BLM,
then in their early or mid-twenties, starting to associate with global Marxists,
especially Third World ones searching for a fifth column inside the United
States. Alicia Garza, who cofounded BLM six years later and became its top
leader, cut her teeth at the 2007 USSF, and she said it was there that she began
to be politicized. Though she was only twenty-six, the new group she had just
joined, a kind of Marxist preparatory called People Organized to Win Employment Rights (POWER), had entrusted her to organize a delegation, half black
and half Hispanic, to attend the USSF in Atlanta.

"It was one of my first trips with POWER, and I was eager to prove myself
by playing a role in helping to coordinate our delegation of about thirty members, along with the staff," Garza wrote in her 2020 book *The Purpose of Power:
How We Come Together When We Fall Apart.* "I was becoming politicized in
this organization."[11] She called the USSF "a major gathering of social justice
activists" that taught her "a lot about how to build relationships with people
with different backgrounds and agendas," skills which, she added, helped her
in Ferguson in 2014.

In light of the latest wave of anti-Israeli protests that took place across the
United States after October 2023, it should be noted that at the first USSF,
there were Palestinian groups. They were there to build early relationships
with American allies, who in turn would help the Palestinians and others by

becoming a fifth column working against a US ally, Israel. The Marxists in attendance were happy to oblige, issuing a resolution calling the creation of Israel
a "catastrophe" and saying that "the Palestinian struggle for self-determination
and freedom reflects the continuing struggles of indigenous peoples, immigrants, and prisoners, poor communities, communities of color and dislocated
people in the United States."[12]

POWER was on the planning committee of the first USSF in 2007, which
means Garza was as well, as was Eric Mann. As we have explained already in
this book, Mann is a former member of the Weather Underground who spent
time in prison for assault and battery, and he has never shied away from telling
anyone that his plan is to dismantle the United States. He recruited Cullors in
2000 (thirteen years before she cofounded BLM), when she was just seventeen,
into his Labor Community Strategy Center in Los Angeles. There he mentored
her from that young age into Marxism, activism, and organizing. By her own
account, it completely changed her. "I'm glad to be part of the left. It has literally
saved my life," said Cullors when she appeared at the USSF Detroit in 2010,
giving Mann's Los Angeles center the credit for channeling her anger. "When I
came to the organization—when I was organized into the organization, I was
seventeen and a half and I was angry. I was really angry. I was really angry, and
I didn't have a direction, I was just spewing anger."[13]

Soon after recruiting Cullors, Mann adopted a strategy he maintains to this
day: centering the revolution on black Americans. It was an idea he picked
up at another international conference, the World Conference against Racism
in Durban, South Africa, in August 2001 (which the United States boycotted
because it equated Zionism with racism and was going to ask for reparations to
Africa). "By 2001, when I returned from the World Conference Against Racism
in Durban, South Africa, the Strategy Center agreed that we needed a specifically Black/Afro-centric campaign," wrote Mann in September 2020—no doubt
pleased how far his strategy had come to fruition in that year's traumatic riots.[14]

For further confirmation that American Marxists set up a US version of the
forum at the behest of America's enemies overseas, to create some breathing
room for them, we also have no less an authority than Garza herself. Speaking
to a gathering in April 2010, in Oakland, California, that was held in advance
of the Detroit forum, Garza explained why the USSF was created. She recounted that as enthusiastic American leftists began to go to WSF meetings in the

early 2000s, leftists overseas expressed annoyance that they were having to travel to places such as Porto Alegre and Nairobi instead of working to start revolutions at home.

"The US Social Forum happened, right? Because folks were recognizing there's all these people coming from the US like 'whooo! build that movement.' And they're like, '*Really*? What are you doing? Take your foot off my neck, right? I need you to go home and talk to your comrades, and your *compañeros*, right? And talk about and figure out what you're gonna do to take your foot off our neck,'" a very animated and youthful-looking Garza says in a video of her talk in Oakland.[15] "So that's where the US Social Forum came from. Out of a recognition that, one, we gotta get together, right? That, two, there is a growing and vibrant set of movements that are being built here and we need to make that visible, right? And not only do we need to make it visible, but we need to get together closely enough to create some room, right? For the rest of the world to get some space and push back. OK? So the first one happened 2007, in Atlanta."[16]

We also have no less an authority than Hugo Chávez, the Marxist dictator of Venezuela. At a huge rally at the 2006 WSF, which was held in Caracas a year before the US affiliate was finally created, Chávez encouraged Americans to take up the revolutionary cudgel. "I think that, finally, distinct movements are rising in the US, movements that each day has gained more power, more conscience, and more unity," he said to great applause from the thousands gathered. "Viva the people of the US!" he shouted, and the crowd responded "Viva!"[17] "We count on you, *compañeros*, we count on you!" Chávez repeated back to his adoring audience of some fifteen thousand, which included Cassen; the Cuban foreign minister Ricardo Alarcón de Quesada; and Cindy Sheehan, the American anti-war activist, who at the time was being lionized by global socialists. Chávez added, "The people can save this world, but essential to this formula to save the world are the people of the US, the conscience of the US people, the resurrection of the US people. United with the people of the Caribbean, the people of Latin America, the people of Asia, Africa and Europe. All of us must unite; join together in a victorious offensive against the empire."

In a speech that lasted an hour and forty minutes, Chávez touched on all the diverse elements, the division of labor, of the war on capitalism and the war on representative democracy, and in favor of participatory democracy—from race to indigenism to climatism (the Bolivarian revolution was late to embrace the LGBTQ+ part of the division of labor, not doing so in full until 2022, under Nicolás Maduro, Chávez's successor[18]). Involvement by the people of the United States in the revolution played a key part: "this will depend especially on the people of the US, on the awakening of the giant that must be sleeping in the souls of those people, the awakening of the giant within US territory, to unite with best causes and the best struggles for equality and liberty." What was needed, he said, was world socialism, with the WSF playing a key organizing role. "For this reason, I call on the World Social Forum.... I think that from the Forum we must push very hard in this direction, in the formation of a grand worldwide anti-imperialist, alternative movement, that will engage the entire world and that has the capacity to connect, grow, and fight." Chávez went on to say that the WSF had to plan an alternative to capitalism because "capitalism is destroying the world—capitalism is destroying the ecological equilibrium of the planet."

The WSF and its offshoots in Caracas exerted their influence in the United States in other ways as well. Later in 2006, as we saw in chapter 4, Bill Ayers went to Caracas to speak at the related World Education Forum, where he praised Chávez for his "profound educational reforms" and for sharing Ayers's belief that "education is the motor-force of revolution."[19] Ayers brought his adopted son Chesa Boudin. Remember that Ayers and Dohrn had raised Boudin ever since his parents, Cathy Boudin and David Gilbert, went to prison for helping murder a policeman in upstate New York during their time with the Weather Underground. After this meeting, Boudin went on to become a translator for Chávez and, in 2019, was elected district attorney of San Francisco, one of several "rogue prosecutors" elected with the financial support of Soros. As DA, he implemented policies he had learned at Ayers's knee and by Chávez's side. An exasperated electorate voted him out of office via referendum in 2022, but not before he had done much damage by refusing to prosecute criminals and releasing others who had been successfully prosecuted before his time in office.

Building the US Network

CHÁVEZ AND others who encouraged building a US network that would help take the "US boot off of the neck" of global Marxist regimes got their money's worth. It was at the Atlanta USSF that organizers founded the National Domestic Workers Alliance (NDWA), an outfit to be financed partly by Soros's many financial tentacles and that was to play a direct role in our nation's veer to the hard left.

Why organize domestic workers? Because, overwhelmingly, they come from the Third World, so organizing them fit with Mann's goal of building an "alliance with Third World people, and overthrow imperialism." The domestic workers were going to be, in the words of the Marxist woman who would lead the NDWA, Ai-Jen Poo, "agents of social change."[20] It wasn't really about domestic work. As Poo continued, "domestic workers have the potential to challenge the labor movement as a whole to see itself as necessarily part of a broader movement for social and global justice."[21] Scale up, as Alinsky told us.

The NDWA has indeed played a pivotal role as an agent of societal transformation, in ways that have nothing to do with the conditions of domestic work. It was the NDWA, as we saw, that sent Garza to Ferguson in 2014, when she turned BLM from a hashtag and a website into a worldwide movement. She told *In These Times*, a Marxist magazine started in 1976 by Julian Bond, Noam Chomsky, and Herbert Marcuse, that in Ferguson, she worked to "make sure the organizations and activists on the ground had the capacity to really hold this moment and extend it into a movement…. I spent some time really sitting with folks and helping them strategize."[22] The NDWA, Garza said, was key at this Ferguson moment. The NDWA "represents 10,000 or more women of color or immigrant women…. We understand the role of gender, race, and class are intricately connected." Her organizing in Ferguson, she added, was informed by "Third World Liberation movements."

In Ferguson, Garza wore at least three hats. One was as BLM cofounder, another was as an officer in the NDWA, and the third was as a member of LeftRoots, a front for the Marxist group Freedom Road Socialist Organization.[23] The fact that Garza was affiliated with these three different groups underscores the link between the revolutionary planning undertaken at the behest of overseas Marxists, and the actual revolution on American streets and in its classrooms, offices, and factories. Others who took part in the USSF and then showed up in Ferguson were AlternateRoots, Project South, Solis's Southwest Workers Union, and the NDWA itself.

A strong contingent of Palestinians from the USSF also turned up in Ferguson, some two hundred strong by some estimates, with speakers including the well-known anti-Semite Linda Sarsour. Just six weeks after the riots in

Ferguson, Cullors herself led a delegation to the West Bank, where she made strong anti-Israel statements. One of the Palestinian groups was taken to Ferguson by National Students for Justice in Palestine, whose anti-Semitic statements in support of Hamas's massacre and gang rapes of Jews on October 7, 2023, were so vile that governor Ron DeSantis ordered Florida universities to disband SJP chapters. Cullors's delegation was organized by Dream Defenders, which associates with the Popular Front for the Liberation of Palestine—which the director of national intelligence calls "a Syria-based terrorist group."[24]

It was these networks, and dozens of others like them, that had shared the BLM hashtag on social media from the moment of the group's creation in 2013, magnifying its messaging and making it a nationally and internationally recognized brand in days.

Today the NDWA is still working hard to realize Chávez's dream of forming "a grand worldwide anti-imperialist, alternative movement" inside the belly of the beast. In 2022, when the Left began to grasp that it was starting to lose the votes of Americans of Latin descent, it was the NDWA's political director, Jess Morales Rocketto, who raised $80 million, some of it Soros's money, to buy eighteen Spanish-language stations across the United States.[25]

The USSF network was created specifically for the type of organizing the revolution required. As Garza put it to the Oakland group, "one of the major things that we want to emphasize for those of you who have never been to a Social Forum . . . is that the Social Forum is *not* a conference." So what was the USSF? "The idea is not that you go and you learn about like twenty different groups' work. . . . It's a movement-building process! The idea behind a Social Forum is to bring together all of our different segments, all of our different sectors, all the work that we're doing, right, and strategize about how we're going to build a better world.

"We come together and we try to build with other sectors, other organizations, other social movements, and we talk about how to make life better for the majority of the world's people. And hopefully what comes out of that is greater cohesion, greater coordination," Garza added.[26]

And the WSF and its USSF subsidiary are but one of the organizing platforms that bring NextGen (and sometimes OldGen) Marxist revolutionaries together with officials of unsavory world regimes, to hatch plans on how to make America an unrecognizable country. There are many others, such as the aforementioned LeftRoots. Yet one more is Left Forum, the new name for the old Socialist Scholars Conference, a creature of the New Left that used to meet annually at the City University of New York.

Left Forum

THE RENAMED and more activist-focused (and thus more confrontational) Left Forum started in 2005. From its first meeting, it demonstrated its international bona fides by bringing representatives from the Venezuelan and Brazilian governments, both Marxist-led, respectively, by Chávez and Lula. At the opening 2005 Left Forum, there was also a heavy contingent of American Marxists, including Frances Fox Piven, Robyn D. G. Kelley, and Rosa Clemente.[27]

China also began sending academics to the Left Forum annual gatherings very early on, in 2006.[28] The next year, 2007, saw the first appearance by Joseph A. Buttigieg, a Notre Dame professor who was by then the country's top Gramsci scholar and the main translator and president of the International Gramsci Society, which he founded to spread Gramsci's teachings around the globe. Buttigieg spoke at a panel titled "Rethinking Marxism." In 2008, Buttigieg spoke on a panel titled "Rethinking Marxism and the Future of Global Struggles." If the name is familiar today, it is because the late Professor Buttigieg is the father of Pete Buttigieg, a 2020 Democratic presidential candidate who serves as secretary of transportation in the Biden administration as of this writing.[29] In 2008, there were several panels on China, with speakers from universities on the Mainland.

Poo, who had just been named head of the NDWA, which had been created months earlier at the first USSF in Atlanta, made her first appearance at a Left Forum in 2008 and from then on became a fixture.[30] Poo returned in 2009 to speak on three panels, one of which—"Left Strategy from the Grassroots"—also included Harmony Goldberg.[31] It was Goldberg's School of Unity and Liberation (SOUL) that had given Garza an internship at the age of twenty-one, just as Mann's Strategy Center did for Cullors at seventeen, and initiated her in the arts of Marxism and organizing. Goldberg, an accomplished academic Gramscian, brings to life with vivid writing how to apply the theories of the twentieth-century Machiavelli to twenty-first-century America. Gramsci's ideas were joined on the stage of the 2009 Left Forum by those of the other twentieth-century European philosopher whose baleful shadow darkens our days, Marcuse. His son Peter, a Marxist professor of urban planning (what else?) at Columbia, spoke on "critical urban theory."

Indeed, we can see in the 2009 Left Forum the perfect combination of philosophy and praxis that, a decade and a half later, has rained on all Americans the changes that so bedevil their lives. It took place in April at Pace University in New York, just three months after Barack Obama had taken office. The three founders of BLM wouldn't start attending for a couple of years. Yet, the hornet's nest that would catapult them to revolutionary leadership was being constructed by activists and ideologues rubbing shoulders as they walked the halls of Pace between collaborative workshops and panels on "building new socialist relations."

Goldberg, the perfect middleman between heavy Gramscian and Marcusian thought, on one hand, and street activism, on the other, was there in 2009. She kept a finger in every pot, from SOUL to the NDWA and the Grassroots Power Project (where her title was, appropriately, "director of praxis"). The NDWA's Poo was also there in 2009, as was Steve Williams, head of POWER, where Garza was still perched in 2009. It is to Williams, according to the Rosa Luxemburg Foundation, that we owe the concept of "transformative organizing" with which Mann was so enamored. It is a set of best (or worst, depending on your view) practices that will help organizers "build up a movement capable of effectively challenging capitalism, hetero-patriarchy, and white supremacy."[32] Williams collaborates with or belongs to several communist organizations, from Freedom Road Socialist Organization to LeftRoots and the Organization for Black Struggle. In 2010, Williams appeared on the same USSF panel with Mann and Cullors, where Cullors explained how Mann's center helped her channel her anger.

By 2010, the presence of officials from the People's Republic of China (PRC) had grown heavy, as world communists looked to the Chinese model as a plausible blueprint. There was a panel in particular titled "Recent Transformations in Chinese Marxism," which included professors from top universities, who were likely to be at least closely associated with the Chinese Communist Party (CCP).

There were no fewer than eight other panels on China at the 2010 Left Forum, in which Chinese officials and a smattering of others participated. There was another panel titled "How to Make a Revolution in the US," which included someone who had thought long about the matter, Goldberg.

The 2011 Left Forum added Mann and Cullors. They participated together in several panels on how to use a black-based multiracial coalition to revolutionize society and on "transformative organizing," which to Mann means the same thing—he says it has to be black-led. Ditto for the year 2012, which again brought officials from the PRC and Venezuela, including its consul in New York, Carol Delgado, and her German husband, Gregory Wilpert, a prominent pro-Chávez activist.

The 2013 Left Forum brought a high dignitary from one of the hemisphere's most radical governments, the Bolivian vice president Álvaro García Linera. Also an ardent Gramscian, Linera spoke at the closing plenary. Opal Tometi, the third cofounder of BLM, started attending in 2013, which saw the same mix of Chinese and Venezuelan dignitaries plotting revolution with American Marxists.[33] The 2013 Left Forum was also held at Pace University in Lower Manhattan, on June 7–9. That means it was the last Left Forum of the pre-BLM era. Just over a month later, on July 13, the jury in Sanford, Florida, acquitted Zimmerman of Martin's murder.

It was during the days following the acquittal that Garza, Cullors, and Tometi created BLM, first as a hashtag rallying point for activism, then, in 2014, in Ferguson as a global network, which is, in fact, called the Black Lives Matter Global Network Foundation (BLMGNF). The work of such platforms as the WSF, the USSF, LeftRoots, and Left Forum had finally borne fruit by producing a Marxist-led movement that was African American–centric and oriented toward the Third World, particularly Latin America. None of the meetings of the different forums would henceforth be the same. From mid-2013 on, the world's Left would focus on BLM, the revolution it had brought to the "belly of the beast."

BLM thus became the locomotive for the revolutionary train. At the Left Forum following Ferguson, Garza delivered a haunting tirade against American society that also mapped out in clear terms what the revolution was after. Her tone and demeanor were dark; she was no longer the happy-go-lucky activist rallying her fellow radicals on behalf of world Marxists, as she had been at the Oakland USSF a mere five years earlier. She was now the leader of a revolutionary movement whose claims were based on grievances, and her mood oscillated between somber and downright surly. Speaking at New York City's John Jay College of Criminal Justice (of all places), Garza said, "Black Lives Matter is much more than a hashtag, in fact, it's an organized network in twenty-six cities globally. It's also intended to be a tactic to help rebuild the black liberation movement—BLM-BLM," she said, extending for emphasis one arm first, then the other.[34]

The stage of anti-capitalist fervor had been set by Paul Jay, CEO and founder of the Real News, an alternative website, who introduced Garza. "Far too few people own far too much. And that's the root of the problem. The class that owns so much, that wields so much political power, is not capable of effecting policy in the interest of the majority of people," said Jay. Jay also emphasized another important theme of the evening: "The super-exploited, the black and Latino workers, will be at the heart of the driving force of this change, they must also be the leadership.... The resistance in Ferguson and Baltimore have opened up a new horizon for building an independent movement for transformational change."[35]

In her speech, Garza smeared the entire arc of American history as being "part of a plan to subvert, to oppress, and in some cases, many cases, especially now, to extinguish black lives." Then, pausing for emphasis, she added, "*To get rid of us.*" BLM's fight, she said, "is absolutely about eradicating police violence and police terrorism, the fight is absolutely about eliminating the criminalization of black people and people of color, and other oppressed people." But the fight was about much more, and so were BLM's ambitions. The fight was against all aspects of American life and against its economic system. Garza launched into a long harangue that presaged the next eight years of our country's life:

But, honestly, this fight is about black liberation, and if I'm going to be honest with you, that cannot be relegated to a hashtag. When we created Black Lives Matter, its intent was not to be limited to narrow visions of what state violence looks like, but it was intended to encompass the struggle for human dignity and self-determination. We understand state violence is criminalization, but we also understand state violence as austerity, that state violence is patriarchy and white supremacy and imperialism. Let me break that down. We understand state violence as thousands of people in Detroit who lack water. Thousands of people in Baltimore who lack access to water. We understand state violence as the attack on public-sector workers and our labor movement. We understand state violence as the lack of access to quality housing and quality education, quality jobs, to a future. It's not possible for a world to emerge where black lives matter if it's under capitalism, and it's not possible to abolish capitalism without a struggle against national oppression and gender oppression. So, the fight against police terror, police violence, state violence, is but one front of many, and it is our duty as human beings, as leftists, to ensure that the fight again police terror and criminalization

NEXTGEN MARXISM | 221

is connected to the conditions of black communities, for the stake of the re-emergence of a vibrant, effective, powerful, black liberation movement.[36]

THAT WAS the oral manifesto of the BLM network, one that had been hatched in Ferguson in late 2014. It was a Marxist movement that was not just black-led and Black-centered but also Third World–aligned, the other element Mann and others thought necessary. This is hardly a surprise, because many of these networks had been activated by Third World Marxists, as we have seen. This brings us to yet another important forum, this one Latin America–focused, that also brought BLM into its fold.

The Foro de São Paulo

THE SÃO Paulo Forum, or in Portuguese, the Foro de São Paulo, was created in that Brazilian city by communist parties and leaders who expressly wanted an "alternative" to capitalism after the collapse of the Soviet Union in 1991. The Foro is strong on Gramsci and his Latin American counterpart, Ernesto Laclau. Both believed in gaining power through stealth, not through the barrel of a gun, and forming a populistic hegemonic bloc. Linera, the Bolivian vice president who closed out the last Left Forum of the pre-BLM era, told an interviewer in 2019 that "Gramsci has been decisive for the development of my own thinking. I began to read him when I was very young.... Since then, unlike so many texts containing economistic analyses or philosophical formulations centered more on the aesthetics of words than on reality, Gramsci has helped me to develop a different way of seeing. He spoke of questions such as language, literature, education or common sense which, though seemingly secondary, actually form the web of daily life for individuals and determine their perceptions and collective political inclinations."[37]

One of the reasons to opt for winning power through "language, literature, education" was that guns had failed Marxists in Latin America. The 1980s was the last time Marxists made a concerted effort to take over the region through armed struggle, in conflagrations that pitted Moscow- and Cuban-backed sides against US-backed opponents. Violent revolts raged in El Salvador, where the Farabundo Martí National Liberation Front faced off against a tenuously elected leader; in Nicaragua, where the Marxist Sandinistas had taken over in a revolution in 1979 and now faced the Reagan-backed Contras guerrillas; and in

Guatemala, where military strongmen held off against an indigenous-centered guerrilla movement. All these Marxist efforts failed, and by the early 1990s, Nicaragua, El Salvador, and Guatemala were all ruled by center-right governments. Mao had said that power came from the barrel of a gun. Mao had been right with regard to China but wrong just about everywhere else, and thus he was thrown in the dustbin of history. Henceforth, we would get digitized Marxism, or Marxism in the sense-making institutions—cultural, or NextGen, Marxism.

There was also a very important exogenous reason for creating the Foro: the Soviet Union had imploded, and Marxists the world over—both the intellectual types and the sort with guns—lost their financial backing as well as their source of ideology. On Christmas Day 1991, the Soviet flag was lowered on the Kremlin for the last time, and the USSR—a truly evil empire responsible for the murder and suffering of millions of Soviet citizens and East Europeans over the decades—broke apart into fifteen separate republics. The writing had been on the wall about communism's collapse behind the Iron Curtain since 1989, when the Berlin Wall was dismantled by thousands of demonstrators armed with simple hammers, and communist regimes in Eastern Europe fell like dominoes in the region's first free elections in decades.

Fidel Castro had watched all this from his Caribbean redoubt with anguished disbelief and fear for his own skin and the vast wealth he had illicitly amassed. Castro's close friend, Lula da Silva, had the same fears, though as simply head of the PT and not yet leader of Brazil, Lula hadn't yet had the opportunity to plunder his country's treasury. They both agreed that something had to be done, so they decided to call for a massive regional summit of hemispheric socialists. On July 4, 1990, of all dates, members from forty-eight socialist and communist parties from around Latin America met in São Paulo, Brazil, at the behest of Castro and Lula, to find a new way forward.

Just as their world appeared to be crumbling, socialist leaders in Latin America decided to unite, share ideas and best practices, and pursue power by means other than bullets. As Lula described the metamorphosis years later in a 2009 speech in Lima, "eighteen years ago, in almost all the countries of South America, there were political currents that believed that the only way to get power was through armed struggle. In 1990, we founded the Foro.... This Foro began to educate the Left to understand that there was a possibility and win through democratic means."[38]

At its second meeting the next year, in Mexico City, the group came to be called the Foro de São Paulo, or the São Paulo Forum. From that point on, the Foro met every year as a large conference, while smaller working conferences were held more frequently to discuss revolutionary tactics. Eventually, BLM was drawn in as well, participating in the Foro held in the Washington, DC, area in July 2017. The BLM representative spoke about how to revolutionize the American street at a panel on "Actions in the US: Objectives and Challenges."[39]

The Final Declaration all the leaders signed at the end of the São Paulo meeting in 1990 laid the foundation for what the forum wanted to achieve. It said that socialism was the most democratic and just answer for the people and that "we reject, therefore, all attempts to benefit from the crisis in Eastern Europe to attempt a restoration of capitalism, annul their social achievements and social rights, and to encourage the illusion of the inexistent tender mercies of liberalism and capitalism."[40] The meeting "reaffirmed in practice," said the manifesto, "the willingness of the left-wing, socialist, and anti-imperialist forces of the sub-continent to share analyses and assessments of their experiences and of the current state of affairs in the world."

The manifesto left no doubt of its socialist and anti-capitalist character. It said that "we know that the pressing needs and the gravest problems of our peoples have their roots in the capitalist system." Yet, it gave plenty of lip service to democratic practices, saying that socialist victory "requires an active commitment to the observance of human rights and to democracy and popular sovereignty as strategic values, putting the left-wing, socialist, and progressive forces before the challenge of constantly renewing their thought and action."

What that word salad meant in practice was that the communists and socialists would from that point on not try to shoot their way into power but would instead work to get elected on populist and reformist planks, concealing their Marxism. The Foro model involved importing academics from Europe who would advise them on how to apply Gramscian principles to change the hegemonic narrative in the culture. Once they got elected, the new leaders could be more open about their Marxism and seek to rewrite constitutions, with constitutional assemblies that would break up the nation into a "plurinational state," where the rights of the indigenous collectives could rise above those of the individual, give absolute power to the president, and make other institutional changes that would impose socialist principles on the population. Once in power, the newly elected Marxists could also then export their revolution to other parts of Latin America and to the United States, creating or fanning street demonstrations that would lead to political crises.

It was a mix that has worked very well in Latin America, whose leaders were often not proper elites but self-serving and self-dealing oligarchs. Their misbehavior created swampy political environments where mistrust of institutions festered, and populist demagogues promising "reform" could logically strike a nerve with a weary population. As a result of the careful application of the Foro de São Paulo playbook, Marxists were, at the time of this writing, in control in Brazil (where Lula is again president), Chile, Colombia, Mexico, Peru, Nicaragua, and Honduras, not to mention, of course, Venezuela, the oil paymaster, and Cuba, the ideological snakehead.

Venezuela's Chávez was the first leader to win elections in this manner, in 1998, and Lula followed suit, winning office in 2002 (these were the two leaders who, lest we forget, had worked for the creation of the WSF and its US affiliate). Chávez had attended the 1993 Havana Foro, and Castro and Lula had been grooming him since then. Chávez thus downplayed his Marxism and ran on a reformist platform against Venezuela's very real corruption. After winning, however, Chávez established his "Bolivarian" revolutions and used his country's vast oil resources to carry out the Foro plan. "Hugo Chávez would spend the next almost two decades systematically transforming Petróleos de Venezuela, S.A. (PDVSA—the Venezuelan national oil company). The result was a multibillion-dollar political and criminal enterprise operating in concert with sympathetic political leaders, economic elites and criminal organizations," wrote the researchers Douglas Farah and Caitlyn Yates in a 2020 study.[41] Tometi has been the BLM founder most associated with the Venezuelan regime, inviting Chávez's successor, Maduro, to Harlem in 2015; acting as an election observer in Venezuela; and writing a manifesto supporting the revolution that same year.

The paths to power of the new presidents who have been elected in the third decade of this century also reveal striking similarities, not just among themselves, but also to BLM's path to power: all used social media–manipulated street violence to score political and cultural victories. This was strictly Gramscian, for, as we said in chapter 2, the war of maneuver—that is, violence—could interrupt the war of positions, and should have, any time a propitious crisis came along—provided that the organic intellectual had done his job of convincing the worker that he had no stake in prolonging capitalism.

Thus street mayhem in Chile in 2019 and in Colombia in 2021 was a carbon copy of the George Floyd riots here in 2020. The riots led in 2021 to the election of Gabriel Boric as president of Chile and in 2022 of Gustavo Petro as president of Colombia, both committed Marxists. In Chile, the issue that galvanized the crowds was a minimal rise in the price of metro rides, in Colombia, a rise in taxes. In both countries, as in the United States, protests organized through social-media quickly mushroomed into widespread national riots. In Chile, churches were looted and a metro station torched, and in all three countries, buildings were ransacked or torched. We have seen similar protest patterns in Ecuador.

In the United States, Joe Biden defeated Donald Trump in the 2020 presidential election and soon started cowriting federal policy with the Black Lives Matter Global Network Foundation, the organization set up by Cullors, Garza, and Tometi.[42] As 2020 progressed, America's cultural and educational elites surrendered to the idea that the United States is oppressive and riven with systemic racism, and deep cultural change accelerated. Even the Audubon Society started changing the names of birds to deemphasize "white supremacy." The heights of finance were conquered. Citigroup, Goldman Sachs, BlackRock, and other financial giants bent a knee and accepted the Chávezian view that their own country was oppressive. "Across social media, America's disproportionately white group of company leaders pronounced themselves 'allies' in the fight against inequality and declared that 'black lives matter,'" wrote the *Financial Times* in 2020.[43] In his 2021 letter to CEOs, BlackRock CEO Larry Fink praised the "wave of historic protests for racial justice in the United States and around the world." Fink demanded that corporations at least partly controlled by BlackRock not only disclose how "their business model will be compatible with a net zero economy" but also that annual disclosures "fully reflect your long-term plans to improve diversity, equity, and inclusion."[44] Fink himself would not in the least be put out by the totalitarian nature of a United States governed by BLM's precepts. "Markets like, actually, totalitarian governments," Fink said in 2011, deriding the wave of revolutions attempting to bring democracy to different parts of the world at the time. "Democracies are very messy, as we know in the United States—we have opinions changing back and forth."[45]

Fanning the Flames of Revolution through Social Media

BUT THE unrest, in the United States and globally, that caused all this did not grow organically, or even domestically. It was planned as a strategy to dismantle capitalism and representative democracy and to introduce totalitarian practices. In the United States, the networks where the plotting festered were created and nurtured for years by global Marxist intellectuals and urged by enemies of the United States. Why hasn't an in-depth study been done on the social media accounts and influencers that fanned the actual flames of protests and riots in US cities in 2020? By its own admission, BLM sent more than 127 million emails that year, and many of the same accounts that promoted protests in Latin America also promoted violence in the United States.[46] In Latin America, the mayhem can be sourced to Foro members. As Farah and Yates found out, the social-media accounts that organized and directed the demonstrations came from outside Colombia and Chile: "It was not just discontent over growing inequality that sustained Chile's unrest. One factor that exacerbated everything was the use of social-media, specifically Twitter, on which accounts from outside Chile were fueling the flames of discontent."[47] They went on to write that an analysis "of 4.8 million tweets from 639,000 Twitter accounts with hashtags in favor of the protests in Chile during the peak of the unrest found that most of the accounts were not Chilean but Venezuelan, Nicaraguan and Cuban. On the other hand, the vast majority of tweets against the protests were Chilean."[48] Florencia Lagos Neumann, a Chilean Communist Party member, openly admitted at a Foro-organized communicators conference in Caracas in December 2019 that the Chilean riots had not been spontaneous at all. "'We are organized, we are more than 100 organizations' whose goal is to overturn the current political structure 'imposed by the United States,'" the researchers quoted her as saying.[49] In the United States in 2020, BLMGNF said that in 2020, "we sent 127,042,508 emails. From these emails, 1,213,992 actions were taken."[50]

The report by Farah and Yates was written a year before the same thing happened in Colombia and two before it was repeated in Peru: in both of those countries as well, the violence was instigated by outside social-media accounts. In Peru in 2022, foreign media accounts activated "indigenous" groups, unions, and other leftist activists to take to the streets after the Maoist president Pedro

Castillo was ousted by the legislature for trying to carry out a power grab. The outside social-media accounts were based in the United States, Argentina, Bolivia, and Mexico and included pro-China, pro-Russia, pro-Iran, and pro-BLM activists.[51]

Farah and Yates wrote that it was at the 2019 Caracas conference that Foro members decided to organize the destabilization of countries not yet governed by the Left. They "had shock troops positioned in Ecuador, Chile and Colombia—almost all trained by the FARC between 2005 and 2016—to successfully carry out a strategy of pushing social discontent to violent actions," they wrote, using the Spanish-language abbreviation of the Revolutionary Armed Forces of Colombia, a narco-terrorist Marxist group.

The street theater was not actually meant to overthrow elected governments, and in fact, none were. They were meant to destabilize governments and institutions and to set up elections where the Marxist alternative, concealing their ideology and presenting themselves as populists, would win. In an example of how it works in practice, Colombia's Gustavo Petro artfully avoided labeling himself a Marxist during the electoral campaign of late 2021 and 2022, preferring to use euphemisms. Even Spain's leftist newspaper *El País* called the strategy "slippery arguments," after trying, in vain, to get Petro to speak clearly about his political beliefs in an interview in late 2021.

When asked whether he was still a Marxist, Petro gave an answer that, when analyzed with the Foro's Gramscian model in mind, actually makes a lot of sense: "It's not that I have been but now I'm not. It's that I have stopped looking at politics in that manner. As a young man I wanted to make armed revolutions, but a lot of things have happened in Colombia and in the world."[52] Of course he had. Petro, a former member of the M19 Marxist terrorist group, is Latin America's version of Bill Ayers: he understood the Foro's lessons. But once elected in June 2022, Petro was freer to speak his mind, increasing his attacks on the market economy by using environmentalism as the excuse. "We are living in times that are the beginning of the extinction of humankind," Petro told a crowd of supporters in a speech at Stanford University in April 2023. "The logical and coherent answer, like the one given at the end of the nineteenth century, is that humanity would have to organize itself to undertake a world revolution against capital."[53]

A Global Network of Revolutionaries

THIS STUDY of global leftist networks and their role in the rise of socialist regimes in Latin America and in fueling BLM suggests that the world's Marxists have developed an effective playbook for taking power. First they fuel social discontent, a sense of grievance and anger. That then spurs violence and social instability—riots, demonstrations, violence—that destabilizes governments and institutions. They use social media to make it seem as if discontent is widespread. Then they ride into power through elections, promising stability and utopian change. Once in power, they support each other across borders to consolidate and further extend their power.

The playbook is grounded in Marx, Lenin, and Gramsci, but its architects are twenty-first-century characters. Stéphane Hessel, who in his youth had been a member of the French Resistance in World War II, in 2010 wrote a manifesto titled "Indignez Vous!" It was officially translated as "Time for Outrage!" but more accurately means "Be Indignant!"[54] He claimed that peace and democracy everywhere were threatened by the tyranny of global capitalism and colonialism, that people everywhere were oppressed, and that the world lay in near environmental ruin. His solution was a return to the communist ideals of the French Resistance. We must abandon the Western obsession with productivity, consumption, and competition, he proclaimed. "It's time to take over. It's time to get angry.... I wish all of you to find your reason for indignation." Hessel's thirty-two-page pamphlet quickly became a global phenomenon, selling millions of copies, and within just several months, large-scale antigovernment demonstrations took place across the globe, from the Arab Spring in January and February 2011 to Los Indignados in Spain in May to Occupy Wall Street in fall 2011.

These were among the first protests in which social media played a pivotal role, and they demonstrated its power to mobilize tens of thousands when combined with the language of indignation and the promise of a utopian future. Hessel's call for indignation put into words what would become a new playbook. It was a group of Spanish academics who then wrote the playbook.

These Spanish academics had already been working together for years on such a playbook, through the Center for Political Social Studies (CEPS), an anti-capitalist consulting firm founded in the 1990s by political science professors from the Universities of Madrid and Valencia, which has been described as an organization that "produces critical thought and cultural and intellectual work to create leftist consensuses."[55] CEPS helped design the political campaigns that brought to power three Latin American Marxist firebrands: Hugo Chávez, who became president of Venezuela in 1999; Evo Morales, who became president of Bolivia in 2006; and Rafael Correa, who became president of Ecuador in 2007. CEPS advised them to adopt the Gramscian strategy of dissimulating their Marxism, to pose as reformists to gain power, and then to reorder society once they had power. The Spaniards helped to write new constitutions, breaking the nations into indigenous "plurinational states," where checks and balances all but disappeared and near-absolute power went to the president. As we wrote in chapter 2, this is a faithful implementation of Gramsci's directive to participate in parliamentary democracy only to gain power and create the conditions for councils or "direct democracy." Then laws were passed to control the press, and other mediating institutions were weakened or dismantled to clear the way for such measures as expropriating property and nationalizing natural resources. The Minister for the economy in the Madrid regional government until July 2022, Javier Fernández-Lasquetty explained in a presentation he gave at the Mont Pelerin Society meeting in Guatemala in 2021 that these were "professors as consultants for the revolution."[56] There was "no financial support from abroad. Nor did arms arrive. Nor military advisers. University professors arrived, grouped in an apparently non-profit consulting firm." The whole thing, Fernández-Lasquetty said, was "based on Gramsci's idea of hegemony" and Laclau's thoughts on collectivism. None of this came cheap. Chávez paid CEPS €3.7 million from Venezuela's public coffers and narco-trafficking profits, money that critics say CEPS used to create the Marxist Spanish party Podemos.[57] Some news reports put Venezuelan payments as high as €7.76 million.[58] From Ecuador, the CEPS academics received some €1.4 million.[59] Spanish news reports also say that Bolivia's Morales used CEPS to fund Podemos in 2014 and 2015, when the party was emerging.[60] The Bolivian Marxist firebrand used a different consulting firm, Neurona, to funnel at least €1.5 million (other reports say it was many millions) to Podemos, according to media reports in Spain.[61] Money also came from Brazil while Dilma Rousseff, Lula's successor, was in power and from Mexico after Andrés Manuel López Obrador, another Marxist, became president.

In this manner, Marxist political scientists from Spanish universities helped South American revolutionaries gain power and become tyrants, writing

230 | "IN THE BELLY OF THE BEAST"

constitutions that impacted the character of these societies. Once in power, these dictators used ill-gotten gains, whether from nationalizations, expropriations, or the illicit international drug trade, to help the academics create their own party back in the mother country and gain power.

And that they did. Podemos, created in January 2014, used its deep pockets to catapult instantly to fame and power, winning 8 percent of the vote in European elections held only four months later. In 2018, it formed a coalition government with the Socialist Party, and Iglesias became deputy prime minister, the second-highest official in the Spanish government. Once in power, it helped introduce gender theory policies and BLM-inspired programs to make Spain's population of African descent (3 percent of the overall population) feel aggrieved.[62] Irene Montero, the Podemos minister behind that project (and Iglesias's common-law wife), has officially joined the Grupo de Puebla, a subgroup of the Foro de São Paulo.

Podemos's manifesto was titled "Move a Piece: Turn Indignation into Political Change." It spelled out the essence of the NextGen Marxist playbook—use indignation to bring about political change:

> Just as with other moments in history, we see today a European continent submerged in perplexity. Whilst the majorities look back with nostalgia on the past that is lost, certain powerful minorities, with no criterion other than their own survival, show that enrichment is their flag and impunity their horizon.... We think it is no longer time for giving up but for making a move and pulling together, by offering tools to outrage and the desire for change. In the streets "Sí se puede" ("Yes, it can be done") is repeatedly heard. We say: "Podemos" ("We can do it").[63]

THE SPANISH academics who had created the playbook now set about implementing it in their own country. They won 8 percent of the vote in the national election, sending five members to the European Parliament, and today it is a member of Spain's ruling coalition, subsumed under a new name, Sumar. But for our purposes, of greatest interest is what we can learn from them about the global networks of new Marxists and the strategies they are using to gain power over unsuspecting populations.

A BLM Globe

THIS IS the international leftist milieu that enabled the emergence of BLM as their agents in "the belly of the beast": Marxist European academics helped South American despots gain power; these tyrants then urged involvement by American Marxists, and a US-based Social Forum was created, where participants plotted how to bring the same blueprint to the United States. And make no mistake: the fate of Venezuelans is the fate that awaits us if we allow the models of Marxist regimes in Venezuela, Bolivia, and so on to be replicated here. But that is exactly what the leaders of BLM are working toward.

"In these last 17 years, we have witnessed the Bolivarian Revolution champion participatory democracy and construct a fair, transparent election system recognized as among the best in the world," wrote Tometi in 2015 of Venezuela's tyrannical government. "We stand with the Venezuelan people as they build a revolutionary and popular democracy based on communal power. *Their struggle is our own.* We denounce the United States of America's continuing intervention and support for the counter-revolution in Venezuela using economic, political, psychological, media and military means…. We reject the hypocrisy of the Venezuelan elite—who like settlers everywhere—cling to their white privilege to the point of even lynching Afrodescendants."[64]

In 2017, Tometi also traveled to Bolivia to meet with that country's Marxist leader, Morales, with whom she said she "discussed human rights, climate change, and the alliances between governments to strengthen global justice."[65] While in La Paz, Tometi was the opening speaker at a conference on "a world without walls," it being the first year of the Trump administration.[66]

BLM did help take the US boot "off the neck" of some of the world's worst regimes, as Garza said was the intent back in 2010. Violeta Tamayo, leader of Bolivia's Revolutionary Workers League, a Trotskyist faction, for example, praised BLM for weakening the United States from within and strengthening Bolivia's socialists from without, going so far as to give BLM partial credit for the victory of the Movimiento al Socialismo socialist party of Linera and Morales at the height of the George Floyd riots. "We believe it's crucial for socialists in the United States to fight to build truly anti-imperialist organizations. For example, the Black Lives Matter movement has been very important in Bolivia for the defeat of the Far Right, because it weakened the interventionist sectors in the

United States and weakened the right wing in our country as well," Tamayo, an indigenous leader, told a leftist publication. "So this shows the importance of the struggles of the revolutionary Left in other countries, of all forms of class struggle, like Black Lives Matter."[67]

Farah and Yates described how these groups use the Foro de São Paulo in this way:

> Militant organizations and groups primarily anchored in the Communist parties or revolutionary movements of their host countries are at the center of the FDSP [Foro de São Paulo]. Under the FDSP umbrella, solidary groups are divided into subgroups by region or social sector. Dozens of organizations or actors are officially invited to a conference and break down into many smaller unions, collectives, or social movements in their home countries. Thus, a single umbrella organization may represent hundreds of other organizations during these events, often with overlapping members and usually quite small individual collectives. From there, these somewhat disparate groups under the umbrella organization can issue similar or identical statements of solidarity with Venezuela and Cuba, condemn the United States and laud Russia and Vladimir Putin as paradigms of anti-imperialist values.[68]

THE STRONG participation by Chinese officials and especially academics at the Left Forum conferences reveals interest in these webs by all our adversaries, not just those in Latin America. China itself has been an ardent amplifier of the BLM rhetoric, making full use of it in its official party press. The Chinese Progressive Association of Boston (CPA Boston), an organization started in the 1970s by the paramilitary, pro-Mao group I Wor Kuen, has cohosted official public events with China's consulate, thus it has an official link to the CCP. CPA Boston has at the same time called on its members and supporters to join BLM marches and protests and to show an unswerving loyalty to BLM's black leadership. During the 2014 organizing in Ferguson, Seeding Change, an umbrella organization that brings CPA Boston and other leftist Chinese-American groups together, posted, for example, a call on its website for members to join the protest. "It is important for Asian American communities to show up for Black Lives and take the lead from Black communities," it said.[69] CPA San Francisco, a separate organization also founded by I Wor Kuen, is meanwhile the financial sponsor of one of BLM's affiliates, the Black Futures Lab.[70] Both CPA Boston and CPA San Francisco also interact extensively with BLM and its leadership through the Left Forum network, Seeding Change, and LeftRoots.[71]

Conclusion

IF YOU look for the reasons that we are living the lives we are in the middle of the century's third decade, with racism imposed in our classrooms through CRT-inspired curricula and in our offices through "antiracist trainings," and why transexual ideology is everywhere, especially in K–12 schools, and why our leaders are considering crippling capitalism in the name of climate change, don't listen to journalists who tell you that it's all part of a "racial reckoning" or a new awareness of the marginalized. There is something much deeper at work here.

In 1968, riots tore through many cities in America following the April 4, 1968, assassination of Martin Luther King Jr. In the nation's capital, more than twelve hundred buildings were burned, with damage climbing to $25 million. Journalists to this day tell you that it was a spontaneous reaction to a particularly evil act. Yet back then, not all journalists were lemmings. Ben Gilbert, a black reporter for *The Washington Post*, found out that the theme was the same as during the far-costlier riots of 2020: Marxism. Gilbert, who later wrote a book about all this titled *Ten Blocks from the White House*, interviewed three men in a hotel who explained to him how they had planned the violence for months and then used the tragedy of the King assassination to strike their blow. "A lot of areas we went into," said one of the Che Guevara–quoting revolutionaries, "there was nothing going on till we got there. But once we started our thing, man, people just took up." These men had a lot of other men working for them. "There is organization. Don't you realize that, as I said, there's a revolution going on; there must be organization! That's the reason that it was not a riot but a rebellion! There is organization. You have your assigned districts that you work with."[72]

The same is true today. So, if you are looking for reasons why our lives are being turned upside down, and the country may be transformed beyond recognition unless we act, don't turn to the mainstream media.

"American media, public intellectuals and government officials have failed to present an accurate assessment of the threat that revolutionary leftist organizations that have declared their allegiance to foreign governments pose to the US Constitution," wrote in 2020 the researcher Ariel Sheen, who has been tracking

234 | "IN THE BELLY OF THE BEAST"

these forums. "The political unrest and media polarization which has accelerated over the past decade is not an organic response to grievances. It is the product of a twenty-year-long strategy developed by anarchists, communists and secessionists in collaboration with foreign government actors. At present we are in year ten of a large-scale, clandestine effort involving tens of thousands of Americans to subvert and eventually annul the Constitution."[73]

So, look at our universities, our philanthropies, our entertainment industry, indeed, our media itself, and all of the other factors of cultural production. Also, look south to politically godforsaken places like Caracas, La Paz, Porto Alegre, and especially Havana. There this transformation into "a better world...another US" (in the words of the US Social Forum, a phrase so often repeated by Marxists that it has become some sort of dog whistle) was envisaged and planned. Only it hasn't been a better world. If we continue to ignore these origins and allow the media to obstruct everything that has been reported in this chapter, then we won't be able to come up with a solution.

And so it is to solutions that we now turn.

9
WHAT TO DO

THE NEXTGEN REVOLUTIONARIES who had been reared on Gramsci, Marcuse, and Alinsky, then politicized and organized by global radical networks, and who later pursued their anti-capitalist and anti-democratic agenda in the name of race, sex, and climate, saw an opportunity to deliver a knockout blow to society in 2020 by seizing on the death of George Floyd. But, simply put, they have overplayed their hand. Yes, they did transform America, making it unrecognizable in many ways: today, we have to submit, or pay lip service, to the bizarre concept that America is an oppressive country and watch as parents let transvestites fondle their minor children. But in the end, what Gramsci called the "sturdy institutions of civil society" have held their ground. The BLM radicals have pushed too hard. Elites may have been thoroughly indoctrinated; everyday Americans have not.

Led by moms and dads, civil society has gotten off its haunches and stands athwart the revolt, yelling, "Stop!" They have forced politicians to take up their cause, electing Glenn Youngkin as Virginia governor in November 2021. They helped give Ron DeSantis an unheard-of twenty-point victory in his reelection as governor of Florida in 2022. The victories are not just electoral. The parents and the rest of civil society have changed the climate of opinion. Three years after BLM's 2020 revolution, the country is turning against the woke agenda of NextGen Marxists, and turning hard.

The moms have bought us time, in other words. We know they have been successful because twice now the Biden administration has tried to label them as domestic terrorists, or hate groups, going so far as to involve a special unit of the FBI. Joe Biden has never given any sign of being a Marxist, NextGen or OldGen. He has always been a retail Delaware politician lacking deep convictions other than his own political survival. In the 2020s, that instinct has made him side with the woke agenda, including by cowriting federal policy with the Marxist founders of BLM, as we showed in chapter 7. So his focus on destroying the mothers' groups is instructive: they matter.

When hundreds of parents in Loudoun County, Virginia, stood up in early 2021 to complain about COVID-19 restrictions in schools, about CRT in the classroom, and about opening girls' bathrooms to boys who claimed they were transgender (leading, in at least one case, to the rape of a minor girl by a skirt-wearing boy[1]), they were starting a counterattack with national repercussions, even if they may not have known it. We traveled the country extensively in 2021 and 2022 to meet with parent groups, and we heard the same refrain, whether in Redmond, Oregon, Aurora, Nebraska, or Cincinnati, Ohio: "Loudoun is Ground Zero!" As far away as Europe, people had heard of Loudoun County.

Up to this point, this book has been about how we got here, detailing how a new generation of Marxists took over the institutions. It has been about the evolution of the ideas that drive them, the development of the strategies that guide them, and the foreign collaborators who support them. This final chapter is about what we can do to fight them. We present strategies to deal with ethnic studies, CRT in classrooms, gender theory, the political use of climate, BlackRock, violent riots in American cities, and so on. But first we answer the question: *Why* must the United States be saved?

Remembering Who We Are

WHY NOT simply let the United States be taken over by NextGen Marxists? Is the effort required for self-government really worthwhile? Some Americans have demonstrated with their behavior that they believe it is not. They do not bother to vote; too many turn out only for presidential elections, as if that one office has a godly power over the character and direction of our communities. Too many leave the education of their children to the "professionals"— the school boards, the teacher's unions, the school administrators. Too many people simply want to attend to the comforts and security of their own lives, their families, their businesses, and not bother with what they see as the messy and uncomfortable business of fighting the NextGen Marxists. But the United States will not function this way. Indeed, the consequence of our neglect is today everywhere apparent. Our first task, therefore, is to reinvigorate our own conviction that the United States is a most worthy subject of our efforts. We must reengage with our history and the ideals that have shaped the United States to rekindle our love for who we are.

When we first started to discuss the idea for this book, both of us had been working to understand and describe the current cultural crisis in the United States. We saw that a number of smart and insightful people were doing the same. But we did not see, either from ourselves or from others, a strategy to reverse the crisis. Nowhere did we see a solid, comprehensive plan for defeating this attack on the United States as the Founders conceived it and as generations of Americans have subsequently improved upon it. A strategy was desperately needed. We looked to several sources for inspiration. One of them was one of the finest strategy documents in US history: the National Security Council policy paper dated April 14, 1950, better known as NSC-68.[2] The report was written in response to concerns about the Soviet Union's development of nuclear weapons and its expansionist and authoritarian intentions. While the report does not bear an author's name, it is known to be the work of Paul Nitze. He was at the time director of policy planning in the US Department of State. The document laid the foundation for the United States' Cold War strategy.

It is not the specific national security assessment or the recommendations of NSC-68 that inspired us. Even though we are again dealing with Marxists, that was a different era, with a different set of security concerns. Rather, it was the way Nitze systemically worked through the problem, and the spare and incisive way he wrote about it, that made us take notice. Most importantly, Nitze wrote that one must start with an understanding of the United States itself, because this determines *why* you fight and *how* you fight. It is worth quoting in full the opening of NSC-68:

> *The fundamental purpose of the United States is laid down in the Preamble to the Constitution: "… to form a more perfect Union, establish Justice, insure domestic Tranquility, provide for the common defense, promote the general Welfare, and secure the Blessings of Liberty to ourselves and our Posterity." In essence, the fundamental purpose is to assure the integrity and vitality of our free society, which is founded upon the dignity and worth of the individual.*
>
> *Three realities emerge as a consequences of this purpose: Our determination to maintain the essential elements of individual freedom, as set forth in the Constitution and Bill of Rights; our determination to create conditions under which our free and democratic system can live and prosper; and our determination to fight if necessary to defend our way of life, for which as in the Declaration of Independence, "with a firm reliance on the protection of Divine providence, we mutually pledge to each other our lives, our Fortunes and our sacred Honor."[3]*

IT IS important to point out, as NSC-68 makes clear, that the Founders were not trying to construct a utopian fantasy, cut off from reality. They sought to create the optimum conditions for human flourishing. They drew from the knowledge and experience of millennia to craft a society that they believed would bring the greatest good to the greatest number. They knew that sin afflicted all men and therefore perfection on this earth was not possible. But they believed they could create a better political order than the monarchies and aristocracies that existed at the time by learning from and building on what had come before.

They succeeded beyond what most Europeans of the time expected. What they created was extraordinary. Never had a country been established with such high aspirations and unbridled optimism. Indeed, never had a country been created with such forethought and planning. In many ways, never had a country been planned or created. As Alexander Hamilton put it in *Federalist 1*, "it seems to have been reserved to the people of this country to decide, by their conduct and example, the important question, whether societies of men are really capable or not, of establishing good government from reflection and choice, or whether they are forever destined to depend, for their political constitutions, on accident and force."[4] What emerged was a country deeply and profoundly committed to liberty.

James Madison, reflecting on the founding, said, "The happy Union of these States is a wonder; their Constitution a miracle; their example the hope of Liberty throughout the world," then added, "Woe to the ambition that would meditate the destruction of either." That dual spirit of aspiration and optimism has allowed Americans, where others might give up or simply not try in the first place, to carve a home out of wilderness, to break free from a great empire, to end the scourge of slavery, and to defy assaults both from without and within. That dual spirit of aspiration and optimism emboldened the America's Founding Fathers to write into the founding documents what Martin Luther King Jr. called the promissory note of equality. "When the architects of our republic wrote the magnificent words of the Constitution and the Declaration of Independence," King said in his famous speech in front of the Lincoln Memorial, "they were signing a promissory note to which every American was to fall heir. This note was a promise that all men would be guaranteed the inalienable rights of life, liberty, and the pursuit of happiness."[5]

In the four hundred years since the first seeds of the American idea were planted with the Mayflower Compact, untold numbers of Americans have experienced extraordinary opportunity, prosperity, and freedom—characteristics which in themselves do not define human flourishing but which are the necessary preconditions. Has it been a perfect experiment? No earthly thing can be. But where it has fallen short, Americans have demonstrated both the flexibility and the will to self-correct. As Abraham Lincoln said on June 26, 1857, the Founders "meant to set up a standard maxim for free society, which should be familiar to all, and revered by all; constantly looked to, constantly labored for, and even though never perfectly attained, constantly approximated, and thereby constantly spreading and deepening its influence and augmenting the happiness and value of life to all people of all colors everywhere."

A standard maxim, familiar to all, revered by all, constantly approximated. This was a formula for human flourishing grounded in an understanding of human nature, of the tendency to corruption and tyranny, of the limitless potential for humans to inflict suffering—but also of the capacity of men to understand better than anyone else their own interests. The American experiment has retained its vibrancy and relevance through the centuries exactly because so many have sought respite from corruption and tyranny—and indeed their suffering found respite here, on American shores.

This is our answer to the question of *why* America should be saved—from Bill Ayers and his stepson Chesa Boudin; from the BLM founders and their Gramscian recruiters and mentors; from the Social Forum, LeftRoots, and Left Forum; from racial and gender theorists; from BlackRock, from our enemies in Venezuela, Cuba, Russia, Iran, and China. Patriots—a combination of disciplined, erudite, commonsense patriots—saved us from Soviet communism. We must now do it from enemies inside the gates, in possession of the commanding heights of the sense-making institutions. In America, the old slogan about socialism meaning "owning the means of production" has turned into "owning the means of producing meaning."

How to Save Our Country: The Role of Individuals

NOW TO the essential and yet difficult question that lies at the heart of this book: *How* can America be saved?

No one magic bullet will get us out of this mess. This self-governing republic is a complex entity, filled with millions of complex humans. The deep and bitter divisions that now wrack the country will not be easily healed. Nor will they ever be fully resolved, but that is part of the fundamental beauty of the United States as the Founders conceived it: it was designed to accommodate diverse viewpoints and beliefs.

But the polarizing and destructive impact of identity politics pushes at the boundaries of what the republic can peacefully withstand. And the peace itself has already been broken, with protests and riots roiling our cities since 2013. The current divisions can and must be addressed. In the past, socialism failed in America because Americans woke up to its tyranny, its abuse of power, its impoverishment, its scarcity, before those acting on behalf of the Soviets or China had been able to take over the country's key institutions. Today we cannot wait for that awakening, because the ideologues have captured so much of the corporate, government, media, and cultural power. The fact that the flag of the transgender movement displaced the American flag at the White House celebration of Flag Day in 2023 speaks volumes.[6]

Therefore the assault of NextGen Marxists, who do not seek to improve upon what we have but to tear it down, must be met with full force, and they must be dislodged from their current thrones in corporate America, in academia, in media, and in government. Their ideas must be exposed for the lies they are, their utopia as nothing more than a formula for tyranny and suffering.

Ten Tactics for Patriots

WE BEGIN our search for strategy by looking for lessons from one of the most successful US efforts in the war of ideas against Marxism: the Active Measures Working Group (AMWG),[7] which was a response to the US government dropping its guard against Soviet subversion.

The Soviet Union had waged its war for global Marxism using a wide array of tools, including propaganda, disinformation, and outright deception. Starting with the case of Saccho and Vanzetti, two immigrant anarchists executed for murder in the 1920s, and the Scottsboro Eight, eight young black men falsely accused of rape in the Deep South in the 1930s, the Soviet Union tried to win the global argument for Marxism by painting the United States, its principal opponent, as racist and anti-immigrant. But then, in the early 1970s, US policymakers decided to stop combating these subversive tactics.

The reason was twofold: the new strategic focus in the relationship with the Soviet Union was arms control; policymakers did not want to poison the atmosphere for détente with unnecessary confrontation. A second major factor was the exposure of tactics by both the CIA and FBI that were attacked as heavy-handed by some, particularly in the 1960s and 1970s against American citizens. These were revealed during Senate Select Committee hearings in 1975 called the Church Committee hearings.

The result was that by the mid-1970s, Soviet deception and disinformation directed against the United States were largely unchecked: "KGB deception activities were only tracked by a handful of CIA analysts who were isolated from broader attempts to characterize Soviet strategic intentions.... Similarly, the FBI, Department of State, and Department of Defense (DOD) had only a few low-level disinformation experts on staff by the late 1970s, and their views were not influential."[8] But three men decided that this state of affairs was not acceptable. Kenneth deGraffenreid and Angelo Codevilla, staffers on the Senate Select Committee on Intelligence, and Herbert Romerstein, a staff member of the House Intelligence Committee, all believed that Soviet disinformation and deception should not be ignored. They worked with significant success to document and expose it. Their work was further supported and encouraged by a handful of academics and members of Congress and led to the creation of the interagency AMWG. What began as the modest efforts of a few individuals grew into an initiative that eventually made its way all the way up into discussions between Ronald Reagan and Mikhail Gorbachev and helped to turn the course of history toward the ultimate defeat of the communist regime in the Soviet Union and the freeing of tens of millions of people from hardship and oppression. This experience leads us to the first of several rules; call them "Ten Tactics for Patriots," and we dedicate them not to Lucifer but to the One who will defeat him.

1. EXPOSE. The single most effective tactic used by the AMWG was to expose the lies, the forgeries, and the propaganda put out by the Soviets and their agents on US soil. Exposing acts of disinformation, such as the story that the United States had deliberately created the AIDS virus, or forgeries, such as the letters forged by the KGB from the Ku Klux Klan threatening athletes from African countries in the run-up to the 1984 Olympic Games in Los Angeles, was an extremely powerful tool in undermining the efficacy of America's enemies.[9] Today, in every area where the NextGen Marxists have tried to take over and corrupt American in-

stitutions, we must expose what they have said about their true intentions. For example, the leaders of BLM acknowledge that they are trained
Marxists.[10] They said they want to destroy the nuclear family and dismantle the foundations of American society, and then they hid those facts.[11]
Education activists have been very effective in exposing the content of
pornographic books in school libraries, in exposing teachers and administrators secretly "transitioning" children. This type of exposure is critical
to helping more people understand the true nature of these organizations
and initiatives and tears away the veil of their claims to be concerned
about racial justice or the welfare of children who are "gender confused."

2. **NETWORK.** A second lesson that can be drawn from the AMWG is the
value of networking and information sharing with like-minded individuals. According to one inside source from that period, "back in the 1970s,
we who were fighting the Soviets and their apologists inside the US government were a fairly lonely lot who were under constant criticism and
pressure to conform to the détente spirit. When we learned of others on
the Hill and elsewhere who had a realistic view of Soviet active measures,
we started networking. That provided vital institutional and moral support."[12] That moral support is so important today, particularly in the early
stage of the fight when the radical Left has managed to cancel so many
people, forcing them out of jobs, silencing them, even physically assault-
ing them. A community of networked individuals is a bulwark against
the Left's strategy of personal destruction. Networking also serves the vital role of information sharing. Zoom calls, conferences, working groups,
and coalitions all help to bolster those who are engaged in the fight, to
share information, to strengthen arguments with evidence and knowledge, and to amplify the important work that is being done.[13]

3. **FOLLOW THE MONEY.** The single biggest factor that favors the NextGen
Marxist radicals right now is the degree to which they have embedded
themselves in key positions in government, corporate America, media,
and Hollywood. The second biggest factor in their favor is the money
they can bring to this fight. Everywhere one turns, the Left is outspend-
ing the right exponentially. Arabella Advisors, the Ford Foundation, the
William and Flora Hewlett Foundation, the Soros organizations, the Bill
and Melinda Gates Foundation—their billions may seem like an impos-

sible weapon to match, but if enough people get angry and speak out against them, it will not matter how much they have. Exposing the sources of funding of the transgender cult, of lurid sex education, of CRT and diversity, equity, and inclusion (DEI), of drag queen story hours, of climate strategies that are barely hidden campaigns to dismantle capitalism, helps weaken their case because it demonstrates that these are in no way authentic grassroots movements but are instead imposed from above.

4. **LIVE WITHIN THE TRUTH.** For every storefront that posted a BLM sign, for every business that flew the "pride" flag, did the proprietors really believe in the ideology behind those symbols? Václav Havel, the dissident and playwright who became Czechoslovakia's first post-communist president, wrote a story about a greengrocer who put in his window a sign that read "Workers of the World, Unite!"—not because he believed it but because it was easy; it's what everybody did. But as Havel pointed out, "by accepting the given rules of the game … he has himself become a player in the game, thus making it possible for the game to go on, for it to exist in the first place."[14] Importantly, what the sign really meant was this: "I am afraid and therefore unquestioningly obedient."[15] What happens if that one greengrocer decides to stop living within the lie? To remove the sign from his window and instead live within the truth? He pays a price, to be sure, but he also exposes the lie for the facade that it is; the facade starts to crumble. As Aleksandr Solzhenitsyn said in *The Gulag Archipelago*, "one man who stopped lying could bring down a tyranny." Today, living within the truth can mean refusing to be silent, even when speaking out will exact a cost. It can mean challenging those who throw out accusations of racism or bigotry or book banning. It can mean explaining the difference between equity and equality—and refusing to accept the former because of the power it puts into the hands of a self-anointed few.

5. **VOTE WITH YOUR WALLET.** One of the reasons Netflix, Amazon, HBO, Hulu, and the rest have produced more and more offensive and out-of-touch content is because Americans have continued watching it. Even if what we saw offended our values, we did not turn it off. So, Hollywood kept forging ahead. The truly profound beauty of the free market is that individuals, not nameless bureaucrats in central planning, make deci-

sions about what products they will or will not buy. But that is a privilege that must be exercised responsibly or it slips away. Finally however, it seems that more Americans are voting with their wallets: one can see it in the massive financial losses of Target, Bud Light, and Disney. The boycott on Anheuser-Busch, made possible partly because Elon Musk's purchase of Twitter made the conservative exchange of ideas possible on social media, particularly bit. The corporation announced in late July 2023 that it would have to lay off four hundred people as its stock price tanked.[16]

6. ENGAGE. Though the right leader, or leaders, are of primary importance, the crisis currently confronting the United States cannot be resolved only by Washington. It will be resolved by the reanimation of American civil society, by the reengagement of millions of Americans in the civil and political life of the country. That is a process that happens one person at a time, and each of us has a role to play. The good news is that what started with parents in Florida and Loudoun County has continued to grow. Those of us who are already engaged must engage our friends and neighbors. We do that by volunteering; by joining our local citizen associations, clubs, and groups; by attending events; by going to school board meetings, asking questions, and inviting others to come along. Most of us will not sign up to attend an event where we won't know anybody, but if a friend invites us, then we are willing to go. Paul Nitze wrote in NSC-68, "The democratic way is harder than the authoritarian way because, in seeking to protect and fulfill the individual, it demands of him understanding, judgment and positive participation in the increasingly complex and exacting problems of the modern world."[17] That positive participation is much more than simply voting. Voting is critical, but it is not enough, and therefore it is not engendered by flyers or emails or texts. A person who is disengaged from civic life, as too many Americans are these days, will either be compelled back in by outrage—and to be sure, there is plenty of that going on—or they will be led back in by love and persuasion. Remember what Alexis de Tocqueville observed when he traveled through the United States in 1831–32:

> *Americans of all ages, conditions and all dispositions constantly unite together.... To hold fetes, found seminaries, build inns, construct churches, distribute books, dispatch missionaries to the antipodes.*

They establish hospitals, prisons, schools by the same method. Finally, if they wish to highlight a truth or develop an opinion by the encouragement of a great example, they form an association.

This is our inspiration: a robust engagement in the civic and political life of the country and an end to atomization that has been fostered by technology and by the ever-growing role of government. Every single one of us can be instrumental in this process.

7. SHOW UP. If you want to win, you have to show up: whether to a school-board meeting, community center, or drag queen story hour, it is not enough to complain. You have to physically step up and be present. At a recent drag queen story hour for toddlers at a local library, a handful of women simply stood outside praying the rosary. It was enough to get the performers to feel uncomfortable and cut the event short, and it has not been repeated since.[18] The fact is that patriots outnumber radicals; the radicals are just noisier, and oftentimes they are better at showing up. We have to show up alongside them and prove that we will not be silenced.

8. PLAY THE LONG GAME. It was seventy years from the publication of *The Communist Manifesto* to the institution of Marxism in Russia. It has been forty years since the NextGen Marxists began their long march through the cultural institutions. Major cultural changes do not happen quickly. We must think about the next election, but we cannot think only about the next election. We must think about how small, seemingly inconsequential actions can have a profound impact. We must plan for the long term and recognize that progress often comes in small, incremental steps.

9. FOCUS INTERNATIONALLY, NATIONALLY, AND LOCALLY. Cultural Marxists have already shown the way. Their long march through the institutions can inform the counterstrategy. While conservatives focused on the high-level aspects of American politics—national races, general elections, presidential campaigns, and policies that were driven from the top down—the Gramscians took monies from left-leaning donors and megafoundations and created global networks that could focus on local issues and then expand them to political and cultural dominance.[19] Their super-networks organized and politicized radicals, who then concentrated at the local level. From using Soros money to fund "social justice"

candidates for district attorney's offices to installing pro-CRT officials on schoolboards, the approach often eschewed the obvious and national for the far more impactful local centers of power. Conservatives are already taking this territory back by running in local races for school or county boards, a trend that must continue. This is cultural trench warfare to win back every inch of political territory ceded to an adversary that thought globally but also acted locally for decades. Many of the different strategies laid out here thus involve action at the state and local levels. Those who want to resist should not look to Washington, DC, for answers but should focus on their own communities.

10. RECLAIM THE CULTURE. We must build a new ecosystem for the provision of cultural content if the ultimate victory against those who hate America is to be achieved. Hollywood is starting to pay the commercial price for the near-absolute wokeness of its output. From the disastrous results of making massive moneymaking franchises like Star Wars and Star Trek woke[20] to the stock market losses incurred as a result by the likes of Netflix and Disney,[21] it is plain that a significant portion of the American people have had enough with the indoctrination on their TV and movie screens. The time is now for those who want to take back the culture to follow the lead of such un-woke movie blockbusters as 2022's *Top Gun: Maverick*. Reagan was right. He who tells the better story will win this war. But conservatives must do more to engage and invest in the culture, and they must recognize that the TV shows and movies their children watch, the books they read, the social media platforms they hang out on, will all profoundly impact their children's worldviews.[22]

FINALLY, A word about the means we can use. Again, looking to the past, there's an invaluable lesson to be learned, in this instance, from the McCarthy hearings. There were two major governmental investigations into communist infiltration in the United States: the House Committee on Un-American Activities, which was formed in 1938, and then the Senate Permanent Subcommittee on Investigations, which initially focused on government waste and abuse but, after Wisconsin's junior senator Joseph R. McCarthy took over the chairmanship in 1953, turned its attention to a communist threat that was very real. Because of all that has been uncovered in the years since then, it is now well documented that concerns about communist subversion and infiltration into the highest reaches of the US government were not unfounded. However, the methods that Senator McCarthy used allowed his critics to permanently discredit the effort. McCarthy did do important work, but he did not help himself, nor the cause of anti-communism, by making allegations he could not substantiate. This mistake must not be made by those fighting NextGen Marxism.

As Selznick warned in his 1952 study of Bolshevik tactics, we must avoid "those excessive reactions which threaten themselves to undermine the foundations of democratic society."[23] Nitze made this point as well in NSC-68: "Compulsion is the negation of freedom, except when it is used to enforce the rights common to all. The resort to force, internally or externally, is therefore a last resort for a free society." In other words, the defense of the nation against NextGen Marxists must strive to remain always constitutional and never stray into the infringement of the rights of American citizens. As Nitze put it, "we have no choice but to demonstrate the superiority of the idea of freedom."[24] Ultimately, it is persuasion, not compulsion, that wins the war of ideas. We must always make the case for the superiority of American freedoms in achieving the greatest good for the greatest number. That means not simply saying the words but living them. We must also demonstrate with our behavior the values we are fighting to uphold.

Having said that, we must also fully acknowledge the fact that from the 1960s, and especially when they took over the institutions in the 1980s, to today, the NextGen Marxists have constituted an ever expanding, ever more totalitarian juggernaut of intolerance and destruction of those who disagree with them. They lie. They conspire. They deceive. Most importantly, they try to silence. But they do not conceal their intentions: time and again, we hear them say that they are out to reshape the country. They do not like what America stands for, and they want to change it. They want to destroy the American experiment. They have dispensed with the primacy of reason in favor of the primacy of power—their power. Indeed, NextGen Marxists are very candid that it is power they seek. "Life without power is death, a world without power would be a ghostly wasteland, a dead planet," wrote Alinsky in *Rules for Radicals*, in which he uses the word "power" seventy-two times. "Organize for power," instructed Alinsky.[25] The BLM founders are equally forthright about their desire for power. "Power is very much about deciding who gets to make decisions, and who doesn't," Garza told Maine leftists in 2019.[26] Indeed, the title of her 2020 book is *The Purpose of Power.*

As they seek to dismantle America and gain power for themselves, the Next-Gen Marxists seek to institute hierarchies based on race, ethnicity, sex, gender, sexual orientation, and sexual preference. Under them, rights are no longer un-alienable but are dispensed by the potentates of DEI. Nature is no longer know-able and rational but whatever they want it to be—it is a "construct" that can be reshaped. Individuals are no longer judged on their own merits but categorically, as members of a collective. It is a chaotic, irrational, and unjust world they are creating, and as history has told us over and over again, a world built on these principles invariably leads to tyranny and profound human suffering.

If we are to fight their grab for power and hold on to what has been be-queathed to us, we need a comprehensive, long-term, multitiered response. Solzhenitsyn wrote in *The Gulag Archipelago,*

> *In keeping silent about evil, in burying it so deep within us that no sign of it appears on the surface, we are implanting it, and it will rise up a thou-sandfold in the future. When we neither punish nor reproach evildoers, we are not simply protecting their trivial old age, we are thereby ripping the foundations of justice from beneath new generations.*[27]

THE NEXTGEN Marxists have gone too far by putting children on the front line of their culture war. Their actions have awakened many Americans to the dev-astating impact that a relentless stress on race and sex can have on our youth, from rising rates of depression to anxiety, suicide, and violence. With the Ten Tactics for Patriots, we provide guidance for the millions of Americans who love this country and want to preserve it, who now recognize that it is our children who are paying the highest price for the assault on our values and our institutions. We are sharing with the reader a range of ways people can engage and bring an end to this culture war by winning.

How to Save Our Country: The Role of Elected Officials

IT IS important also to see the instances when Americans, especially those who have run for office, have already made a difference. This should both inform the reader and help the reader discern which candidates take the threat of NextGen

Marxism seriously. The Ten Tactics for Patriots can be applied by individuals across the nation to deal with the different ways the NextGen Marxists are trying to change our society. Those same principles can also be used by government to fight this scourge at the policy and legislative levels. We have focused on nine main areas where the battle can be waged, first in the realm of ideas, and then at the political level, and we catalog what can be done or what is already being done:

1. the takeover of the universities
2. CRT in K–12 schools
3. gender theory, in schools and elsewhere
4. wokeness in the military
5. BLM, global networks, and "peaceable protests"
6. climate change
7. environmental, social, and corporate governance (ESG)
8. woke corporations
9. funding

LET'S TAKE a brief look at what has been done—or needs to be done—in these areas.

Education

THE FIGHT over education covers a lot of ground and has to do with CRT, ethnic studies, reversing the NextGen Marxist takeover of the university, and much more. As we contemplate it, we must bear in mind that the leftists who took over the universities, the architects of CRT and the founders of ethnic studies, were all clear about their goals. They wanted to revolutionize society; as Derrick Bell said, they had a subversive agenda. As Stokely Carmichael put it, it was "precisely the job of the black educator to train his people how to dismantle America, how to destroy it."[28] What we are confronting when we face down these disciplines is revolution.

University Reform

WE CANNOT discuss the efforts being undertaken in the realm of university reform without mentioning the free state of Florida and its governor. Ron DeSantis, a candidate for the Republican nomination for president at the time of this writing, moved against the College Board's ethnic studies; prohibited DEI and CRT in schools, colleges, and universities; elevated classical education and the teaching of great books; reformed the accreditation process; and increased the accountability of tenured professors. It's hard to find a better suite of policies that aim at the heart of the NextGen Marxist project.

In rejecting the College Board's pilot class that was ostensibly an Advanced Placement African American history course, DeSantis was indeed disallowing a Marxist course. The course intended to teach Angela Davis—a former Black Panther on the FBI Ten Most Wanted Fugitives list who ran twice as vice president on the Communist Party USA ticket—the works of BLM's Black Lives Movement and the Movement for Black Lives; and D. G. Kelley, a self-described "Marxist, surrealist feminist." Also included in the course were the pearls of wisdom of the Marxist radical feminist Gloria Jean Watkins, who goes by the pen name bell hooks.[29] The College Board agreed to rewrite the course.

On April 19, 2022, the governor also signed into law Senate Bill 7044, which brought competition to the accreditation process by forcing universities to vary accreditors in consecutive cycles. The bill also increased accountability for tenured professors by empowering the state's seventeen-member board of governors that oversees the state's public university system to conduct performance reviews, whereas before, universities were forced to keep tenured professors even if they were acting with political motivation.

In May 2023, DeSantis signed into law three additional bills: Senate Bill 266 prohibited the expenditure of monies on DEI programs; established the Hamilton Center for Classical and Civic Education, a new college at the University of Florida; and provided further resources to the Adam Smith Center for Economic Freedom, a free-market think tank at Florida International University. Additionally, House Bill 931 prohibited public institutions from requiring that professors and students sign DEI pledges, which are basically unconstitutional political loyalty oaths.[30]

Texas, Ohio, Georgia, Arkansas, Montana, Idaho, Iowa, North and South Dakota, Kansas, Oklahoma, and Alabama, among other states, have begun the necessary work of dismantling the race agenda. The University of Arkansas at Fayetteville eliminated its DEI office and relocated its staff. We hope that other states will follow.

Critical Race Theory

JUST AS we cannot talk about university reform without mentioning the Free Sunshine State, we cannot speak about the fight against CRT without mentioning Chris Rufo. It was Rufo who first brought the issue of CRT to the national fore, identifying for the country the intellectual root of all the madness Americans were seeing all around them in classrooms and the rest of society.

"It's absolutely astonishing how critical race theory has pervaded every aspect of the federal government," Rufo told Tucker Carlson in an interview on September 2, 2020. "This is an existential threat to the United States. And the bureaucracy, even under Trump, is being weaponized against core American values. And I'd like to make it explicit: The President and the White House—it's within their authority to immediately issue an executive order to abolish critical-race-theory training from the federal government. And I call on the President to immediately issue this executive order—to stamp out this destructive, divisive, pseudoscientific ideology."[31]

One powerful person was watching at the White House, Donald J. Trump, who immediately got his chief of staff, Mark Meadows, on the phone. Meadows in turn called Rufo the next morning and set in motion the process that, in a matter of a few short weeks, resulted in an executive order that would bar federal workers and contractors from CRT indoctrination. Federal officials would henceforth prohibit so-called diversity training programs in the federal workforce.[32] Biden ended all that four months later with Executive Order 13985.

But Rufo's even greater contribution was arguably the following: he framed all of the radicalism that had suddenly burst through our institutions after 2020 under the banner of "critical race theory." And it stuck, driving the Left crazy. In a couple of tweets in early 2021, Rufo candidly explained his strategy:

We have successfully frozen their brand—"critical race theory"—into the public conversation and are steadily driving up negative perceptions. We will eventually turn it toxic, as we put all of the various cultural insanities under that brand category.[33]

The goal is to have the public read something crazy in the newspaper and immediately think "critical race theory." We have decodified the term and will recodify it to annex the entire range of cultural constructions that are unpopular with Americans.[34]

RUFO HAD described in his tweets how the Right could win—by defining what the Left was doing in a concise and yet accurate way that the public could readily grasp.

Rufo further explained, "We are no longer going to let the Left set the terms of debate. The truth is that politics is a form of conflict and rhetoric is its primary weapon."[35]

Rufo's experience provides us with five important lessons: (1) set the terms of the debate—you don't have to use the Left's terminology or way of doing things; (2) state things clearly—avoid euphemisms and recondite phrases (avoid using the word *recondite*); (3) be accurate—Rufo got CRT exactly right; (4) be strategic—once you've chosen a fight, plan it out; and, perhaps most importantly; and (5) be courageous and take risks—you will have to talk about sex, race, and Marxism, so speak clearly and avoid doublespeak. The other side accuses those who take action of racism, homophobia, and McCarthyism. But the fear that this will happen is far more damaging than the actual abuse, because it leads to conservatives clamming up about these issues, which is what the Left wants. When the actual insults come, they are far less damaging than anticipated. The Left has so overused these epithets that they are now valueless. This is the law of diminishing returns at work. It is a shame, as a word like *racist* should be potent. It is truly awful to hate someone because of his race. But the Left has so abused this word that it is now practically meaningless. Those who want to wage a battle of ideas against NextGen Marxists would do well to take a page from Rufo's work. He has fought that battle and not flinched on camera when discussing issues that the Left has made taboo.

As we later found out, Biden's pen was less mighty than he thought, and if he believed that he would unleash CRT on the nation by rescinding Trump's ban, he was greatly mistaken. The states soon took up where the federal government had stopped, spurred to act by moms and dads.

Overall, from the time that Biden foolishly thought he could bring CRT back with his signature to the completion of this book, 40 percent of all states have passed laws banning or restricting CRT notions being used by teachers. The best efforts, the ones that will have the best success in both courts of law and the court of public opinion, are not those laws that ban the teaching of CRT but those that do not allow practices that violate the Constitution's First

Amendment ban on compelling speech, the Fourteenth Amendment's equal protection clause, or the Civil Right Act's Title VI prohibition of racial discrimination in schools, public or private, that take taxpayer money. Solid bills also include "parental bills of rights" that ensure the rights of parents to morally educate their children and to be fully informed about important matters regarding their children. Generally, efforts that are opaque or that ban ill-explained ideas, such as "divisive concepts," will leave even well-intentioned teachers frustrated and lose parental support. Another negative in these bills is banning the concept that one race is superior to the other, a worthwhile effort, but those who know CRT may come back and rightly ask, "Show us where any of us have claimed that?"

Overall, twenty-one states—Arkansas, Georgia, Kansas, Oklahoma, Missouri, Florida, Texas, Alabama, Idaho, Iowa, Kentucky, Montana, Ohio, Mississippi, New Hampshire, North and South Dakota, South Carolina, Tennessee, Utah, and Virginia—have passed some sort of anti-CRT bill, and others are preparing bills for the 2024 legislative session. They represent nearly all regions—from the South to the Midwest, the West, the mountain states, and New England. The only region missing is the West Coast.

Georgia's HB 1084 restricts discussion of race at school and includes the "divisive concepts" language, which may make it overly broad, but it does the right thing by banning the teaching that the United States is "fundamentally racist," which would fall under compelled speech. In Arkansas, Governor Sarah Huckabee Sanders signed in her first day in office, on January 11, 2023, an executive order that bans any indoctrination of students that conflicts "with the principle of equal protection under the law." Oklahoma's bill, one of the earliest, having come in spring 2021, also prevents teachers from making students believe that racism is ingrained in the country and impacts lawmaking. As he was signing the bill, Governor Kevin Stitt wisely said that the bill would not prevent the teaching of slavery and racism but that "we can and should teach this history without labeling a young child as an oppressor."[36] Governor Ron DeSantis signed Florida's bill a year later and was equally forceful: "We believe an important component of freedom in the state of Florida is the freedom from having oppressed ideologies imposed upon you without your consent."[37] In Virginia, Governor Glen Youngkin used an executive order to ban the imposition of CRT concepts, saying that children should not be taught to see all of life through the lens of race.

It is important to emphasize again that, though all these were the actions of politicians, behind these twenty-one instances were committed parents who risked their own positions in society, and their children's social standing—and often much more—to make sure that their children would be free of these indoctrinations. They changed the climate of opinion in America and, in so doing, changed the course of history.

Ethnic Studies

ETHNIC STUDIES, as we have seen, was from its inception a subversive attempt to undermine Western and American society, and it laid the groundwork for CRT. Given the revolutionary potential of ethnic studies, the fact that it is the "intellectual arm of the revolution," many radical outfits dedicated to training and indoctrinating teachers on it have spread around the nation. One of the most radical ones is the Xicanx Institute for Teaching and Organizing (XITO), which has featured the BLM founder Cullors as a speaker. XITO describes itself as "a grassroots, urban education consulting collective and non-profit organization committed to training teachers, school districts, and higher education institutions in decolonial and re-humanizing pedagogies and curriculum development."[38] It has consulting sites all over California, a few in Washington State, and one each in Colorado and New Mexico.

Some mom activists have clearly understood the threat posed by ethnic studies and fought back. One such mom is Kelly Schenkoske, a force of nature from Monterrey who has spent years researching ethnic studies and other attempts to reshape education, such as a program called Whole School, Whole Community, Whole Child. Schenkoske doesn't just research these issues but spends a great deal of time sharing this valuable information through Zooms large and small, through her podcast *A Time to Stand*, and by traveling the country to advise other parents.

Importantly, Schenkoske provided evidence in a suit won in January 2022 by the California Foundation for Equal Rights (CFER; on whose advisory board one of us, Gonzalez, sits) against the California Department of Education and the state's Board of Education. The legal settlement removed Aztec and Ashe chants and other affirmation prayers from the state's ethnic-studies curriculum, showing that even in Gavin Newsom's Golden State, energized parents can win. "Having the progressive state of California voluntarily agreeing to take out two problematic religious chants from the ethnic studies model curriculum is an important victory," Wenyuan Wu, the executive director of CFER, said in a release. "We will continue to monitor each school district to ensure that they don't teach the deleted chants and teach ethnic studies in a constructive rather than a divisive ideological manner."[39]

In fact, throughout the state, Californians are fighting against other forms of ethnic studies, now that Newsom has signed a law that made the state the first to make ethnic studies mandatory for high school graduation. Thus, in Los Alamitos, parents organized in 2022 to fight the introduction of not just ethnic studies but also gender ideology, all part of the Learning for Justice curriculum being pushed in the school district. "Los Alamitos School District is introducing Critical Race Theory (CRT) into the students' curriculum under the disguise of an elective Ethnic Studies, mandatory K–12 Social Justice Standards, and Culturally Responsive Instruction for teachers," the organizers wrote to parents. "These sound like very reasonable and even positive additions, however the courses are filled with hate for America and all America stands for."[40] Parents in Orange County, Santa Clara, and other Golden State localities also organized. In Boston, ethnic studies will be a graduation requirement as of 2026, according to a law passed in 2022. Parents Defending Education obtained documents from the Boston Teachers Union Ethnic Studies Now! committee that explained that the focus of the course is "on the construction and transformation of identity."[41]

Parents Defending Education is one of the best groups that has emerged to fight back against the surge of NextGen Marxists in educational fields. Its practical "Indoctrination Map"[42] reveals problems around the United States, for example, how the Scottsdale Unified School District has a "gender support plan" that was copied from the radical group Gender Spectrum, and what is being done about it, in this case, investigative work by Arizona Independent News.

In bullet-point fashion, the following are some steps that can be taken in the education realm:

- Eliminate the DEI bureaucracy, which is the enforcement mechanism of NextGen Marxism.
- Encourage, incentivize, and, if necessary, enforce a diversity of views among the professoriate.
- Protect freedom of speech on campus.

- Reform the accreditation process, to ensure that ideology is not mandatory.
- Remake boards of trustees.
- Pass legislation banning the imposition of CRT notions used to compel belief, which is unconstitutional.
- Eliminate ethnic studies or subject it to more rigorous vetting through the accreditation process.

ELECT SCHOOL board members who will protect the rights of parents and keep the focus on educational excellence, rather than imposing radical ideologies.

Taking on Gender Theory

THE BIDEN administration has not stopped at a complete embrace of a divisive race agenda; it has also elevated gender ideology in such a breathless fashion that it is borderline pathological. From the campaign trail, Biden had announced that in his first hundred days in office, he would amend the Civil Rights Act of 1964 to ban discrimination based on gender identity and sexual orientation. As Margaret Harper McCarthy, a professor of theological anthropology, put it, the Equality Act is "at war with reality." At stake, she wrote in *The Wall Street Journal*, was not women's sports or bathrooms; "at stake is the freedom of rational human beings to use a common vocabulary when speaking about what all can see. Also at stake are the countless vulnerable souls falling prey to the tyrannizing 'gender identity' ideology and the medical atrocities that go with it."[43]

In his first months in office, the president then sent a letter to all state attorneys general insisting that the Constitution allows minors to undergo medical procedures and makes it possible for people to choose "X" as their sex on their passports, saying that this would "improve their travel experience." In his first week in office, Biden lifted the ban on openly transgender service members from serving. Also, during "Pride Month" in 2023, dozens of our embassies posted social media videos of diplomats dancing with drag queens and even furries.

With support for gender ideology coming all the way from the top of the US government, how can lawmakers fight this insidious problem? Understanding that gender theorists are at war with reality is a good place to start. It is imperative that politicians, as well as individuals, confronting this most disturbing of all the NextGen Marxist attacks call things by their names. Never, ever, must someone who lives not by lies speak of "gender-affirming care," "genital surgery," "puberty suppression," "pretissue transfer," or any other euphemism. Proponents of gender theory want to allow children to *mutilate* their bodies, *amputate* the perfectly healthy breasts of minor girls, *castrate* boys, and invert their penises. The gender acolytes seek incoherence because you cannot fight something that you cannot name or identify. But gender ideology *can* be named, and we can fight back by rejecting the Left's deceptive terminology and using instead the actual descriptors of what is being done to children. Similarly, we must speak openly and forcefully about the fact that these practices will lead to a lifetime of *infertility, incontinence,* and *sexual dissatisfaction.* We must be clear that this is what the president of the United States is supporting when he calls for "gender-affirming care." Equally, although it is a matter of personal choice to call someone by the name the person chooses (the authors, for example, have no compunction about calling a man "Sally" if that is the name by which he wants to be known), it is to participate complicitly in a lie to refer to that man as "she." Grammar and linguistic rules exist to help mankind interpret the world around us, to explain the natural world, and to communicate these facts. They are therefore above the personal whims of individuals.

All the critical theories—but above all the sexual theories—are based on this fundamental denial of nature and the espousal of a constructionist view of life. Reality can, and must, be deconstructed, they contend. Liberation depends on it. Lest we forget, Gramsci believed that Marx's greatest innovation was the idea that nature was not fixed but constantly evolving, along with one's relationship with other humans. "That 'human nature' is the 'ensemble of social relations' is the most satisfying answer, because it includes the idea of becoming—man becomes, he changes continuously with the changing of social relations," wrote Gramsci, quoting approvingly from Marx's "Theses on Feuerbach."[44] This attachment to the mutability of reality has in fact been the only immutable characteristic of Marxists since. Economic determinism has been abandoned, the working class has been thrown overboard, and the expectation of constant revolution has been rethought. But the ability of man to alter reality, nature, truth itself, has been a constant. And nowhere is it more in evidence than in gender theory, in this sense, the most Marxist of the NextGen Marxists' radical theories.

Gender acolytes, says Jay Richards, rarely speak clearly. "But don't be fooled. When you see these confusing terms deployed to explain away what you know to be true, you can be quite sure you're not dealing with sound science or sound philosophy, but with an incoherent kludge of concepts that we may rightly call gender ideology."[45]

Speaking the truth, living not by lies—in Solzhenitsyn's words, and the title of Rod Dreher's great book—may seem simple, but it isn't in our times. Because the gender-theory militants are so intent on imposing their truth-distorting view of human existence on the population, by coercion if necessary, turning back their gains will require money, strategizing, and, above all, courage. University students who refuse to go along with the gender lies face at best social isolation and at worst expulsion from the university. Those who speak out can even face physical threats, as we saw in April 2023, when the swimmer Riley Gaines dared to speak out at San Francisco State University (SFSU) against having to compete against Lia Thomas, a man who took first prize. Activists organized by SFSU's Queer and Trans Resource Center rushed into her speech, surrounded Gaines, and physically attacked her.[46]

California parents who refuse to go along with the obvious lie that their child was born into the wrong sex and want a treatment for their gender dysphoria that does not involve either amputation or toxins face the threat of Child Protective Services showing up at their door and taking their child away, all because of Assembly Bill 957. Another measure, Assembly Bill 665, allows children as young as twelve to receive sex therapy without parental consent.[47] In Michigan, House Bill 4474 would make it a "hate crime" felony to "misgender" someone.[48] The so-called Pride Month in summer 2023 saw a parade of horribles being forced on families and young children who visit ballparks. Most abominably, the Los Angeles Dodgers not only invited but celebrated and gave an award to a satanic group that sexualizes Christ on the cross.

The bills in question are being challenged in the courts even as we write, but even if they are overturned, the NextGen sexual Marxists will come back with others. Unlike with the same-sex marriage campaign, when advocates sought buy-in from American society through a well-thought-out marketing strategy, the transgender movement simply wants to impose its view by force of law and has found willing allies in politicians on the Left. The strategy against gender ideology must therefore also include legislation and "lawfare."

Banning Grotesque Medical Practices

MANY STATES are taking the lead in banning extreme medical procedures on youth. Texas became the largest state to make it impossible for children to receive puberty blockers and hormone therapies, never mind surgeries, when Governor Greg Abbott signed into law Senate Bill 14 on June 2, 2023.[49] The Lone Star State thus became the eighteenth state to restrict surgeries or chemical therapies for minors, who do not have the maturity to make these life-changing, irreversible decisions. In addition, five states—Idaho, North Dakota, Oklahoma, Florida, and Alabama—have made it a felony for doctors to engage in medical transitioning for minors. In the case of Alabama, the provision of puberty blockers, hormones, and medical procedures to minors is a felony punishable by up to ten years in prison.

Gender Identity Promotion

SCHOOLS IN many states have also been actively promoting gender ideology to minors, often leaving parents in the dark, so legislatures can and do help. Ohio's House Bill 616 would, for example, ban sex discussion in K–3 in public and private schools. After that, the treatment of the matter would have to be age appropriate. Teachers who ignore this rule and decide they know what's best for other people's children could lose their teaching licenses. Georgia's Senate Bill 222 requires parental involvement before a child can be subjected to these notions. South Dakota's ban on the promotion of gender dysphoria goes all the way to seventh grade. Florida, once again, leads in this area. Its ban on discussion of sexual matters in schools was expanded in 2023 by the state's Board of Education. Its new rule stated that schools "shall not intentionally provide classroom instruction to students in grades 4 through 12 on sexual orientation or gender identity unless such instruction is expressly required by state academic standards."[50]

Men Playing on Women Teams

TO PROTECT girls' and women's sports from participation by boys and men, legislation has become a very powerful tool. In 2020, only Idaho had passed legislation to prevent men from competing in women's sports. By 2022, legislation had been passed in twenty-three states. But the pushback continues:

fairness-in-women's-sports legislation is supported almost only by Republicans, while it is attacked by Democrats. And many Republican legislators remain fearful of taking on this issue at both the state and federal levels. The Protection of Women and Girls Sports Act passed in the Republican-majority house has stalled in the Democrat-held Senate. This will no doubt continue to be one of the front lines in NextGen Marxists' assault on America. Therefore we must fight smartly and effectively. Riley Gaines has found that it is women—those who are impacted by this problem—who must go to bat for it and speak out against it. She says that the issue is best framed in a way that is pro-woman, rather than anti-trans. The actual language we use is also critical:

> When I started speaking out, I referred to myself as a biological woman. But then I realized that when I add that modifier, it's as if I am admitting there is an unbiological alternative to being a woman, which is scientifically wrong. The same is true of terms such as "sex-reassignment surgery." I stopped using that because in fact you cannot reassign sex. We have to stop using their language and be mindful of the words we use. When we start adhering to these changes in our language, it contributes to a cultural shift. Even subconsciously you don't even know you are doing it until it is too late.[51]

"Book Banning"

PERHAPS NO other issue has been more demagogued by the Left than laws restricting access to sexually explicit content by young children. Several states have passed laws that allow school authorities to remove sexually explicit material from reading lists or library shelves. Trying to explain to a progressive that just because *Penthouse* is not available at the school library does not mean that *Penthouse* has been banned will not work. The gender acolytes want the material out there for children to access, so they can plant their questions and skepticism about reality in their young minds; they don't care about adults, whose brains are harder to mold. Still, it is important to reassure fair-minded Americans in the middle, people busy with their lives who have decided—for their own reasons—not to delve too deeply into what they would see as the "culture wars," that there is no book banning taking place.

Luckily, our colleagues Jay Greene and Robert Pondiscio, respectively, at Heritage and the Thomas B. Fordham Institute, have run the numbers, and the critics are wrong. "If we define banned as 'not shelved' or placed out of the immediate reach of children, then the vast majority of published books have been banned. If we count only works included in official school curriculums, then only a few hundred works in all of human history could be said to be 'approved,'" but obviously those are ridiculous standards, they write.[52] One of five books that were removed from a school district in Florida, out of 156 challenged, was described by the publisher as "immersed into the minds and hearts of lesbian, bisexual, transgender, gay, queer, and questioning young people" and aimed at young adults, who obviously are no longer in K–12 classrooms.

Foreign Policy

LAST, BUT of the utmost importance, the State Department, the US Agency for International Development, and other government agencies must stop exporting gender ideology to other countries. As the Family Research Council (FRC) wrote in an important report released in June 2023, our government has engaged in what can only be called "ideological colonialism." "American embassies around the world are the most prominent platform from which the Biden administration outwardly displays its prioritization of LGBT ideology," the report said. FRC researchers analyzed the websites and social media platforms of US embassies "and found that in 2022 at least 132 US embassies released Pride Month statements via social media or their website, at least 99 US embassies flew Pride or Progress flags, and at least 49 embassies had staffers who participated in Pride parades. The mark of this ideological push is widespread, and the harms will be as well."[53]

Of course, fixing this problem, and many others, will have to wait until January 2025:

· Protect children by passing state laws banning sexually explicit books below a certain age.

· Elect school boards that prioritize the interests of students and their families.

· End amputations—mastectomies and castration of minors—and the administration of toxins and puberty blockers through various means, including through "lawfare."

· End the teaching of the view, in this realm as in racial theories, that all of reality, including biology, human nature, and sexual differences, comprises conceptual constructs, mere products of a value system.

Nextgen Marxism in the Military

THIS IS another issue that may have to wait until a new administration before any real change can come. The president is, after all, commander in chief of the armed forces, and that man is (as of this writing, and, we hope, until January 2025) Joseph R. Biden. Congress, and regular Americans, can, in the meantime, do some things to attenuate the damage.

First, there is the power of exposure and, when necessary, the anvil of ridicule. We saw, for example, how in May 2022, the navy yanked Ibram X. Kendi and other controversial CRT writers from its recommended reading list.[54] The chief of naval operations, Admiral Michael Gilday, had included Kendi's racial poison (in the book in question, Kendi openly advocates for discrimination) and other controversial material on race and gender ideology but was buried under a ton of criticism, from writers such as ourselves and, most importantly, from members of Congress. The members of our military have volunteered to risk their lives in defense of the Constitution. It is unfair to them—and it would be national suicide—to suggest that they read material that slanders these very founding documents.

Congress, indeed, has an important role to play. In 2021, members of Congress grilled three of the top DOD brass—Admiral Gilday; secretary of defense Lloyd Austin, a retired army general; and then chairman of the Joint Chiefs of Staff, General Mark Milley—over the reading list and a questionable DOD program to combat "extremism." Critics rightly saw this as a witch hunt against conservatives, since leftist extremism, in the form of CRT and BLM, was not only ecouraged, but actively promoted. The Florida Republican Representative Mike Waltz called the reading list "destructive." Milley made things worse for himself and the military services with a series of offhand, ill-considered comments. His comment "I want to understand White Rage. And I'm white... So, what is it that caused thousands of people to assault this building and try to overturn the Constitution of the United States of America? What caused that? I want to find that out" made clear to all that he associated the riot that took place at the US Capitol on January 6, 2021, with racism, or at least with "white rage"—a questionable academic concept from a CRT professor—although there is no evidence of a link.[55]

In 2023, Biden sought to replace Milley as chairman of the Joint Chiefs with an even more woke successor, Air Force General Charles Q. Brown. Brown boasts of hiring based on race and has also pushed gender ideology. While he was chief of staff of the air force, cadets were ordered to no longer call their parents "Mom and Dad," as this is "divisive language." Thirty leaders of the conservative movement sent the US Senate, which must vote on the nomination, a letter asking that Brown be rejected. "With such a poor record of leadership, confirmation of Gen. Brown as Chairman of the Joint Chiefs of Staff would jeopardize national security," they said.[56] This is a good example of how civil-society institutions can organize to combat NextGen Marxism in the military.

We asked our friend Matthew Lohmeier, the space force lieutenant colonel whom the administration relieved of command in 2021 for writing a book on NextGen Marxists in the military—*Irresistible Revolution: Marxism's Goal of Conquest and the Unmaking of the American Military*—what he would recommend to rid the armed forces of this threat. He responded:

The men and women in uniform are an absolutely critical part of the solution to wokeness in the Uniformed Services. From where they sit, they can do more to exert respectful and necessary pressure on senior military leaders than almost anyone else can. However, the difficulty for them lies in the fact that they have been trained to be relatively apolitical and most of them do a good job conducting themselves in a relatively apolitical manner (that is, all but the woke activists, and they exist at all ranks). When leftist talking points become part of military culture, especially by way of formal military training, your average service member will shy away from sharing an alternative view that is more aligned with their own values. That's because they wish to avoid the appearance of acting in a politically partisan manner. It's a rather unfortunate dilemma they're in.

The suggestions in my book for servicemen and women who want to act are the following:

· *Believe that every one of us has an important role to play as events unfold.*
· *Avoid anger; don't forget to smile.*
· *But be courageous…*
· *Get educated. Read up on things.*
· *That way you can speak up with an informed opinion.*
· *Live not by lies. Live by truth.*
· *Pay attention. Be aware.*

COMPLEMENTING THIS advice from our friend Matt, we offer the following bullet points of our own:

· Eliminate the entire DEI construct from all DOD efforts.
· Eliminate instruction of CRT notions in the academy.
· Bar the use of appropriated dollars for race-conscious hiring, promotion, or other activity through acts of Congress.
· Ensure that fields of study at military academies respond to military needs.
· Stop telling young men and women who have volunteered to defend the country and its Constitution, and even lay down their lives for their country, that America is systemically racist or oppressive.
· Review whether senior officers have engaged in political or politicized activity or speech.

Black Lives Matter, Global Networks, and Their "Peaceable Protests"

AMERICANS HAVE constitutional rights to free speech, free association, life, property, and so on. These include Garza, Cullors, Tometi, Abdullah, Mann, Goldberg, and all the other BLM leaders and their communist mentors—even though their expressed wish is to overthrow the Constitution and how the country is constituted. But victims of street mayhem, whether store owners whose businesses were destroyed during the riots of 2020, or in previous years, or those who had their peace disturbed in our streets—or those who were killed in 2020 or earlier owing to something called the "Ferguson effect"—also indeed had their rights, and they were violated because of BLM's action. Government has to protect the rights of all citizens, and in a manner that does not violate the rights of those who peacefully argue for the destruction of society.

But peaceful 2020 was not. The Armed Conflict Location and Event Data Project, housed at Princeton University, coded more than 660 of the some 12,000 protests that took place in 2020 as riots.[57] These riots caused some $2 billion in property damage,[58] the costliest disturbance in US history, and at least twenty-five people had died as of Halloween that year.[59] The murder rate in 2020 went up 30 percent, blowing past the previous record spike of 12 percent in 1968—another politically charged year. The press did not question whether some sort of "Ferguson" or "Minneapolis" effect was at play, whereby homicides and other crimes rise because police pull back after riots.[60] But some brave researchers have. In a July 2023 study, Dae-Young Kim, an associate professor in the Department of Criminal Justice at SUNY Buffalo, argued that "the increases in gun, non-domestic, and gang homicides were significantly associated with decreased police stops in the wake of the pandemic and Floyd protests."[61] In a 2021 study revised in 2023, Travis Campbell, a researcher at the University of Massachusetts, revealed that murders had gone up 11.5 percent in parts of the country where BLM rioted between 2014 and 2019, "which is over 3,000 additional homicides."[62]

Congressional Hearings

BLM's VIOLENCE gives elected officials reason to investigate the group and its leaders, and in fact such hearings would be an important tool in the fight against NextGen Marxism. That members of Congress have not done this yet is a testament to how scared our leaders can be when it comes to matters of race, sex, or climate, precisely the areas the Left uses to make its inroads into society. But congressional hearings are one of our society's best self-defense mechanisms. Congress must therefore put Cullors, Garza, Abdullah, Tometi, and others under oath and ask them how much of the mayhem they, or the Black Lives Matter Global Network Foundation, coordinated. If laws were broken during the riots, looting, and burnings, Congress can refer the matter to the FBI.

While they have the architects of BLM, the National Domestic Workers Alliance, Left Forum, and others on the stand, members of Congress can also ask about their ideological goals. It is a recognized right to espouse Marxism; the US Supreme Court has held that espousal of communism is not sufficient grounds for denying an American employment or security clearances, for instance. But it would be great for the American people to be able to hear from the lips of Cullors and the others their concrete political aims. BLM's founding architects have called for the "complete transformation" of "all branches of government"[63] and for "dismantling the organizing principle of this society."[64] They then went about trying to achieve this through the Gramscian combination of infiltration, indoctrination, and, when necessary, intimidation and violence. Congress can ask whether the BLM organizations still want to dismantle the family[65] or embrace central planning—as LeftRoots, the coordinating committee of which Garza is a member, aims to do.[66] Members can ask Garza directly what she meant when she said that "it's not possible for a world to emerge where black lives matter if it's under capitalism. And it's not possible to abolish capitalism without a struggle against national oppression and gender oppression," statements she made at the 2015 annual convention of the Marxist organization Left Forum.[67] Members should ask Tometi what she meant when she lauded Nicolás Maduro's "participatory democracy"[68] or when she discussed the "alliances between governments to strengthen global justice" with Bolivia's Marxist firebrand Evo Morales.[69] They can ask Cullors why she wants not only to defund the police but also to abolish the prison and court systems.[70] What, pray tell, does she think will happen to society as a result, and is the dismantling of society precisely what she intends through all these steps?

A congressional panel looking into BLM must of course avoid the credibility deficits that plagued the January 6 committee. Both parties must be allowed to appoint members, because cross-examination is indispensable in eliciting the truth. The BLM leadership has the right to try to convince fellow Americans *peacefully* that it would be best to overthrow the country and start anew, and the committee can give it that opportunity. But their fellow Americans also have a right to know what BLM stands for and what it is working toward. This is all the more true given the enormous resources the Fortune 500 and everyday Americans have poured into BLM, which in 2020 alone reached almost $100 million. Ordinarily, this would have been the job of the press, but whether because of newsroom coercion or because they were ideologically in sync, journalists not only refused to do their job but even prepared the ground for BLM's work by changing the language itself.

Peaceable?

IT IS important to revisit as well the changes that were made during the civil rights era that shifted the definition of "peaceable assembly" to allow more rights for protestors. As Mia Gradick, a law student at Regent University School of Law, has written in an as yet unpublished paper, the Court has chosen to "practice judicial restraint[71] from defining a clear definition of 'peaceable' assemblies."[72]

Expose the Networks

THERE IS also the fact that, whereas Americans have constitutional rights,

foreigners—and foreign entities—do not. America has the right to subject organizations such as the World Social Forum or the Foro de São Paulo, which
have expressly stated their desire to change our Constitution, to surveillance
and/or intelligence gathering. Media, especially independent media, must report on these gatherings, to shine a light on their plans and subject them to
greater scrutiny. The Foro de São Paulo—which, lest we forget, includes BLM
in its meetings—held its twenty-sixth meeting in Brasília from June 29 to July
2, 2023, cohosted by Lula's Partido dos Trabalhadores and Brazil's Communist
Party. Only leftist outfits covered this conference. This is not the kind of scrutiny
it merits.

At that meeting, for example, Lula dropped all previous inhibitions and declared himself to be the communist he is. He said that conservatives "accuse us
of being communist, thinking that this will offend us. But that does not offend
us…. To call us communist or socialist never will offend us. Never. On the contrary, it makes us proud." Lula also openly discussed how the Left fights norms
and the family. "Here in Brazil, we confront a narrative of traditions, a narrative
of family, a narrative of patriotism. So here we confront all these narratives that
the people have historically learned to fight." For good measure, he celebrated
the victories of "our comrade Hugo Chávez."[73]

Why isn't this news? This is the man whom the Biden administration chose
to support in elections in 2022. In fact, sources tell us that Juan Gonzalez, a
senior director at the National Security Council, told a meeting in Washington
that Biden knew that Lula would create foreign-policy problems, and still he
chose to support him over his rival, President Jair Bolsonaro, a conservative
who was friendly with President Trump.

Given the impact that these forums, especially Brazilian-origin ones, have
on our domestic peace, conservative outlets would do well to report on them,
to expose their plans and desires. As early as 2009, the Brazilian philosopher
Olavo de Carvalho explained that the media goes out of its way to ignore the
Foro—and the impact this has. "Thus, the São Paulo Forum, which is the vastest
and most powerful political body that has ever existed in Latin America, goes
on unknown to the American and, by the way, also worldwide public opinion,"
Carvalho wrote. He explained that the media, both in Brazil and here, simply
concluded, "against all evidence, that the São Paulo Forum was only a debate
club, with no decisional power at all." But the minutes and final resolutions of the

Foro meetings showed "that discussions ended up becoming resolutions, unanimously signed by the members present. Debate clubs do not pass resolutions."[74]

We offer the following strategies for combating the Marxist networks that are trying to undermine the American constitutional order:

· Authorities must investigate BLM, LeftRoots, the World Social Forum, the Foro de São Paulo, and any other organizations or networks that have expressly stated their desire to change our Constitution.

· Media, especially independent media, must report on these gatherings and shine a light on their plans, subjecting them to greater scrutiny.

· The US Supreme Court's expansion of the right to assemble throughout the civil-rights movement has allowed BLM to challenge our constitutional order. The courts need to define what is in fact considered "peaceable," considering today's events. Local legislatures should also be empowered to interpret what truly "peaceable" assembly means.

· US authorities must investigate the 2020 protests, especially the 660 some odd that turned into riots—and probe why police did not intervene and why rioters did not end up in jail.

Climate Change

THE FORO de São Paulo's vast use of environmentalism alerts us, once more, to how this is merely a front of the NextGen Marxists' assault. As we have explained, NextGen Marxists use the threat of climate change to kneecap capitalism, as environmentalism is one of the tentacles of the division of labor. Greenpeace's founder, Patrick Moore, sounded the alarm early, writing in 1994 that the same takeover of the universities by Marxists that occurred in the 1980s was being replicated in environmentalism. The makeup of Greenpeace's workforce changed dramatically after the collapse of the Soviet Union, he said, because communism's demise behind the Iron Curtain transmuted into anti-corporate extremism. "Suddenly, the international peace movement had a lot less to do. Pro-Soviet groups in the West were discredited. Many of their members moved into the environmental movement, bringing with them their eco-Marxism and pro-Sandinista sentiments. These factors have contributed to a new variant of the environmental movement that is so extreme that many people, including myself, believe its agenda is a greater threat to the global environment than that posed by mainstream society," Moore wrote for the *Leadership Quarterly* in

1994.[75] Greenpeace then became filled with "former Soviet apologists."[76]

The resulting new "eco-extremism" then became, Moore wrote, "anti-human," "anti-technology and anti-science," "anti-organization," "anti-trade, "anti-free enterprise," "anti-democratic," and "basically anti-civilization." The NextGen Marxist eco-extremists developed a deep disdain for humans, whom they wished would disappear from Earth; a longing for a return to primitive society; a "dislike of national governments"; and an expectation for the "whole world to adopt anarchism." Its new antidemocratic nature was "perhaps the most dangerous aspect of radical environmentalism. The very foundation of our society, liberal representative democracy, is rejected," wrote Moore.

Is there a more totalizing vision of today's NextGen Marxism? With this background, we can see why Van Jones, President Obama's "green jobs czar" for a few weeks, found it so easy to go from being a self-described communist who, in 1994, cofounded a collective that trained young activists on Marx and Lenin, Standing Together to Organize a Revolutionary Movement (STORM), to joining the Apollo Alliance, which promoted environmental efforts, after STORM disintegrated in 2002.[77] Jones, of course, did not stay long on the job after his communist background came out in the press, causing the new president a great deal of embarrassment. It also becomes clear why Greta Thunberg, the Swedish environmentalist who has become the darling of the global climate change movement, has come out as an anti-capitalist leftist. There is no "back to normal," she told a large crowd at London's Royal Festival Hall in October 2022. "Normal," she was reported as saying, was the "system" that gave the world the climate crisis, a system of "colonialism, imperialism, oppression, genocide," of "racist, oppressive extractionism."[78]

It is no wonder that Governor DeSantis said at a press conference in December 2021, "People, when they start talking about things like 'global warming,' they typically use that as a pretext to do a bunch of left-wing things that they would want to do anyways. We're not doing any left-wing stuff. What we're doing though, is just reacting to the fact that okay, we're a flood-prone state."[79] DeSantis is, however, showing how climate hysteria can be defanged by spending money on climate adaption, for example, by funneling "hundreds of millions of dollars to communities across the state" to help them cope with flooding, as *Time* wrote in 2022, rather than by chasing the capitalism-killing chimera of carbon reduction.

President Donald Trump must also be commended for unilaterally withdrawing the United States from the Paris Agreement, a colossal, multinational agreement under which his predecessor, Obama, had committed the country to cut carbon emissions by 25 percent, an impossible goal if you expect the economy to grow. Americans must demand an end to a climate hysteria that would push us away from reliable, traditional sources of energy, bypassing nuclear energy options, and on to unreliable, "renewable" forms that will drive us into the antihuman and anticivilization fever dreams of the NextGen eco-Marxists.

We offer the following recommendations:

· Expose the leftist and Marxist ideologues who are driving environmental alarmism as a means for bringing down the free-market system.
· Use the bully pulpit of government to fight the outlandish claims of eco-extremists. Open the White House, Congress, and state governors' offices and legislatures to alternative voices.
· Create alternative boards of scientists who dare question the current climate orthodoxy.
· Allow market mechanisms to continue to innovate clean and energy-efficient solutions and stop the distorting and corrupting impact of government intervention.

Environmental, Social, and Corporate Governance

ESG IS downstream from climate change and another area where the states are leading the fight against corporate NextGen Marxists. This will remain the case until there is a change at the White House, in 2024 or at a future time. A change in the presidency would allow the federal government to take many steps, through executive orders or working with Congress, against the violations of their fiduciary responsibilities by such large asset managers as BlackRock and State Street, because they vote not the financial interests of the funds they hold but the political interests of their CEOs.

But the campaign against ESG must have a state-led front, given that state pension funds controlled by state financial officers are asset behemoths that can get the attention of woke financial companies. A dozen states are drafting plans to punish banks and other financial asset managers that impose ESG rules on companies in their states. State financial officers in Arizona, Arkansas, Florida, Idaho, Kentucky, Louisiana, North Dakota, Oklahoma, South Carolina, Texas,

Utah, and Wyoming have enacted laws, or are considering doing so, barring major financial asset managers from doing business with the state.

They were led by West Virginia's state treasurer Riley Moore, who, on July 28, 2022, placed five major financial institutions—Larry Fink's BlackRock, as well as the Goldman Sachs Group, JPMorgan Chase, Morgan Stanley, and Wells Fargo—on a "Restricted Financial Institution List" that constrains their activities in the state because of their boycott of the fossil fuel sector.[80] Inclusion on the list authorizes the state treasurer to take the following actions:

· disqualify a restricted financial institution from the competitive bidding process or from any other official selection process;
· refuse to enter into a banking contract with a financial institution based on its restricted financial institution status;
· require, as a term of any banking contract, an agreement by the financial institution not to engage in boycott of energy companies for the duration of the contract.

"WE'RE NOT going to pay for our own destruction, we're not going to subsidize that," Moore told *Fox Business* in an interview. "They [ESG activists] have weaponized our tax dollars against the very people and industry that have generated them to begin with. That is why we're pushing back against this ESG movement."[81] Moore scored an immediate victory when Bancorp pledged not to boycott fossil fuels to avoid being placed on the list. The CFO in DeSantis's Florida agrees, saying in July 2022 that "for years now, the cult of ESG economic activists has been working overtime to infuse unwanted, woke ideology into the American economic system because they know their social policies wouldn't pass the sniff test from voters. It's anti-American, anti-freedom, a deliberate attempt to subvert our democracy and not in the best interest of Florida businesses, retirees, or investors."[82] Governor DeSantis himself proposed legal and administrative actions banning fund managers of the State Board of Administration from surrendering to ESG scoring for Florida's investments under the state's retirement system.[83] All this has potentially huge ramifications at all levels across American politics and culture, and it shows that state leaders can fight and resist cultural Marxism.

We offer the following recommendations:

· Ban fund managers who practice ESG from managing state pension funds, and otherwise boycott firms, such as BlackRock, State Street, and Vanguard, that engage in practices inimical to the values of the citizens of a state. Divest state pensions from ESG portfolios.

· Launch shareholder lawsuits. Sue the CEO if he refuses to ignore his fiduciary responsibilities in the name of his preferred policy outcome.

· State legislators should pass laws restricting insurance companies from considering ESG factors and standards when setting rates.

Fighting Woke Corporations

WOKE CORPORATIONS engage not just in ESG but across a number of fronts. There are many ways to fight them. Aside from the boycotts already covered earlier in this chapter in our Ten Tactics, we have the examples of governors such as Ron DeSantis jousting with the likes of Disney. The governor went into action after the woke megacorporation, one of Florida's largest employers because of Disney World,[84] announced that it was not just opposed to but would support efforts to repeal one of DeSantis's key pieces of legislation, the Parental Rights in Education law.[85] Signed by DeSantis on March 28, 2022, the law was itself proof that DeSantis takes gender theory seriously. It says simply that "classroom instruction by school personnel or third parties on sexual orientation or gender identity may not occur in kindergarten through grade 3 or in a manner that is not age-appropriate or developmentally appropriate for students in accordance with state standards."

Banning instruction on sexual orientation to children aged eight or younger would seem common sense to most Americans, but it led to a torrent of criticism from the Left and its media stenographers, who quickly named the law the "Don't Say Gay" act. The Disney CEO Bob Chapek told shareholders in early March that he had called the governor to oppose the then bill because "it could be used to unfairly target gay, lesbian, nonbinary and transgender kids and families."[86] The call itself prompted no action. But when Disney issued a Twitter statement on the day of the law's enactment saying that "our goal as a company is for this law to be repealed by the legislature or struck down in the courts, and we remain committed to supporting national and state organizations working to achieve that,"[87] DeSantis had seen enough. Three weeks later, he signed into law a bill that terminated the Reedy Creek Improvement District, which for decades had allowed Disney to self-govern the geographical area that

Disney World occupies. The governor's actions were all the better for the fact that he was eliminating a government-granted privilege. They were anti–crony capitalism, not an interference in the free market.

Before signing the bill, DeSantis made a statement that put Disney and everyone else on notice that woke actions would come with a heavy price and should be a call to action for all who want to join the Reconquista: "You're a corporation based in Burbank, California, and you're going to marshal your economic might to attack the parents of my state? We view that as a provocation, and we're going to fight back against that."[88] DeSantis's action against Disney shifted the universe of how government at all levels can deal with woke corporations. No longer will corporate giants think they can walk astride America and make decisions that reflect only the views of a NextGen Marxist world. It is an example for others.

We offer the following recommendations:

· Limit the power of corporations to impel employees to adhere to political views or sign what amounts to loyalty oaths that are political in character.
· Organize boycotts of woke corporations' virtue signaling, as has already been successfully done to Disney, Anheuser-Busch, Target, and Ben and Jerry's.

Stop Funding the Left

NEXTGEN MARXISTS have cleverly convinced governments to support their pet projects financially, and government, of course, means taxpayers—of both the Left and the Right. Conservatives, for some reason, are not nearly as good at this. This should not be totally unexpected, as one of the goals of NextGen Marxists is to concentrate power over our lives in the hands of unaccountable experts said to be disinterested, as the Heritage analyst David Ditch wrote in 2013: "a largely unnoticed aspect of these fierce political and societal debates is that one side—the progressive Left—has secured hundreds of billions of dollars in annual federal subsidies for its projects and institutions."[89]

The projects of NextGen Marxism get funded through payments to education; research grants to Big Science; foreign aid—which, as Ditch rightly observes, "has become an appendage of the progressive movement, exporting overseas a radical woke agenda of gender ideology, abortion, and climate fanaticism, which also benefits Communist China's global ambitions"[90]—and payments to

Big Art and public broadcasting. Continuing the status quo would therefore hardly be neutral—it would accrue power to the Left. Although it is impossible to put a precise number on the total, Ditch wrote to us in an email, "Religious congregations take in ~$75 billion per year from donors, who give freely. We're giving a comparable amount every year to organizations controlled by the left, and we don't have much of a choice when it comes to paying our taxes."

The solution here is simple: it's time for Congress to step in and reduce the appropriations, if not altogether defund (e.g., in the cases of the Corporation for Public Broadcasting and the US Agency for International Development) all these projects.

Conclusion

AS WE have demonstrated in this book, the NextGen Marxists who started taking over our institutions in the 1980s were Sixties radicals who, having first tried and failed to overthrow the United States through violence, then opted for Dutschke's Long March. These are strategies that owe their origins to the intellectual response that Marxists had to the failure of their council revolts in Germany and Italy immediately after the end of World War I. The NextGen activists were organized along Alinsky lines and received a helping hand from foreign Marxists who also drew inspiration from the Italian and German models and who also wanted the overthrow of the United States, professing that "another world is possible." As in Latin America, and as the Frankfurt scholars did, they sometimes try to conceal their Marxism. But whether they inhabit the sexual, racial, or climate space, they share a constructivist view of the world that denies nature and is at war with reality; they despise representative democracy, the free markets, and the family, seeking to move the latter out of the way so they can indoctrinate the next generation; and they cast themselves as champions of the oppressed, yet wherever their theories have been put into practice, tyranny has triumphed. Whether they profess to overthrow "heteronormativity," "white supremacy," or "oppressive extractionism," what they want to do is subjugate us, make us poorer, and enslave us.

We have written this book because we want to open America's eyes to what all these activists have in common, describe their strategies, and offer modest proposals on how to counter them. Our society and our political system have been infiltrated. As Mark Levin says in *American Marxism*, "the counterrevolution of the American Revolution is in full swing. And it can no longer be dismissed or ignored, for it is devouring our society and culture."[91] Americans must reverse the gains the NextGen Marxists have made, not contenting themselves only with conserving what little terrain remains uncontested. This is our contribution to the great and consequential battle of ideas that our compatriots are waging, and we explicitly seek to change the nation's climate of opinion. Ultimately, the battle will be won, or lost, in two places: in civil society and in politics. Long before the United States was even a country, its strength resided in the engagement of its citizens, their active participation in their communities, and their commitment to both their individual welfare and also to the common good. This civic attitude was then enshrined in the Constitution. We chose not to be a nation ruled by a monarch or an all-powerful leader but to be a nation of self-governing citizens. That takes work. We cannot sit back and pray that a solution to our current ills will magically sweep in and save us. It depends on each one of us. At the same time, those whom we chose to represent us in local, state, and federal government do have an important role to play. We are, after all, a nation of laws. Therefore the individual who holds this book in his hands must engage in the process of ensuring that this nation is governed responsibly, whether as a voter, a poll watcher, a party official, an election officer, a campaign volunteer, a candidate, or all of these. Again, there is no army of angels or experts who will fulfill these roles for us. It is up to each one of us. Finally, as voters, we must judge politicians asking for our vote against the challenges we have laid out. The time is now. We have a country to save.

ACKNOWLEDGMENTS

No BOOK IS solely the product of its authors. Many people have contributed with ideas, suggestions, editing, etc. We would like to name just a few of the many people who helped us with *NextGen Marxism*. We apologize in advance to those who helped us whose names we have unintentionally left out.

As is the case with any endeavor of this type, our families suffered from our absence during the writing and crafting of this book. As Seb Gorka said to Mike after the book was finished, "Thank you for letting me have my wife back!" So we thank them for their forbearance.

Seb Gorka helped us not only by enduring Katie's absence, but he explained the field of grand strategy, which was helpful for a book of this kind. Our interns Rachel Hazelip, Braden Spurlock, Hannah Balash, and Kurt Gmunder were also crucial in the writing of this book.

A special thanks must be given to Ariel Sheen, a researcher whose profound understanding of global leftist networks, and pathbreaking writings on this issue, were fundamental for our comprehension of the role they had played in the unravelling of America.

At Heritage, we thank President Kevin Roberts and Vice President Derrick Morgan for their leadership, education supremo Lindsey Burke for her ideas and editing, Eric Korsvall, Rob Bluey and John Backiel for supporting the project, and James Carafano, Mike's boss of many years, for his support of this project.

There are many others who helped, but because they are government officials, we have to leave their names out. They know who they are, and how grateful we are. The same is true for others in the corporate and educational world who also helped us. Their well-founded fear of retribution is one of the main reasons we wrote this book. Nobody should be afraid to express their political beliefs in our free country.

ENDNOTES

Introduction

1 Olavo de Carvalho, *The Revolutionary Mentality, Know Your Enemy: An Introduction to the Revolutionary Mentality* (n.p.: Inter-American Institute for Philosophy, Government and Social Thought, 2007), 1.

2 Karl Marx, "Theses on Feuerbach," 1845, https://www.marxists.org/archive/marx/works/1845/theses/theses.htm.

3 Nuno Ornelas Martins, "The Nature of the Cambridge Heterodoxy," *Revue de philosophie économique* 14 (2013): 49–71, https://www.cairn.info/revue-de-philosophie-economique-2013-1-page-49.htm.

4 Karl Marx and Frederick Engels, *The Manifesto of the Communist Party* (Peking: Foreign Languages Press, 1975).

5 For example, 18 percent of social science professors self-identify as Marxists, as opposed to 5 percent who identify as conservatives, and the share of Marxists goes up as high as 25 percent in sociology. See Bryan Caplan, "The Prevalence of Marxism in Academia," *EconLog* (blog), March 31, 2015, https://www.econlib.org/archives/2015/03/the_prevalence_1.html. As Caplan says, "if 18% of a discipline fully embrace a body of nonsense, there is also probably a large bloc of nonsense sympathizers—people who won't swallow the nonsense whole, but nevertheless see great value in it. Suppose, plausibly, that there is one fellow traveler for every true believer.... That would bring the share of abject intellectual corruption to fully 35%—and 51% in sociology." *See also* Jenna Lawrence, "AEI Panel: Marxists Outnumber Conservatives in Social Sciences," *Campus Reform*, June 13, 2016, https://www.campusreform.org/article?id=7678.

6 Alfonso Aguilar, Mike Gonzalez, and Joshua Trevino, "The Smithsonian's Latino Exhibit Is a Disgrace," *The Hill*, August 11, 2022, https://thehill.com/opinion/international/3596470-the-smithsonians-latino-exhibit-is-a-disgrace/.

7 Brenda Hafera, "A Tale of Three Presidential Homes: The Good, the Bad and the Ugly," Heritage Foundation, July 27, 2022, https://www.heritage.org/conservatism/report/tale-three-presidential-houses-the-good-the-bad-and-the-ugly.

8 Sexuality Information and Education Council of the United States, *Guidelines for Competitive Sexual Education, 3rd ed.* (Washington, DC: SIECUS, 2021), https://npin.cdc.gov/publication/guidelines-comprehensive-sexuality-education-3rd-edition.

9 SIECUS, "Our History," https://siecus.org/about-siecus/our-history/.

10 Felicity Barringer, "Education: The Mainstreaming of Marxism in US Colleges," *The New York Times*, October 25, 1989.

11 Derrick A. Bell, "Who's Afraid of Critical Race Theory?," *University of Illinois Law Review* 1995, no. 4 (1995): 893.

12 Eric Mann, "Lost Radicals," *Boston Review*, January 15, 2014, https://www.

bostonreview.net/articles/eric-mann-michael-dawson-radical-black-left-history/.

13   Marx's favorite phrase, "Everything that exists deserves to perish," was a line from Goethe's Mephisto (the devil): Paul Kengor, *The Devil and Karl Marx* (Gastonia, NC: Tan Books, 2020), 36.

14   In the *Manifesto*, Marx and Engels write that collectivization "cannot be effected except by means of despotic inroads on the rights of property" (26).

15   SocioPhilosophy, "Max Horkheimer on Critical Theory," YouTube video, 1:27, https://www.youtube.com/watch?v=OBaYo9Qi-wo.

16   Barringer, "Education."

17   Barringer.

18   Eric Mann, interview with Laura Flanders on *The Laura Flanders Show*, 2015, https://lauraflanders.nationbuilder.com/ericmann.

19   David Horowitz, *Barack Obama's Rules for Revolution: The Alinsky Model* (Sherman Oaks, CA: David Horowitz Freedom Center, 2008).

20   Cornel West, "The Struggle for America's Soul," *The New York Times*, September 15, 1991.

21   Alicia Garza, "No Justice, No Peace: Confronting the Crises of Capitalism and Democracy," speech given at the Left Forum, May 29–31, 2015, https://cryptome.org/2015/05/left-forum-2015.pdf.

22   Marina Karides, Walda Katz-Fishman, Rose M. Brewer, and Jerome Scott, eds., *The United States Social Forum: Perspectives of a Movement* (Chicago: Changemaker, 2010), 251.

23   Karides et al., 228.

24   Karides et al., 251.

25   Karides et al., 180.

26   Karides et al., 222.

27   John McGough and Isaac Steiner, "The 1st US Social Forum: A Festival of Radical Energy," *Europe Solidaire Sans Frontiere*, September 2007, http://europe-solidaire.org/spip.php?article10101.

28   Garza, "No Justice, No Peace."

29   Cory Fischer-Hoffman, "The US Social Forum: Building the People's Platform for 2016," teleSUR, June 24, 2015, https://www.telesurenglish.net/opinion/The-US-Social-Forum-Building-the-Peoples-Platform-for-2016—20150624–0028.html.

30   Garza, "No Justice, No Peace," 21:40.

31   Daniel Silva, "The Circulation of Violence in Discourse," Tilburg University paper 109, September 2014, 1.

32   Matthew Continetti, *The Right: The Hundred-Year War for American Conservatism* (New York: Basic Books, 2022), 95.

33   Carvalho, *Revolutionary Mentality*, 2.

34   George Will, "Wokeness in All Its Self-Flattering Moral Vanity Comes for a Statue at Princeton," *The Washington Post*, January 6, 2023, https://www.washingtonpost.

com/opinions/2023/01/06/wokeness-attack-on-princeton-statue/.

35 They were Rachel Levine, appointed assistant secretary of health at HHS, and Sam Brinton, a deputy assistant secretary at the Department of Energy. The latter was fired in late 2022 after he kept getting arrested stealing luggage at airports.

36 Jeffrey M. Jones, "LGBT Identification in US Ticks Up to 7.1%," Gallup, February 17, 2022, https://news.gallup.com/poll/389792/lgbt-identification-ticks-up.aspx.

37 Ironically, this could be a limiting principle. Many of the former children who had healthy parts of their bodies amputated are now suing, as can be seen in the case of Chloe Cole, who had her breasts surgically removed as part of her "gender-affirming care" at fifteen and was, at the time of this writing, suing her doctors at age eighteen. *See* James Reinl, "It's Like Nazi Era Experiments," *Daily Mail*, January 10, 2023, https://www.dailymail.co.uk/news/article-11619823/Detransitioner-Chloe-Cole-slams-breast-removal-op-endured-aged-15-child-protection-appeal.html.

38 James Lindsay, private seminar held in Washington, DC, January 9, 2023.

39 Robert R. Reilly, *America on Trial: A Defense of the Founding* (San Francisco: Ignatius Press, 2021), 251.

40 Paul Piccone, "Gramsci's Marxism: Beyond Lenin and Togliatti," *Theory and Society* 3, no. 4 (1976): 485–512, https://www.jstor.org/stable/656811.

41 Encontro de Partidos e Organizações de Esquerda da América Latina e Caribe, "Declaración de São Paulo," https://forodesaopaulo.org/wp-content/uploads/2014/07/01-Declaracion-de-Sao-Paulo-19901-1.pdf.

42 Oakland Social Forum, "USSF Oakland Meeting 001.AVI," YouTube video, 10:03, https://www.youtube.com/watch?v=CAUlaQm4sDA.

Chapter 1: Background of the Present Crisis

1 Jonathan Murphy and Mark Kramer, *The Black Book of Communism: Crimes, Terror, Repression*, trans. Stephane Courtois et al. (Boston: Harvard University Press, 2000), 72.

2 Stéphane Courtois, "Introduction: The Crimes of Communism," in Murphy and Kramer, 4–10.

3 James H. Billington, *Fire in the Minds of Men: Origins of the Revolutionary Faith* (New Brunswick, NJ: Transaction, 2006), 17.

4 Sir Francis Bacon, "The New Atlantis," https://www.gutenberg.org/files/2434/2434-h/2434-h.htm.

5 Bacon.

6 Steve Pejovich, "From Socialism in the 1900s to Socialism in the 2000s: The Rise of Liberal Socialism," *Post-Communist Economies* 30, no. 1 (2018): 118, https://doi.org/10.1080/14631377.2017.1398527.

7 Robert R. Reilly, *America on Trial: A Defense of the Founding* (San Francisco: Ignatius Press, 2021), 9.

8   Ellis Sandoz, "Philosophical and Religious Dimensions of the American Founding," in *Arguing Conservatism: Four Decades of the "Intercollegiate Review"* (Wilmington, DE: ISI Books, 2008), 251.

9   Cited in Reilly, *America on Trial*, 13.

10   Robert A. Nisbet, "Rousseau and Totalitarianism," *Journal of Politics* 5, no. 2 (1943): 100.

11   Jean-Jacques Rousseau, *Du Contrat Social*, ed. Charles E. Vaughan (Manchester: University Press, 1918).

12   Thomas Carlyle, quoted in Benjamin Wiker, *10 Books That Screwed Up the World* (Washington, DC: L. Regnery, 2008), 2.

13   Nisbet, "Rousseau and Totalitarianism," 102.

14   Alexis de Toqueville, *Democracy in America*, ed. and trans. Harvey C. Mansfield and Delba Winthrop (Chicago: University of Chicago Press, 2000).

15   Nisbet, "Rousseau and Totalitarianism," 96.

16   Cited in Reilly, *America on Trial*, 274.

17   Richard Pipes, *A Concise History of the Russian Revolution* (New York: Vintage Books, 1996).

18   V. I. Lenin, *What Is to Be Done?* (New York: International, 1969).

19   Cited in Jack S. Bakunin, "Pierre Leroux on Democracy, Socialism, and the Enlightenment," *Journal of the History of Ideas* 37, no. 3 (1976): 456.

20   Edmund Wilson, *To the Finland Station* (New York: Farrar, Straus, and Giroux, 1972), 95–96.

21   https://www.marxists.org/archive/marx/works/1845/holy-family/index.htm.

22   Thomas Sowell, *Marxism: Philosophy and Economics* (London: Taylor and Francis, 2012), 170.

23   Robert Payne, *Marx* (New York: Simon and Schuster, 1968), 124.

24   Karl Marx and Frederick Engels, *The Manifesto of the Communist Party* (Peking: Foreign Languages Press, 1975), 32.

25   Marx and Engels, 36.

26   Marx and Engels, 56.

27   Marx and Engels, 77.

28   Quoted in Billington, *Fire in the Minds of Men*, 292.

29   From the notes of Karl Marx, cited in Wilson, *To the Finland Station*, 151.

30   Richard M. Ebeling, "How Marx Got on the Wrong Side of History," June 16, 2017, https://fee.org/articles/how-marx-got-on-the-wrong-side-of-history/.

31   Ebeling.

32   Karl Korsch, "The Marxism of the First International," http://www.marxists.org/.

33   Address of the International Working Men's Association to Abraham Lincoln, President of the United States of America, presented to US ambassador Charles

Francis Adams, January 28, 1865, written by Karl Marx, https://www.marxists. org/archive/marx/iwma/documents/1864/lincoln-letter.htm.

34   Billington, *Fire in the Minds of Men*, 16.

35   E. H. Carr, *The Bolshevik Revolution 1917–1923* (New York: Penguin Books, 1984), 19.

36   Cited in Pipes, *A Concise History of the Russian Revolution*, 103.

37   Pipes, 154.

38   W. Bruce Lincoln, *Red Victory: A History of the Russian Civil War* (New York: Simon and Schuster, 1989), 384.

39   Herbert Marcuse, "Recent Literature on Communism," http://www.marcuse.org/.

40   Lenin, *What Is to Be Done?*

41   Pipes, *A Concise History of the Russian Revolution*, 1.

42   Minutes of the Second Congress of the Communist International, First Session, July 19, 1920, https://www.marxists.org/history/international/comintern/2nd-congress/ch01.htm.

43   Minutes of the Second Congress of the Communist International.

44   Theodore Draper, *The Roots of American Communism* (New York: Viking Press, 1957), 11.

45   Draper, 13.

46   *Social Service* (published by the American Institute for Social Service) 3, no. 2 (April 1901): 109.

47   Katharine C. Gorka, *Cornell Iron Works: The History of an Enduring Family Company* (Mountain Top, PA: Cornell Cookson, 2013), 156.

48   Gorka, 160–61.

49   Draper, *Roots of American Communism*, 101–2.

50   See, e.g., Fletcher Schoen and Christopher J. Lamb, *Deception, Disinformation, and Strategic Communications: How One Interagency Group Made a Major Difference*, Institute for National Strategic Studies Strategic Perspective 11 (Washington, DC: National Defense University Press, 2012).

51   Reilly, *America on Trial*, 251.

52   Stephen Koch, *Double Lives: Spies and Writers in the Secret Soviet War of Ideas against the West* (New York: Free Press, 1994).

53   Koch, 36.

54   See, e.g., Annika Neklason, "Saccho and Vanzetti's Trial of the Century Exposed Injustice in 1920s America," *Smithsonian Magazine*, May 27, 2021, and Dr. Laura Kuykendall, "Prejudice at the Trial of Saccho and Vanzetti," https://smarthistory. org/seeing-america-2/sacco-and-vanzetti-sa/.

55   "The 1928 Comintern Resolution on the Negro Question in the United States," https://www.revolutionarydemocracy.org/archive/CIResNNQ.pdf.

56   "1928 Comintern Resolution."

57   Oscar Berland, "Nasanov and the Comintern's American Negro Program," *Science and Society* 65, no. 2 (2001): 226–28, https://www.jstor.org/stable/40403897.

58   Oscar Berland, "The Emergence of the Communist Perspective on the 'Negro Question' in America: 1919–1931: Part Two," *Science and Society* 64, no. 2 (2000): 194–217, https://www.jstor.org/stable/40403839.

59   Glenda Elizabeth Gilmore, *Defying Dixie: The Radical Roots of Civil Rights, 1919–1950* (New York: W. W. Norton, 2008), 119.

60   Koch, *Double Lives*, 31, 42.

61   Berland, "Emergence of the Communist Perspective," 210.

62   Angela Davis, keynote address, Brandeis University, February 2019, https://www.brandeis.edu/now/2019/february/video-transcripts/angela-davis.html.

63   Testimony of John Charles Moffitt before the House Committee on Un-American Activities (HUAC), October 1947, https://historymatters.gmu.edu/d/6441.

64   Lenin, *What Is to Be Done?*, 68.

65   Lenin, 70.

Chapter 2: The Cultural Awakening

1   Antonio Gramsci, *"The Modern Prince" and Other Writings* (Paris: Foreign Language Press, 2021), 137.

2   Frank Rosengarten, "The Gramsci–Trotsky Question (1922–1932)," *Social Text* 11 (Winter 1984–85): 68.

3   E.J. Hobsbawm, "Gramsci and Political Theory," *Marxism Today*, July 1977, 208.

4   Megan Trudell, "Gramsci: The Turin Years," *International Socialism*, April 9, 2007, https://www.marxists.org/history/etol/writers/trudell/2007/xx/gramsci.html.

5   Gwyn A. Williams, *Proletarian Order* (New York: Pluto Press, 1975), 56, quoted by WorkersControl.net, December 30, 2015, https://www.workerscontrol.net/theorists/proletarian-power-turin-factory-councils-1919-1920.

6   Andreas Møller Mulvad and Benjamin Ask Popp-Madsen, "From Neo-Republicanism to Socialist Republicanism," *Theoria* 69, no. 171 (2022): 115n2, https://www.berghahnjournals.com/view/journals/theoria/69/171/th6917106.xml.

7   Trudell, "Gramsci."

8   Antonio Gramsci, *Selections from Political Writings 1910–1920* (London: Lawrence and Wishart, 1977), 126, quoted by Trudell, "Gramsci."

9   Gramsci, 76.

10   Gramsci, 76.

11   Gramsci, 129.

12   Trudell, "Gramsci."

13   Williams, *Proletarian Order*, 241.

14 WorkersControl.net, https://www.workerscontrol.net/theorists/proletarian-power-turin-factory-councils-1919-1920.

15 Trudell, "Gramsci."

16 Gramsci, *Selections*, 191.

17 Quoted in Duncan Hallas, *The Comintern* (London: Haymarket, 2008), 60, an online reproduction of which can be found at https://www.marxists.org/archive/hallas/works/1985/comintern/ch3.htm#s1.

18 Alastair Davidson, "Gramsci and Lenin, 1917–1922," *Socialist Register* 11 (1974): 137, https://socialistregister.com/index.php/srv/issue/view/402.

19 Antonio Gramsci, "The Revolution against Capital," November 24, 1917, https://www.marxists.org/archive/gramsci/1917/12/revolution-against-capital.htm.

20 Antonio Gramsci, "The Price of History," *L'Ordine Nuovo*, June 7, 1919, https://www.marxists.org/archive/gramsci/1919/06/price-history.htm.

21 Rosengarten, "Gramsci–Trotsky Question," 72.

22 Davidson, "Gramsci and Lenin," 145.

23 Davidson, 146.

24 See Paul Piccone, "Gramsci's Marxism: Beyond Lenin and Togliatti," *Theory and Society* 3, no. 4 (1976): 502, http://www.jstor.org/stable/656811.

25 Rosengarten, "Gramsci–Trotsky Question," 78.

26 Leon Trotsky, *The First Five Years of the Communist International*, 2:220–22, quoted in Rosengarten, 79–80.

27 Rosengarten, 84.

28 See the "Chronological Outline" in Antonio Gramsci, "Socialism and Culture," in *The Gramsci Reader: Selected Writings 1916–1935*, ed. David Forgacs (New York: New York University Press, 2000), 58, http://ouleft.org/wp-content/uploads/gramsci-reader.pdf.

29 Hobsbawm, introduction to Gramsci, *Gramsci Reader*, 13.

30 Gramsci, 189.

31 Quintin Hoare and Geoffrey Nowell Smith, *Selections from "Prison Notebooks"* (London: Electric Book Company, 1999), 145.

32 Hoare and Smith.

33 Antonio Gramsci, *L'Ordine Nuovo*, June 21, 1919, in Quintin Hoare and John Matthews, *Selections from "Political Writings"* (London: Lawrence and Wishart, 1977), 67–68.

34 Gramsci, 68.

35 Gramsci, *Gramsci Reader*, 57.

36 Gramsci, "*Modern Prince*," 100.

37 Mulvad and Popp-Madsen, "From Neo-Republicanism to Socialist Republicanism."

38 Forgacs, in Gramsci, *Gramsci Reader*, 424.

39   Harmony Goldberg, *Hegemony, War of Position, and Historic Bloc: A Brief Introduction to Antonio Gramsci's Strategy Concepts* (Berkeley, CA: Grassroots Power Project, 2017), 21.

40   Eric Mann, "LA's 'Defund the Police' Battle: Breakthrough," *LA Progressive*, August 23, 2020, https://www.laprogressive.com/education-reform/anatomy-of-the-breakthrough.

41   Hoare and Smith, *Selections*, 494.

42   Hoare and Smith, 209–10.

43   Hoare and Smith, 489.

44   Hoare and Smith 489.

45   Hoare and Smith 489.

46   Goldberg, *Hegemony*, 16. Here she quotes Gramsci, which corresponds to Hoare and Smith, *Selections*, 451.

47   Gramsci, *L'Ordine Nuovo*, July 12, 1919, in Hoare and Matthews, *Selections*, 76–77.

48   Nicolás Maduro (@NicolasMaduro), "Se cumplen 131 años del natalicio del político y teórico italiano Antonio Gramsci," Twitter, January 22, 2022, 10:22 AM, https://twitter.com/nicolasmaduro/status/1484909297540677638.

49   Joseph Gravina, "Gramsci's Philosophy of Praxis," University of Malta, https://www.um.edu.mt/library/oar/bitstream/123456789/53661/1/13%20Joseph%20Gravina%20149-58.pdf.

50   Karl Marx, "Theses on Feuerbach," 1845, https://www.marxists.org/archive/marx/works/1845/theses/theses.htm.

51   Derrick A. Bell, "Who's Afraid of Critical Race Theory?," *University of Illinois Law Review* 1995, no. 4 (1995): 893.

52   Alicia Garza, *The Purpose of Power* (New York: OneWorld, 2020), 204.

53   Gerhard P. Bassler, "The Communist Movement in the German Revolution, 1918–1919," *Central European History* 6, no. 3 (1973): 243.

54   "Interview with Lothar Popp 1978 (extractions)," *Renate and Klaus Kuhl—Sailors' Revolt in Kiel* (blog), http://www.kurkuhl.de/en/novrev/popp_interview.html.

55   Murray Bookchin, *The Third Revolution: Popular Movements in the Revolutionary Era* (London: Continuum, 2005), 19.

56   Bassler, "Communist Movement," 242.

57   Bassler, 244. It is very interesting, and telling, that Bassler admits this, given that he goes to great lengths to defend the councils and present them as agents, not of Bolshevization, but of "direct democracy" in action.

58   Bookchin, *Third Revolution*, 21.

59   Quoted by Bookchin, 25.

60   Bookchin, 28.

61   Bookchin, 32.

62   Rosa Luxemburg, "The National Assembly," *Die Rote Fahne*, November 20, 1918,

https://www.marxists.org/archive/luxemburg/1918/11/20.htm.

63   Clara Zetkin, "Rosa Luxemburg's Attitude toward the Russian Revolution after the November Revolution in Germany," 1922, https://www.revolutionarydemocracy.org/rdv19n2/zetkin.htm.

64   Bookchin, *Third Revolution*, 63.

65   Rosa Luxemburg Stiftung, "About Us," https://www.rosalux.de/en/foundation/about-us.

66   Bookchin, *Third Revolution*, 34.

67   Rolf Wiggershaus, *The Frankfurt School: Its History, Theories, and Political Significance* (Cambridge, MA: MIT Press, 1995), 11.

68   Quoted by John Abromeit in his biography *Max Horkheimer and the Foundations of the Frankfurt School* (Cambridge: Cambridge University Press, 2011), 56.

69   Wiggershaus, *Frankfurt School*, 13.

70   Mario Rapoport, *Bolchevike de Salón, Vida de Felix J. Weil, el fundador argentino de la escuela de Frankfurt* (Buenos Aires: Sudamérica, 2014).

71   Ian Gardner reproduces a 1944 report that Horkheimer wrote to the president of Columbia University, where the Frankfurt School scholars had to flee during the Nazi era, in "The First Marxist Workweek," *The Mallard*, October 20, 2020, https://ian-gardner.medium.com/the-first-marxist-work-week-an-argentine-riddle-wrapped-in-mystery-inside-an-enigma-22a3d1b15cb2. The report says, "The Institut fur Sozialforschung was conceived in the fall of 1919 by Felix J. Weil." As Gardner writes, "it seems unlikely that Horkheimer would have deliberately lied about the creation of Weil's brainchild to the President of a University that was so generously hosting the Institute's activities." The report can be found online at https://sammlungen.ub.uni-frankfurt.de/horkheimer/content/pageview/6624087.

72   Abromeit, *Max Horkheimer*, 61.

73   Max Horkheimer, *Dawn and Decline* (New York: Seabury Press, 1978), 21.

74   Wiggershaus, *Frankfurt School*, 44.

75   Quoted in Abromheit, *Max Horkheimer*, 50.

76   Horkheimer, *Dawn and Decline*, 27.

77   Horkheimer, 29–30.

78   Abromheit, *Max Horkheimer*, 62.

79   Gardner, "First Marxist Workweek."

80   Abromeit, *Max Horkheimer*, 62.

81   Karl Korsch, *Three Essays on Marxism* (New York: Monthly Review Press, 1971), 6.

82   Paul Mattick, "Karl Korsch: His Contribution to Revolutionary Marxism," 1962, 1, https://www.marxists.org/archive/mattick-paul/1962/korsch.htm.

83   Although Zoltan Tarr, in his book on the Frankfurt School, says that *critical* is used first by Emmanuel Kant, to mean that human understanding of nature created natural law. Tarr, *The Frankfurt School: The Critical Theories of Max Horkheimer and Theodor W. Adorno* (New York: John Wiley, 1977), 13. See also

"Immanuel Kant," in *Stanford Encyclopedia of Philosophy*, ed. Edward N. Zalta, https://plato.stanford.edu/entries/kant/.

84   Tom Meisenhelder, *"The Contemporary Significance of Karl Korsch's Marxism," Nature, Society, and Thought 14, no. 3 (2001)*, https://omnilogos.com/contemporary-significance-of-karl-korsch-marxism/.

85   Korsch, *Three Essays on Marxism*, 65.

86   David Craven, "Meyer Schapiro, Karl Korsch, and the Emergence of Critical Theory," *Oxford Art Journal* 17, no. 1 (1994): 46.

87   Georg Lukács, "Tactics and Ethics," https://www.marxists.org/archive/lukacs/works/1919/tactics-ethics.htm.

88   Victor Zitta, *Georg Lukács' Marxism: Alienation, Dialectics, Revolution* (Berlin: Springer, 2016), 106, quoted in Stephen R. Soukup, *The Dictatorship of Woke Capital* (New York: Encounter Books, 2021), 37, 38.

89   Wiggershaus, *Frankfurt School*, 13.

90   Spartacus Educational, "Richard Sorge: The Greatest Spy of the 20th Century?," *Spartacus* (blog), https://spartacus-educational.com/spartacus-blogURL127.htm.

91   House Committeee on Un-American Activities, *The Communist Conspiracy: Communism outside the United States*, 79, https://www.google.com/books/edition/The_Communist_Conspiracy_Communism_outsi/c48rAQAAMAAJ.

92   See the record of the testimony to the US Senate Subcommittee to Investigate the Administration of the Internnal Security Act, August 7, 1951, 273, https://www.google.com/books/edition/Institute_of_Pacific_Relations/OlQsAAAAMAAJ.

93   Wiggershaus, *Frankfurt School*, 16.

94   Wiggershaus, 24.

95   Recounted by Aleksander Matkovic in "A Yugoslav in the Frankfurt School?," *Research and Alternatives* (blog), May 22, 2021, https://aleksandarmatkovic.wordpress.com/2021/05/22/a-yugoslav-in-the-frankfurt-school/.

96   Here John Riddell quotes Zetkin, "Die Lehren des deutschen Eisenbahnerstriks," *Kommunistische Internationale* 20 (1922), in "Clara Zetkin's Struggle for the United Front," *Marxist Essays and Commentary* (blog), March 3, 2011, https://johnriddell.com/2011/05/03/clara-zetkins-struggle-for-the-united-front/.

97   Riddell.

98   Quoted in Wiggershaus, *Frankfurt School*, 35.

99   Abromeit, *Max Horkheimer*, 61.

100   Martin Jay, *The Dialectical Imagination* (Boston: Little, Brown, 1973), 19.

101   Max Horkheimer, *Critical Theory: Selected Essays*, trans. Matthew J. O'Connell et al. (New York: Continuum, 2002), 196, http://blogs.law.columbia.edu/critique1313/files/2019/09/Horkheimer-Traditional-and-Critical-Theory-2.pdf. See also Jeffrey A. Standen, "Frankfurt Criticalism Asserted That Instrumentalized Reason Had Become the Vehicle of Domination," *Virginia Law Review* 72, no. 5 (1986): 993.

102   Horkheimer, *Critical Theory*, 246.

103 Horkheimer, 194.

104 Horkheimer, 207.

105 Horkheimer, 219.

106 Movieclips, "Blue Pill or Red Pill—The Matrix (2/9) Movie CLIP (1999) HD," YouTube video, 2:40, https://www.youtube.com/watch?v=zE7PKRjrid4.

107 Horkheimer, *Critical Theory*, 197.

108 Horkheimer, 199.

109 Horkheimer, 226.

110 Horkheimer, 207.

111 Horkheimer, 241.

112 Mike Gonzalez, "At Least Nikole Hannah-Jones Is Honest about the 1619 Project's Goals," *Washington Examiner*, February 25, 2023, https://www.washingtonexaminer.com/restoring-america/patriotism-unity/at-least-nikole-hannah-jones-is-honest-about-the-1619-projects-goals.

Chapter 3: The (Old) New Left

1 Herbert Marcuse and Karl Popper, *Revolution or Reform? A Confrontation* (Chicago: Precedent, 1976), 57.

2 Barry M. Katz, "Praxis and Poiesis: Toward an Intellectual Biography of Herbert Marcuse [1898–1979]," *New German Critique*, no. 18 (1979): 14, https://doi.org/10.2307/487844.

3 Marcuse and Popper, *Revolution or Reform*, 57; Douglas Kellner, *Herbert Marcuse and the Crisis of Marxism*, quoted by Caroline Ashcroft, *From the German Revolution to the New Left: Revolution and Dissent in Arendt and Marcuse* (Cambridge: Cambridge University Press, 2021), 838.

4 Douglas Kellner, introduction to Herbert Marcuse, *The New Left and the 1960s*, Collected Papers of Herbert Marcuse 3 (London: Routlege, 1968), 2.

5 Marcuse, *The New Left and the 1960s*, 122.

6 Ashcroft, *From the German Revolution*, 853.

7 Tom Hyaden, "The Port Huron Statement," Students for a Democratic Society, June 15, 1962, 9.

8 C. Wright Mills, "Letter to the New Left," *New Left Review*, no. 5 (September–October 1960), republished at https://www.marxists.org/subject/humanism/mills-c-wright/letter-new-left.htm.

9 Graham Allison, "Fidel Castro at Harvard: How History Might Have Changed," *Boston Globe*, April 25, 2015, https://www.belfercenter.org/publication/fidel-castro-harvard-how-history-might-have-changed.

10 Marcuse, *The New Left and the 1960s*, 126, emphasis added.

11 Marcuse, 125.

12   Herbert Marcuse, *One Dimensional Man* (1964; repr. London: Routledge, 2001), 260–61.

13   Howard Zinn, "Marxism and the New Left," in *Dissent: Explorations in the History of American Radicalism*, ed. Alfred L. Young (DeKalb: Northern Illinois University Press, 1968), 370.

14   Marcuse, *The New Left and the 1960s*, 125–26.

15   Marcuse, 127.

16   Students for a Democratic Society, digital history exhibit, https://digilab.libs.uga.edu/exhibits/exhibits/show/civil-rights-digital-history-p/students-for-a-democratic-soci.

17   Students for a Democratic Society, Port Huron Statement, June 15, 1962, https://history.hanover.edu/courses/excerpts/111huron.html.

18   Zinn, "Marxism and the New Left," 357.

19   Port Huron Statement, The Sixties Project, University of Virginia at Charlottesville, http://www2.iath.virginia.edu/sixties/HTML_docs/Resources/Primary/Manifestos/SDS_Port_Huron.html.

20   Todd Gitlin, *The Sixties: Years of Hope, Days of Rage* (New York: Bantam, 1993), 2.

21   Marcuse, *The New Left and the 1960s*, 129.

22   "Cuba: Year of the Firing Squad," *Time*, February 3, 1961, https://content.time.com/time/subscriber/article/0,33009,872043,00.html.

23   Michelle Chase, "C. Wright Mills' Cuban Summer," *Jacobin*, September 2017, https://jacobin.com/2017/09/c-wright-mills-listen-yankee-cuban-revolution-trevino-review.

24   Kirby Smith and Hugo Llorens, "Renaissance and Decay: A Comparison of Socioeconomic Indicators in Pre-Castro and Present Day Cuba," *Annual Proceedings of the Association for the Study of the Cuban Economy* 8 (1998). The authors show through statistics the strong position Cuba was in in 1959, when Castro took over, and how it had even regressed in, for example, daily caloric intake.

25   C. Wright Mills, *The Politics of Truth: Selected Writings of C. Wright Mills* (Oxford: Oxford University Press, 2008), 250, quoting from "Listen Yankee."

26   Marcuse, *The New Left and the 1960s*, 2.

27   Marcuse.

28   Quoted by Kellner, introduction, 20, from Marcuse's *Reflections on the French Revolutions*.

29   Irving Howe, "The Decade That Failed," *New York Times Magazine*, September 19, 1982, 83, https://www.nytimes.com/1982/09/19/magazine/the-decade-that-failed.html.

30   David Horowitz, *Barack Obama's Rules for Revolution: The Alinsky Model* (Sherman Oaks, CA: David Horowitz Freedom Center, 2008).

31   Marcuse and Popper, *Revolution or Reform*, 57. Quoted by Ashcroft, *From the German Revolution*, 838.

32   Herbert Marcuse, "An Essay on Liberation," 1969, https://www.marxists.org/reference/archive/marcuse/works/1969/essay-liberation.htm.

33   "A Conversation with Theodor W. Adorno," from *Der Spiegel*, 1969, *Communists In Situ* (blog), https://cominsitu.wordpress.com/2015/09/01/a-conversation-with-theodor-w-adorno-spiegel-1969/.

34   Mills, "Letter to the New Left."

35   Marcuse, *One Dimensional Man*, 1.

36   SocioPhilosophy, "Max Horkheimer on Critical Theory," YouTube video, 1:27, https://www.youtube.com/watch?v=OBaYo9Qi-wo.

37   Herbert Marcuse, "Repressive Tolerance," in *A Critique of Pure Tolerance*, by Robert Paul Wolff, Barrington Moore Jr., and Herbert Marcuse (Boston: Beacon Press, 1969), 120.

38   Marcuse, *One Dimensional Man*, 255–56.

39   Kellner, introduction, 160.

40   Marcuse, *One Dimensional Man*, 9.

41   Marcuse, 261.

42   Herbert Marcuse, *Eros and Civilization: A Philosophical Inquiry into Freud* (Boston: Beacon Press, 1955), 201.

43   Marcuse, *The New Left and the 1960s*, 154–55.

44   Marcuse, 129.

45   Staughton Lynd, "The New Left," *Annals of the American Academy of Political and Social Science* 382 (1969): 65, http://www.jstor.org/stable/1037115.

46   The files can be seen at https://vault.fbi.gov/Howard%20Zinn%20/Howard%20Zinn%20Part%2001%20of%2004%20.

47   Zinn, "Marxism and the New Left," 359.

48   Zinn, 356–57.

49   Marcuse, *The New Left and the 1960s*, 49.

50   Barbarella Fokos, "The Bourgeois Marxist," *San Diego Reader*, August 23, 2007, https://www.sandiegoreader.com/news/2007/aug/23/bourgeois-marxist/.

51   Zinn, "Marxism and the New Left," 358.

52   Zinn, 359.

53   John T. McQuiston, "Abbie Hoffman, 60s Icon, Dies; Yippie Movement Founder," *The New York Times*, April 14, 1989.

54   Myra MacPherson, "Jerry Rubin," *The Washington Post*, October 18, 1981, https://www.washingtonpost.com/archive/lifestyle/1981/10/18/jerry-rubin/beb88e6b-ba7e-4839-80ac-4442f6d47809/.

55   Neil MacFarquhar, "Murders Spiked in 2020 in Cities across the United States," *The New York Times*, September 21, 2021.

56   Bryan Burrough, *Days of Rage: America's Radical Underground, the FBI, and the Forgotten Age of Revolutionary Violence* (New York: Penguin Press, 2015), 59, 60.

57   Burrough, 65.

58   "You Don't Need a Weatherman to Know Which Way the Wind Blows," June 18, 1969, https://www.sds-1960s.org/sds_wuo/weather/weatherman_document.txt.

59   Abbie Hoffman, *Steal This Book* (Pirate Editions, 1971), 1.

60   Herbert Marcuse, *Marxism, Revolution and Utopia*, Collected Papers of Herbert Marcuse 6, ed. Douglas Kellner and Clayton Pierce (Abingdon, UK: Routledge, 2014), 336.

61   Herbert Marcuse, *Counterrevolution and Revolt* (Boston: Beacon Press, 1972), 55.

62   Marcuse, *The New Left and the 1960s*, 156.

63   Marcuse.

Chapter 4: The Metamorphosis

1   Sol Stern, "The Bomber as School Reformer," *City Journal*, October 6, 2008, https://www.city-journal.org/html/bomber-school-reformer-10465.html.

2   Ben Joravsky, "The Long, Strange Trip of Bill Ayers," *Chicago Reader*, November 8, 1990, https://chicagoreader.com/news-politics/the-long-strange-trip-of-bill-ayers/.

3   Joravsky.

4   Howard Zinn, "Marxism and the New Left," in *Dissent: Explorations in the History of American Radicalism*, ed. Alfred L. Young (DeKalb: Northern Illinois University Press, 1968), 370.

5   "You Don't Need a Weatherman to Know Which Way the Wind Blows," June 18, 1969, https://www.sds-1960s.org/sds_wuo/weather/weatherman_document.txt.

6   Lucinda Franks, "The Seeds of Terror," *New York Times Magazine*, November 22, 1981, https://www.nytimes.com/1981/11/22/magazine/the-seeds-of-terror.html.

7   Burrough, *Days of Rage*, 73.

8   Ian Tuttle, "Progressives' Plan B: Violent Protest or Principled Opposition," *National Review*, January 3, 2017, https://www.nationalreview.com/2017/01/demo-crats-march-washington-anti-trump-protests-violent-or-peaceful/.

9   Burrough, *Days of Rage*, 78–79.

10   Arthur M. Eckstein, *Bad Moon Rising: How the Weather Underground Beat the FBI and Lost the Revolution* (New Haven, CT: Yale University Press, 2016), 69.

11   Eckstein, 70.

12   Eckstein, 81.

13   Marcia Froelke Coburn, "No Regrets," *Chicago Magazine*, August 1, 2001, https://www.chicagomag.com/chicago-magazine/august-2001/no-regrets/.

14   Frank Wilkins, "The Murder of Sharon Tate by the Manson Family," Reel Reviews, https://www.reelreviews.com/shorttakes-56/sharontate/sharontate.

15   Charles Manson, biography, https://www.biography.com/crime/charles-manson.

16   Susan Atkins, "Susan Atkins' Story of 2 Nights of Murder," December 14, 1969, https://www.cielodrive.com/archive/susan-atkins-story-of-2-nights-of-murder/.

17   Burrough, *Days of Rage*, 85.

18   Daniel Patrick Moynihan, *Daniel Patrick Moynihan: A Portrait in Letters of an American Visionary* (New York: PublicAffairs, 2010), 217.

19   Patricia Lear, "Rebel without a Pause," *Chicago Magazine*, May 1, 1993, https://www.chicagomag.com/chicago-magazine/may-1993/rebel-without-a-pause/.

20   Lear.

21   Mark Rudd, *Underground* (New York: HarperCollins, 2009), 189.

22   Paul Kengor, "Charles Manson and the Weather Underground," *American Spectator*, November 21, 2017, https://spectator.org/charles-manson-and-the-weather-underground/.

23   Wilkins, "Murder of Sharon Tate."

24   Franks, "Seeds of Terror."

25   Kengor, "Charles Manson and the Weather Underground."

26   Kevin D. Williamson, "Charles Manson's Radical Chic," *National Review*, November 20, 2017, https://www.nationalreview.com/2017/11/charles-manson-1960s-radicals-loved-him/.

27   Moynihan, *Daniel Patrick Moynihan*, 217.

28   Kengor, "Charles Manson and the Weather Underground."

29   Eckstein, *Bad Moon Rising*, 81.

30   Franks, "Seeds of Terror."

31   Burrough, *Days of Rage*, 98.

32   Burrough, 77, quoting Weatherman Gerry Long.

33   Joy James, " 'Concerning Violence': Frantz Fanon's Rebel Intellectual in Search of a Black Cyborg," *South Atlantic Quarterly* (Winter 2013), https://sites.williams.edu/jjames/files/2019/06/black-cyborg.pdf.

34   Coburn, "No Regrets."

35   Franks, "Seeds of Terror."

36   Eckstein, *Bad Moon Rising*, 83.

37   Eckstein, 83.

38   Burrough, *Days of Rage*, 121.

39   Eckstein, *Bad Moon Rising*, 85.

40   Deroy Murdock, "Obama Taking Ayers' Cash Another Red Flag," *CT Insider*, October 30, 2008, https://www.ctinsider.com/local/opinion/article/Obama-taking-Ayers-cash-another-red-flag-1289768.php.

41   Burrough, *Days of Rage*, 56.

42   Burrough, 159.

43   Franks, "Seeds of Terror."

44   Burrough, *Days of Rage*, 362.

45   Burrough, 364.

46   Burrough, 368–69.

47   "Weather Underground Splits," *Women and Revolution*, no. 14 (Spring 1977), 2, https://www.marxists.org/history/etol/newspape/w&r/WR_014_1977.pdf.

48   Sol Stern, "The Bomber as School Reformer," *City Journal*, December 23, 2015, https://www.city-journal.org/html/bomber-school-reformer-10465.html.

49   Dinitia Smith, "No Regrets for a Love of Explosives, in a Memoir of Sorts, a War Protester Talks of Life with the Weathermen," *The New York Times*, September 11, 2001.

50   Franks, "Seeds of Terror."

51   William Voegeli, "Days of Rage, Years of Lies," *Claremont Review of Books* 11, no. 3 (2011), https://claremontreviewofbooks.com/days-of-rage-years-of-lies/.

52   Bill Ayers, Phil Smith Lecture, 2011, https://files.eric.ed.gov/fulltext/EJ960323.pdf.

53   Paul Berman, *A Tale of Two Utopias: The Political Journey of the Generation of 1968* (New York: W. W. Norton, 1997), 56.

54   The description of Berman's thoughts came in Gerald Sorin, *Irving Howe: A Life of Passionate Dissent* (New York: New York University Press, 2002), 207.

55   Voegeli, "Days of Rage."

56   Sorin, *Irving Howe*, 206.

57   Sorin, 65.

58   Smith, "No Regrets."

59   Jennifer Allen, "Woody's Children," *New York* magazine, December 6, 1982, 22.

60   Sol Stern, "Ayers Is No Education 'Reformer,'" *The Wall Street Journal*, October 16, 2008, https://www.wsj.com/articles/SB122411943821339043.

61   Sol Stern, "The Ed Schools' Latest—and Worst—Humbug," *City Journal*, Summer 2006.

62   See note 9.

63   William H. Schubert, "My Friend and Colleague, Bill Ayers," October 20, 2008, https://www.mail-archive.com/sixties-l@googlegroups.com/msg00331.html.

64   Joravsky, "Long, Strange Trip of Bill Ayers."

65   Joravsky.

66   Mary Grabar, "Did Bill Ayers Get His Teaching Job "the Chicago Way"?, *America's Survival*, May 15, 2017.

67   Stern, "Ayers Is No Education Reformer."

68   Grabar, "Did Bill Ayers Get His Teaching Job?," 7.

69   Paulo Freire, *Pedagogy of the Oppressed*, trans. Myra Bergman Ramos (New York: Penguin Books, 1993), 11.

70   Freire, 16.

71   Lisa Klope, "Humanizing Education: Paulo Freire's Legacy," January 21, 2022, https://www.usfca.edu/education/humanizing-education-paulo-freires-legacy.

72   Elliott D. Green, "What Are the Most-Cited Publications in the Social Sciences (According to Google Scholar)?," LSE Research Online, London School of Economics and Political Science, May 12, 2016.

73   Jay Schalin, "Radically Transforming the Nation: Our Politicized Schools of Education," James G. Martin Center for Academic Renewal, February 20, 2019, https://www.jamesgmartin.center/2019/02/radically-transforming-the-nation-our-politicized-schools-of-education/.

74   Billy Ayers, Bernadine Dohrn, Jeff Jones, Celia Sojourn, Prairie Fire, Prairie Fire Distributing Committee, July 1974, 1, https://www.sds-1960s.org/PrairieFire-reprint.pdf.

75   Ron Chepesiuk, *Sixties Radicals, Then and Now* (Jefferson, NC: McFarland, 1995), 102.

76   Grabar, "Did Bill Ayers Get His Teaching Job?," 8.

77   Grabar.

78   Bill Ayers, World Education Forum, November 7, 2006, https://billayers.org/2006/11/.

79   Stanley Kurtz, "Obama and Ayers Pushed Radicalism on Schools," *The Wall Street Journal*, September 23, 2008, https://www.wsj.com/articles/SB122212856075765367.

80   Murdock, "Obama Taking Ayers' Cash Another Red Flag."

81   Ben Smith, "Obama Once Visited '60s Radicals," *Politico*, February 22, 2008, https://www.politico.com/story/2008/02/obama-once-visited-60s-radicals-008630.

82   *People's Daily World*, June 19, 1986, 18-A.

83   Drew Griffin and Kathleen Johnson, "Ayers and Obama Crossed Paths on Boards, Records Show," CNN Election Center, https://www.cnn.com/2008/POLITICS/10/07/obama.ayers/.

84   Scott Shane, "Obama and '60s Bomber: A Look into Crossed Paths," *The New York Times*, October 3, 2008.

85   Smith, "Obama Once Visited '60s Radicals."

86   Stern, "Bomber as School Reformer."

87   Franks, "Seeds of Terror."

Chapter 5: The Takeover

1   Kayla Corbin, "A Rhetorical History of Black Studies: Black Power and Epistemology" (honors thesis, University of Richmond, 2021), 2.

2   The study by James Kindgren, "Measuring Diversity: Law Faculties in 1997 and 2013," *Harvard Journal of Law and Public Policy* 39 (2016): 144, 149, came in Michael Conklin, "Political Ideology and Law School Rankings," *University of*

Illinois Law Review 2020 (2020): online178, https://illinoislawreview.org/online/political-ideology-and-law-school-rankings/.

3   Jay Schalin, "The Politicization of University Schools of Education: The Long March through the Education Schools," James G. Martin Center for Academic Renewal, February 2019, 1, https://www.jamesgmartin.center/2019/02/schools-of-education/.

4   Evelyn Hu-DeHart, "The History, Development, and Future of Ethnic Studies," *Phi Delta Kappan* 75, no. 1 (1993): 51, 52, http://www.jstor.org/stable/20405023.

5   For a treatment of this process, please see Mike Gonzalez, *The Plot to Change America: How Identity Politics Is Dividing the Land of the Free* (New York: Encounter Books, 2020).

6   Hu-DeHart, "History," 52.

7   For the list of fifteen demands, see https://diva.sfsu.edu/collections/strike/bundles/187915.

8   https://diva.sfsu.edu/collections/strike/bundles/187915.

9   "Interview: Jason Ferreira," *Socialist Worker*, December 13, 2018, https://socialistworker.org/2018/12/13/1968-the-strike-at-san-francisco-state.

10   C. Vann Woodward, *The Strange Career of Jim Crow* (New York: Oxford University Press, 1955), 198, 199, 200,

11   One can read an account of the affair given by Barbarella Fokos, "The Bourgeois Marxist," *San Diego Reader*, August 23, 2007, https://www.sandiegoreader.com/news/2007/aug/23/bourgeois-marxist/.

12   College Factual, "Best Ethnic Studies Bachelor's Degree Schools," 2023, https://www.collegefactual.com/majors/ethnic-cultural-gender-studies/ethnic-studies/rankings/top-ranked/bachelors-degrees/.

13   Haley Smith, "Angela Davis Proclaims She's a "Lifelong Communist," Audience Erupts in Applause," *New Guard*, March 31, 2016.

14   Bonner Center for Civics Engagement, University of Richmond, 2020 Engage for Change Awards, https://engage.richmond.edu/events/awards/awards2020.html.

15   Corbin, "Rhetorical History," 3.

16   Corbin, 5, 8.

17   University of Richmond, Schools of Arts and Sciences, Africana Studies, https://africana.richmond.edu/#about.

18   Bret Stephens, "California's Ethnic Studies Follies," *The New York Times*, March 9, 2021.

19   *Harvard Crimson*, "A Critical Decision: Save the CLS Program," December 5, 1985, https://www.thecrimson.com/article/1985/12/5/a-critical-decision-save-the-cls/.

20   Paul L. Caron, "98% of Harvard Law Faculty Political Donations Go to Democrats," *TaxProf Blog*, May 2, 2015, https://taxprof.typepad.com/taxprof_blog/2015/05/98-of-harvard-law-faculty-.html.

21   Mari Matsuda, "Looking to the Bottom," a 1987 essay that appeared in the *Harvard Civil Rights–Civil Liberties Law Review* and then was reprinted in the

tome that serves as the foundational book of CRT, *Critical Race Theory: The Key Writings That Formed the Movement*, ed. Kimberlé Crenshaw, Neil Gotanda, Gary Peller, and Kendall Thomas (New York: New Press, 1996), 63.

22   R. S. Radford, "The Public Interest. Not Just for the Left Anymore," Pacific Legal Foundation, July 27, 2010, https://pacificlegal.org/the-public-interest-not-just-for-the-left-any-more/.

23   Walter Olson, "The Ford Foundation: Shaping America's Laws by Re-making Her Law Schools," Capital Research Center, July 1, 2023, https://capitalresearch.org/article/the-ford-foundation-shaping-americas-laws-by-re-making-her-law-schools/.

24   Olson.

25   Michelle Fabio, "What Is a Legal Clinic in Law School?," ThoughtCo, https://www.thoughtco.com/what-is-a-legal-clinic-2154873.

26   Minna J. Kotkin, "Clinical Legal Education and the Replication of Hierarchies," Harvard Law School's Center on the Legal Profession, January/February 2020, https://clp.law.harvard.edu/knowledge-hub/magazine/issues/clinical-legal-education/clinical-legal-education-and-the-replication-of-hierarchy/.

27   Radford, "Public Interest."

28   Olson, "Ford Foundation."

29   Mike Gonzalez, *The Plot to Change America* (New York: Encounter Books, 2020), 14.

30   MALDEF, "MALDEF Successfully Pushed to Expand the Voting Rights Act to Language Minorities," March 19, 2020, https://www.maldef.org/2020/03/maldef-successfully-pushed-to-expand-the-voting-rights-act-to-language-minorities/.

31   Charles Du, "Securing Public Interest Law's Commitment to Left Politics," Yale Law Journal Forum, October 21, 2018, 244, https://www.yalelawjournal.org/forum/securing-public-interest-laws-commitment-to-left-politics.

32   "Critical Legal Theory," Cornell Law School Legal Information Institute, https://www.law.cornell.edu/wex/critical_legal_theory.

33   William Blackstone, "Commentaries on the Laws of England," 1765, https://constitutioncenter.org/the-constitution/historic-document-library/detail/william-blackstonecommentaries-on-the-laws-of-england-1765-69#:~:text=It%20is%20binding%20over%20all,or%20immediately%2C%20from%20this%20original.

34   Stefan Sciaraffa, "Critical Legal Studies: A Marxist Rejoinder," *Legal Studies* 5, no. 2 (1999): 201–219, https://doi.org/10.1017/S1352325299052040.

35   Duncan Kennedy, *The Critique of Rights in Critical Legal Studies* (Durham, NC: Duke University Press, 2002), 182.

36   Cornell Law School Legal Information Institute, "Critical Legal Theory."

37   Duncan Kennedy, "Critical Labour Theory: A Comment," 4 *Indiana Law Journal* 4 (1981): 506, quoted in Alan Hunt, *The Theory of Critical Legal Studies* (London: Oxford University Press, 1984), note 2.

38   Kennedy.

39   Allan C. Hutchinson and Patrick J. Monahan, "Law, Politics, and the Critical Legal Scholars: The Unfolding Drama of American Legal Thought," *Stanford Law Review* 36, no. 1/2 (1984): 200, https://doi.org/10.2307/1228683.

40   Kennedy, *Critique of Rights*, 218.

41   Quoted by Hutchinson and Monahan, "Law, Politics, and the Critical Legal Scholars," 232.

42   Kennedy, *Critique of Rights*, 183.

43   James R. Hackney Jr., *Legal Intellectuals in Conversation* (New York: New York University Press, 2012), 23.

44   Duncan Kennedy, "Antonio Gramsci and the Legal System," *ALSA Forum* 6, no. 1 (1982): 31–32, http://www.duncankennedy.net/documents/Photo%20articles/Antonio%20Gramsci%20and%20The%20Legal%20System.pdf.

45   Kennedy, 24.

46   Kennedy, 25.

47   Kennedy, 36.

48   Jennifer A. Kingson, "Harvard's Tenure Battle Puts Critical Legal Studies on Trial," *The New York Times*, August 30, 1987.

49   Paul D. Carrington, "Of Law and the River," *Journal of Legal Education* 34 (1984): 227.

50   Mari J. Matsuda, "Looking to the Bottom: Critical Legal Studies and Reparations," *Harvard Civil Rights–Civil Liberties Law Review* 22 (1987): 327, 325.

51   Martsuda, 345–46.

52   Crenshaw et al., *Critical Race Theory*, xxvi.

53   See a video of the 2019 event: American Studies Association, "Presidential Session: Intersectionality and Critical Race Theory," YouTube video, 1:43:37, https://www.youtube.com/watch?v=elaIUgX-zZE.

54   "Living History Interview with Richard Delgado and Jean Stefancic," *Transnational Law and Contemporary Problems* 221 (2011): 225, https://digitalcommons.law.seattleu.edu/cgi/viewcontent.cgi?article=1039&context=faculty.

55   Richard Delgado, "The Imperial Scholar: Reflections on a Review of Civil Rights Literature," *University of Pennsylvania Law Review* 132 (1984): 4, https://papers.ssrn.com/sol3/papers.cfm?abstract_id=1992111.

56   Crenshaw et al., *Critical Race Theory*, xix.

57   John O. Calmore, "Critical Race Theory, Archie Shepp, and Fire Music: Securing an Authentic Intellectual Life in a Multicultural World," in Crenshaw et al., 326.

58   Derrick A. Bell, "Who's Afraid of Critical Race Theory?," University of Illinois Law Review 1995, no. 4 (1995): 893.

59   Derrick A. Bell, "Strangers in Academic Paradise: Law Teachers of Color in Still White Law Schools," *USF Law Review* 20 (1986): 387.

60   Tim Pearce, "Biden's Supreme Court Pick Championed Advocates of Critical Race Theory in Lectures, Speeches," *Daily Wire*, March 17, 2022, https://www.

dailywire.com/news/bidens-supreme-court-pick-championed-advocates-of-critical-race-theory-in-lectures-speeches.

61   Paulo Freire, *Pedagogy of the Oppressed* (New York: Continuum, 1970), 47.

62   Kimberlé Crenshaw, "Race, Reform and Retrenchment," *Harvard Law Review* 101, no. 7 (1988): 1386.

63   Roger Severino, presentation to staff at the Heritage Foundation.

64   Kennedy, *Critique of Rights*, 180–81.

65   "Black Lives Matter Co-founder Patrisse Cullors on Abolition and Imagining a Society Based on Care," Democracy Now!, January 31, 2022, https://www.democracynow.org/2022/1/31/patrisse_cullors_an_abolitionists_handbook.

66   Willmoore Kendall, *The Conservative Affirmation* (Washington, DC: Regnery, 1963), 149–22.

Chapter 6: Organizing for Revolution

1   Saul Alinsky, *Rules for Radicals* (New York: Vintage Books, 1971), ix.

2   Hillary D. Rodham, "There Is Only the Fight …" (thesis, Wellesley College, 1969), 8, https://blogs.chicagotribune.com/files/hillaryclintonthesis-ocr.pdf.

3   Rodham, 1.

4   Vladimir Lenin, *What Is to Be Done?* (1902), 17, https://www.marxists.org/archive/lenin/works/1901/witbd/.

5   Lenin, 34.

6   Lenin.

7   Back of the Yard Neighborhood Council, http://www.encyclopedia.chicagohistory.org/pages/100.html.

8   Lenin, *What Is to Be Done?*, 50.

9   Arto Artinian, "Lenin Reloaded Again: A Critical Book Review of Tamas Krausz's Reconstructing Lenin: An Intellectual Biography," *Situations* 7, no. 1 and 2 (2018): 127.

10   Artinian, 139.

11   Alinsky, *Rules for Radicals*, 37.

12   Quoted from the recollections of the evening by Ludwig Lore, who had hosted the meeting in his Brooklyn home, in Theodore Draper, *The Roots of American Communism* (New York: Viking Press, 1957), 81.

13   Louis Fraina, *Revolutionary Socialism* (1918), quoted in Draper, 91.

14   The Programme of the Communist International, Comintern Sixth Congress 1929, https://www.marxists.org/history/international/comintern/6th-congress/ch06.htm.

15   Programme of the Communist International.

16   Comintern Sixth Congress, "Section VI—The Strategy and Tactics of the Com-
      munist International in the Struggle for the Dictatorship of the Proletariat, 1. Ide-
      ologies among the Working Class Inimical to Communism," in *The Programme
      of the Communist International Together with the Statutes of the Communist
      International*, trans. Mike NacNair (London: Modern Books, 1929), 23.

17   See, e.g., Michael J. Austin and Neil Betten, "Intellectual Origins of Community
      Organizing, 1920–1939," *Social Service Review* 51, no. 1 (1977): 155–70, http://www.
      jstor.org/stable/30015463.

18   Philip Selznick, *The Organizational Weapons: A Study of Bolshevik Strategy and
      Tactics* (Santa Monica, CA: RAND Corporation, 1952), 96.

19   Saul Alinsky, quoted in Marion K. Sanders, *The Professional Radical: Conversa-
      tions with Saul Alinsky* (New York: Harper and Row, 1967), 27.

20   "Saul Alinsky: A Candid Conversation with the Feisty Radical Organizer,"
      Playboy, March 1972, http://documents.theblackvault.com/documents/fbi-
      files/100-BA-30057.pdf.

21   Stanley Kurtz, "Why Hillary's Alinsky Letters Matter," *National Review Online*,
      September 22, 2014, https://www.nationalreview.com/corner/why-hillarys-alin-
      sky-letters-matter-stanley-kurtz/.

22   Rodham, "There Is Only the Fight … ," 5, emphasis added.

23   Alinsky, *Rules for Radicals*, 3.

24   John Kretzmann, "Post-Alinsky Community Organizing," The Citizen's Hand-
      book, https://www.citizenshandbook.org/postalinsky.html.

25   Alinsky, *Rules for Radicals*, xxxiii.

26   TheStrategyCenter, "Transformative Organizing Theory (USSF 2010 Workshop),"
      YouTube video, 25:40, https://www.youtube.com/watch?v=rQvoszih8l4.

27   Alinsky, *Rules for Radicals*, 69.

28   Alinsky, 17.

29   Alinsky, 15.

30   Sanford Horwitt, *Let Them Call Me Rebel: Saul Alinsky—His Life and Legacy*
      (New York: Knopf, 1992), 526.

31   Horwitt, 525.

32   Alinsky, *Rules for Radicals*, 130.

33   Robert B. Westbrook, review of *The League for Industrial Democracy: A Docu-
      mentary History*, 3 vols., by Bernard K. Johnpoll and Mark R. Yerburgh, *Interna-
      tional Labor and Working-Class History*, no. 20 (1981): 73–78, http://www.jstor.
      org/stable/27671382.

34   Westbrook.

35   *Students in Revolt: The Story of the Intercollegiate League for Industrial Democracy*
      (New York: League for Industrial Democracy, 1933), 3, accessed via https://archive.
      org/details/StudentsInRevoltTheStoryOfTheIntercollegiateLeagueForIndustrial.

36   Quoted in Beatrice Hansen, "A Political Biography of Walter Reuther: The

Record of an Opportunist,"
August 1969, https://www.marxists.org/history/etol/document/swp-us/misc-1/hanon-reuth.htm.

37 Aryeh Neier, *Taking Liberties: Four Decades in the Struggle for Rights* (New York: PublicAffairs, 2003), xviii.

38 Neier, xx.

39 Jack London and Upton Sinclair had been founders of the Intercollegiate Socialist Institute.

40 For Mencken's influence on one of the original SDS leaders, see Todd Gitlin, *The Sixties: Years of Hope, Days of Rage* (New York: Bantam, 1993), 1.

41 Gitlin, 31.

42 https://snccdigital.org/inside-sncc/alliances-relationships/sds/.

43 Gitlin, *The Sixties*, 147.

44 Gitlin, 165. See also Richard Rothstein, "A Short History of ERAP," Online Archive of California, https://oac.cdlib.org/view?docId=kt4k4003k7.

45 Quoted in Eugene H. Methvin, *The Riot Makers: The Technology of Social Demolition* (New Rochelle, NY: Arlington House, 1970), 28.

46 Some of the content in this section was previously published: Katharine C. Gorka, "How the 1960s Riots Foreshadow Today's Communist Weaponization of Black Pain," *The Federalist*, September 14, 2020, https://thefederalist.com/2020/09/14/how-the-1960s-riots-foreshadow-todays-communist-weaponization-of-black-pain/.

47 See, e.g., David Horowitz, "Tom Hayden, L.A. and Me," *Salon*, March 3, 1997, https://www.salon.com/1997/03/03/horowitz970303/, and Sol Stern, "American Turncoat: The Meaning of Tom Hayden's Life," *City Journal*, November 4, 2016, https://www.city-journal.org/article/american-turncoat.

48 Quoted in Methvin, *Riot Makers*, 27.

49 Methvin.

50 Methvin, 32.

51 Tom Hayden, "A Special Supplement on the Occupation of Newark," *The New York Times Review of Books*, August 24, 1967, https://www.nybooks.com/articles/1967/08/24/a-special-supplement-the-occupation-of-newark/.

52 Paul Solman, "Racism, Riots and Economics: If History Is the Guide, Why Baltimore Won't Recover Soon," PBS.org, May 15, 2015, https://www.pbs.org/newshour/economy/racism-riots-economics-baltimore-recovery.

53 Sean Wilentz, "General Editor's Introduction," in *The Kerner Report: The National Advisory Commission on Civil Disorders* (Princeton, NJ: Princeton University Press, 2016), x.

54 Dan Berger, *Outlaws of America: The Weather Underground and the Politics of Solidarity* (Chico, CA: AK Press, 2006), 95.

55 Stanley Kurtz, *Radical-in-Chief: Barack Obama and the Untold Story of American*

Socialism (New York: Threshold, 2010), 46.

56   Kurtz, 131.

57   https://midwestacademy.com/.

58   Eric Mann, "Transformative Organizing," in *Race, Poverty, and the Environment* 17, no. 2 (2010): 84.

59   Mann, 85.

60   Mann, 86.

61   Robert J. Alexander, *Maoism in the Developed World* (Westport, CT: Praeger, 2001), 34.

62   University of California Television, "Growing Activism: Labor/Community Strategy Center," YouTube video, 0:15, https://www.youtube.com/watch?v=BO6MR-2S4a0s.

63   Mike Gonzalez, *BLM: The Making of a New Marxist Revolution* (New York: Encounter, 2020), 87–88.

64   Eric Mann, "Building the Anti-Racist, Anti-Imperialist United Front: Theory and Practice from the Strategy Center and Bus Riders Union," September 6, 1996, https://thestrategycenter.org/1996/09/06/building-the-anti-racist-anti-imperialist-united-front-theory-and-practice-from-the-l-a-strategy-center-and-bus-riders-union/.

65   Eric Mann, *Playbook for Progressives* (Boston: Beacon Press, 2011), 24.

66   Labor Community Strategy Center, *Case Study*, 21, http://www.ferntiger.com/pdf/Bus_Riders_Union.pdf.

67   Mike Gonzalez, "To Destroy America," *City Journal*, September 1, 2020.

68   Patrisse Cullors, *When They Call You a Terrorist* (New York: St. Martin's Griffin, 2018), quoted in Gonzalez, 87.

69   Mann, *Playbook*, 25.

70   Mann, "Building the Anti-Racist."

71   Dignity and Power Now, "About Us," https://dignityandpowernow.org/about-us/.

72   Peter Byrne, "SOUL Trainers," *SF Weekly*, October 16, 2002.

73   https://www.schoolofunityandliberation.org/.

74   https://www.schoolofunityandliberation.org/.

75   Darnell Moore and Patrisse Cullors, "5 Ways to Never Forget Ferguson," *The Guardian*, September 4, 2014.

76   Patrisse Cullors, "We Didn't Start a Movement. We Started a Network," Neighborhood Funders Group, February 21, 2016, https://medium.com/@patrissemariecullorsbrignac/we-didn-t-start-a-movement-we-started-a-network-90f9b5717668.

77   Barbara Ransby, *Making All Black Lives Matter* (Oakland: University of California Press, 2018), 21.

78   Christopher Dawson, *The Crisis of Western Education* (New York: Sheed and

Ward, 1961), 3.

79   LeftRoots, "Why LeftRoots?," https://leftroots.net/why-leftroots/.

80   Elyse Lightman Samuels, *From "The Help" to "Roma": How the National Domestic Workers Alliance Is Transforming Narratives in Pop Culture* (New York: Pop Culture Collaborative, 2019), 4, https://www.domesticworkers.org/wp-content/uploads/2021/05/Roma-Case-Study.pdf.

81   Methvin, *Riot Makers*, 187.

82   Dan Neumann, "Black Lives Matter Co-founder: Maine Can Be a Leader in Dismantling White Nationalism," Beacon: A Project of the Maine People's Alliance, June 28, 2019, https://mainebeacon.com/black-lives-matter-co-founder-maine-can-be-a-leader-in-dismantling-white-nationalism/.

83   Selznick, "Organizational Weapons," 97.

84   Selznick, 315.

85   Selznick, 318.

Chapter 7: Sexualizing Children and the Attack on the Family

1   Gergely Szilvay, *A Critique of Gender Theory* (Budapest: Center for Fundamental Rights, 2002), 35.

2   Carl R. Trueman, *The Rise the Triumph of the Modern Self: Cultural Amnesia, Expressive Individualism, and the Road to Sexual Revolution* (Wheaton, IL: Crossway, 2020), 21.

3   Robert Owen, quoted in Holly Jackson, *American Radicals: How Nineteenth-Century Protest Shapes the Nation* (New York: Crown Books, 2019), x.

4   Mike Gonzalez, *BLM: The Making of a New Marxist Revolution* (New York: Encounter Books, 2021), 99.

5   Michael Walsh, *The Devil's Pleasure Palace: The Cult of Critical Theory and the Subversion of the West* (New York: Encounter Books, 2015), 32.

6   Paul Kengor, *The Devil and Karl Marx: Communism's Long March of Death, Deception, and Infiltration* (Gastonia, NC: Tan Books, 2020), 81.

7   Karl Marx and Friedrich Engels, *The Manifesto of the Communist Party* (Peking: Foreign Languages Press, 1975), 56.

8   Marx and Engels, 77.

9   Robert Owen, *Two Discourses on a New System of Society, as Delivered before the US Congress* (Manchester, UK: A. Heywood, [1839]).

10 Victoria C. Woodhull, *The Origins, Tendencies and Principles of Government* (New York: Woodhull, Claflin, 1871).

11 Victoria Woodhull, quoted in Jackson, *American Radicals*, 286.

12 See esp. Sigmund Freud, *Civilization and Its Discontents*, trans. James Strachey, ed. Samuel Moyn (New York: W. W. Norton, 2022).

13 Freud, 20.

14 Freud, 20.

15 Freud, 40.

16 Freud, 43.

17 Freud, 41.

18 Biography of Wilhelm Reich, https://wilhelmreichmuseum.org/about/biography-of-wilhelm-reich/.

19 See, e.g., Myron Sharaf, *Fury on Earth: A Biography of Wilhelm Reich* (Boston: Da Capo Press, 1994).

20 Wilhelm Reich, *The Sexual Revolution*, rev. ed., trans. Theodore Wolf (New York: Farrar, Straus, and Giroux, 1963), x.

21 Reich.

22 Austen Ruse, "Cultural Marxism Is at the Heart of Our Moral Disintegration," *CRISIS Magazine*, 2015.

23 Reich, *Sexual Revolution*, xviii.

24 Reich, xviii.

25 Winston Churchill, *The World Crisis, 1911–1918* (New York: Free Press, 2005), 291.

26 Georg Lukács, preface to *History and Class Consciousness* (London: Merlin Press, 1967).

27 Lukács, quoted by Marxist.org, https://www.marxists.org/archive/lukacs/works/history/lukacs67.htm.

28 Reich, *Sexual Revolution*, xi.

29 Reich, xi.

30 Max Horkheimer and Theodor W. Adorno, *Dialectic of Enlightenment: Philosophical Fragments*, ed. Gunzelin Schmid Noerr, trans. Edmund Jephcott (Stanford, CA: Stanford University Press, 2002), 1.

31 Horkhiemer and Adorno, 1.

32 Theodore Adorno, *Minima Moralia: Reflections from the Damaged Life* (1951), 6, https://www.marxists.org/reference/archive/adorno/1951/mm/ch01.htm.

33 Marcuse, epilogue to *Eros and Civilization*, 241, https://www.marxists.org/reference/archive/marcuse/works/eros-civilisation/epilogue.htm.

34 Marcuse, 241.

35 Marcuse, 242.

36 Marcuse, xv.

37 Richard Kearney and Herbert Marcuse, "Interview with Herbert Marcuse," *Crane Bag* 1, no. 1 (1977): 77, http://www.jstor.org/stable/30060134.

38 Marcuse, *Eros and Civilization*, xv.

39   Marcuse, 201.

40   Jeffrey Escoffier, "The Sexual Revolution, 1960–1980," http://www.glbtqarchive.com/ssh/sexual_revolution_S.pdf.

41   Christopher F. Rufo, "How the Trans Movement Conquered American Life," YouTube video, 0:30, https://www.youtube.com/watch?v=Xwsekb5QReo&t=72s.

42   Rufo.

43   Walsh, *Devil's Pleasure Palace*, 10.

44   Rosa Lee, quoted in Rufo, "How the Trans Movement Conquered American Life."

45   These titles can be found variously in "Dr. Jack Hyles Books Collection," Jack Hyles, Internet Archive, https://archive.org/stream/jackhylesbooks/Grace-and-Truth_djvu.txt, and in Craig Yoe, ed., *The Best of Sexology: Kinky and Kooky Excerpts from America's First Sex Magazine* (Philadelphia: Running Press, 2008).

46   "Isadore Rubin, 58, Wrote Sex Texts," unsigned obituary, *New York Times*, August 3,1970, https://timesmachine.nytimes.com/timesmachine/1970/08/03/78798307.html?pageNumber=31.

47   https://www.govinfo.gov/content/pkg/GPO-CRECB-1969-pt23/pdf/GPO-CRECB-1969-pt23-2-3.pdf.

48   Centers for Disease Control and Prevention, National Prevention Information Network, "Sex Ed State Law and Policy Chart: SIECUS State Profiles: Aug. 2021," https://npin.cdc.gov/publication/sex-ed-state-law-and-policy-chart-siecus-state-profiles-aug-2021.

49   SIECUS, "Our History," https://siecus.org/about-siecus/our-history/.

50   SIECUS, *Sex, Race, and Politics in the US* (Washington, DC: SIECUS, 2022), 5, https://siecus.org/wp-content/uploads/2022/06/2022-Racial-Justice-Resource.pdf.

51   Aleksandr Solzhenitsyn, "The Bluecaps," in *The Gulag Archipelago, 1918–1956: An Experiment in Literary Investigation* (New York: HarperCollins, 2007), 173–74.

Chapter 8: "In the Belly of the Beast"

1   Micha Frazer-Carroll, "What I Learned from Founding Black Lives Matter," *Dazed*, December 19, 2019, https://www.dazeddigital.com/politics/article/47167/1/opal-tometi-what-i-learned-from-founding-black-lives-matter.

2   Travis Campbell, "Black Lives Matter's Effect on Police Lethal Use of Force," May 13, 2021, 23, https://static1.squarespace.com/static/5b7ea2794cde7a79e-7c00582/t/632b227c09baca06926c874b/1663771266815/black+lives+matters-police+lethal.pdf.

3   For a specific look at all these facts, please see Mike Gonzalez, *BLM: The Making of a New Marxist Revolution* (New York: Encounter Books, 2020).

4   Bret Stephens, "I Was Wrong about Trump Voters," *The New York Times*, July 21, 2022.

5   Bernard Cassen, "On the Attack," *New Left Review*, January/February 2003,

https://newleftreview.org/issues/ii19/articles/bernard-cassen-on-the-attack.

6   Ruben Solis Garcia, "History of Social Justice Movements in the US since 1999," in *National Social Movement Agenda*, US Social Forum 2010, Detroit, MI, June 26, 2010, https://www.projectsouth.org/wp-content/uploads/2012/06/ActionPlan-Summary-FINAL.pdf.

7   Marina Karides, Walda Katz-Fishman, Rose M. Brewer, and Jerome Scott, eds., *The United States Social Forum: Perspectives of a Movement* (Chicago: Change-maker, 2010), 339.

8   Karides et al., 256.

9   *National Social Movement Agenda.*

10   Eric Mann, "Pt 1 Transformative Organizing Theory (US Social Forum 2010 Workshop)," YouTube video, 22:53, https://www.youtube.com/watch?v=Abm-34FzgwoE.

11   Alicia Garza, *The Purpose of Power: How We Come Together When We Fall Apart* (New York: OneWorld, 2020), 189.

12   Karides et al., 311.

13   Patrisse Cullors, "Pt 4 Transformative Organizing Theory (USSF 2010 Work-shop)," YouTube video, 17:22, https://www.youtube.com/watch?v=suN8QTM0-jEY&t=2s.

14   Eric Mann, "The Black-Led Defund the Police Movement Wins Great Break-through in Los Angeles: An Organizer's Interpretation," *Portside*, September 5, 2020, https://portside.org/2020-09-05/black-led-defund-police-movement-wins-great-breakthrough-los-angeles-organizers.

15   *Compañeros* is the word used by Cuban communists for the Soviet comrade, and it is how one addresses others in Cuba since the revolution.

16   Alicia Garza, "USSF Global Meeting, April 13, 2010," YouTube video, 10:03, https://www.youtube.com/watch?v=CAUlaQm4sDA.

17   Venezuela Analysis, "President Chavez's Speech to the 6th World Social Forum—Americas," March 6, 2006, https://venezuelanalysis.com/analysis/1728. Also partly transcribed by the authors from Chávez's speech in Spanish, which can be found here: https://www.arcoiris.tv/scheda/es/501/.

18   Mike Gonzalez, "Nicolás the Woke," *Daily Signal*, June 21, 2022, https://www.heritage.org/americas/commentary/nicolas-the-woke.

19   Bill Ayers, "World Education Forum," November 7, 2006, https://billayers.org/2006/11/.

20   Ai-Jen Poo, Andrea Cristina Mercado, Jill Shenker, Xiomara E. Corpeno, and Allison Julien, "National Domestic Workers Alliance," in Karides et al., *United States Social Forum*, 158.

21   Poo et al., 165.

22   Julia Wong, "As Ferguson 'Weekend of Resistance' Begins, Organizers Weigh How to Turn a Moment into a Movement," *In These Times*, October 10, 2014, https://inthesetimes.com/article/from-a-moment-to-a-movement.

23 LeftRoots was one of many groups or networks that took part both in the USSF process between 2007 and 2013 and in organizing the movement in Ferguson in 2014.

24 "Popular Front for the Liberation of Palestine–General Command (Pflp-Gc)," https://www.dni.gov/nctc/ftos/pflp_gc_fto.html.

25 Mike Gonzalez, "Soros-Backed Media Consortium Is Buying, to Censor, Conservative Radio Stations," *Daily Signal*, June 9, 2022, https://www.dailysignal.com/2022/06/09/soros-backed-media-consortium-is-buying-to-censor-conservative-radio-stations/.

26 Garza, "USSF Global Meeting, April 13, 2010."

27 For the attendance at the Left Forums, we have relied mostly on the good work of Trevor Loudon, who curates these meetings at the site called KeyWiki. For 2005, the list of attendees can be found at http://keywiki.org/Left_Forum_2005.

28 Left Forum 2006, Columbia University, http://www.columbia.edu/~lnp3/mydocs/american_left/leftforum2006.htm.

29 *Rethinking Marxism*, http://rethinkingmarxism.org/audio/index.html.

30 Left Forum 2008, https://www.keywiki.org/Left_Forum_2008.

31 Left Forum 2009, https://www.keywiki.org/Left_Forum_2009.

32 Steve Williams, "Organizing Transformation," *Rosa Luxemburg Stiftung*, June 2015, https://www.rosalux.de/publikation/id/1116/organizing-transformation.

33 Left Forum 2013, program guide, https://www.yumpu.com/en/document/read/15573023/left-forum-2013-program-guide.

34 "Left Forum 2015—Saturday Evening Event," *Other Voices, Other Choices* (blog), May 30, 2015, http://othervoicesotherchoices.blogspot.com/search/label/Alicia%20Garza.

35 "Left Forum 2015."

36 "Left Forum 2015."

37 Marcelo Musto, "Bolivian Vice President Alvaro Garcia Linera on Marx and Indigenous Politics," *Truthout*, November 9, 2019, https://truthout.org/articles/bolivian-vice-president-alvaro-garcia-linera-on-marx-and-indigenous-politics/.

38 Agence France-Presse, "Foro de São Paulo ajudou a democratizar esquerda latino-americana, diz Lula," May 17, 2008, https://g1.globo.com/Noticias/Mundo/0,,MUL473012-5602,00-FORO+DE+SAO+PAULO+AJUDOU+A+-DEMOCRATIZAR+ESQUERDA+LATINOAMERICANA+DIZ+LULA.html.

39 "Memoria del Segundo Encuentro Anual del Foro de São Paulo del Area de Washington DC, Maryland y Virginia," July 11, 2017, https://forodesaopaulo.org/memoria-del-2do-encuentro-anual-del-foro-de-sao-paulo-del-area-de-washington-dc-maryland-y-virginia/.

40 *DECLARAÇÃO FINAL dos Encontros do Foro de São Paulo (1990–2012)*, translated from the Portuguese by the authors, published by the PT's International Relations Secretariat, June, 2013, 11–15, http://5c912a4babb9d-3d7cce1-6e2107136992060ccfd52e87c213fd32.r10.cf5.rackcdn.com/wp-content/files/Foro-Maio2013.pdf.

41 Douglas Farah and Caitlyn Yates, *Turmoil in the Western Hemisphere: The Role of the Bolivarian Joint Criminal Enterprise in Latin America's Unrest*, Parry Center Occasional Paper (Washington, DC: William Perry Center for Hemispheric Defense Studies, National Defense University, 2020), 9, https://www.ibiconsultants. net/_upload/mediaandpublications/document/turmoil-in-the-western-hemisphere-published.pdf.

42 For an example of this, see David A. Ditch, Mike Gonzalez, Hans A. von Spakovsky, and Erin Dwinell, "President Biden's 'Equity Action Plans' Reveal Radical, Divisive Agenda," *Heritage Foundation Backgrounder*, no. 3710 (May 25, 2022), https://www.heritage.org/sites/default/files/2022-05/BG3710.pdf.

43 Andrew Edgecliffe-Johnson, "Company Chiefs Join Outrage at Police Killings of African-Americans," *Financial Times*, June 1, 2020, https://www.ft.com/content/2e26831f-af45-43b2-856f-9db698845b27.

44 Larry Fink's 2021 letter to CEOs, https://www.blackrock.com/us/individual/2021-larry-fink-ceo-letter.

45 Eduardo Corrochio, "BlackRock CEO Larry Fink: 'Markets Like Totalitarian Governments' (2011)," YouTube video, 0:22, https://www.youtube.com/watch?v=RmY4AvoPIoA.

46 Mike Gonzalez, "What Happens in the Andes Does Not Stay in the Andes," *Daily Signal*, December 19, 2022, https://www.heritage.org/progressivism/commentary/what-happens-the-andes-does-not-stay-the-andes.

47 Farah and Yates, *Turmoil in the Western Hemisphere*, 14.

48 Farah and Yates. The two writers cite "Análisis Twitter Protestas en Chile," ConnectalLabs, November 26, 2019, https://github.com/connectalabs/riots_chile_analisis/blob/master/analisis_tweets_sobre_levantamiento_social.md.

49 Lagos Neumann can be seen saying that here: https://www.youtube.com/watch?v=z0657Nc7_pw.

50 Black Lives Matter, *Black Lives Matter 2020 Impact Report* (Los Angeles, CA: BLM, 2020), https://blacklivesmatter.com/wp-content/uploads/2021/02/blm-2020-impact-report.pdf.

51 Gonzalez, "What Happens in the Andes."

52 Jan Martinez Ahrens and Inez Santaeulalia, "Gustavo Petro: 'Colombia no necesita socialismo, necesita democracia y paz,'" *El Pais*, September 18, 2021, https://elpais.com/internacional/2021-09-19/gustavo-petro-colombia-no-necesita-socialismo-necesita-democracia-y-paz.html.

53 Clifton Parker, "Colombian President Gustavo Petro Urges Transition to Green Energy," Stanford University, April 20, 2023, https://fsi.stanford.edu/news/colombian-president-gustavo-petro-urges-transition-green-energy.

54 Stéphane Hessel, *Time for Outrage*, trans. Marion Duvert (New York: Twelve, Hatchett, 2011).

55 "Podemos vuelve a sus origene y confiara a la Fundacion CEPS su estructura valenciana," *ValenciaPlaza*, January 3, 2014, http://epoca1.valenciaplaza. com/ver/144704/podemos-vuelve-a-sus-origenes-y-confiara-a-la-fundacion-ceps-su-estructura-valenciana.html.

56   One of the authors was at the meeting and has the PowerPoint presentation.

57   Francisco Mercado, "Foundation Linked to New Party Podemos Received E3.7m from Hugo Chavez," *El Pais*, June 18, 2014, https://english.elpais.com/elpais/2014/06/18/inenglish/1403082454_361529.html.

58   M. A. Ruiz Coll, "Las pruebas de que los lideres de Podemos han cobrado 7,7 millones del Gobierno de Venezuela," *OK Diario*, July 23, 2017, https://okdiario.com/investigacion/pruebas-que-lideres-podemos-han-cobrado-77-millones-del-gobierno-venezuela-1183326.

59   Carlos Cuesta, "Iglesias y su equipo de la fundación CEPS también recibieron 369.019 E a titulo personal de Ecuador," *OK Diario*, September 11, 2020, https://okdiario.com/espana/pablo-iglesias-equipo-fundacion-ceps-tambien-recibieron-369–019-euros-titulo-personal-ecuador-6125834.

60   Alejandro Entrambasaguas, "El colonel boliviano que denuncio a Iglesias," *OK Diario*, October 4, 2012, https://okdiario.com/investigacion/coronel-boliviano-que-denuncio-iglesias-evo-pago-podemos-mediante-ceps-que-no-quedara-rastro-6217330.

61   Luis Costantini, "Podemos involucro a IU en la firma de contratos polémicos Neurona," *Voz Populi*, January 24, 2020, https://www.vozpopuli.com/espana/politica/podemos-involucro-iu-contratos-nuerona_0_1321369297.html.

62   See, e.g., the questionnaire that Spain's Equality Ministry, headed by Podemos's Irene Montero (Iglesias's common-law wife), released in 2021 for Spain's Afro-descendants: "Aproximacion a la poblacion Africana y Afrodescendiente en Espana," https://www.igualdad.gob.es/wp-content/uploads/Aproximacion-a-la-poblacion-africana-y-afrodescendiente-en-Espana.pdf.

63   "Podemos—Translated Manifesto," January 20, 2014, https://hiredknaves.wordpress.com/2014/01/20/podemos-translated-manifesto/.

64   Opal Tometi, "Black Lives Matter Network Denounces US 'Continuing Intervention in Venezuela,'" *Venezuela Analysis*, December 26, 2015, https://venezuelanalysis.com/analysis/11789.

65   "Evo Morales recibe a representante de Alianza Negra de EEUU," https://www.telesurtv.net/news/Evo-Morales-recibe-a-representante-de-Alianza-Negra-de-EE.UU.--20170621-0007.html.

66   Ricardo Gomez, "Conferencia para un mundo sin muros," *Comunicacion para la Integración*, June 21, 2017, https://www.integracion-lac.info/es/node/39189.

67   Violeta Tamayo, "The MAS Victory, the Coup, and the Fight for Socialism," *LeftVoice*, October 28, 2020, https://www.leftvoice.org/the-mas-victory-the-coup-and-the-fight-for-socialism-interview-with-a-bolivian-revolutionary/.

68   Farah and Yates, *Turmoil in the Western Hemisphere*, 10.

69   "We Choose Resistance: Listen to the Call on Black and Asian Solidarity," Seeding Change, December 18, 2014, https://www.seeding-change.org/wechooseresistance-listen/.

70   Support Black Futures Lab, https://cpasf.ourpowerbase.net/civicrm/contribute/transact?reset=1&id=45.

71   See, e.g., Seeding Change, "Meet Our 2023 Host Sites," https://www.seed-ing-change.org/meet-our-2023-potential-host-sites/.

72   Cited by Mark Judge, "How Riot Ideology Destroyed American Cities," *Washington Standard*, June 6, 2023, https://www.washingtonexaminer.com/restor-ing-america/patriotism-unity/how-riot-ideology-destroyed-americas-cities.

73   Ariel Sheen, "American CastroChavismo: Why Venezuela Matters," *Ariel Sheen* (blog), November 12, 2020, https://arielsheen.com/index.php/2020/11/12/ameri-can-castrochavismo-why-venezuela-matters/.

Chapter 9: What to Do

1   Max Eden, "What Happened in Loudoun Schools," *RealClearEducation*, Decem-ber 1, 2022, https://www.realcleareducation.com/articles/2022/12/13/what_hap-pened_in_loudoun_schools_110798.html.

2   The document was originally classified top secret, then declassified in 1975 by then secretary of state Henry Kissinger.

3   NSC 68, 5.

4   Alexander Hamilton, *Federalist* no. 1, https://avalon.law.yale.edu/18th_century/fed01.asp.

5   Martin Luther King Jr., "I Have a Dream" (speech, Washington, DC, August 28, 1963), available from American Rhetoric, http://www.americanrhetoric.com/speeches/mlkihaveadream.htm.

6   Kerry J. Byrne, "White House Flew Controversial New Transgender Flag That Troubles Some Critics in the Gay Community," *Fox News*, June 14, 2023, https://www.foxnews.com/lifestyle/white-house-flew-controversial-transgen-der-flag-troubles-some-critics-gay-community.

7   The material from this description is largely taken from Fletcher Schoen and Christopher J. Lamb, *Deception, Disinformation, and Strategic Communications: How One Interagency Group Made a Major Difference* (Washington, DC: Center for Strategic Research, Institute for National Strategic Studies, National Defense University, 2012), http://www.ndu.edu/inss/docuploaded/Strategic%20Perspec-tives%2011_Lamb-Schoen.pdf. Some of this content was previously published in Katharine C. Gorka, "Lessons Re-engaging in the War of Ideas: Lessons from the Active Measures Working Group," Westminster Institute, February 1, 2013, https://westminster-institute.org/articles/re-engaging-in-the-war-of-ideas-lessons-from-the-active-measures-working-group/. For more on Western efforts to counter Soviet active measures, see also Nicholas J. Cull, Vasily Gatov, Peter Pomerantsev, Anne Applebaum, and Alistair Shawcross, *Soviet Subversion, Disinformation and Propaganda: How the West Fought against it—an Analytic History, with Lessons for the Present* (London: LSE Consulting, 2017), https://www.lse.ac.uk/iga/assets/documents/arena/2018/Jigsaw-Soviet-Subversion-Disinformation-and-Propa-ganda-Final-Report.pdf.

8   Schoen and Lamb, *Deception, Disinformation, and Strategic Communications*, 19.

9   Schoen and Lamb, 52–53.

10   Mike Gonzalez, "Marxism Underpins Black Lives Matter Agenda," September 8, 2021, https://www.heritage.org/progressivism/commentary/marxism-underpins-black-lives-matter-agenda.

11   Anthony Leonardi, "Black Lives Matter 'What We Believe' Page That Includes Disrupting 'Nuclear Family Structure' Removed from Website," *Washington Examiner*, September 21, 2020, https://www.washingtonexaminer.com/news/black-lives-matter-what-we-believe-page-that-includes-disrupting-nuclear-family-structure-removed-from-website.

12   Interview with the author.

13   See, e.g., the importance of networking to the left-wing effort to control the 2019 election in Molly Ball, "The Secret History of the Shadow Campaign That Saved the 2020 Election," *Time*, February 4, 2021, https://time.com/5936036/secret-2020-election-campaign/.

14   Vaclav Havel, "The Power of the Powerless," in *Without Force or Lies: Voices from the Revolution of Central Europe 1989–90*, ed. William M. Brinton and Alan Rinzler (San Francisco: Mercury House, 1990), 53.

15   Havel, 49.

16   Ari Blaff, "Anheuser Busch Lays Off Nearly 400 Corporate Workers as Bud Light Backlash Continues," *National Review*, July 27, 2023, https://www.nationalreview.com/news/anheuser-busch-lays-off-nearly-400-corporate-workers-as-bud-light-backlash-continues/.

17   NSC-68, 23.

18   Heather Zwicker, "Drag Queen Storybook Hour Gets Mixed Review," *Fairfax County Times*, July 16, 2021, https://www.fairfaxtimes.com/articles/drag-storybook-hour-gets-mixed-reviews/article_70635b4c-e575-11eb-9bd1-076bb587b678.html.

19   Note, e.g., George Soros's efforts to elect radical prosecutors. See, e.g., Charles D. Stimson and Zack Smith, " 'Progressive' Prosecutors Sabotage the Rule of Law, Raise Crime Rates, and Ignore Victims," Heritage Foundation Legal Memorandum 275, October 29, 2020, https://www.heritage.org/crime-and-justice/report/progressive-prosecutors-sabotage-the-rule-law-raise-crime-rates-and-ignore.

20   Christian Toto, "Can Woke Hollywood Survive Biden's Recession?," *Hollywood in Toto*, August 6, 2022, https://www.hollywoodintoto.com/woke-hollywood-biden-recession/.

21   Charles Gasparino, "Thumbs Down on 'Woke': 'Disney Debacle' Lesson for CEOs," *New York Post*, May 7, 2022, https://nypost.com/2022/05/07/thumbs-down-on-woke-disney-debacle-lesson-for-ceos/.

22   See also Andrew Klavan, *The Crisis in the Arts: Why the Left Owns the Culture and How Conservatives Can Begin to Take It Back* (Sherman Oaks, CA: David Horowitz Freedom Center, 2014).

23   Phillip Selznick, *The Organizational Weapon: A Study of Bolshevik Strategy and Tactics* (New York: McGraw-Hill, 1952), 315.

24   NSC-68, 11.

25   Saul D. Alinsky, *Rules for Radicals: A Practical Primer for Realistic Radicals* (New York: Vintage Books, 1989), 53, 10.

26   Dan Neumann, "Black Lives Matter Co-Founder: Maine Can Be a Leader in Dismantling White Nationalism," *Beacon*, June 28, 2019.

27   Aleksandr I. Solzhenitsyn, *The Gulag Archipelago, 1918–1956: An Experiment in Literary Investigation* (New York: HarperCollins, 2007), 178.

28   C. Vann Woodward, *The Strange Career of Jim Crow* (New York: Oxford University Press, 1955), 198, 199, 200.

29   Lindsey Burke and Mike Gonzalez, "DeSantis Exposes Marxist Slant of African American History Course, Demands Rewrite," *Daily Signal*, January 23, 2023, https://www.dailysignal.com/2023/01/23/desantis-exposes-marxist-slant-of-african-american-history-course-demands-rewrite/.

30   "Governor Ron DeSantis Signs Legislation to Strengthen Florida's Position as National Leader in Higher Education," May 15, 2023, https://www.flgov.com/2023/05/15/governor-ron-desantis-signs-legislation-to-strengthen-floridas-position-as-national-leader-in-higher-education/.

31   Benjamin Wallace-Wells, "How a Conservative Activist Invented the Conflict over Critical Race Theory," *The New Yorker*, June 18, 2021, https://www.newyorker.com/news/annals-of-inquiry/how-a-conservative-activist-invented-the-conflict-over-critical-race-theory.

32   Christopher F. Rufo, " 'White Fragility' Comes to Washington," *City Journal*, July 18, 2020, https://www.city-journal.org/white-fragility-comes-to-washington; Rufo, "The Truth about Critical Race Theory," *Wall Street Journal*, October 4, 2020, https://www.wsj.com/articles/the-truth-about-critical-race-theory-11601841968; Rufo, "Department of Homeland Security Training on 'Microinequities,' " August 3, 2020,   https://christopherrufo.com/p/the-smallest-injustice.

33   Chris Rufo (@realchrisrufo), "We have successfully frozen their brand—'critical race theory'—into the public conversation and are steadily driving up negative perceptions," Twitter, March 15, 2021, 3:14 PM, https://twitter.com/realchrisrufo/status/1371540368714428416.

34   Chris Rufo (@realchrisrufo), "The goal is to have the public read something crazy in the newspaper and immediately think 'critical race theory,' " Twitter, March 15, 2021, 3:17 PM, https://twitter.com/realchrisrufo/status/1371541044592996352.

35   Chris Rufo (@realchrisrufo), "We are no longer going to let the Left set the terms of debate," Twitter, June 18, 2022, 2:50 PM, https://twitter.com/realchrisrufo/status/1538232677459009537.

36 Sarah Polus, "Oklahoma Governor Signs Bill That Prevents Schools from Teaching Critical Race Theory," *The Hill*, May 7, 2021, https://thehill.com/homenews/state-watch/552451-oklahoma-governor-signs-bill-that-prevents-schools-from-teaching.

37 Emily McCain, "Governor Signs 'Stop Woke Act,' Special District Bill into Law," *ABC Action News*, April 22, 2022, https://www.abcactionnews.com/news/state/governor-desantis-signs-so-called-stop-woke-act-into-law.

38 https://www.xicanxinstitute.org/.

39 Christopher Tremoglie, "Parents Join Anti–Critical Race Theory Group and Win Lawsuit against Radical School Curriculum in California," *Washington Examiner*, January 17, 2022, https://www.washingtonexaminer.com/restoring-america/community-family/parents-join-anti-critical-race-theory-group-and-win-lawsuit-against-radical-school-curriculum-in-california.

40 "Dear Concerned Parents, Grandparents and Community Members," https://docs.google.com/document/u/0/d/1eTNNnLUriptjbkad4otJPKOXHbz0GL2im-wKLF2loMOI/mobilebasic.

41 Parents Defending Education, "Boston Public Schools' Ethnic Studies Curriculum Focuses on Oppression and 'Pillars of White Supremacy,'" https://defendinged.org/incidents/boston-public-schools-ethnic-studies-curriculum-focuses-on-oppression-and-pillars-of-white-supremacy/.

42 Parents Defending Education, "Indoctrination Map," https://defendinged.org/map/.

43 Margaret Harper McCarthy, "The Equality Act Is at War with Reality," *The Wall Street Journal*, March 30, 2021, https://www.wsj.com/articles/the-equality-act-is-at-war-with-reality-11617143549.

44 Nuno Ornelas Martins, "The Nature of the Cambridge Heterodoxy," *Revue de philosophie économique* 14 (2013): 49–71.

45 Jay Richards, "What Is Gender Ideology?," *The Daily Signal*, July 7, 2023, https://www.heritage.org/gender/commentary/what-gender-ideology.

46 Mike Gonzalez, "Riley Gaines and Judge Duncan: Americans against Trans Totalitarianism," *The Daily Signal*, April 19, 2023, https://www.heritage.org/gender/commentary/riley-gaines-and-judge-duncan-americans-against-trans-totalitarianism.

47 Charles Haubner, "California Bill Would Include Child's Gender in Custody Cases," *CBS News*, June 13, 2023, https://www.cbsnews.com/sacramento/news/california-gender-affirming-bill-controversy-capitol/.

48 Giulia Carbonaro, "Michigan's Pronouns Law 'Probably Is Unconstitutional,'" *Newsweek*, July 6, 2023, https://www.newsweek.com/michigan-pronoun-bill-probably-unconstitutional-first-amendment-1811232.

49 Alex Nguyen and William Melhado, "Gov. Gregg Abbott Signs Legislation Barring Trans Youth from Accessing Transition-Related Care," *The Texas Tribune*, June 2, 2023, https://www.texastribune.org/2023/06/02/texas-gender-affirming-care-ban/.

50   Lynn Hatter, "Florida's Education Board Issues Near-Ban on Gender Identity
     and Sexual Orientation Instruction in Public Schools," WFSU, April 19, 2023,
     https://news.wfsu.org/state-news/2023-04-19/floridas-education-board-is-
     sues-near-ban-on-gender-identity-and-sexual-orientation-instruction-in-pub-
     lic-schools.

51   Interview with the author, November 23, 2023.

52   Jay Greene and Robert Pondiscio, "Who Decides What Children Read? Au-
     thoritarians Slander Parent Groups as 'Book Banners,'" *The Daily Signal*,
     September 29, 2023, https://www.heritage.org/education/commentary/who-de-
     cides-what-children-read-authoritarians-slander-parent-groups-book.

53   Arielle Del Turco and Chris Gacek, "Exporting LGBT Ideology," Family Research
     Council, June 2023, https://downloads.frc.org/EF/EF23F21.pdf.

54   Brent Sadler, "Navy 'Eases the Rudder' with Its Recommended Readings," *The
     Daily Signal*, May 16, 2022, https://www.heritage.org/defense/commentary/na-
     vy-eases-the-rudder-its-recommended-readings.

55   Stephanie Weaver, "Gen. Mark Milley: 'I Want to Understand White Rage,'" *Fox
     News*, June 24, 2021, https://www.fox10phoenix.com/news/gen-mark-milley-i-
     want-to-understand-white-rage.

56   "Conservatives Oppose Confirmation of General Charles Q. Brown," Conserva-
     tive Action Project, July 12, 2023, https://conservativeactionproject.com/conser-
     vatives-oppose-confirmation-of-general-charles-q-brown/.

57   This information comes from the Armed Conflict Location and Event Data Proj-
     ect, which coded more than 660 events as riots in September 2020. The Microsoft
     Excel sheet containing the information has been removed from the website, but
     the authors have a record of it.

58   Jennifer Kingston, "Exclusive: $1 billion-plus riot damage is most expensive in
     insurance history." Axios, Sept. 16, 2020, https://www.axios.com/2020/09/16/ri-
     ots-cost-property-damage.

59   Lois Beckett, "At Least 25 Americans Were Killed during Protests and Political
     Unrest in 2020," *The Guardian*, October 31, 2020, https://www.theguardian.com/
     world/2020/oct/31/americans-killed-protests-political-unrest-acled.

60   Paul Cassell, "Explaining the Recent Homicide Spikes in US Cities," Utah Law
     Faculty Scholarship, September 2020, https://dc.law.utah.edu/cgi/viewcontent.
     cgi?article=1216&context=scholarship.

61   Dae-Young Kim, "Did De-Policing Contribute to the 2020 Homicide Spikes?,"
     Police Practice and Research, advance online publication, https://doi.org/10.1080/1
     5614263.2023.2235056.

62   Travis Campbell, "Black Lives Matter's Effect on Police Lethal Use of Force," Uni-
     versity of Massachusetts Amherst, July 2, 2023, https://www.umass.edu/econom-
     ics/news/black-lives-matters-effect-police-lethal-use-force-travis-campbell.

63   Patrisse Cullors and Darnell Moore, "Ferguson Protests to #FergusonNext: 5
     Paths to Progress after Non-Indictment," *The Guardian*, November 24, 2014,
     https://www.theguardian.com/commentisfree/2014/nov/24/ferguson-pro-
     tests-progress-non-indictment-grand-jury.

64 Dan Neumann, "Black Lives Matter Co-Founder: Maine Can Be a Leader in Dismantling White Nationalism," *Maine Beacon*, June 28, 2019, https://mainebeacon.com/black-lives-matter-co-founder-maine-can-be-a-leader-in-dismantling-white-nationalism/.

65 Anthony Leonardi, "Black Lives Matter 'What We Believe' Page That Includes 'Disrupting Family Structure' Removed from Website," *New York Post*, September 21, 2020, https://www.washingtonexaminer.com/news/black-lives-matter-what-we-believe-page-that-includes-disrupting-nuclear-family-structure-removed-from-website.

66 LeftRoots, "We Need a Radical and Grounded Left," https://leftroots.net/why-leftroots/.

67 Nick Kangadis, "Flashback, BLM Co-Founder in 2015, 'It's Not Possible' for Black Lives to Matter Unless We Abolish Capitalism," MRC TV, https://www.mrctv.org/blog/flashback-blm-co-founder-2015-its-not-possible-black-lives-matter-until-capitalism-abolished.

68 "Black Lives Matter Network Denounces US 'Continuing Intervention in Venezuela,'" https://venezuelanalysis.com/analysis/11789.

69 "Evo Morales recibe a representante de Alianza Negra de EEUU," https://www.telesurtv.net/news/Evo-Morales-recibe-a-representante-de-Alianza-Negra-de-EE.UU.--20170621-0007.html.

70 "Black Lives Matter Co-Founder Patrisse Cullors on Abolition and Imagining a Society Based on Care," Democracy Now!, January 31, 2020, https://www.democracynow.org/2022/1/31/patrisse_cullors_an_abolitionists_handbook.

71 Judicial restraint is a type of legal interpretation in which judges do not inject their own opinions into precedence, can remand cases to lower courts, or do not rule on a case due to it being more legislative than judicial in nature.

72 Mia Gradick, "The Championing of Freedom of Assembly from the Civil Rights Movement to Black Lives Matter," unpublished manuscript, 3.

73 Poder360, "Lula discursa no Foro de São Paulo," YouTube video, 29:08, https://youtu.be/rJPL1Rz4l4I.

74 "Olavo de Carvalho Explains Lula and the São Paulo Forum," interview with Alek Boyd, October 22, 2009, https://olavodecarvalho.org/olavo-de-carvalho-explains-lula-and-the-sao-paulo-forum/.

75 Moore reprinted his essay on his blog, *Dr. Patrick Moore: The Sensible Environmentalist*, http://ecosense.me/2012/12/30/key-environmental-issues-4/.

76 Rick Cohen, "Former Greenpeace Founder Supports Nuclear Power," *Nonprofit Quarterly*, March 24, 2011, https://nonprofitquarterly.org/former-greenpeace-founder-supports-nuclear-power/.

77 Eliza Strickland, "The New Face of Environmentalism," *East Bay Express*, November 2, 2005, https://eastbayexpress.com/the-new-face-of-environmentalism-1/.

78 Nicholas Harris, "Greta Thunberg Throws in Her Lot with the Anti-Capitalist Left," *Unherd*, October 31, 2022, https://unherd.com/thepost/greta-thunberg-throws-her-lot-in-with-the-anti-capitalist-left/.

79   Justin Worland, "Ron DeSantis Is at the Forefront of New Republican Climate Politics," *Time*, October 4, 2022, https://time.com/6219326/ron-desantis-climate-florida/.

80   Treasury of the State of West Virginia, "Restricted Financial Institution List," https://wvtreasury.com/portals/wvtreasury/content/legal/memorandum/Restricted-Financial-Institutions-List.pdf.

81   Thomas Catenacci, "Republican States Are Planning an All-Out Assault on Banks: 'We Won't Do Business with You,'" *FoxBusiness*, August 4, 2022, https://www.foxbusiness.com/politics/republican-states-planning-assault-woke-banks-wont-do-business.

82   Thomas Catenacci, "Republican States Are Planning an All-Out Assault on Woke Banks," *FoxBusiness*, August 3, 2022, https://www.foxbusiness.com/politics/republican-states-planning-assault-woke-banks-wont-do-business.

83   Ron DeSantis, "Governor Ron DeSantis Eliminates ESG Considerations from State Pension Investments," news release, August 23, 2022, https://www.flgov.com/2022/08/23/governor-ron-desantis-eliminates-esg-considerations-from-state-pension-investments/.

84   "Employer Database," Florida Insight, https://floridajobs.org/wser-home/employer-database.

85   Florida Senate, HB 1557, https://www.flsenate.gov/Session/Bill/2022/1557.

86   D'Angelo Gore, "DeSantis vs. Disney Q&A," Annenberg Public Policy Center, May 5, 2022, https://www.factcheck.org/2022/05/desantis-vs-disney-qa/.

87   Walt Disney Company (@WaltDisneyCo), "Statement from The Walt Disney Company on signing of Florida legislation," Twitter, March 28, 2022, 1:22 PM, https://twitter.com/WaltDisneyCo/status/1508494672817123330.

88   The Hill (@thehill), "@GovRonDeSantis: 'Disney says we are going to work to repeal parents' rights in Florida and I'm just thinking to myself you're a corporation based in Burbank, California and you're going to marshal your economic might to attack the parents of my state?,'" Twitter, April 23, 2022, 8:16 PM, https://twitter.com/thehill/status/1518020897923387392.

89   David Ditch, "Defunding the Left, Reducing Handouts to States, Eliminating Waste: Priority Appropriations Savings for Congress," Heritage Foundation, May 18, 2023, 2, https://www.heritage.org/budget-and-spending/report/defunding-the-left-reducing-handouts-states-eliminating-waste-priority.

90   Ditch, citing Max Primorac and James M. Roberts, "Congress Must Stop Biden's Misuse of US Foreign Aid to Impose His Radical Social Agenda on the World," *Heritage Foundation Backgrounder*, no. 3706 (May 10, 2022), https://www.heritage.org/sites/default/files/2022-05/BG3706.pdf.

91   Mark Levin, *American Marxism* (New York: Threshold, 2021), 1.

INDEX

Abbott, Greg, 259

Abdullah, Melina, 146, 163, 265

ACLU Women's Rights Project, 150

Active Measures Working Group (AMWG), 240–48

Adams, John, 30–31

Adorno, Theodor, 87, 99, 154, 198

Africana Studies Faculty Learning Community, 147

Afro American Student Union, 144

Ahmen, Hassan Jeru, 178

Alinksy, Saul, 175, 247; Alinsky method, 165–66; stealth socialism and, 180–81; translating Marxist-Leninist organizational strategy, 171–74

Alinsky, Saul, 152, 165

Allen, James, 48

Alpert, Jane, 123–23

Althusser, Louis, 70

American Civil Liberties Union, 151

American Civil War, 40

American Revolution, 29–31

American War of Independence, 40

Annenberg Foundation, 133

Annenberg, Walter, 135

Armed Conflict Location and Event Data Project, 264–65

Artelt, Karl, 71

Artinian, Arto, 167

Asian American Political Alliance, 144

Assembly Bill 665, 258

Assembly Bill 957, 258

Association for the Taxation of Financial Transactions and for Citizens Action (ATTAC), 208–9

Austin, Lloyd, 262

Austro-Hungarian Empire, 194–95

Avanti!, 58

Ayers, Thomas, 113

Ayers, William, 95, 106, 138–39, 239; background of, 113–17; becoming Long Marcher, 127–135; Days of Rage and, 116–17; and death of Weathermen, 124–27; Manson murders and, 117–20; New Red Army and, 120–24; relationship with Obama, 135–37

Bachert, Katherina, 77

Back of the Yards Neighborhood Council, 167

Bacon, Francis, 28

Bakunin, Mikhail, 36, 44

Barringer, Felicity, 11–13, 131, 141; "Education; the Mainstreaming of Marxism in US Colleges," 10–11; and failure of class consciousness, 14–17

Bassler, Gerhard, 71

Batista, Fulgencio, 92

Bator, Paul M., 157

Bell, Derrick, 11, 69, 158, 160–61, 249

Benjamin, Walter, 103, 104

Berman, Paul, 128

Biden, Joe, 235, 251–53, 262–63, 267

Biennio Rosso, 54–58

Billington, James, 27

Black Americans, 143, 158,160, 212

Black Liberation Army, 126

Black Lives Matter (BLM), 7–8, 11, 16–17; Left Forum and, 219–21; network building and, 231–34; peaceable protests an, 264–65; sowing seeds of revolution, 183–87

Black Lives Matter Global Network Foundation (BLMGNF), 219, 225

Black Panthers, 95, 108, 117, 144, 211, 250

Black Revolutionary Communist League, 182

Black Student Caucus, 146

Black Student Union, 144

Blackstone, William, 154

Blanco, Carlos, 146

Bolshevik Revolution, 26–27, 41–43, 64; bringing to United States, 46–50; international aspirations of, 43–46; ten months before, 168

Bolsonaro, Jair, 267

Bond, Julian, 215

book banning, 260–61

Bookchin, Murray, 72–73

Booth, Heather, 181

Boston Review, 12

Boudin, Cathy, 214

Boudin, Chesa, 131, 239

Boudin, Kathy, 121, 126

bourgeois democracy. *See* representative democracy

Boyte, Harry, 181

Brecht, Bertolt, 80

Breines, Paul, 79

Brezhnev, Leonid, 95

Brown, Charles Q., 263

Buck, Marilyn, 126

Bukharin, Nikolai, 57, 168

Bundy, McGeorge, 92

Burrough, Brian, 107, 121

Burton, Bill, 138

Bus Riders Union (BRU), 182–83

bus riders, sowing seeds of revolution among, 181–83

Buttigieg, Joseph A., 217

California Foundation for Equal Rights (CFER), 254–55

Calmore, John O., 160

Calvert, Gregory, 177

Carlson, Tucker, 251

Carmichael, Stokely, 145, 177, 249

Carr, E. H., 41

Carrington, Paul D., 157

Carvalho, Olavo de, 9, 267–68

Cassen, Bernard, 208

Castro, Fidel, 92, 107, 118, 222

Center for Political Social Studies (CEPS), 228–29

Centers for Disease Control (CDC), 10

Chace, Michelle, 97

Chapek, Bob, 272

Chavez, Cesar, 165

Chávez, Hugo, 113, 135, 213–14, 224

Chesimard, Joanne, 126

Chicago Citizen of the Year Award, 132

Chicago Reader, 114, 115, 132

children, sexualization of, 203–4; "trinity of the most monstrous evils," 192–97; gender theory, 189–91; twentieth-century crises as influence, 197–203

Chile, 62, 207, 224–27

China, 26, 42–43, 50, 109, 115, 125, 145, 182, 192, 217–18, 222, 227, 232, 239–40

Chinese Communist Party (CCP), 218

Chinese Progressive Association of Boston (CPA), 232–33

Chinese Progressive Association of San Francisco, 145

Chomsky, Noam, 215

Churchill, Winston, 197

Cicero, Marcus, 32

Civil Rights Act, 256

Civil Rights Movement, 107

civil society, community organization, 169–71

Clark, Judy, 126

Clemente, Rosa, 217

climate change, 268–70

Climate Justice: The US Left and the Problem of the State (film), 15

Clinton, Hillary Rodham, 137, 171

Closing of the American Mind, The (Ayers), 138–39

College Board, 249–50

College Factual, 146

Collier, Peter, 119, 126

Collins, William, 179

Colombia, 62, 224–26

common good, 31–33

Communist International (Comintern), 43, 47–48, 59–62, 82–83, 104, 138

Communist Manifesto, The (Marx), 9, 37–39, 43, 193, 200, 245

Communist organizational mode, community organization, 169–71

Communist Party USA (CPUSA), 9, 136

community organization, 187–88; Alinsky borrowing from Lenin, 165–67; Black Lives Matter (BLM), 183–87; bus riders, 181–83; civil society and, 169–71; ghettoes and, 175–79; socialism coming to United States, 168–69; stealth socialism, 180–81; translating Marxist-Leninist organizational strategy, 171–74

compañeros, 113, 213, 304n15

conferences, 15–16

congressional hearings, 265–66

consent, 29, 33, 43, 63, 128, 188, 190, 203, 253, 258

Constituent Assembly, 167

Corbin, Kayla, 147

Craven, David, 80

Crenshaw, Kimberlé, 9, 158, 162

crises, as influences, 197–203

Critical Legal Studies (CLS), 142, 148–50, 153–59

critical Marxism, 80

critical race theory (CRT), 11–12, 38–39, 142; ethnic-studies revolution and, 159–64; fighting against, 251–54

critical theory, red pill of, 82–87

crits of color, 159–60

Croly, Herbert, 127

Cuba, 26, 42–43, 50, 92, 95–97, 107–8, 115, 129, 145, 173, 192, 224, 232, 239

Cullors, Patrisse, 11–12, 66, 163, 183–85, 205, 212, 254, 265

cultural awakening: Frankfurt School, 82–87; in Germany, 70–75; important figures, 76–82; in Italy, 53–70; lessons from revolutionary fiasco, 75–76

cultural Marxist, assessment of, 12–14

Cultural Revolution, 125

culture, reclaiming, AMWG, 246

Daily Worker, 176

Daley, Richard, 132

Das Kapital, 40

Davidson, Alastair, 60

Davis, Angela, 49–50, 95, 105, 106, 154, 183, 250

Davis, Rennie, 95

Days of Rage, 107–8, 112, 116–17

Debray, Regis, 107

Declaration of Independence, 30

Declaration of the Comintern's Sixth Congress, 168–69

Declaration of the Rights of Man and of the Citizen, 33

Delgado, Richard, 158, 160

Dellinger, David, 95, 104

Democratic Socialists of America (DSA), 180

Der Spiegel, 99

DeSantis, Ron, 216, 235, 249–50, 269–73

Detwiler, Jim, 113

Dewey, John, 127

Die Internationale, 79

Die Linke, 75

Die Rote Fahne (The Red flag), 72–74, 82

Dignity and Power Now, 184

direct democracy, 55, 127–30

Disease Control and Prevention (CDC), 202

Disney, 272–73

Dissent, 129

Ditch, David, 273–74

diversity, equity, and inclusion (DEI), 49, 243

Dohrn, Bernadine, 95; Manson Family and, 117–20

Dohrn, Bernardine, 113, 115, 136; and death of Weathermen, 124–27; New Red Army and, 120–24

Draper, Theodore, 44–45
Dream Defenders, 216
Dreher, Rod, 258
Dreier, Peter, 180
Drucker, Peter, 31
Du, Charles, 153
dual tyranny, 31–34
Dutschke, Rudi, 109

Eberling, Richard, 39
Eckstein, Arthur M., 116, 122
Economic Research and Action Project (ERAP), 177
Ecuador, 225, 227, 229
Ehrenreich, Barbara, 180
El Salvador, 221–22
elected officials, role of, 248–49
engagement, AMWG, 244–45
Engels, Friedrich, 10, 36–40
Enlightenment, 29
Environmental Defense Fund, 151
environmental, social, and governance (ESG), 205, 270–72
Equality Act, 256
Eros and Civilization (Marcuse), 103, 199
"Essay on Liberation" (Marcuse), 98–99
ethnic studies: creation of, 142–48; fighting against, 254–56
ethnic-studies revolution, 141–42; critical legal studies (CLS), 153–59; Critical Legal Studies (CLS), 148–50; critical race theory (CRT), 159–64; ethnic studies, 142–48; public interest law, 150–53
expose, AMWG, 241–42

Fabio, Michelle, 151
Faces at the Bottom of the Well (Bell), 161
false consciousness, 82–83, 85, 173
Family Research Council (FRC), 261
family, attack on. *See* children, sexualization of
Family, cult. *See* Manson, Charles

Fanon, Frantz, 121
Far Left, 16, 80, 112, 124, 133, 206, 209–10
Far Right, 231–32
Farabundo Martí National Liberation Front, 221–22
Farah, Douglas, 224, 226, 232
February Revolution of 1917, 42
Ferguson effect, 206
Ferguson, Missouri, unrest in, 183–87
Fernández-Lasquetty, Javier, 229
Ferreira, Jason, 144–45
First International, 40
Floyd, George, 7, 68, 235
focus, AMWG, 245–46
Fonda, Jane, 179
Ford Foundation, 151
foreign policy, 261–62
Forgacs, David, 62
Formation of the Intellectuals, The (Gramsci), 63
Foro de São Paulo (São Paulo Forum), 207, 221–25, 267–68
Foucault, Michel, 155, 200–201
Fourth World Congress, 59
Fraina, Louis, 168
Franco-Prussian War, 40
Frankfurt School, 75–76, 198, 200; cultural awakening and, 82–87; explaining jettison of worker, 99
Frankfurter, Felix, 47
Franks, Lucinda, 115, 121–22
Freedom Road Socialist Organization, 215, 218
Freire, Paulo, 9, 133, 141, 161–62
French Revolution, 27, 29, 31–34
Freud, Sigmund, 194–95
Froines, John, 95
Fromm, Erich, 199
Frykowski, Wojciech, 118
Fuerzas Armadas de Liberacion Nacional (Armed Forces of National Liberation), 108
Fugitive Days (Dohrn), 116

funding, stopping, 273–75

Galilei, Galileo, 27–28
Gardner, Ian, 79
Garza, Alicia, 16, 163, 184–85, 205, 248, 265
Gates, John, 176
gender identity, promoting, 259
gender theory: attack on family, 189–91; taking on, 256–58
George C. Fuller Company, 45
German Communist Party (KPD), 71, 74, 79
Germany, revolution in, 70–75
Get-Together Club, 45
ghetto population, 93, 102
ghettoes, sowing seeds of revolution in, 175–79
Gilbert, Ben, 233
Gilbert, David, 214
Gilday, Michael, 262
Gitlin, Todd, 174, 175, 177
Gold, Ted, 121
Goldberg, Harmony, 66, 217–18
Gonzalez, Juan, 267
Gorbachev, Mikhail, 241
Gordon, Robert W., 155
Gorz, André, 180
Gotanda, Neil, 158, 160
Grabar, Mary, 133, 134–35
Gradick, Mia, 266
Grajew, Oded, 208
Gramsci Reader, The, 62
Gramsci, Antonio, 9, 49, 155, 235, 257; Biennio Rossio and, 54–58; Black Americans and, 158–59; and hegemony theory, 63–65; and historic bloc, 66; influencing Duncan Kennedy, 154–57; legacy of, 53–54; other ideas of, 68–70; prison years, 61–62; Soviets and, 58–61; war of positions/maneuvers, 66–68
Grassroots Global Justice Alliance

(GGJ), 210
Grathwold, Larry, 121–22
Gravina, Joseph, 69
Greene, Jay, 260
Greene, Maxine, 141
Greenpeace, 15, 268–69
Grupo de Puebla, 207
Guardian, 90, 92, 185
Guevara, Che, 107
Gulag Archipelago, The (Solzhenitsyn), 243, 248
Gumperz, Julian, 82
Guterres, António, 210

Hackney, James R., Jr., 156
Hafera, Brenda, 10
Hamas, 7
Hamilton, Alexander, 238
Hampton, Fred, 117
Hannah-Jones, Nikole, 86, 106
Harrington, Michael, 180
Harvard Crimson, The, 148
Harvard Law School, coup at, 148–49
Havel, Václav, 243
Hayakawa, Samuel Ichiye, 144
Hayden, Tom, 91, 95, 104, 106, 129, 171, 174, 175–79
HB 1084, Georgia, 253
Hegel, G.W. F., 36
hegemony, 63–65
Heine, Heinrich, 36
Hessel, Stéphane, 228
heteronormativity, abolishing, 201
Hindenburg, Paul von, 87
Hiss, Alger, 9
historic bloc, 66, 211
History and Class Consciousness (Lukács), 82
Hitler, Adolf, 87
Hobsbawm, Eric, 54, 62, 68, 70, 109
Hoffman, Abbie, 95, 106
"Holy Family, The" (Marx), 36

Honecker, Erich, 95
Hoover, J. Edgar, 118
Horkheimer, Max, 13, 77–79, 100, 154, 155, 198
Horney, Karen, 200
Horowitz, David, 98, 119, 126
Horowitz, Marxist David, 14–15
Horwitt, Sanford D., 174
House Bill 4474, 258
House Bill 616, 259
House Bill 931, 250
House Committee on Un-American Activities, 246
House Un-American Activities Committee, 202
Howe, Irving, 98, 129
Hu-DeHart, Evelyn, 142–43
"Human Pride" (Marx), 35–36
Hutchinson, Allan, 155

I Wor Kuen, 145, 182, 232
ideological direction, lack of (New Left), 103–10. See also New Left
Iglesias, Pablo, 70
Il Grido del Popolo, 64
In These Times, 185, 215
Independent Social Democratic Party (USPD), 71
individuals, role of, 239–40
Institut für Marxismus (Institute for Marxism). See Frankfurt School
Institute for Social Research, 75
Intercollegiate Socialist Society (ISS), 175
International Council (IC), 210
International Working Men's Association, 40, 42
Italian Communist Party (PCI), 58
Italy, Marxism in, 53–54; Biennio Rosso, 54–58; Gramsci and Soviets, 58–61; hegemony theory, 63–65; historic bloc, 66; prison years, 61–62

Jackson, Ketanji Brown, 161

Jacobin, 96
Jay, Paul, 220
Jefferson, Thomas, 30–31
Jobs With Justice, 210
Johnson, Lyndon B., 115, 151
Jones, Jeff, 122
Joravsky, Ben, 132

Kelley, Robyn D. G., 217
Kellner, Douglas, 97, 110
Kendi, Ibram X., 262
Kengor, Paul, 119–20, 137
Kennedy, Bobby, 107
Kennedy, Duncan, 154–57, 162
Kennedy, John F., 92
Kerner Report, 279
Khrushchev, Nikita, 10
Kim, Dae-Young, 265
Kind and Just Parent: The Children of Juvenile Court, A (Ayers), 137
King, Martin Luther, Jr., 107, 181, 233, 238
Kinsey, Albert, 200
Klavan, Andrew, 191
Kollontai, Alexandra, 168
Kolpe, Lisa, 134
Korsch, Karl, 76, 79–80
Kotkin, Minna, 151
Kretzman, John, 172
Kun, Bela, 104
Kurtz, Stanley, 137, 171

L'Ordine Nuovo, 55
Labor Community Strategy Center, 11–12, 16, 181–83, 212
labor, communist division of, 14–17
Lassalle, Ferdinand, 44
Lawrence, Charles, 158, 160
Lawson, John Howard, 49–50
Lawyers Committee for Civil Rights under Law, 150
League for Industrial Democracy (LID), 175

League of Revolutionary Struggle, 182

Lee, Rosa, 201–2

Left Forum, 15–17, 217–21

Left Root, 207

LeftRoots, 215

Lenin, Vladimir, 10, 26, 41–45, 118, 165–67

Lerner, Jon, 117

Levin, Mark, 274

Liebknecht, Karl, 72

Lincoln, Abraham, 239

Linera, Álvaro García, 219, 221, 231

Locke, John, 28, 29, 30

Lohmeier, Matthew, 263

London, Jack, 175

long game, playing, AMWG, 245

Long March through the Institutions, 68

Long Marcher, Ayers becoming, 127–35

Loudoun County, Virginia, 235–36

Löwenthal, Leo, 87

Lukács, Georg, 76, 80–82, 198

Lumumba, Patrice, 145

Lydegraf, Clayton Van, 125

Machiavelli, Niccolò, 53

Madison, James, 238

Maduro, Nicolás, 69, 266

Maercker, Georg von, 74

Malcolm X, 121

Mann, Eric, 11–12, 14–16, 66, 106, 166, 173, 181–83, 211–14

Manson, Charles, 117–20

Marcuse, Herbert, 42, 68, 70, 76, 93–94, 110–12, 114, 145, 196, 215; as "Guru of the Sexual Revolution," 103; on Marxism as right alternative, 101–2; on nature of civilization, 198–200

Margo, Robert, 179

Marquis de Sade, 191

marriage, "trinity of the most monstrous evils," 192–97

Martin, Trayvon, 184, 205

Marx–Engels Institute, 104

Marx, Karl, 8, 9, 118, 155; and culture of revolution, 35–40

Marxism, 7–10; community organization and, 165–88; cultural awakening of, 53–87; ethnic-studies revolution and, 141–64; and failure of class consciousness, 14–17; New Left and, 89–112; origins of, 25–27; in year 1989, 10–14

"Marxism and the New Left" (Zinn), 105

Marxist Workweek, 79–80, 104, 82083

Matsuda, Mari, 149, 158–60

Max, Steve, 181

May 19th Communist Organization, 109

Mayflower Compact, 29–31, 239

McCarthy, Joseph R., 246–47

McCarthy, Margaret Harper, 256

Meadows, Mark, 251

medical practices, banning, 259

Mencken, H. L., 177

Methvin, Eugene, 187

Metropolitan Transportation Authority, LA, 183

Mexican American Legal Defense and Education Fund (MALDEF), 150, 152

middle class, shaping image of, 176–77

military, NextGen Marxism in, 262–64

Milley, Mark, 262–63

Mills, C. Wright, 91–92, 97, 100, 106

Minh, Ho Chi, 118

"Modern Prince, The" (Gramsci), 53–54

Monahan, Patrick, 155

Monde diplomatique, Le, 209

money, following, AMWG, 242–43

Montesquieu, 28–29

Moore, Darnell, 185

Moore, Patrick, 15–16, 268–69

Moore, Riley, 271

More, Thomas, 27

Moses, Bob, 177

"Move a Piece: Turn Indignation into

Political Change," manifesto, 230
Movimiento Estudiantil Chicano de Aztlan, 146
Moyers, Bill, 101, 110–12
Moynihan, Daniel Patrick, 118–20
Mulvad, Andreas Møller, 55, 65
Münzenberg, Willi, 47, 82, 104

NAACP Legal Defense Fund, 151
Nation, The, 148
National Domestic Workers Alliance (NDWA), 186–87, 214–16
National Review, 120
National Students for Justice in Palestine, 216
National Women's Law Center, 150–51
Native American Rights Fund, 150
Natural Resources Defense Council, 151
Neier, Aryeh, 176
neoliberalism, 208
NetRoots, 207
network building: BLM globe, 231–34; building US network, 214–17; Foro de São Paulo, 221–25; Left Forum, 217–21; overview of, 205–8; playbook for, 228–30; social media and, 226–27; US Social Forum (USSF), 210–14; World Social Forum (WSF), 208–10
network, AMWG, 242
networks, exposing, 267–68
Neumann, Florencia Lagos, 226
Neumann, Franz Leopold, 91
New Atlantis, 28
New Left, 89–91; abandoning worker, 97–101; and direct democracy, 127–30; embracing Cuba, 96–97; failure of, 110–12; ghetto population and, 93–94; groups under, 94–96; power elite and, 91; shaping, 91–103; strength of, 92–93; term, 91–92; violence outbreaks, 103–10; workers and, 93
New Left Review, 100, 109

New Red Army, 120–24
New York Times, 2–6, 126, 130, 131, 147, 177; Cornel West article in, 15; "Education; the Mainstreaming of Marxism in US Colleges," 10–11
New York Times Magazine, 98, 115, 127
New York Times Review of Books, 178
Newark Community Union Project, 129
Newsom, Gavin, 146–48
Newton, Isaac, 27
NextGen Marxism, 7–10; community organization and, 165–88; cultural awakening, 53–87; ethnic-studies revolution and, 141–64; and failure of class consciousness, 14–17; foundations of, 25–51. See also present crisis, background of; historic bloc and, 66; metamorphosis, 113–39. See also Ayers, William; in military, 262–64; network building, 205–34; New Left and, 89–112; overview of, 17–24; saving United States, 235–75; sexualization of children, 189–204; Soviet communism and, 41–43; and year 1989, 10–14
Nicholas II, tzar, 168
1989, year, 10–14
Nisbet, Robert, 32–34
Nitze, Paul, 244, 247
Nixon, Richard F., 93, 126
North Korea, 26
North Vietnam, 26
NSC-68, 237–38, 244

Obama, Barack, 113, 128, 135–37, 171
Obrador, Andrés Manuel López, 229–30
October Coup, 42
October Revolution, 62, 71
Old Left, 97, 104, 106, 174
OldGen Marxism, 216, 236
Olson, Walter, 150
One Dimensional Man (Marcuse), 93, 100, 102–3
Open Society Institute, 176

operationalism, 105
Other America, The (Harrington), 180
Oughton, Diana, 113, 115, 121
Owen, Robert, 192–93

Pacific Legal Foundation, 151
País, El, 227
Palmer, Alice, 135–36
Parent, Steven, 118
Parents Defending Education, 255–56
Paris Agreement, 270
Paris Commune, 40, 42
Parker, Dorothy, 47
parliamentary democracy, 68–70
participatory democracy, 55, 69, 128–32, 167, 174, 213, 231, 266
Partido dos Trabalhadores (PT), 208–9
patriots, ten tactics for, 240–48
Payne, Robert, 37
peaceable assembly, 266
peaceable protests, 264–65
Pedagogy of the Oppressed (Freire), 133–34, 141, 161–62
Peller, Gary, 158
Penthouse, 260–61
People Organized to Win Employment Rights (POWER), 211–12
People's Daily World, 136
People's Republic of China (PRC), 218
Petro, Gustavo, 227
Petróleos de Venezuela, S.A. (PDVSA), 224
Piccone, Paul, 60
Pipes, Richard, 34
Piven, Frances Fox, 180, 217
Plato, 25–27
Playbook for Progressives (Mann), 183
Podemos, 230
Polanski, Roman, 117
Politico, 136, 138
Pollock, Friedrich, 77
Pondiscio, Robert, 260

Poo, Ai-Jen, 215
Popp-Madsen, Benjamin Ask, 55, 65
Popp, Lothar, 71
Popular Front for the Liberation of Palestine, 216
Port Huron Statement, 96, 107–8, 115
Porter, Katherine Anne, 47
power elite, 91
Prairie Fire Distribution Committee, 124
Prairie Fire Organizing Committee (PFOC), 124
praxis, philosophy, 69
present crisis, background of, 49–50; culture of revolution, 34–40; international aspirations, 43–46; origins of Marxism, 25–27; reform *versus* revolution, 29–34; revolution coming out of wilderness, 41–43; secular revolution, 27–28
Prison Notebooks (Gramsci), 54, 60–62
private property, "trinity of the most monstrous evils," 192–97
Protection of Women and Girls Sports Act, 259–60
Proudhon, Pierre-Joseph, 36–37
public interest law, 150–53
Puerto Rican Legal Defense Fund, 150
Purpose of Power, The (Garza), 211

Quesada, Ricardo Alarcón de, 213

racial minorities, 143
Radek, Karl, 82, 104
Rader, Dotson, 107
Radford, R. S., 150–52
RAND Corporation, 170
Ransby, Barbara, 186
Rapoport, Mario, 77
Reagan, Ronald, 126, 144, 241
Real News, 220
Rebel without a Cause (film), 96
Red Terror, 42
reform, revolution *versus,* 29–34

Reich, Wilhelm, 195–98
Reign of Terror, 34, 40
Reilly, Robert, 20, 31, 46
religion, "trinity of the most monstrous evils," 192–97
representative democracy, 12, 34, 55, 69, 73, 106, 127–29, 160–61, 213, 269, 274
"Repressive Tolerance" (Marcuse), 100–101, 174
Restricted Financial Institution List, 271
Reuther, Walter, 175–76
Reveille for Radicals (Alinsky), 172
revolution: coming out of wilderness, 41–43; culture of, 34–40; reform *versus*, 29–34
revolutionary consciousness, 44, 50–51, 55–58, 60, 82, 114, 166, 168
Riazanov, 104
Ricardo, David, 38
Richards, Jay, 257–58
Richards, B. J., 130–3`
Robbins, Terry, 121
Robinson, Cedric, 147
Rocketto, Jess Morales, 216
Rosenberg, Susan, 126
Rosengarten, Frank, 54
Rousseau, Jean-Jacques, 28, 31–34
Rousseff, Dilma, 229
Roybal, Ed, 152
Rubin, Isadore, 202
Rubin, Jerry, 95, 106
Rudd, Mark, 119
Rufo, Chris, 191, 201, 251–52
Rules for Radicals (Alinsky), 165, 167, 171, 174, 247
Ruse, Austen, 196
Russia, war of positions/maneuvers in, 66–68
Russian Revolution, 59

Sacco, Nicola, 46–47
Saint-Simon, Henri de, 35

San Francisco State University (SFSU), 144–45, 258
Sanders, Bernie, 207–8
Sanders, Sarah Huckabee, 253
Sandoz, Ellis, 31
Sartre, Jean-Paul, 121
Savage Songs (Marx), 35–36
Savinkov, Boris, 81
Schenkoske, Kelly, 254
Schmuckle, Karl, 82
School of Unity and Liberation (SOUL), 184–85, 217–18
Schubert, William H., 131
Schucht, Julia, 59
Scientific Revolution, 27
Scottsboro Nine, 48–50
Seale, Bobby, 95
Second International, 40
secular revolution, 27–28
Selznick, Philip, 187–88, 247
Senate Bill 14, 259
Senate Bill 222, 259
Senate Bill 266, 250
Senate Bill 7044, 250
Severino, Roger, 162
Sex Ed for Social Change (SIECUS), 10, 202–3
Sexology, 202
Sexual Revolution, The (Reich), 196
Sexual Struggle of Youth, The (Reich), 196
sexuality, 97, 147, 191, 194–201, 203–4
Shaull, Richard, 133–34
Sheehan, Cindy, 213
Sheen, Ariel, 233, 277
showing up, AMWG, 245
Sierra Club Legal Defense Fund, 151
Sieyès, Abbé, 33
Silva, Luiz Inácio Lula da, 208
Sinclair, Upton, 175
Small Schools Workshop, 132–33
Smith, Adam, 38
Smith, Ben, 136, 138

Smith, Robert, 144

Social Contract, The (Rousseau), 31

Social Democratic Party (SPD), 71–75

social media, fanning flames of revolution through, 226–27

Socialism and the Coming Decade, 181

Socialist Society for Sexual Counseling and Sex-Research, 196

Socialist Worker, 144

Soldatenräte (soldiers' councils), 71

Solzhenitsyn, Aleksandr, 203, 243, 248

Sorge, Richard, 82

Soros, George, 176, 210

Southern Worker, 48

Soviet Union, 26–27, 240–41

sports, protecting, 259–60

Standing Together to Organize a Revolutionary Movement (STORM), 269

stealth socialism, 180–81

Steinem, Gloria, 200

Stephens, Bret, 147–48, 206

Stern, Sol, 131

Struve, Peter, 41

Student League for Industrial Democracy (SLID), 175–76

Student Nonviolent Coordinating Committee (SNCC), 94–96, 144

Students for a Democratic Society (SDS), 115, 171; direct democracy and, 127–30; as flagship organization, 94–96; sowing seeds of revolution, 175–79

Summer Youth Organizing Academy, 182–83

Supreme Soldiers Council, 71–72

Susskind, Heinrich, 82, 104

Szilvay, Gergely, 190

"Tactics and Ethics" (Lukács), 81

Tamayo, Violeta, 231–32

Tate, Sharon, 117–20

Teachers College (TC), 131

Ten Blocks from the White House

(Gilbert), 233

Ten Tactics for Patriots, 240–48

Tet Offensive, 115

theoria, 76

Third International. *See* Communist International (Comintern)

Third World, 12, 66, 106, 115, 133, 142, 145, 211, 215

Third World Liberation Front (TWLF), 144–45

Third World Marxists, 107–8, 115, 221

Thomas, Lia, 258

Three Essays on Marxism (Korsch), 80

Thunberg, Greta, 269

Tocqueville, Alexis de, 244–45

Tometi, Opal, 184, 231, 265

"Traditional and Critical Theory" (Horkheimer), 84

transformative organizing, 181–83

Transgender Marxism (Lee), 201–2

"trinity of the most monstrous evils," 192–97

Trotsky, Leon, 59–61, 168

Trudell, Megan, 55–57

Trueman, Carl, 190, 191

Trump, Donald, 251, 267, 270

truth, living within, AMWG, 243

Turati, Filippo, 55

tyranny, 25–26

Unger, Mangabeira, 155–56

United States: Active Measures Working Group (AMWG), 240–48; banning medical practices, 259; Black Lives Matter, 264–65; book banning, 260–61; bringing Bolshevik Revolution to, 46–50; climate change, 268–70; congressional hearings, 265–66; critical race theory, 251–54; environmental, social, and governance (ESG), 270–72; ethnic studies, 254–56; exploiting race relations in, 47–49; exposing networks, 267–68; fighting woke corporations, 272–73; foreign policy, 261–62; gender identity promotion, 259; intellectual vanguards in, 49–50; Loudoun County, Virginia, 235–36; Marxist–Leninist organizing coming to, 168–69; Marxists seeding ideas in, 46–47; mean playing on women teams, 259–60; NextGen Marxism in military, 262–64; peaceable assembly, 266; rekindling love for, 236–39; remembering who we are, 236–39; role of elected officials, 248–49; role of individuals in, 239–40; role of individuals, 239–40; stop funding Left, 273–75; taking on gender theory, 256–58; ten tactics for patriots, 240–48; translating Marxist-Leninist organizational strategy in, 171–74; university reform, 249–50

universities, reforming, 249–50
University of California (UC), 144
University of Illinois Chicago (UIC), 124, 131–32
US Constitution, 33
US network, building, 214–17
US Peace Council, 136
US Social Forum (USSF), 15–16, 207, 210–14

Vanzetti, Bartolomeo, 46–47
Venezuela, 26, 62, 135, 213, 219, 224, 229, 231, 239
Vietnam War, 93
violence, New Left creating, 103–10
Voegeli, William, 127, 130
Voting Rights Act (VRA), 152, 154
vulgar Marxism, 80, 124

Wall Street Journal, 256
wallet, voting with, AMWG, 243–44
Walsh, Michael, 192–93
Waltz, Mike, 262
Walzer, Michael, 129

war of maneuvers, 66–68, 109
war of positions, 66–68
War on Poverty, 180
war, sex and, 197–203
Washington Post, 233
Watkins, Gloria Jean, 250
"We Didn't Start a Movement. We Started a Network" (Cullors), 185
Weather Underground, 11, 107–10, 212; and Days of Rage, 115–17; and death of Weathermen, 124–27; Manson murders and, 117–20; New Red Army and, 120–24
Weather Underground Organization (WUO), 125
Webb, Lee, 174, 175
Weber, Max, 155
Weil, Félix, 76–77
Weiner, Lee, 95
Wells, H. G., 47
West Village, bombing in, 121–23
West, Cornel, 16
What Is to Be Done? (Lenin), 43, 166
When They Call You a Terrorist (Cullors), 183
Whitaker, Chico, 208
whitewashing, 175–79
Whole School, Whole Community, Whole Child, 254
Wiener, Jonathan M., 13–14
Wiggershaus, Rolf, 76, 82
Wilbrandt, Robert, 76
Wilhelm II, kaiser, 70
Wilkerson, Cathlyn, 121, 123
Wilkins, Frank, 120
Williams, Gwyn Alfred, 55
Williams, Steve, 218
Williamson, Kevin D., 120
Wilpert, Gregory, 219
Wilson, Edmund, 35
Wittfogel, Karl, 82
woke corporations, fighting, 272–73
Woodhull and Claflin's Weekly, 193

Woodhull, Victoria, 193
worker, abandoning, 97–101
WorkersControl.net, 57
World Council of Churches, 134
World Social Forum (WSF), 16, 207,
    208–10, 267
World War II, 196, 200, 228

Xicanx Institute for Teaching and Orga-
    nizing (XITO), 254

Yale Law Journal, 153
Yates, Caitlyn, 224, 226, 232
Yezhovshchina, 104
Ylvisaker, Paul, 152
Youngkin, Glenn, 235, 253

Zapata, Emiliano, 145
Zetkin, Clara, 59, 76–77
Zetkin, Konstantin, 77
Zimmerman, George, 184, 205, 207
Zinn, Howard, 93–95, 104–6, 114
Zinoviev, Grigory, 57